AF794499

NORFOLK PAUPER INVENTORIES
*c.*1690–1834

Records of Social and Economic History is a British Academy Research Project.

The British Academy, established by Royal Charter in 1902, is the national academy for the humanities and social sciences, promoting, sustaining and representing advanced research. As an academy composed of senior scholars throughout the UK, it gives recognition to academic excellence and achievement, and plays a leadership role in representing the humanities and social sciences nationally and internationally. As a learned society, the British Academy facilitates the research of individuals and groups of scholars.

More information can be found at *www.thebritishacademy.ac.uk*

RECORDS OF SOCIAL AND ECONOMIC HISTORY
NEW SERIES 59

NORFOLK PAUPER INVENTORIES *c.*1690–1834

EDITED BY
JOSEPH HARLEY

Published for THE BRITISH ACADEMY
by OXFORD UNIVERSITY PRESS

Oxford University Press, Great Clarendon Street, Oxford OX2 6DP

© The British Academy 2020
Database right The British Academy (maker)

First edition published in 2020

All rights reserved. No part of this publication may be reproduced, stored in a retrieval system, or transmitted, in any form or by any means, without the prior permission in writing of the British Academy, or as expressly permitted by law, by licence or under terms agreed with the appropriate reprographics rights organization. Enquiries concerning reproduction outside the scope of the above should be sent to the Publications Department, The British Academy, 10–11 Carlton House Terrace, London SW1Y 5AH

You must not circulate this book in any other form and you must impose this same condition on any acquirer

British Library Cataloguing in Publication Data
Data available

Library of Congress Cataloging in Publication Data
Data available

Typeset by
New Leaf Design, Malton, North Yorkshire
Printed in Great Britain by
TJ International Ltd, Padstow, Cornwall

ISBN 978–0–19–726665–6

Foreword

Whatever its faults, the English and Welsh 'Old Poor Law' (1601-1834) was a remarkable institution, helping many of the neediest in society to make ends meet. Here was John Clare's 'parish state' in action, with local people financing and administering relief according to statutory requirements, but exercising considerable discretion as they did so. The rich records produced have been used by historians for around a century in showing power relations at work, the operation of the 'economy of makeshifts', and local variations within national histories. In recent decades poor law historians, building upon E. P. Thompson's call to rescue the poor cottager and others from the 'enormous condescension of posterity', have shown just how active were the poor themselves in negotiating with the authorities over relief.

A previous volume in this series, edited by Thomas Sokoll, reproduced dramatic 'pauper letters' from Essex, clearly demonstrating that the poor were far from simply passive recipients of relief under the Old Poor Law. They knew the law and argued their case with the authorities. This volume introduces a further dimension by reproducing 230 inventories of the property of paupers who had been caught up with the poor law in Norfolk – such inventories were especially common in East Anglia. What these documents, carefully transcribed and edited by Dr Harley, show is that some paupers on relief were far from completely destitute, with their property providing a sort of collateral that the authorities might seek to claim at a later date by way of recompense for the relief provided. The inventories shed new light on the goods possessed by some poor people, many of them women, adding to our knowledge of the world of goods at the time, where the focus of historians has often been upon less day to day and more expensive commodities. These inventories will, therefore, be of great use to historians not only of the Old Poor Law and the dynamics of local society, but of consumption and gender.

Professor Rosemary Sweet shepherded this volume to the production stage, where Professor Harding, the general editor of the series, guided it through to publication. I am very grateful to these colleagues for their considerable efforts.

Julian Hoppit, Chair, Records of Social and Economic History Committee
April 2019

Contents

List of figures and maps

Tables

Acknowledgements

I would like to start by thanking the various organisations that have given me funding over the years, including the Arts and Humanities Research Council (ah/k503101/1) and the Economic History Society (EHS-AppRFGS07/2013/0028; EHS-AppRFGS/1477901217899016; and Postan junior research fellowship 2016–17). My research into pauper inventories would not have been possible without their generous help. Parts of this book were published in Joseph Harley, 'Consumption and Poverty in the Homes of the English Poor, c. 1670–1834', *Social History*, 43 (2018), pp. 81–104 and Joseph Harley 'Pauper Inventories, Social Relations and the Nature of Poor Relief under the Old Poor Law, England c. 1601–1834', *Historical Journal*, 62 (2019), pp. 375–398. This material has been reprinted with permission from Taylor & Francis and Cambridge University Press. Thanks are also due to Norfolk Record Office for allowing me to consult and reproduce material in their custody.

My interest in pauper inventories stems from my undergraduate studies at the University of Leicester. In a module entitled 'Peopling the Industrial Revolution', Steve King opened my eyes to numerous historical sources relating to poverty and the fascinating literature on the everyday lives of ordinary people. I am particularly grateful to Steve for his support during the early stages of planning my research. While undertaking my Master's degree at Warwick, I studied pauper inventories for my dissertation and was immeasurably helped by Thomas Sokoll and Pete King, who both kindly allowed me to use their transcriptions of pauper inventories from Essex. From there I went on to start my PhD under the supervision of Pete. His knowledge of pauper inventories is unrivalled and without his help my thesis (and subsequently this book) would have been much more difficult to write and far less enjoyable.

I owe my biggest academic debt to Roey Sweet. She has been extremely generous with her time, offering advice over countless email conversations and reviewing all my articles and this volume in full. Many others have also offered me support, help, and advice, including Aaron Andrews, Julie Attard, Jennie Brosnan, Justin Colson, Paul Elliott, Simon Gunn, Tim Hitchcock, Vicky Holmes, Jen Kain, Mark Knights, Paul Maddrell, Charmian Mansell, Katy Roscoe, Keith Snell, Jon Stobart, Deborah Toner, Emily Whewell, and Chris White. Thank you all. As General Editor, Vanessa Harding has read this volume in full and with a keen eye she has done some excellent work cutting out errors and helping me to improve the text.

I would like to end by thanking my family, including my sister and Barrie and Vicky Bishop, for their support over the years. Although she will never read this, Bonnie also deserves to be recognised for always being by my side and distracting me at just the right times. I would like to particularly highlight the role of my parents, Sue and Rob Harley, and my wife, Claire. My parents have helped me in too many ways to name and have always encouraged my research, even when they did not always fully understand it! Claire challenges me intellectually every day but also has the profound ability to make me laugh with the crudest comments. She has been there through the highs and lows and has had an unshakeable belief in my abilities. Without her love and support this volume would not have been possible.

Abbreviations

BPP	British Parliamentary Papers
CCAL	Canterbury Cathedral Archives and Library, Canterbury
DHC	Dorset History Centre, Dorchester
ERO	Essex Record Office, Chelmsford
KHLC	Kent History Library Centre, Maidstone
LRO	Lancashire Record Office, Preston
NRO	Norfolk Record Office, Norwich
ROLLR	Record Office for Leicestershire, Leicester and Rutland, Wigston
WAS	Wigan Archives Service, Leigh

Chapter 1

Pauper inventories as a historical source

Under the old poor law of 1601–1834, poor law officials would sometimes visit the homes of parishioners and take an inventory of their possessions in return for help from the parish. The paupers would then continue to use their belongings and at a later date, usually when they died, the goods would revert back to the parish. Most of these inventories do not survive, but where they do, they are very important documents for social, economic, and cultural historians. The inventories capture some of the poorest people in society and can be used to study entitlement to relief, the material nature of poverty, and social relations between parish authorities and the indigent. They can be used to piece together the domestic lives of the poor and to research a considerable range of topics, including consumption, everyday life, household production, domestic management, household structure, and room use. They open up questions relating to standards of living and the wider economy, including fuel use and food consumption. Pauper inventories also allow us to consider important historiographical debates, such as the extent to which the country underwent a consumer, industrial, and industrious revolution over the long eighteenth century.

Much like pauper letters, which were sent to poor law authorities by claimants asking for poor relief, pauper inventories can be used to assess entitlement and the attitudes of the individuals that distributed help to paupers such as overseers of the poor and churchwardens.[1] The majority of pauper inventories were written by overseers, sometimes assisted by churchwardens or members of the vestry. Authorities entered paupers' homes, invited or not, and went through their possessions writing down items as they went. This is likely to have had a significant impact on the relationship between the parish and the indigent. One could argue, for example, that authorities used the system of inventorying parishioners' goods to punish paupers and dissuade future applicants. Alternatively, because the practice often guaranteed people relief and meant that recipients could keep their goods until they no longer needed them, the exercise could be viewed as

[1] Thomas Sokoll, ed., *Essex Pauper Letters, 1731–1837* (Oxford, 2001); Steven King, Thomas Nutt, and Alannah Tomkins, eds., *Narratives of the Poor in Eighteenth-century Britain*, vol. 1, *Voices of the poor: poor law depositions and letters* (London, 2006); Steven King, *Writing the Lives of the English Poor, 1750s–1830s* (London, 2019).

benevolent.[2] Vestries and overseers would normally use their discretion to decide whether somebody was 'deserving' of relief based on claimants' morality, devoutness, sobriety, respectability, industriousness, and deference.[3] With pauper inventories, it was not only people's character that was assessed to qualify for relief, but also their belongings.[4] Pauper inventories were technically made 'from above' (by those in charge), but in many respects they allow us to study the nature of poverty 'from below' (from the poor's perspective), as they are very personal documents and capture the poor's worldly goods in a space where they rested and felt safest.

Pauper inventories are particularly important documents for the items that they list. They record a relatively representative collection of household goods owned by paupers, allowing us to study the domestic and material lives of the poor. Historians have long used inventories to assess these topics, but have been almost wholly reliant on probate inventories, which list the possessions of deceased people for the purposes of inheritance and debt.[5] Probate inventories are one of the most abundant and important sources that early modern historians have at their disposal, but they tend to capture the material lives of the middling sort and elite of society and omit the poor.[6] By law, for example, only the goods of people with an estate worth at least £5 were inventoried for probate.[7] Although appraisers sometimes neglected this procedure,[8] many poor people were nonetheless excluded from the process when they fell beneath this threshold. Furthermore,

[2] This is discussed further in chapter 2 and Joseph Harley, 'Pauper Inventories, Social Relations and the Nature of Poor Relief under the Old Poor Law, England c. 1601–1834', *Historical Journal*, 62 (2019), pp. 375–398.

[3] Steve Hindle, *On the Parish? The micro-politics of poor relief in rural England c. 1550–1750* (Oxford, 2004), pp. 379–398; Samantha A. Shave, *Pauper Policies: Poor law practice in England, 1780–1850* (Manchester, 2017), pp. 127–130.

[4] This is not to say that people were denied relief because they owned very little. Subsequent chapters show that pauper inventories capture a range of people with very different levels of material wealth.

[5] For example, Lorna Weatherill, *Consumer Behaviour and Material Culture in Britain 1660–1760*, 2nd edn. (London, 1996); Carole Shammas, *The Pre-industrial Consumer in England and America* (Oxford, 1990); Carl B. Estabrook, *Urbane and Rustic England: Cultural ties and social spheres in the provinces 1660–1780* (Manchester, 1998), pp. 128–191; John Beckett and Catherine Smith, 'Urban Renaissance and Consumer Revolution', *Urban History*, 27 (2000), pp. 31–50; Mark Overton, Jane Whittle, Darron Dean, and Andrew Hann, *Production and Consumption in English Households, 1600–1750* (London, 2004); Henry French, *The Middle Sort of People in Provincial England 1600–1750* (Oxford, 2007).

[6] It is important to note that recent work by Craig Muldrew and Ken Sneath uses labourers' probate inventories to examine the material lives of the poor. Craig Muldrew, *Food, Energy and the Creation of Industriousness: Work and material culture in agrarian England, 1550–1780* (Cambridge, 2011); Ken Sneath, 'Consumption, Wealth, Indebtedness and Social Structure in Early Modern England' (Ph.D. thesis, University of Cambridge, 2008); Ken Sneath, 'A Consumer Revolution in Huntingdonshire?', *The Local Historian*, 41 (2011), pp. 229–238.

[7] Shammas, *Pre-industrial Consumer*, p. 19.

[8] Muldrew, *Food*, p. 186.

recent research on the probate inventories of the few labourers whose goods went through probate has indicated that they represent the belongings of a minority of the poor who were materially richer than most, as they often had access to land to rear animals and grow crops, meaning that they had greater means to stave off poverty than most. Pauper inventories, on the other hand, appear to represent a more typical subgroup of the poor that had little access to land, struggled to make do due to life-cycle-related problems such as sickness and old age, and owned most types of goods in smaller numbers.[9]

Historians have frequently lamented that we cannot study the consumer behaviour of the poor because there are not enough sources to do so,[10] and some have even suggested that there is little point in researching the group since they could not afford anything more than food and a few basic household necessities.[11] Because pauper inventories are generally formulaic and similar to probate inventories in structure and layout, they allow us to address this imbalance in the literature and systematically assess the material lives of the poor. This is important as the study of consumption has become a cornerstone of early modern and modern history during the past 30–40 years.[12] The items recorded in pauper inventories, for example, can be used to examine the quantity and variety of belongings that paupers owned; bundling/assembling of goods (i.e. collections of related objects);[13] the financial value of items; and the disappearance or lack of certain

[9] These findings are based on the study of Kent, in: Joseph Harley, 'Consumption and Poverty in the Homes of the English Poor, c. 1670–1834', *Social History*, 43 (2018), pp. 81–104. Also see: Weatherill, *Consumer Behaviour*, pp. 191–194; Barry Coward, *The Stuart Age: England, 1603–1714*, 3rd edn. (Harlow, 2003), p. 55; Sneath, 'Consumption, Wealth', p. 102; Peter King, 'Pauper Inventories and the Material Lives of the Poor in the Eighteenth and early Nineteenth centuries', in Tim Hitchcock, Peter King, and Pamela Sharpe, eds., *Chronicling Poverty: The voices and strategies of the English poor, 1640–1840* (Basingstoke, 1997), pp. 155–191.

[10] Weatherill, *Consumer Behaviour*, p. 194; Norman J. G. Pounds, *Hearth & Home: A history of material culture* (Bloomington, 1989), p. 184; Overton et al., *Production and Consumption*, p. 170.

[11] Robert W. Malcolmson, *Life and Labour in England 1700–1780* (London, 1981), p. 149; E. P. Thompson, *The Making of the English Working Class* (London, 1991, reprint of 1963 ed.), p. 351.

[12] For an introduction to the topic, see: Frank Trentmann, ed., *The Oxford Handbook of the History of Consumption* (Oxford, 2012); Janine Maegraith and Craig Muldrew, 'Consumption and Material Life', in Hamish Scott, ed., *The Oxford Handbook of Early Modern European History, 1350–1750*, vol. 1, *Peoples and place* (Oxford, 2015), pp. 369–397; Sara Horrell, 'Consumption, 1700–1870', in Roderick Floud, Jane Humphries, and Paul Johnson, eds., *The Cambridge Economic History of Modern Britain*, vol. 1, *1700–1870*, 2nd edn. (Cambridge, 2014), pp. 237–263; Avner Offer, 'Consumption and Affluence, c. 1870–2010', in Roderick Floud, Jane Humphries, and Paul Johnson, eds., *The Cambridge Economic History of Modern Britain*, vol. 2, *1870 to the present*, 2nd edn. (Cambridge, 2014), pp. 205–228. Also see note 5.

[13] On this, see: Jan de Vries, *The Industrious Revolution: Consumer behaviour and the household economy, 1650 to present* (Cambridge, 2008), pp. 31–37; Jon Stobart, *Sugar and Spice: Grocers in provincial England 1650–1830* (Oxford, 2013), passim; Woodruff D. Smith, *Consumption and the Making of Respectability, 1600–1800* (London, 2002), pp. 122–123; Sidney W. Mintz, *Sweetness and Power: The place of sugar in modern history* (New York, 1985), p. 214; Mary Douglas and Baron C. Isherwood, *The World of Goods: Towards an anthropology of consumption* (London, 1979), p. 72;

objects. They can be subjected to linguistic analysis through the examination of the adjectives used to describe items, such as 'new' and 'old'.[14] The origins, production techniques, and uses of objects can also sometimes be inferred from the inventories, when foreign woods such as mahogany are mentioned; when items of furniture are described as 'joined'; or when goods are described by their function such as a '*dining* table'. Through this, one can examine how the households of the poor were organised and managed.

In a similar manner, the inventories reveal the ownership of items related to domestic work and production, such as spinning wheels, churns, brushes, and looms. This is important as it enables historians to study a considerable range of domestic activities such as spinning, weaving, knitting, carding, farming, brewing, distilling, baking, dairy work, cleaning, washing, and food preservation such as salting meats. Probate inventories have long been used to study these topics,[15] but because they largely do not capture the poor we have relatively little understanding of the nature of production in poor homes.[16] Forty-three of the 230 inventories (19 per cent) in this collection record the rooms in which items were found, albeit sometimes in a casual manner, allowing us to further examine the material lives of the poor and assess the arrangement and organisation of the home. By identifying where certain items were found, we can study the importance and functions of rooms such as kitchens, bedrooms, and parlours.[17]

Joseph Harley, 'Material Lives of the English Poor: A regional perspective, c. 1670–1834' (Ph.D. thesis, University of Leicester, 2016), passim.

[14] On linguistic analysis, see: Mary C. Beaudry, 'Words for Things: Linguistic analysis of probate inventories', in Mary C. Beaudry, ed., *Documentary Archaeology in the New World* (Cambridge, 1988), pp. 43–50; Overton et al., *Production and Consumption*, pp. 114–116; Muldrew, *Food*, p. 200; Harley, 'Material Lives of the English Poor: A regional perspective', pp. 210–216. Also see: Adrian B. Evans, 'Enlivening the Archive: Glimpsing embodied consumption practices in probate inventories of household possessions', *Historical Geography*, 36 (2008), pp. 49–54.

[15] For example, W. G. Hoskins, 'The Leicestershire Farmer in the Seventeenth century', *Agricultural History*, 25 (1951), pp. 9–20; Mark Overton, *Agricultural Revolution in England: The transformation of the agrarian economy, 1500–1850* (Cambridge, 1996); Joan Thirsk, *The Agrarian History of England and Wales*, vol. 5, *1640–1750*: Parts 1–2 (Cambridge, 1984–1985); Overton et al., *Production and Consumption*, pp. 33–86.

[16] There are some notable exceptions to this, such as: John Styles, 'Fashion, Textiles and the Origins of Industrial Revolution', *East Asian Journal of British History*, 5 (2016), pp. 161–189. It is also important to note that Thomas Sokoll briefly used pauper inventories to illustrate the importance of spinning in poor Essex household economies: Thomas Sokoll, *Household and Family among the Poor: The case of two Essex communities in the late eighteenth and early nineteenth centuries* (Bochum, 1993), p. 187.

[17] Scholars of material culture have increasingly turned their attention to studying individual rooms. For example, see: Sara Pennell, *The Birth of the English Kitchen, 1600–1850* (London, 2017); Vicky Holmes, *In Bed with the Victorians: The life-cycle of working-class marriage* (Cham, 2017); Lesley Hoskins, 'Social, Economic and Geographical Differences in mid-Nineteenth-century Homes: The evidence from inventories', *Regional Furniture*, XXVIII (2013), pp. 93–119.

Through being able to systematically examine the material lives of the poor, historians can analyse change over time and address key areas of debate such as the consumer, industrious, and industrial revolutions. In 1982, Neil McKendrick argued that Britain witnessed the world's first 'consumer revolution' during the third quarter of the eighteenth century. He claimed that levels of spending were 'unprecedented in the depth to which it penetrated the lower reaches of society'.[18] Many historians have disagreed with McKendrick's ideas and have argued that changes in consumer behaviour were more long-drawn-out and started much earlier in the 1550s.[19] Nevertheless, the ideas have remained influential and numerous academics continue to claim that the eighteenth century saw a consumer revolution.[20] The study of pauper inventories offers a fresh approach to this debate. Changes in consumer behaviour are also integral to Jan de Vries' argument that north-western Europe and North America underwent an 'industrious revolution' during the long eighteenth century. Proponents of the theory argue that the household shifted its production from self-provisioning and worked harder for longer hours in production for the market, to earn a cash income which could be used to purchase market-produced goods. It is argued that these changes at the level of the household had a considerable impact on the economic development of Britain and the wider world by preceding and preparing the way for the industrial revolution,[21] whereby production moved away from homes to workshops and factories.[22] These areas of debate are some of the most fertile areas of research today and it is currently unclear whether empirical data supports or

[18] Neil McKendrick, 'The Consumer Revolution of Eighteenth-century England', in Neil McKendrick, John Brewer, and J. H. Plumb, *The Birth of a Consumer Society: The commercialisation of eighteenth-century England* (London, 1982), pp. 9–33; Neil McKendrick, 'Introduction', in McKendrick, Brewer, and Plumb, *Consumer Society*, pp. 1–6.

[19] John Brewer, 'The Error of our Ways', Lecture to the Cultures of Consumption programme, The Royal Society, 2003, Working paper no. 12 [From: www.consume.bbk.ac.uk/publications.html. Accessed 26/11/2010]; John Styles, 'Manufacturing, Consumption and Design in Eighteenth-century England', in John Brewer and Roy Porter, eds., *Consumption and the World of Goods* (London, 1993), pp. 527–554; Ben Fine and Ellen Leopold, *The World of Consumption* (London, 1993), pp. 62–72; Ben Fine, *The World of Consumption: The material and cultural revisited*, 2nd edn. (London, 2002), pp. 155–175; Jean-Christophe Agnew, 'Coming up for Air: Consumer culture in historical perspective', in Brewer and Porter, *World of Goods*, pp. 19–39.

[20] For example, Jon Stobart, 'A History of Shopping: The missing link between retail and consumer revolutions', *Journal of Historical Research in Marketing*, 2 (2010), pp. 342–349; Sneath, 'Consumption, Wealth'; Sneath, 'Consumer Revolution', pp. 229–238.

[21] Jan de Vries, *Industrious Revolution: Consumer behaviour*; idem, 'The Industrial Revolution and the Industrious Revolution', *Journal of Economic History*, 54 (1994), pp. 249–270.

[22] Of course, this is a rather simplified discussion of the industrial revolution. For an introduction to the vast literature on the topic and further context, see: Peter N. Stearns, *Debating the Industrial Revolution* (London, 2015); E. A. Wrigley, *The Path to Sustained Growth: England's transition from an organic economy to an industrial revolution* (Cambridge, 2016).

disproves the concept.[23] More work is clearly needed to examine changes in consumption and production in the homes of the poor, to uncover whether people at the lower echelons of society had any part in these so-called revolutions.

Despite their obvious importance, very little research has been conducted on pauper inventories. This is somewhat to be expected, as the sources are notoriously difficult to locate and contextualise. On the other hand, the lack of research on the sources is particularly surprising as historians have known about the practice for decades. There are, for example, numerous succinct references to the policy in the notable works of Sidney and Beatrice Webb, F. G. Emmison, E. M. Hampson, and W. E. Tate.[24] More recently, pauper inventories have been used to study the mechanisms of poor relief and negotiation between the parish and the indigent. Steven King used fifty-six inventories such as pauper and rent-arrear inventories to assess negotiation and entitlement to relief. He contended that numerous parishes would step in to help the poor while they still owned a reasonably extensive collection of possessions, suggesting that paupers did not need to be materially destitute before they were entitled to assistance.[25] Alongside Joan Kent, King has further argued that the practice shows that the authorities had a 'hard-nosed, money conscious attitude' and wanted the poor to contribute more towards their own relief.[26] Other historians have briefly linked the making of pauper inventories to control, deterrence, and the penalisation of the poor. Paul Fideler used the policy as an example to illustrate the uncertainty of a parish pension.[27] Steve Hindle argued that the practice shows that poor relief was not unconditional, and Anthea Newman claimed that the inventorying of parishioners' goods 'must have acted as a powerful deterrent to accepting parish relief'.[28]

[23] For instance, see: Muldrew, *Food*; Hans-Joachim Voth, *Time and Work in England 1750–1830* (Oxford, 2000); Overton et al., *Production and Consumption*; Alexandra Shepard, *Accounting for Oneself: Worth, status, and the social order* (Oxford, 2015).

[24] Sidney Webb and Beatrice Webb, *English Local Government: English poor law history*, part 1, *The old poor law* (London, 1927), p. 169; F. G. Emmison, *The Relief of the Poor at Eaton Socon, 1706–1834* (Aspley Guise, 1933), pp. 30, 33–34; E. M. Hampson, *The Treatment of Poverty in Cambridgeshire 1597–1834* (Cambridge, 1934), pp. 79–80, 83, 108–109, 182–183, 185, 276–277; W. E. Tate, *The Parish Chest: A study of the records of parochial administration in England*, 3rd edn. (Cambridge, 1969), pp. 207, 303 endnote 33.

[25] Steven King, *Poverty and Welfare in England 1700–1850: A regional perspective* (Manchester, 2000), pp. 93–97. Similar argument are also made in: Barbara Cornford, 'Inventories of the Poor', *Norfolk Archaeology*, 35 (1970–1973), p. 125; Paul A. Fideler, *Social Welfare in Pre-industrial England* (London, 2006), pp.148–150.

[26] Joan Kent, 'The Rural "middling sort" in Early Modern England, circa 1640–1740: Some economic, political and socio-cultural characteristics', *Rural History*, 10 (1999), p. 35; idem and Steven King, 'Changing Patterns of Poor Relief in some English Rural Parishes circa 1650–1750', *Rural History*, 14 (2003), pp. 137–138.

[27] Fideler, *Social Welfare*, p. 112.

[28] Hindle, *On the Parish*, p. 282; A. E. Newman, 'The Old Poor Law in East Kent, 1606–1834: A social and demographic analysis' (Ph.D. thesis, University of Kent, 1979), pp. 153–154.

Pauper inventories have most commonly been used to consider the consumer behaviour of the poor. Barbara Cornford was one of the earliest writers to assess empirically the material lives of the poor in the early 1970s. She used fifteen pauper inventories from Martham village in Norfolk to show that paupers owned a wide range of consumer goods despite being on poor relief.[29] In 1997 Peter King used fifty-one pauper inventories to assess the material lives of paupers in Essex. The results built substantially upon Cornford's findings to suggest that goods such as looking glasses, tea-related items, and timepieces became more prevalent in Essex pauper households over the long eighteenth century.[30] Adrian Green studied 206 Norfolk inventories alongside archaeological evidence to assess the living conditions of the poor. In a similar manner to King and Cornford, he argued that the inventories demonstrated that people's material lives were improving over the eighteenth century. Green called the inventories he used 'pauper inventories'; however, because the sources were not checked against other poor law records, around one-third of the sample did not relate to the recipients of relief; rather their goods had been inventoried for other reasons such as debt.[31] Ruth Mather recently used seven pauper and rent-arrears inventories alongside fifty probate inventories from London and the Pennine region, to argue that the working class owned a range of goods and furnished their homes with a range of materials between 1790 and 1820.[32] Overall, then, the literature on the practice is based on only a small number of pauper inventories from parts of Essex and a handful of other settlements.[33] Likewise, the research on the mechanisms of poor relief and negotiation between the parish and the indigent has generally been based on negligible numbers of inventories and handfuls of overseers' accounts and vestry minutes, which only note the presence of the practice.

This volume is the first ever published collection of pauper inventories and helps to bring the poor to the forefront in areas where they have often been neglected by researchers. With this in mind, the following chapters are intended

[29] Cornford, 'Inventories of the Poor', pp. 118–125.

[30] King, 'Pauper Inventories', pp. 155–191.

[31] Adrian Green, 'Heartless and Unhomely? Dwellings of the poor in East Anglia and north-east England', in Joanne McEwan and Pamela Sharpe, eds., *Accommodating Poverty: The housing and living arrangements of the English poor, c. 1600–1850* (Basingstoke, 2011), pp. 69–101.

[32] Ruth Mather, 'The Home-Making of the English Working Class: Radical politics and domestic life in late-Georgian England, c. 1790–1820' (Ph.D. thesis, Queen Mary, University of London, 2016), pp. 34–36, 77–78, 93, 124–125, 188–189.

[33] My research has been addressing this imbalance. To date, I have collected 60 pauper inventories from Dorset, 61 from Kent, 228 from Essex, 11 from Lancashire, 72 from Leicestershire and Rutland, and 230 from Norfolk. See: Joseph Harley 'Material lives of the Poor and their Strategic use of the Workhouse during the final decades of the English Old Poor Law', *Continuity and Change*, 30 (2015), pp. 71–103; idem, 'Consumption and Poverty', pp. 81–104; idem, 'Pauper Inventories, Social Relations'; idem, 'Consumption and the Life-cycle of English Paupers: The perspective from Essex, 1750–1834', (M.A. thesis, University of Warwick, 2011); idem, 'Material Lives of the English Poor: A regional perspective'.

to offer a guide to readers on the inventories and further outline their importance to researchers. It is also hoped that the subsequent chapters will lay the groundwork for new avenues of research and will motivate readers to collect additional samples of inventories. Chapter 2 examines the legality of taking inventories of paupers' goods and the customary aspects that underpinned the practice. It is found that the system of making inventories of parishioners' belongings had no legal basis and that the impetus to make pauper inventories instead came from local practices and policies, created at the discretion and initiative of individual officials, ratepayers, and vestrymen. Motivated by a perceived need to reduce rates, the inventorying of paupers' goods was a method that parishes used to recoup money and get the poor to contribute towards their own relief. The mindsets and attitudes of parish officers and ratepayers also appear to have been crucial in underpinning their decisions to appraise the belongings of parishioners. Sometimes paupers' goods were enumerated in an inventory for benevolent reasons, or at the very least with benign consequences, as the practice ensured that many people received parish assistance until they died. This meant that people did not have to sell their possessions before they were seen as 'deserving' and helped to legitimise their claim. However, parishes appear to have increasingly inventoried claimants' belongings in a more punitive manner and used it as a method to dissuade people from applying for relief by the late eighteenth century.

Chapter 3 starts by analysing the numerous types of inventories that were found in Norfolk Record Office, showing that parish and miscellaneous archive collections contain a multitude of different types of inventories which can be used to examine numerous topics such as debt, the economy of makeshifts, and the nature of poor relief. The geographical, socio-economic, and chronological distribution of the 230 pauper inventories from Norfolk is then examined. It is found that most pauper inventories were created between the 1720s and 1770s in rural agricultural areas of southern and central Norfolk, where there were difficult farming conditions and a much higher dependence on poor relief than in wider Norfolk and in England and Wales. The final section of the chapter considers the types of people whose possessions were inventoried, to assess the extent to which the people captured in the sources are representative of pauper populations as a whole. The results show that overall parishes made inventories of similar types of paupers and that pauper inventories are broadly representative of many other claimants whose goods were not appraised by the parish. Women were most likely to have their possessions inventoried by parochial officials between the seventeenth and late eighteenth century, but after this inventories were increasingly made of goods in male-headed households. Parishes tended to make inventories of the possessions of longer-term recipients, who were particularly expensive to relieve and received pensions for life-cycle-related problems such as sickness, old age, and infirmity.

The final chapter scrutinises examples of pauper inventories and the items listed in the sources, to illustrate how they were formatted and how representative the goods in the documents are for paupers who did not have their goods appraised by the parish. It is argued that pauper inventories are difficult sources to examine for similar reasons to probate inventories, and that they should never be viewed as complete as items may be missing. Nevertheless, because they are potentially representative of the ownership of the goods of millions of people at the point that they turned to poor relief and capture a wide range of belongings, they are very useful sources for studying a range of topics related to material culture, the history of the home, and the poor's everyday lives.

Chapter 2

The context and practice of making pauper inventories

During the old poor law of 1601–1834, the parish was established as an administrative unit for distributing poor relief to people who needed help for reasons such as sickness, lack of work, and old age. The system was administered by one or more overseers of the poor, aided by churchwardens, who were responsible for raising a tax (poor rate) to fund the system and deciding which parishioners should be given assistance. Parishes had their own vestries which were made up of ratepayers who had a say on how the taxes should be spent. Local magistrates and justices of the peace also had powers to monitor and overrule overseers' decisions to ensure that the system was administered fairly. This overarching system remained in place between 1601 and 1834, but was altered on numerous occasions through the passing of hundreds of national and local acts which impinged directly on how the poor would be helped and the powers that parochial officials had.[1] From the 1690s, for example, local and national acts led to the extensive establishment of workhouses as a form of support (indoor relief),[2] and the settlement laws meant that paupers could only be relieved in their 'home' parish.[3] Moreover, with the

[1] For further reading on the statutory basis of the old poor law, see: Geoffrey W. Oxley, *Poor Relief in England and Wales 1601–1834* (London, 1974), pp. 14–33; Paul Slack, *Poverty and Policy in Tudor and Stuart England* (London, 1988), pp. 113–131; Jonathan Healey, *The First Century of Welfare: Poverty and poor relief in Lancashire 1620–1730* (Woodbridge, 2014), pp. 4–12; King, *Poverty and Welfare*, pp. 18–47, 272–274; Shave, *Pauper Policies*, pp. 56–149; Lynn Hollen Lees, *The Solidarities of Strangers: The English poor laws and the people, 1700–1948* (Cambridge, 1998), passim; Anthony Brundage, *The English Poor Laws, 1700–1930* (London, 2002), pp. 9–36; Derek Fraser, *The Evolution of the British Welfare State*, 4th edn. (London, 2009), pp. 38–69; S. J. Thompson, 'Population Growth and Corporations of the Poor, 1660–1841', in Chris Briggs, P. M. Kitson, and S. J. Thompson, eds., *Population, Welfare and Economic Change in Britain 1290–1834* (Woodbridge, 2014), pp. 189–225.

[2] On workhouses, see for instance: Kathryn Morrison, *The Workhouse: A study of poor-law buildings in England* (Swindon, 1999); James S. Taylor, 'The Unreformed Workhouse, 1776–1834', in E. W. Martin, ed., *Comparative Development in Social Welfare* (London, 1972), pp. 57–84; Tim Hitchcock, 'The English Workhouse: A study of institutional poor relief in selected counties, 1696–1750' (D.Phil. thesis, University of Oxford, 1985).

[3] By the late seventeenth century, people's 'home' parish or place of settlement was determined in numerous ways. A child's settlement was the same as their father's, but children born out of wedlock had settlement in the parish where they were born. Women took the parish of their husband at marriage. Settlement could also change when a boy served an apprenticeship (usually

system being organised into nearly 15,000 parishes in England and Wales which each had differing local needs and their own officials (who often changed every 6–12 months), a highly discretionary and complex patchwork of systems was in place during the old poor law.[4] It is from this complicated structure that the practice of inventorying paupers' goods was born.

Legality of the practice

Pauper inventories were made to record the possessions that a claimant owned at one point in time. The paupers would then continue to use their goods and at a later date, usually when they died, the goods would revert to the parish when they would then be sold, given to other paupers as relief in kind, or be used to furnish the parish poorhouse/workhouse. Some parishes also took paupers' lands and homes,[5] though much more rarely since few people owned their own properties.[6] Under the old poor law there was no direct legal statute which allowed parish officers to inventory and later take claimants' goods in this way in return for support. The impetus to make

lasting seven years) in another parish, or when somebody was in continuous employment for a full year or more in another settlement. One could also pay poor rates or rent a property with a yearly value of £10 or more in another parish to qualify for a new settlement. For further information, see: James S. Taylor, 'The Impact of Pauper Settlement 1691–1834', *Past and Present*, 73 (1976), pp. 42–74; James S. Taylor, *Poverty, Migration, and Settlement in the Industrial Revolution: Sojourners' narratives* (Palo Alto, 1989); K. D. M. Snell, *Parish and Belonging: Community, identity and welfare in England and Wales* (Cambridge, 2006), esp. pp. 81–161; Tim Hitchcock and Robert Shoemaker, *London Lives: Poverty, crime and the making of a modern city, 1690–1800* (Cambridge, 2015), pp. 42–52.

[4] For more information on the discretionary and complex nature of the old poor law and local systems governance, see: Hindle, *On the Parish*; King, *Poverty and Welfare*; Shave, *Pauper Policies*; Peter King, *Crime, Justice and Discretion in England 1740–1820* (Oxford, 2000); Peter King, 'The Summary Courts and Social Relations in Eighteenth-century England', *Past and Present*, 183 (2004), pp. 125–172; Peter King, *Crime and Law in England, 1750–1840: Remaking justice from the margins* (Cambridge, 2006); David Sugarman and G. R. Rubin, 'Towards a New History of the Law and Material Society in England 1750–1914', in G. R. Rubin and David Sugarman, eds., *Law, Economy and Society, 1750–1914: Essays in the history of English law* (Abingdon, 1984), pp. 47–52; Joanna Innes, *Inferior Politics: Social problems and social policies in eighteenth-century Britain* (Oxford, 2009); Hitchcock and Shoemaker, *London Lives*; Richard Dyson, 'The Extent and Nature of Pauperism in five Oxfordshire Parishes, 1786–1832', *Continuity and Change*, 28 (2013), pp. 421–449.

[5] See for instance the 1804 vestry minutes of Tetney, Lincolnshire, in John Wild, *Tetney, Lincolnshire: A history* (Grimsby, 1901), pp. 95–96. Also see John Broad, 'Housing the Rural Poor in Southern England, 1650–1850', *Agricultural History Review*, 48 (2000), p. 166.

[6] Amanda Vickery, for example, estimated that only around one in ten people owned their own homes. Moreover, those who owned their own homes are likely to have been the middling sort and elite. Amanda Vickery, *Behind Closed Doors: At Home in Georgian England* (New Haven, 2009), p. 7.

pauper inventories instead came from local customs and policies, created at the discretion and initiative of individual officials, ratepayers, and vestrymen.[7]

Parishes often felt that they were legally justified in taking paupers' goods despite having little authority to do so. Some parish officials, for example, among the opening lines of inventories wrote that the goods were appraised in a 'lawful' or 'legal' manner. The pauper inventory of Francis Karrington of Shelton was apparently made 'as ye Law requires' **(171)**. Occasionally parishes made paupers sign legal documents which stated that they were entitled to their goods because they had given them relief. The inventory of Henry Wells of Bressingham stated that the parish was entitled to his possessions as they had paid his rent **(10)**:

> in Considderation of the sume of one pound and seventenn shillings & six pence paid by Thomas fullcher & Edmund Briant Churchwarden and Overseer of ye pa[ri]sh of Brisingham … to my Landlord weaxd for me ye said Henry wells of Brisingham and for and in Consideration of a sartaine Rent to be paid me ye said Henry wells he [h]ath Bargained and solde and by this p^{r}[e]sent writing doth grant Bargaine and sell unto ye said Thomas fullcher and Edm[un]^{t} Briant of Brisingham …

Samuel Hunt had a similar written agreement with St. Mary in the Marsh in Norwich **(123)**. It was made when he started receiving casual relief, declaring that:

> I do hereby Acknowledge that ye above Goods Furniture and Things are in my Possession and that the same are the property of the Officers of ye Parish of St Mary in ye Marsh in ye Close, and I do promise not to Embezzle any [Par]t there of and that I will deliver up ye same to ye Officers of ye said Parish of St Mary in ye Marsh when I am call'd upon so to do …

This was clearly a device that some authorities used to take parishioners' goods legally and avoid prosecution.

Most parishes did not go to the trouble of creating legal agreements and some justices of the peace may have even supported the inventorying of pauper goods, even though parishes lacked the requisite legal authority to do so. For instance, though probably referring to workhouse admittance-related inventories, Deal (Kent) borough quarter sessions in 1722 recorded that:

> It is ordered that noe person or persons whatsoever applying to the proper officers of the s[ai]^{d} Town of Deal for Releife Shall receive any Weekly Allowance untill that the said Officers shall have taken an account of what Goods and Effects Such persons have and there order be reccieved to the Town house appointed for the Same[?] up and then Entred into a Book there kept & belong

[7] See note 4.

to the said house and the persons there to be kept according to the Rules of the said house.[8]

The frequency with which the poor appealed to local justices to complain about their goods being inventoried probably varied regionally and depended upon how understanding claimants thought their local justice was.[9] Moreover, it is possible that some of the poor were not aware of their legal right to petition justices or may have been fearful of retribution or an unfavourable decision, such as the refusal of relief or being forced into the workhouse, if they complained to a justice.[10] Nonetheless, where evidence has survived it appears that many justices helped to protect paupers' belongings, and that overseers wanted to avoid disputes over goods reaching justices. In 1814, for example, the justice Samuel Whitbread stopped the parish of Wilstead, Surrey, from taking 'an old bed and sheets' from John Monday.[11] The autobiography of the labourer Joseph Mayett records one instance when the parish of Quainton in Buckinghamshire took his deceased brother's possessions. Instead of letting this happen, Mayett went to the overseer and 'told him if he did not deliver everything into my hands the next morning I would put the law in force against him'. The threat of the legal action worked and the following morning the overseer 'Came and delvered them up to me and my youngest brother'.[12] As a result, justices of the peace are only rarely listed as appraisers or witnesses in pauper inventories as they might have stopped the process.

A detailed example of a justice stopping a parish from taking a pauper's belongings has survived from Wingham in Kent. It was written by a local justice, Edward Mills, and concerned the pauper John Beach, who had received a weekly allowance of 1s. 6d. or 2s. from the parish of Wingham for 20 years. John's daughter Ann and her husband forced John out of his home and took his possessions, following Ann's constant abuse and beatings of her father. The parish claimed that Ann had no right to the goods as they had been promised to the parish around 10–12 years ago. An inventory had been

[8] KHLC De/JQs1, Deal quarter sessions book, 1719–1778.

[9] Peter King, 'The Rights of the Poor and the Role of the Law: The impact of pauper appeals to the summary courts, 1750–1834', in Peter Jones and Steven King, eds., *Obligation, Entitlement and Dispute under the English Poor Laws, 1600–1900* (Cambridge, 2015), pp. 252–253, 257, 260–261; King, *Poverty and Welfare*, pp. 31–32; Peter Dunkley, 'Paternalism, the Magistracy and Poor Relief in England, 1795–1834', *International Review of Social History*, 24 (1979), pp. 371–397.

[10] The current state of research suggests that most paupers had a reasonable understanding of the poor laws which they used to negotiate relief. Snell, *Parish and Belonging*, pp. 87–93; Steven King, 'Negotiating the Law of Poor Relief in England, 1800–1840', *History*, 96 (2011), pp. 410–435; King, 'Rights of the Poor', pp. 253–254; Hitchcock and Shoemaker, *London Lives*.

[11] Alan F. Cirket, ed., *Samuel Whitbread's Notebooks 1810–11, 1813–14* (Bedford, 1971), p. 125.

[12] Ann Kussmaul, ed., *The Autobiography of Joseph Mayett of Quainton (1783–1839)* (Chesham, 1986), pp. 83–84.

made to prove this.[13] The justice ruled that Ann could not keep John's belongings, but also questioned whether the parish had had the right to take the goods in the first place. Mills decided that parishes had no authority to inventory and take pauper possessions to reimburse themselves for some of the money that they had previously paid out in relief. He also said that parishes could not use the act of 5 Geo. I c.8. 1718–19, which allowed parishes to distrain the goods of runaway parents or partners, to justify the taking of paupers' goods.[14] Although this source does not relate to Norfolk, it is particularly interesting as it shows that some justices were aware that the appraising and taking of paupers' goods had no legal basis and indicates that if they saw such abuses sometimes they stopped them. The fact that Mills had to point out that parishes were not allowed to use the act of 5 Geo. I c.8. 1718–19 to take paupers' belongings indicates that some parochial officials misused existing statute to justify their actions. Furthermore, it shows that assistance could be conditional and withheld if claimants did not allow the parish to inventory their possessions.

Parish motives to make pauper inventories

The question why parishes made pauper inventories is difficult to answer, since every inventory was made at a local level under the initiative and discretion of parish officers and vestrymen. This also means that it is difficult to assess pauper inventories from one county as a single collection, as systems of poor relief varied from parish to parish and local practice was dependent upon the economic, legal, and cultural conventions of the respective parishes.[15] Despite this, two key reasons emerge which developed organically through disputes, worries, and shared values among overseers, ratepayers, vestries, and paupers. The first of these reasons is financial. Many of these paupers cost considerable amounts of money to help and so inventorying their goods was a method that parishes used to raise money and get the poor to contribute something to the parish pot. While the amounts that parishes received from pauper belongings were generally small, symbolically these sums of money were very important to many ratepayers. Secondly, the

[13] Unfortunately, this inventory does not appear to have survived.

[14] CCAL U3/269/16/1, Wingham case for opinion, 1766.

[15] King, *Poverty and Welfare*; Samantha A. Shave, 'The Dependent Poor? (Re)constructing the lives of individuals "on the parish" in rural Dorset, 1800–1832', *Rural History*, 20 (2009), pp. 67–97; Samantha Williams, *Poverty, Gender and Life-cycle under the English Poor Law 1760–1834* (Woodbridge, 2011); Hindle, *On the Parish*; Barry Reay, *Rural Englands: Labouring lives in the nineteenth century* (Basingstoke, 2004); Dyson, 'Pauperism in five Oxfordshire Parishes', pp. 421–449.

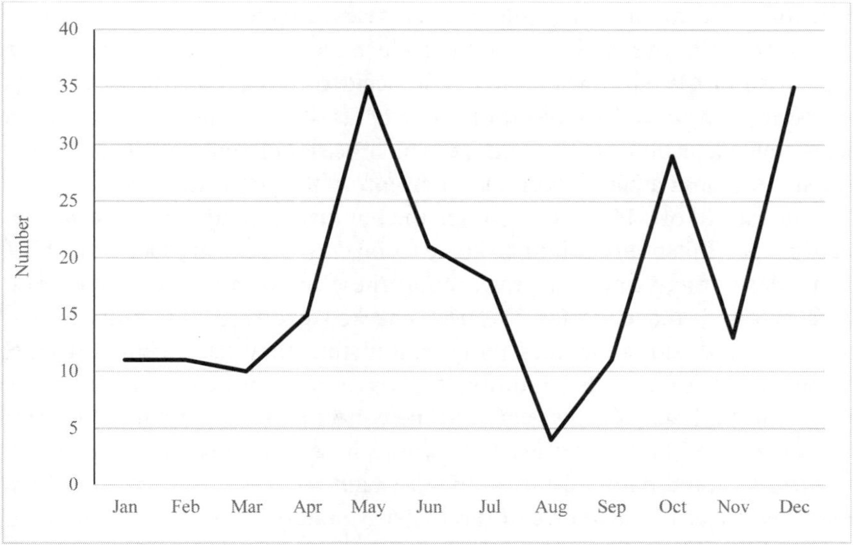

Figure 2.1 Months when the Norfolk pauper inventories were made, c.1690–1834

attitudes of parochial authorities and ratepayers appear to have been crucial in underpinning their decisions to inventory the goods of paupers. Although the practice had no legal basis, the appraising of paupers' belongings can be linked to benevolence as it guaranteed many people parish assistance until they died and it meant that they did not have to sell off their goods before they were entitled to help from the parish. Their possessions gave the poor an important card to play when applying for long-term relief and helped to strengthen their claim. However, although there is some chronological overlap, parishes appear to have increasingly appraised the possessions of claimants as a method to dissuade further applications and control the numbers of people on poor relief by the late eighteenth century.

Figure 2.1 shows the months when the pauper inventories from Norfolk were made. The fewest pauper inventories were made in August. This may arise from seasonal reasons, as the vast majority of inventories came from rural areas and August was when agricultural seasonal unemployment was generally lowest and when there was least pressure on parochial funds.[16] If the overseers were farmers this was also the time in the year when they were preoccupied with other matters. From October, seasonal unemployment increased and more people tended to apply for relief, which may explain the

[16] The geographical distribution of the inventories is discussed further in chapter 3.

growth in the number of pauper inventories in October and December.[17] Nineteen of the inventories that were made in December, however, came from the parish of Cawston when the parish decided to make inventories 'of All the poore that Rec[ei]ve Colecttion' in 1699 **(25–43)**. As such, it is difficult to accurately determine the extent to which seasonal unemployment was a decisive factor in a parish deciding to inventory the goods of its parishioners.

The month of May stands out for the number of pauper inventories that were made. Taken alongside the spike in inventories during October, this is particularly interesting as it was around these times in the year when rates were assessed and collected. Vestries checked overseers' accounts around these months and sometimes they realised that they had spent too much money or that they needed additional funds to support the poor over the next 6–12 months. Likewise, it was around these months when most new overseers were appointed and many of these would have had ideas of their own to reduce the amounts of rates that people paid. Many overseers would have also been eager to make inventories of parishioners' goods for personal reasons, as they might otherwise have ended up using their own money if they overspent parochial funds while they were in charge. These sums of money could be considerable and if the vestry thought that overseers were irresponsible then they could be out of pocket for months or not receive their money back at all.[18] Justices could also force overseers to spend more money than was intended if pauper appeals to them to override parish decisions were successful.[19] Arguments, disagreements, conflicts, and negotiations over money at vestry meetings were ubiquitous.[20] Overseers and many larger ratepayers appear to have consequently often welcomed the inventorying of pauper goods in the hope that it would reduce rates, diminish the chance that the parish would get into debt, and ensure that the poor contributed something towards their own relief.

Appraisers sometimes mentioned in vestry minutes or the inventories themselves how the money expended on somebody had influenced their decision to appraise their goods. Such evidence indicates that because paupers were given relief the parish felt entitled to their possessions. In Shelton, the goods of Francis Karrington were appraised 'upon his craweing collection of

[17] K. D. M. Snell, *Annals of the Labouring Poor: Social change and agrarian England, 1660–1900* (Cambridge, 1985), pp. 15–66.
[18] For example, in 1820 the overseer of Little Walsingham, William Groom, had his goods distrained by justices of the peace for overspending £87 7s. 12d. of parish funds. NRO PD 582/108, Order for distress against William Groom, 1820. Also see: Newman, 'Old Poor Law', p. 134; L. A. Botelho, *Old Age and the English Poor Law, 1500–1700* (Woodbridge, 2004), p. 68.
[19] Williams, *Poverty, Gender*, pp. 91–100; King, 'Rights of the Poor', pp. 235–262; Dunkley, 'Paternalism', pp. 371–397.
[20] Hindle, *On the Parish*, pp. 365–378; Williams, *Poverty, Gender*, pp. 69–100.

Table 2.1 Income from selling paupers' goods in Bressingham parish, 1715–1729

Date (half year ending)	Total parish income	Income from selling pauper goods	Percentage of total parish income from selling pauper goods
Apr 1715	£9 1s. 6d.	£0 17s. 6d.	9.6
Apr 1719	£20 8s. 5d.	£0 2s. 6d.	0.6
Apr 1722	£24 16s. 0d.	£1 0s. 6d.	4.1
Apr 1724	£16 7s. 5d.	£4 7s. 6d.	26.7
Sep 1724	£26 12s. 3d.	£5 16s. 0d.	21.8
Oct 1726	£31 19s. 1d.	£3 18s. 6d.	12.3
Apr 1728	£36 12s. 10d.	£0 2s. 0d.	0.3
Apr 1729	£43 7s. 6d.	£1 5s. 0d.	2.9

Source: NRO PD 295/93, Bressingham overseers' accounts, 1692–1729.

ye Town' **(171)**. In the same parish an inventory was made of Katherine Jex's possessions 'upon her taken Collection' **(178)**. In Hingham, the inventory of Widow Little's belongings was made because 'She was fon'd to be Reliev'd by the Parish' **(60)**. William Car's goods were inventoried by Bressingham parish 'for ye Reliefe of himselfe and his famelye' **(14)**. A pauper inventory was made of Thomas Cullam's possessions 'for Collection ... [from] the parish of Forncett S^{t} peter' **(44)**. On 14 December 1699, Cawston parish made pauper inventories 'of All the poore that Rec[ei]ve Colecttion' **(25–43)**. Parishes would thus appraise the possessions of paupers at a range of life-cycle points: some were made of the goods of individuals who had received poor relief for long periods of time; some were made of the possessions of people as soon as they started to receive support from the parish; and some were made because the parish expected to pay out large sums of money in the near future. In total, 35 per cent of Norfolk pauper inventories were made around the point when people started receiving regular or casual relief from the parish, and 65 per cent were made of the belongings of paupers who were already on regular or casual assistance.[21]

The income from selling pauper belongings was mostly small, but symbolically it was very important to parish officials and larger ratepayers who wanted the poor to contribute towards their own support. In Frampton, Lincolnshire, for instance, the parish raised over £126 from selling the possessions of parishioners over a 118-year period. This, however, only equated to an average income of around £1 1s. 4d. every year.[22] The goods of John Cooper

[21] 'Already on relief' is defined as receiving relief for two months or more before the pauper inventory was made. Most people in this category, however, had been on some sort of relief for years. Unfortunately, it was not possible to determine exactly when paupers started receiving relief in around one-third of the inventories.

[22] Hindle, *On the Parish*, p. 281; idem, 'Power, Poor Relief, and Social Relations in Holland Fen, c. 1600–1800', *Historical Journal*, 41 (1998), p. 94.

were worth £2 18s. 2d. at his death in Eaton Socon, Bedfordshire, but this figure made up only 16 per cent of the total money that the parish had paid out to relieve him.[23] In Martham, Elizabeth Smith and/or her husband had been in receipt of between 6d. and 2s. per week for ten years almost without break, and were also frequently given money during times of sickness, clothing, rent payments, and fuel. Yet their goods only raised £1 15s. when they were sold by the parish around late 1771 or early 1772 **(90)**. Table 2.1 shows the parish of Bressingham's total income and the revenue that they received from selling paupers' goods between 1715–1729. The results show that the income from selling parishioners' goods was relatively high in 1724 and 1726, but that during most years income from the practice was small as it rarely exceeded more than 10 per cent of total parish takings.[24] Moreover, it is important to note that the revenue from selling parishioners' goods was zero most years. The system ultimately depended upon a pauper, who had previously had an inventory made of their goods, passing away. As a result, income from the selling of claimants' belongings was unpredictable and sporadic from year to year.

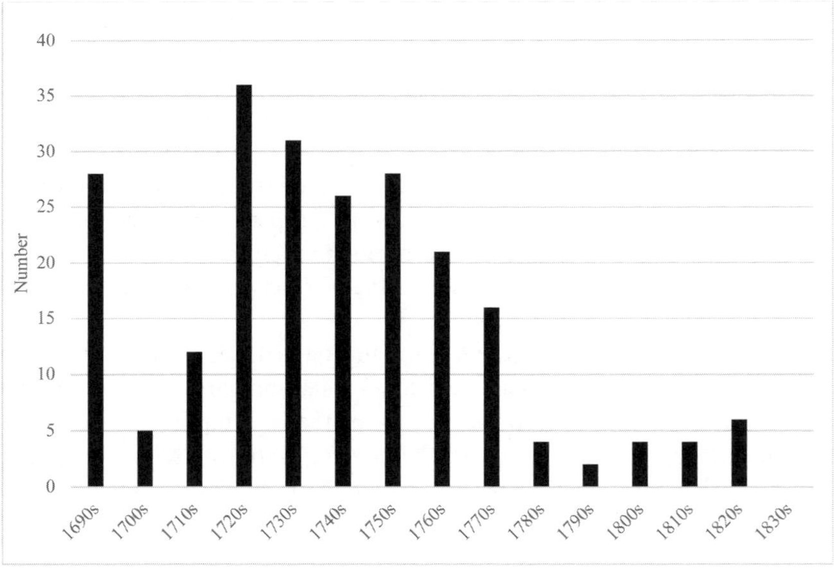

Figure 2.2 Chronological distribution of the Norfolk pauper inventories, c.1690–1834

[23] Hindle, *On the Parish*, p. 281; Emmison, *Relief of the Poor*, pp. 33–34.

[24] A number of pauper inventories from Bressingham during these years appear not to have survived.

In most cases, parishes experimented with this policy for several years but then stopped. Sometimes parishes ceased making inventories when justices prohibited them from doing so;[25] however, most of the time it appears that the practice stopped when a new overseer decided that they did not want to apply the policy, or when parishes realised that they did not make as much money from it as they hoped. This means that in a single parish the making of pauper inventories usually did not continue for more than a few years.[26] One should not, however, use this as evidence to suggest that the policy was insignificant. The practice was a highly formative part of claimants' experience of poor relief when applied and had a considerable influence on notions of entitlement and how paupers and officials interacted with one another.[27]

Historians such as Keith Snell and Mark Blaug have characterised southern and eastern rural parishes as 'miniature welfare states' in the decades before 1780, as support was generally more benevolent, generous, and encompassing at this time, helping people in a number of creative and pragmatic ways.[28] By the late eighteenth century, however, the poor law system was seen to be in 'crisis' as rates significantly increased and growing numbers of able-bodied men applied for relief.[29] The making of pauper inventories can be related to this more general chronology. Most pauper inventories were made between the 1720s and 1770s (Figure 2.2).[30] As these were the years when parishes were often flexible and generous, this may indicate that, in addition to financial considerations, parishes inventoried the goods of paupers for benevolent reasons, or at the very least the policy had benign consequences. Their possessions gave the poor a bargaining chip which they could use to negotiate support and when their goods were inventoried this essentially acted as official recognition that they were deemed worthy of parish assistance. Moreover, inventorying paupers' goods but allowing them to use them until they died was a better option from the poor's point of view than being

[25] See for instance the example of Edward Mills and Wingham parish above.

[26] There are, of course, exceptions. In Redenhall with Harleston and Wortwell, for example, pauper inventories can be found from 1708 to 1828 **(124–167)**. Moreover, many more pauper inventories were made but have not survived for the parish.

[27] This is discussed at length in: Harley, 'Pauper Inventories, Social Relations'.

[28] Snell, *Annals*, pp. 105–107; Mark Blaug, 'The Poor Law Report reexamined', *The Journal of Economic History*, 24 (1964), p. 229.

[29] Snell, *Annals*, pp. 108–114; King, *Poverty and Welfare*, pp. 164–167; Peter Dunkley, *The Crisis of the Old Poor Law in England 1795–1834: An interpretive essay* (London, 1982); J. R. Poynter, *Society and Pauperism: English ideas on poor relief, 1795–1834* (London, 1969); Fraser, *British Welfare State*, pp. 46–57; Brundage, *English Poor Laws*, pp. 25–69; Bernard Harris, *The Origins of the British Welfare State: Social welfare in England and Wales, 1800–1945* (London, 2004), pp. 42–47. Also see: John Broad, 'Parish Economies of Welfare', *Historical Journal*, 42 (1999), pp. 985–1006.

[30] The chronological distribution of the pauper inventories is discussed further in chapter 3.

made to sell their belongings before they were entitled to relief. The lines between paying rates and ending up on the parish could be very thin.[31] Consequently, many lesser ratepayers would not have supported a policy that could have forced them to sell off their possessions immediately if they were ever to end up on relief themselves.[32]

Parishes appear to have inventoried the goods of parishioners less often from 1780 (Figure 2.2). Despite this, the evidence suggests that by the late eighteenth and early nineteenth centuries the appraising of paupers' goods was closely linked to a negative shift in the attitudes of ratepayers and parochial authorities, who increasingly wanted to pay less towards the support of the poor, dissuade people from applying for relief, and help only the most deserving and desperate of people. The infamous Royal Commissioners' report of 1834 praised the practice of taking paupers' goods. They wrote that the application of the policy in Northumberland 'frequently has a salutary effect, as instances occur of poor persons returning what they had received, when they discovered that they had been paid from the assessment, saying, "I would sooner want it than have my goods looked over, and seized when I die"'.[33]

Some parishes branded paupers' goods with the initials or name of the parish after they were inventoried by authorities. For example, in 1821 in East Harling, the belongings of Rhoda Wretham and Widow Whitehead were marked 'EHP' **(51–52)**. In Cowpe Lenches, New Hall Hey, and Hall Carr parish in Lancashire, the goods given to paupers were branded with a 'P' or 'CLP' during the 1810s.[34] 'Old' Warren and his wife's goods were marked 'A.P' by parochial officials in Ardleigh, Essex in 1822.[35] Examples of parishes branding parishioners' belongings are difficult to find before the late eighteenth century, suggesting that the practice was not very common even though most pauper inventories were made between 1720 and 1770 (Figure 2.2). Recipients' goods were branded to stop paupers from selling or pawning their

[31] Tim Hitchcock, Peter King, and Pamela Sharpe, 'Introduction: Chronicling poverty—the voices and strategies of the English poor, 1640–1840', in Hitchcock, King, and Sharpe, *Chronicling Poverty*, p. 10; Williams, *Poverty, Gender*, pp. 69–100, 125–129; Healey, *First Century of Welfare*, pp. 113–126.

[32] It is important to note that in Lancashire and other northern counties, parishes appear to have conversely generally taken and/or made paupers' sell their goods before they were entitled to relief. For more information on this and the reasons for it, see: Harley, 'Pauper Inventories, Social Relations'; idem, 'Material Lives of the English Poor: A regional perspective', pp. 32–78.

[33] BPP, 1834, XXIX.1, *Report from his Majesty's Commissioners for Inquiring into the Administration and Practical Operation of the Poor Laws. Appendix A: Reports of assistant commissioners, part II*, p. 195a.

[34] LRO MBRA/acc9017/11, Cowpe Lenches, New Hall Hey, and Hall Carr overseers' accounts, 1806–1850.

[35] ERO D/P 263/12/8, Ardleigh overseers' accounts, 1821–1824.

belongings. Parishes also used the practice to build up a stock of goods that could be given to other claimants or be used to furnish the parish pesthouse, poorhouse, or workhouse. The branding of paupers' goods, however, could also deliberately or inadvertently act as a way in which to identify, discriminate, and shame the poor. As the work of Steve Hindle has shown, for example, when people were made to wear badges on their clothing to show that they were paupers, the badges were used to shame and stigmatise the poor. It was also hoped by parochial authorities that wearing them would further dissuade people from applying for assistance unless they really needed it.[36] In a similar manner, the act of branding parishioners' goods could have had the same effect.

When the parish of Helpston in Northamptonshire came to inventory the goods of the labouring poet John Clare's father around the 1800s or 1810s, he was especially disgusted when the parish branded each item. Clare wrote that 'as soon as he went to the parish for relief they came to clap the town brand on his goods and set them down in their parish books because he shoud not sell or get out of them'. Clare bitterly resented this policy, lamenting that he 'felt utterly cast down for I coud not help them sufficient to keep them from the parish'.[37] The subject of appraising parishioners' goods appeared in one of Clare's most well-known poems, *The Parish: A Satire*:

> Tasking the pauper [his] labours to stand
> Or clapping on his goods the Parish Brand
> Lest he shoud sell them for the want of bread
> On parish bounty rather pind then fed
> Or carrying the parish book from door to door
> Claiming fresh taxes from the needy poor
> And if ones hunger overcomes his hate
> And buys a load with what shoud pay the rate
> He instant sets his tyrant laws to work
> In heart and deed the essence of a turk
> Brings summons for an eighteen penny rate
> And gains the praises of the parish state
> Or seizes goods and from the burthend clown
> Extorts for extra trouble half a Crown
> Himself a beggar that may shortly take
> A weekly pittance from the rates they make ...[38]

[36] Steve Hindle, 'Dependency, Shame and Belonging: Badging the deserving poor, c. 1550–1750', *Cultural and Social History*, 1 (2004), pp. 6–35; Hindle, *On the Parish*, pp. 433–445; Steve Hindle, 'Technologies of Identification under the Old Poor Law', *The Local Historian*, 36 (2006), esp. pp. 229–231.

[37] Eric Robinson, ed., *John Clare's Autobiographical Writings* (Oxford, 1983), p. 115.

[38] John Clare, *The Parish: A satire*, ed. Eric Robinson (London, 1985), pp. 63–64.

If paupers were caught selling or pawning their branded possessions the parish might withhold relief. It is also possible that some people were prosecuted if they sold their goods or if others were caught handling them. Though there were no laws which allowed parishes to brand paupers' goods, there were laws which protected parish property. Under these regulations people were fined or imprisoned if they were caught selling or handling stolen branded workhouse goods.[39] Parishes could have potentially manipulated this law to apply to people on outdoor relief, as pauper goods were viewed as parish property after they were inventoried, even though the indigent continued to use them.

A number of contemporaries argued that the appraising and seizing of pauper goods was cruel. In 1773, the Quaker poet and writer John Scott wrote that:

> In some of those few parishes, where allowance out of the workhouse is permitted, an unkind and indelicate practice frequently obtains. The parish vouchsafes a trifling pittance of a pension; and an industrious son or daughter, from the earnings of their industry, supplies the remainder of the maintenance of the aged or decrepit parent. In such cases, an inventory of what little household furniture may be in the pauper's possession is immediately taken, in order that it may revert to the parish at his decease. The poor have sensibility; and it is really cruel to treat as criminals, whose property is confiscated, those who in this respect have no crime but inevitable poverty.[40]

As we saw above, Joseph Mayett also opposed the system and threatened to report the overseer to a justice.[41] Occasionally some paupers even tried to hide their goods, showing that they resisted the policy.[42]

Newspaper reports help to illustrate how ratepayers increasingly applied a hard-nosed attitude to parishioners' goods by the early nineteenth century. Between 1818 and 1819, numerous newspapers around the country reported on a pauper named Barksby who deceived officials and exploited the parish by receiving relief that he did not need. The 77-year-old pauper had been in receipt of relief for twenty years when he asked the parish of Stanley in Derbyshire for additional help to pay his rent, claiming that he was starving and would have to sell his goods to make do. The overseer was subsequently 'induced' to visit Barksby's home and make an inventory of his possessions. In a small box, the overseer found 'in notes, gold and silver, the sum of 114*l.* 8s. 6d. besides a note of hand for 4*l.* and 19 dishonoured 1*l.* notes of

[39] Michael Nolan, *A Treatise of the Laws for the Relief and Settlement of the Poor*, vol. 2, 4th edn. (London, 1825), p. 390.

[40] John Scott, *Observations on the Present State of the Parochial and Vagrant Poor* (London, 1773), p. 48.

[41] See above.

[42] Elizabeth Melling, ed., *Kentish Sources*, vol. 4, *The poor* (Maidstone, 1964), p. 104; *The Northampton Mercury*, 2 Jan 1819, p. 4; *Evening Mail*, 13 Jan 1830, p. 2.

Belliers' bank; and a further sum of 1*l.* 10s. was found afterwards in the miserable dwelling'.[43] Newspapers called Barksby a 'wretch' and widely reported their 'disgust' at his abuse of the system. Several publications stated that 'Such impositions have a tendency to lock up the feeling of compassion, and to harden the human heart'.[44] In January 1830, another story was widely circulated regarding the widowed pauper Biddy Green. She died while living in the home of a woman called Widow Speight, who proceeded to examine the deceased's bed where she found 'hidden treasure', including:

> 22 guineas of the reigns of George II. and III., 37 half guineas of ditto, one sovereign ... two piece of foreign gold coin, value 36s. each; one gold watch, one silver watch, one silver pint, one silver cream-jug, twelve silver tea-spoons, six silver table-spoons, one silver gravy spoon, and various other articles of considerable value!!![45]

News about the goods in Widow Speight's home eventually reached the authorities and they were taken by the parish.[46] Although Barksby and Biddy Green were clearly abusing the system if these stories are true, they nonetheless help to demonstrate the distrust that paupers faced. Such scandals were rare, but they were widely circulated and would have led some people to believe that paupers were being treated too kindly and that they were taking advantage of the system. Calls for poor law reform were becoming particularly insistent from the late eighteenth century, for numerous reasons including rising poor rates and growing numbers of able-bodied men applying for relief.[47] Such stories relating to people's possessions are another feature of this demand for a harsher poor law regime, and would have led to the distrust of paupers on the ground and a tougher stance when it came to inventorying the goods of parishioners.

[43] Quote from: *The Public Ledger and Daily Advertiser*, 25 Dec 1818, p. 2.

[44] Among others, the story was reported in: ibid., p. 2; *The Bury and Norwich Post, or Suffolk, Essex, Cambridge, Ely, and Norfolk Telegraph*, 30 Dec 1818, p. 832; *Chester Courant and Anglo Welsh Gazette*, 12 Jan 1819, p. 4; *Newcastle Courant*, 2 Jan 1819, p. 2; *The Northampton Mercury*, 2 Jan 1819, p. 4; *Royal Cornwall Gazette, Falmouth Packet, and Plymouth Journal*, 2 Jan 1819, p. 4.

[45] Quote from: *The Manchester Courier and Manchester General Advertiser*, 16 Jan 1830, p. 3.

[46] Among others, the story was printed in: ibid., p. 3; *Evening Mail*, 13 Jan 1830, p. 2; *The Hull Packet Humber Mercury or Yorkshire and Lincolnshire Advertiser*, 19 Jan 1830, p. 3; *The Ipswich Journal; and Suffolk, Norfolk, Essex, and Cambridgeshire Advertiser*, 16 Jan 1830, p. 2.

[47] Snell, *Annals*, pp. 108–114; King, *Poverty and Welfare*, pp. 164–167; Dunkley, *Crisis of the Old Poor Law*; Poynter, *Society and Pauperism*; Brundage, *English Poor Laws*, pp. 25–69; Fraser, *British Welfare State*, pp. 46–57; Harris, *British Welfare State*, pp. 42–47.

Conclusion

The poor law was a highly complex system and there are conflicting issues that must be considered to fully understand it, such as the law, finances, and the subjective opinions of overseers, ratepayers, vestries, and paupers. It is from these myriad factors that the illegal, discretionary, and customary practice of inventorying parishioners' goods was created. Motivated by a perceived need to reduce rates, the appraisal of claimants' possessions was a method that parishes used to get paupers to contribute items to town stock or extra funds to the parish chest. Sometimes paupers' goods were appraised for relatively compassionate reasons or with benign consequences, since the practice guaranteed many people support until they passed away and they did not need to be materially destitute before they were entitled to parish assistance. As the work of Beverly Lemire and others has shown, it was common for people to use their goods as a form of credit or savings and to go through cycles of acquiring, pawning, or selling their belongings to purchase food, pay bills, and address cashflow problems.[48] Thus, when parishes inventoried parishioners' goods, it was not an unusual practice for people to exchange their goods for something else. At least this way they could acquire relief, keep their belongings a little longer, and create a more comfortable home than would otherwise have been possible. By the late eighteenth century, however, parishes increasingly appear to have inventoried people's belongings in a more disciplinary manner and used the practice as a method to control pauper populations. In this sense, the making of pauper inventories can be linked to the hardening of attitudes and calls for a harsher poor law system, which eventually resulted in the Poor Law Amendment Act of 1834.

A handful of paupers refused relief as soon as they realised that their possessions would be inventoried. Through desperation others took whatever help they could get and let their goods be listed with little resistance. More commonly, there appears to have been a process of negotiation between parishioners and officials. For example, around 35 per cent of paupers started receiving relief after their goods were appraised and also made more frequent requests for items such as clothing. Other claimants started receiving higher regular relief payments the week after their goods were appraised. The poor thus had agency and could make agreements with officials. There was an element of trust between the two parties. The pauper had faith in overseers to

[48] Beverly Lemire, *The Business of Everyday Life: Gender, practice and social politics in England, c. 1600–1900* (Manchester, 2005), pp. 82–109; Melanie Tebbutt, *Making Ends Meet: Pawnbroking and working-class credit* (Leicester, 1983); Alannah Tomkins, *The Experience of Urban Poverty, 1732–82: Parish, charity and credit* (Manchester, 2006), pp. 204–234; Shepard, *Accounting for Oneself*.

give them long-term relief, and the authorities trusted the indigent not to pawn or sell the goods after they were appraised. The relationship was partially built on self-interest: the poor endeavoured to be independent and keep their belongings, while the parish wanted to help the most deserving of people and control expenditure. However, there was also mutual understanding and an element of give and take. If the parish was simply interested in maintaining its financial solvency and/or punishing the poor, they would have taken the goods of every pauper who applied for relief and only left parishioners with a few basic necessary items. Instead, they generally targeted people who needed long-term relief and wanted the assurance of receiving relief until they died. Many officials thus strove to help the poor and allow them the dignity of staying in their own home with their possessions. Likewise, although many paupers disliked the policy, many also appear to have understood that it was a necessary part of receiving assistance and keeping their independence. The next chapter continues to examine the practice by focusing on the county of Norfolk and the sample of inventories transcribed in this volume.

Chapter 3

The sample of Norfolk inventories

Pauper inventories are very difficult to find as they are largely not documented in archive catalogues and are generally only located through the laborious task of looking through thousands of pages of overseers' accounts, bills, receipts and vouchers, vestry minutes, churchwardens' accounts, and workhouse records. As this chapter will show, the practice of making pauper inventories was relatively common in Norfolk, meaning that a larger than usual number of inventories are indexed in Norfolk Record Office. It is on these catalogued inventories that this research on Norfolk is primarily based. This means that this volume is not exhaustive as there are almost certainly other inventories which remain to be unearthed at the repository. The chapter starts by discussing the 539 located inventories from which the core sample of 230 pauper inventories is drawn, before moving on to examine the geographical, socio-economic, and chronological distribution of the pauper inventories from Norfolk. The types of paupers whose goods were appraised by parishes in Norfolk is then considered.

The sample

Numerous types of inventories can be found in record offices in addition to pauper inventories. Many of these relate to the possessions of paupers, but considerable numbers of them were made of the belongings of people who were clearly not poor, based on the fact that they paid large amounts of money in taxes, received no poor relief or help from charities, and sometimes had many hundreds of pounds worth of stock and goods. Because of this, every inventory identified from the archival catalogue has been cross-referenced to other sources such as overseers' accounts, quarter sessions papers, and vestry minutes to determine why it was made and whose belongings it lists. It is important to do this since many of the inventories are superficially similar but were clearly made for very different reasons.

Five hundred and thirty-nine inventories were found at Norfolk Record Office in Norwich in total (Table 3.1). One hundred and eighteen of the inventories are classed as 'unknown' as relevant background information could not be found to classify them and determine whose goods had been

Table 3.1 Types of inventories found among Norfolk parish and miscellaneous archival collections, c.1643–1834

Type of inventory	Number
Pauper inventories	230
Unknown	118
Goods-given	51
Debt-related (rates, rent, unknown debt)	34
Poorhouse/workhouse contents	31
Goods-taken	28
Other	23
Almshouse-related	13
Poorhouse/workhouse admittance-related	7
Family abandonment	3
Bastardy-related	1
Total	**539**

appraised. The 230 pauper inventories among this sample are the principal focus of this volume. The remaining inventories are not transcribed here, unless they relate to the possessions of somebody who also had a pauper inventory made of their possessions. It is, nonetheless, important to discuss these other inventories to show the reader how the inventories were categorised, how they are different to pauper inventories, and to highlight the vast potential there is for future research.

Goods-given inventories, which list the items given to people by the parish, are the second most common type of inventory found among parish and miscellaneous archival records (Table 3.1). On occasion they only list a few basic items such as beds and bedding, but at other times they record a considerable range of goods which could be used to furnish an entire home. Of the fifty-one goods-given inventories, thirty-six were successfully linked to other sources to confirm that the person in the inventory was receiving poor relief when the goods were given to them. These inventories could be made for a substantial number of reasons. Sometimes goods were given to inmates when they left the poorhouse/workhouse to help them get back on their feet. For example, £2 worth of goods were given to James Wright in April 1828 by Marlingford parish 'in his leaving the House of Industry'.[1] On occasion, people received goods from the parish when they moved out of their parents' home into a house with their partners.[2] The parish gave items to some

[1] NRO PD 404/54, Marlingford town book, 1776–1829.

[2] William Cobbett, *Two-Penny Trash: Politics for the poor* (London, 1831), p. 195; Steven King, 'Chance Encounters? Paths to household formation in early modern England', *International Review of Social History*, 44 (1999), pp. 34–37; Steven King, 'Too Poor to Marry? "Inheritance", the poor and marriage/household formation in rural England 1800–1840s', in Anne-Lise Head-

parishioners when their old goods had been distrained for non-payment of debts or taxes.[3] At times, paupers needed new belongings when they were removed from their host parish to their home parish under the laws of settlement. Often paupers were able to cart back some of their goods with them, however this was not always possible.[4]

Almshouse-related and poorhouse/workhouse contents inventories were made to catalogue the items that were held in almshouses or poorhouses/workhouses. They were made to keep the goods safe and monitor whether items had been stolen or broken, and to determine if any further items were needed. They could also be created when the poorhouse/workhouse was given over to a contractor, who was paid a weekly fee for every pauper that resided in the house.[5] Among workhouse records, there are inventories of inmates' belongings which were taken in the period immediately before they entered the poorhouse/workhouse (poorhouse/workhouse admittance-related inventories). Some admittance-related inventories record the storage of inmates' goods, which were subsequently given back to the parishioner if they left the poorhouse or workhouse. Others document inmates' belongings that were sold, given to other paupers, or were used to furnish buildings such as the parish pesthouse, poorhouse, or workhouse.[6]

Debt-related inventories were made for the purpose of distraining somebody's possessions to pay back a debt of some sort. By law, creditors would make an inventory of the debtor's goods and give them five days to pay back the money or lose their belongings. The goods were impounded and creditors were only allowed to seize enough items to pay the debt. Nor were creditors allowed to take goods which would affect a man's livelihood such as his tools. If not enough sellable items could be found to repay the debt, then defaulters could be imprisoned.[7] Of the thirty-four debt inventories,

König, ed., *Inheritance Practices, Marriage Strategies and Household Formation in European Rural Societies* (Turnhout, 2012), p. 148.

[3] The accounts of Abram parish (Lancashire), for example, show that on 11 February 1809 new goods were given to a parishioner after a bailiff had seized their old belongings. WAS TR/Ab/5–7, Abram particulars of disbursements of the overseers, constables and supervisors, c. 1691–1800.

[4] See, for instance, the goods-given inventory of Edward Lane of Lydlinch, Dorset. DHC PE-LYD/OV/1/1 Lydlinch overseers' accounts, 1734–1781. Also see: Sokoll, *Essex Pauper Letters*, p. 358.

[5] For example, inventories were made of Ightham workhouse in Kent when it was under the care of the contractor Thomas Yowel between 1789 and 1797 and William Bridger between 1798–1800. KHLC P202/8/1, Ightham vestry church volume, 1782–1813.

[6] For further information on these sources, see: Harley, 'Material Lives of the Poor and their Strategic use of the Workhouse', pp. 71–103; Tomkins, *Experience of Urban Poverty*, pp. 36–78; Susannah R. Ottaway, *The Decline of Life: Old age in eighteenth-century England* (Cambridge, 2004), pp. 247–276.

[7] On the legal side of this, see: Thomas Jonathan Wooler, *Every Man his own Attorney* (London,

twenty-two relate to arrears of rent. It is unknown whether the others were made for rent arrears or for other reasons such as non-payment of poor rates. The debt-related inventories were made of the goods of a range of people and only thirteen of them related to paupers' belongings. Many of these inventories have ended up in parish collections as debtors sometimes approached their local overseer in the hope that they would pay the debt for them.

Goods-taken inventories were made to record the possessions that the parish took from parishioners. These goods were then sold, recycled around the community, used in the poorhouse/workhouse, or destroyed. Twenty-two of the twenty-eight goods-taken inventories were made of the belongings of paupers. Goods-taken inventories have commonly been mistaken for pauper inventories of the kind discussed here, as they sometimes record the final process when the goods of a deceased pauper, which had previously been promised to the parish in a pauper inventory, were taken. However, goods-taken inventories could be made for a variety of different reasons and so should be viewed as distinct from pauper inventories. Over half of these inventories were made of the goods of people who were still alive, and so were not made to record the final stage of the pauper inventory process when the parish took a deceased pauper's belongings. Some goods-taken inventories record the parish taking back the items that they had previously given to a claimant.[8] On occasion goods could be taken from one pauper and given to another in exchange for being looked after.[9] Sometimes the parish only took a small number of goods to pay the funeral expenses of a spouse or child. For example, in June 1724 twelve items of John Hansford were sold for 10s. by Hingham parish, to contribute to the 13s. 3d. burial expenses of his wife.[10] Consequently, many of these inventories were made for very different reasons to pauper

1830); Richard Burn, *The Justice of the Peace and Parish Officer*, vol. 1, 12th edn. (London, 1772), pp. 170, 480–481, 448–449; Burn, *Justice of the Peace*, vol. 3, pp. 489–491; Richard Burn, *The History of the Poor Laws* (London, 1764), p. 251; William Dickinson, *A Practical Exposition of the Law relative to the Office and Duties of a Justice of the Peace*, vol. 1, pp. 413–416; Thomas Walter Williams, *The Whole Law relative to the Duty and Office of a Justice of the Peace*, vol. 1, pp. 786–804; Robert Gardiner, *Compleat Constable*, 3rd edn. (London, 1708), pp. 79–80, 125–126; Nolan, *Treatise of the Laws*, vol. 1, p. 251; Giles Jacob, *The Compleat Parish-officer*, 10th edn. (London, 1744), pp. 7, 32–35, 84; David Englander, *Landlord and Tenant in Urban Britain 1838–1918* (Oxford, 1983), pp. 22–33; Joanna Innes, 'The King's Bench Prison in the later Eighteenth Century: Law, authority and order in a London debtors' prison', in John Brewer and John Styles, eds., *An Ungovernable People: The English and their law in the seventeenth and eighteenth centuries* (London, 1980), pp. 250–298.

[8] See the example of John Monday, in Cirket, *Samuel Whitbread's Notebooks*, p. 125.

[9] For instance, in 1629 the goods of William Feind were given to John Bundock in return for Bundock caring and providing for Feind. ERO D/P 54/18/1, Stock bond to maintain a pauper for three years in consideration of receiving his goods, 1629.

[10] NRO PD 575/128, Hingham inventories, 1706–1731; NRO PD 575/124, Hingham lists of poor people in receipt of weekly collection, 1700–1746.

inventories and often record only a handful of items rather than representing the entire contents of a pauper's home.

Family abandonment inventories were made to record the distraint of the goods of husbands and/or wives who had deserted their family and left them chargeable to the parish. This practice was established in 1718/19 under the act of 5 Geo. I c.8. 1718–19,[11] though there is evidence to suggest that people's goods were informally distrained for the same reasons before this date.[12] Similarly, bastardy-related inventories recorded the distraint and sale of the belongings of putative mothers and/or fathers of a child born out of wedlock.[13] Although some of the people recorded in these inventories technically became paupers and were sometimes from labouring backgrounds, a number of these inventories relate to the belongings of people from middling trades.

There are numerous other inventories among archival records but they are too many to discuss at length. Some of the inventories record the clothes that a person owned or the clothing that they wanted. For example, in the early 1780s inventories were made to record the clothing of inmates in Ashill workhouse and what they needed.[14] Inventories could be made of the goods of people who had broken the law. For instance, if people were caught selling ale or hawking without a license their possessions could be distrained by a justice of the peace.[15] When individuals did not pay levies such as tithes, window taxes, and highway rates, their belongings could be distrained to cover the cost of the tax.[16] The possessions of people who had been declared insane could be legally seized by poor law authorities.[17] Overseers and other parish officers could equally have their goods distrained to pay fines if they were

[11] Burn, *Justice of the Peace*, vol. 3, pp. 505–507; Burn, *History of the Poor Laws*, p. 101; Williams, *Whole Law*, vol. 3, pp. 673, 740; Dickinson, *Exposition of the Law*, vol. 2, pp. 685–686; Nolan, *Treatise of the Laws*, vol. 3, p. 86; Jacob, *Compleat Parish-officer*, p. 187; George Nicholls, *A History of the English Poor Law*, vol. 2 (London, 1854), pp. 6–7.

[12] See for example the inventory of Samawell Bailers in KHLC P41/5/1, Brabourne churchwardens' assessments and disbursements, 1693–1735, and vestry minutes dated 8 January 1678/79 in KHLC P339/11/3, Smarden poor rate book, 1675–1690.

[13] Burn, *History of the Poor Laws*, p. 96; Burn, *Justice of the Peace*, vol. 3, p. 207; Dickinson, *Exposition of the Law*, vol. 1, pp. 170, 176; Williams, *Whole Law*, vol. 1, pp. 267–268; Jacob, *Compleat Parish-officer*, pp. 175–176; Nolan, *Treatise of the Laws*, vol. 2, pp. 279–280, 337.

[14] NRO PD 548/71, Ashill inventories, 1780–1786.

[15] Ruth Paley, ed., *Justice in Eighteenth-century Hackney: The justicing notebook of Henry Norris and the Hackney petty sessions book* (London, 1991), pp. 14, 81–82, 94; Gwenda Morgan and Peter Rushton, eds., *The Justicing Notebook (1750–64) of Edmund Tew, Rector of Boldon* (Woodbridge, 2000), p. 40; Healey, *First Century of Welfare*, p. 138.

[16] Burn, *Justice of the Peace*, vol. 4, p. 357; Jacob, *Compleat Parish-officer*, pp. 117, 206–208, 227.

[17] Williams, *Whole Law*, vol. 3, pp. 4–5, 9–10; Nolan, *Treatise of the Laws*, vol. 3, pp. 116–117; Dickinson, *Exposition of the Law*, vol. 2, p. 53; Burn, *Justice of the Peace*, vol. 3, p. 112; ERO D/P 245/18/11, Colchester order to seize estate of Elizabeth Hart to defray her lunacy maintenance, 1770; ROLLR DE 400/64, Ullesthorpe order to distrain, 1830.

charged with neglecting their duties, not making paupers wear badges, not keeping accurate accounts, or refusing somebody relief who had an order from a justice.[18]

With there being such a considerable range of inventories among parish records, it is imperative to cross-reference each inventory to other primary sources to determine why it was made and whose goods were appraised. Most of these inventories have not hitherto been used by historians, meaning that there is vast potential for future research. Goods-given inventories, for example, can be used to study the generosity of parishes or the makeshift economies that the poor used to acquire goods. Poorhouse/workhouse-related inventories allow us to study material life in institutions of the old poor law. The inventories of non-paupers can be used to study the middling sort during the late eighteenth and early nineteenth century, when the numbers of probate inventories significantly decline. The remainder of the chapter focuses on the sample of 230 pauper inventories from Norfolk.

Geographical and socio-economic distribution of pauper inventories

Inventories were made of claimants' goods in Europe and North America in locations such as Denmark, Prussia, and New Jersey.[19] In Britain, evidence has been found that the inventorying of pauper goods happened in various parishes in most English counties during the old poor law. The system also probably operated in parts of Wales where poor law statutes were identical to England. The frequency with which the practice happened, however, could vary considerably according to location. Current research shows that the practice was most common in the east of England, as large samples have been located for Norfolk and Essex.[20] Poor law officials also made pauper inventories in Dorset, Kent, Leicestershire, and Rutland, but not to the same extent as parishes in East Anglia. For the northern county of Lancashire only eleven pauper inventories have been located, as parishes appear to have generally taken and/or made paupers' sell their goods before they were entitled to relief

[18] Dickinson, *Exposition of the Law*, vol. 2, p. 720; Williams, *Whole Law*, vol. 3, pp. 354, 603, 694, 696, 708; Jacob, *Compleat Parish-officer*, pp. 89, 144, 186; Nolan, *Treatise of the Laws*, vol. 3, pp. 64–66, 127–128, 151.

[19] BPP, 1834, XXXIX.1, *Report from his Majesty's Commissioners for Inquiring into the Administration and Practical Operation of the Poor Laws. Appendix F: Foreign Communications*, pp. xvii, 149, 287, 457; Samuel Nevill, *The Acts of the General Assembly of the Province of New-Jersey, from the year 1753*, vol. 2 (Woodbridge, NJ, 1761), pp. 226–227.

[20] On Essex pauper inventories, see: King, 'Pauper Inventories', pp. 155–191; Harley, 'Consumption and the Life-cycle of English Paupers'.

there.[21] Similarly, very few inventories (of any kind) were found from Durham in Green's study on the households of the poor.[22] Collectively, this suggests that the practice of inventorying paupers' goods was most common in the east of England, followed by the south. Then moving northwards and westwards, the practice became gradually less common.[23]

Norfolk is the fourth largest county in England and its 740 parishes went through considerable changes over the long eighteenth century.[24] At the beginning of the period, Norfolk boasted the country's largest provincial city, Norwich, which acted as an important administrative, political, cultural, religious, economic, and social centre to Norfolk and beyond.[25] Norwich and other parts of the county were enjoying the benefits of a thriving woollen textile industry that was sold to consumers in England and Europe.[26] Towns such as Great Yarmouth and King's Lynn were also relatively prosperous, bringing in exports of grain and coal to the county and supplying its hinterland with a range of foodstuffs, manufactured goods, and services.[27] There were over thirty market towns across the county, which supplied their immediate areas with a range of amenities between the late seventeenth and early eighteenth centuries.[28]

Over the eighteenth century, however, textile production was in terminal decline as producers in Norfolk struggled to earn a living and most production moved to the north of England.[29] This led to a number of knock-on

[21] For more information on the regional distribution of pauper inventories and the reasons for this, see: Harley, 'Pauper Inventories, Social Relations'; idem, 'Material Lives of the English Poor: A regional perspective'.

[22] Green, 'Heartless and Unhomely?', p. 81.

[23] These findings are in line with other interpretations. Historians have generally found that poor law practice was different between the south and north of England. In the south, paupers could expect to receive more support from a better-funded system particularly before 1780, while in the north people generally appear to have received lower allowances and found it more difficult to get relief. The reasons for these differences have generated much debate. For two contrasting arguments, see: King, *Poverty and Welfare* and Hindle, *On the Parish*, pp. 282–295.

[24] Anne Digby, *Pauper Palaces* (London, 1978), p. 15.

[25] Joyce Ellis, 'Regional and County Centres', in Peter Clark, ed., *The Cambridge Urban History of Britain*, vol. 2, *1540–1840* (Cambridge, 2000), pp. 673–704; Carole Rawcliffe and Richard Wilson, eds., *Norwich since 1550* (London, 2004); *Pigot and Co.'s National Commercial Directory* (London, 1830), pp. 557–587.

[26] John Patten, *English Towns 1500–1700* (Folkestone, 1978), pp. 252–294; Susanna Wade Martins, *A History of Norfolk* (Chichester, 1984), pp. 73–78; Richard Wilson, 'The Textile Industry', in Rawcliffe and Wilson, *Norwich*, pp. 219–241.

[27] Patten, *English Towns*, pp. 252–294; Martins, *History of Norfolk*, pp. 78–80; Digby, *Pauper Palaces*, pp. 17–18; *Pigot and Co.'s*, pp. 549–554, 598–607.

[28] Alan Dyer, 'Small Market Towns 1540–1700', in Clark, *Cambridge Urban History*, p. 433; Martins, *History of Norfolk*, pp. 82–83; Susanna Wade Martins, *Norfolk: A changing countryside* (Chichester, 1988), pp. 81–98; Patten, *English Towns*, pp. 252–294; *Pigot and Co.'s*, pp. 527–607.

[29] Digby, *Pauper Palaces*, pp. 18–20; Steven King and Geoffrey Timmins, *Making Sense of the*

effects as the textile industry involved the labours of considerable numbers of people who reared sheep and worked in the trading and selling of textiles.[30] In 1797 the social commentator Frederick Morton Eden claimed that 'The Norwich trade has for some years been in declining state' and that weavers and spinners received low wages that had not improved in twenty years.[31] Once famed for its handloom production of attractive and inexpensive worsted goods, agricultural production became much more important to the economy of Norfolk over the eighteenth century. The county is often identified as one of the forerunners of the so-called 'agricultural revolution', owing to its adoption of innovative farming practices such as four-course crop rotation.[32] Large parts of Norfolk were enclosed by 1750 to expand the amount of cultivatable land and create larger farms.[33] These changes brought greater profits to farmers, but for the wider population this led to more precarious lives and deepening poverty. Agricultural wages in Norfolk were some of the lowest in the country and with enclosure many of the poor lost their access to commons and waste grounds to gather food or fuel and graze animals.[34] The total Norfolk population increased substantially from around 230,919 people in 1700 to 390,054 in 1831,[35] meaning that unemployment and underemployment became increasingly common over the period.[36] This led to rising poor rates and greater spending on the poor to relieve their poverty. In 1803, 12s. 5d. was spent on poor relief per head of the population compared to 8s. 11d. for England and Wales. At the eve of the passing of the new poor law in 1834, spending had increased to 15s. 9d. per head compared to a national figure of 9s. 1d. per capita.[37]

Pauper inventories have been found for thirty-four (4.6 per cent) of Norfolk's 740 parishes (Figure 3.1). The vagaries of record survival and

Industrial Revolution (Manchester, 2001), pp. 41–44; Wilson, 'Textile Industry', pp. 219–241; Martins, *History of Norfolk*, pp. 72–75.

[30] Penelope J. Corfield, 'East Anglia', in Clark, *Cambridge Urban History*, p. 40.

[31] Frederic Morton Eden, *The State of the Poor*, vol. 2 (London, 1797), pp. 477–479.

[32] Martins, *Changing Countryside*, pp. 26–42; Martins, *History of Norfolk*, pp. 53–58.

[33] Michael Turner, *English Parliamentary Enclosure: Its historical geography and economic history* (Folkestone, 1980), pp. 46–48, 79; Digby, *Pauper Palaces*, p. 24; Roger J. P. Kain, John Chapman, and Richard R. Oliver, *The Enclosure Maps of England and Wales 1595–1918* (Cambridge, 2004), pp. 96–101; Martins, *History of Norfolk*, pp. 54–56.

[34] Snell, *Annals*, pp. 23–57, 138–227, 375–376, 411–417; J. L. Hammond and Barbara Hammond, *The Village Labourer, 1760–1832: A study in the government of England before the reformation bill*, 2nd edn. (London, 1920); J. M. Neeson, *Commoners: Common Right, Enclosure and Social change in England, 1700–1820* (Cambridge, 1993), esp. pp. 158–184; Martins, *Changing Countryside*, pp. 55–56; King, *Poverty and Welfare*, p. 123.

[35] E. A. Wrigley, 'Rickman Revisited: The population growth rates of English counties in the early modern period', *Economic History Review*, 62 (2009), p. 721; *Census, 1831*.

[36] King, *Poverty and Welfare*, p. 123.

[37] Digby, *Pauper Palaces*, p. 84. Also see Table 3.2 below.

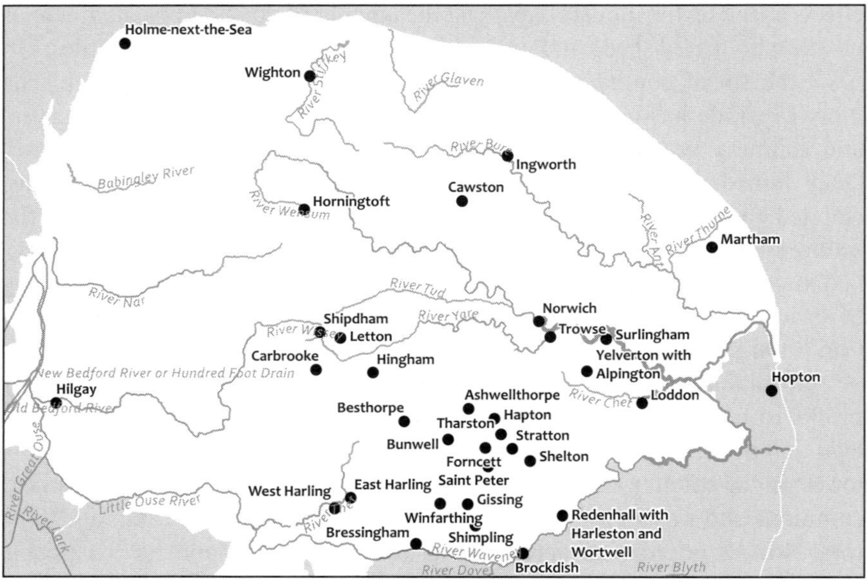

Figure 3.1 Settlements in Norfolk with surviving pauper inventories, c.1690–1834

systems of archival cataloguing, however, make it difficult to determine whether what has survived represents the types and numbers of parishes that typically made inventories of parishioners' goods. Rather, the majority of inventories in this volume were identified from archive catalogues and so may only represent parishes that are particularly well indexed at Norfolk Record Office. Nevertheless, it is worth discussing the sample to contextualise the inventories and draw some tentative conclusions about local and inter-regional differences in poor relief practice.

Pauper inventories have been located for numerous parts of the county. However, only four inventories were found from coastal settlements (Holme-next-the-Sea and Hopton) and only one was found from the west of the county (Hilgay). The vast majority of inventories were made in the stiff loams and clay lands of central and southern Norfolk, where there were difficult mixed farming conditions leading to less available employment for labourers.[38] The bulk of the pauper inventories were made in relatively well-connected areas. A number of them were made within a twenty-mile radius of the major commercial centre Norwich and were close to turnpikes and/or coaching routes that connected people to major ports such as Yarmouth and

[38] Digby, *Pauper Palaces*, p. 16; Green, 'Heartless and Unhomely?', p. 82; Martins, *History of Norfolk*, p. 51; Martins, *Changing Countryside*, p. 26.

the rest of England.[39] Other market towns such as Attleborough, Buckenham, Bungay, Diss, East Harling, Hingham, Redenhall, and Wymondham were also often within walking distance of the settlements in which the inventories were made.

Table 3.2 has been constructed to further understand the local economic and social conditions in the parishes where inventories survive. The findings are primarily based on census data from 1801 and the parliamentary report *Abstract of Answers and Returns ... relative to the Expenses and Maintenance of the Poor in England* taken between 1802 and 1803.[40] The report offers the most comprehensive record of national poor law statistics before the passing of the new poor law in 1834, such as figures on the amounts of money raised by poor rates and the numbers and types of paupers on relief. The report's reliability, however, has often been questioned.[41] For example, it is possible that parishes occasionally misinterpreted what they were supposed to do and returned the average number of parishioners relieved rather than the total number.[42] Furthermore, these figures are based on the early nineteenth century and so it is highly questionable whether they can be applied to parishes which made inventories of parishioners' goods in the late seventeenth and eighteenth centuries. Thus, the figures are tentative, but they nonetheless offer a revealing picture as to why certain parishes may have inventoried paupers' belongings.

The most striking feature of Table 3.2 is that parishes with surviving pauper inventories tended to spend much more on poor relief and have greater proportions of paupers in their populations than either Norfolk taken overall or England and Wales. This is particularly interesting considering that a relatively high proportion of the Norfolk population as a whole was already on poor relief.[43] Just over one in ten people (11.4 per cent) were paupers in England and Wales between 1802–3, but nearly one in five people (18.6 per

[39] M. J. Daunton, *Progress and Poverty: An economic and social history of Britain 1700–1850* (Oxford, 1995), pp. 285–317; Michael Freeman, 'Transport', in John Langton and R. J. Morris, eds., *Atlas of Industrializing Britain, 1780–1914* (London, 1986), pp. 80–93; Patten, *English Towns*, p. 291; Digby, *Pauper Palaces*, p. 16; Martins, *History of Norfolk*, pp. 82–84; John Hatcher, *The History of the British Coal Industry*, vol. 1, *Before 1700: towards the age of coal* (Oxford, 1993), pp. 2–3.

[40] BPP, 1803–4, XIII, *Abstract of Answers and Returns... relative to the Expenses and Maintenance of the Poor in England.*

[41] In spite of this, we still lack detailed studies which examine its usefulness.

[42] It is important to stress that this probably only happened rarely, as the proportions of paupers relieved is remarkably consistent across thousands of parishes. See: Williams, *Pauperism to Poverty*, p. 147.

[43] Approximately Norfolk had England's eighth largest proportion of paupers. In order of magnitude: Sussex (22.6 per cent), Wiltshire (22.1 per cent), Berkshire (20.0 per cent), Oxfordshire (19.4 per cent), Buckinghamshire (17.7 per cent), Suffolk (16.6 per cent), and Essex (16.4 per cent). From: ibid., pp. 149–150.

Table 3.2 Extract of poor law administration and expenditure in Norfolk, c.1801–1803

Parish	**Population 1801**	**Rate in the pound 1802–3**	**Total expenditure on poor relief 1802–3**	**Expenditure on relief per head of population**	**Proportion of paupers in population * (%)**
Ashwellthorpe	314	8s.	£254 1s.	16s. 2d.	24.2
Besthorpe	391	4s. 3d.	£318 7s. 7d.	16s. 3d.	28.4
Bressingham	650	6s. 3d.	£619 9s. 1d.	19s. 1d.	20.8
Brockdish	370	8s.	£247 2s. 6d.	13s. 4d.	17.6
Carbrooke	536	2s. 3d.	£364 14s. 8d.	13s. 7d.	17.4
Cawston	840	8s. 9d.	£917 15s. 6d.	£1 1s. 10d.	42.5
Forncett St. Peter	538	7s.	£350 12s. 1d.	13s.	23.0
Gissing	444	9s. 3d.	£624 6s.	£1 8s. 1d.	55.0
Hapton	172	4s. 8d.	£109 13s.	12s. 9d.	18.6
East Harling	674	8s. 10d.	£583 17s. 6d.	17s. 4d.	15.6
West Harling	122	3s. 8d.	£132 10s. 3d.	£1 1s. 9d.	72.1
Hilgay	759	3s. 1d.	£457 18s. 6d.	12s. 1d.	7.1
Hingham	1,203	4s. 8d.	£790 2s.	13s. 2d.	9.7
Holme-next-the-Sea	165	2s. 10d.	£112 17s. 7d.	13s. 8d.	16.4
Horningtoft	197	2s. 2d.	£94 7s. 4d.	9s. 7d.	8.6
Ingworth	181	9s. 11d.	£144 7s. 6d.	15s. 11d.	11.6
Letton	131	2s.	£70 8s. 10d.	10s. 9d.	9.2
Loddon	799	1s. 4d.	£184 1s. 6d.	4s. 7d.	1.0
Martham	639	5s. 6d.	£158 18s. 1d.	5s.	8.6
Gr./Lt. Moulton	354	6s. 9d.	£316 0s. 11d.	17s. 10d.	33.9
Norwich, St. Mary	1,018	6s. 6d.	£373 14s. 4d.	7s. 4d.	4.9
Redenhall with Harleston and Wortwell	1,845	6s.	£1020 0s. 3d.	11s. 1d.	15.8
Shelton	220	4s.	£260 10s.	£1 3s. 8d.	16.8
Shipdham	1,250	2s. 8d.	£821 9s.	13s. 2d.	10.3
Stratton St. Mary	549	5s. 6d.	£526 18s. 7d.	19s. 2d.	18.0
Surlingham	308	5s. 4d.	£217 1s. 6d.	14s. 1d.	22.7
Trowse (with Newton)	428	8s.	£447 13s. 11d.	£1 0s. 11d.	24.8
Yelverton with Alpington	163	3s. 4d.	£82 8s.	10s. 1d.	5.5
<u>Comparative figs. (mean)</u>					
Norfolk sample	**528**	**5s. 6d.**	**£380 11s. 9d.**	**15s. 4d.**	**18.6**
Norfolk (all)	**371**	**5s. 2d.**	**£254 7s. 3d.**	**12s. 5d.**	**15.2**
England and Wales	**578 ~**	**4s. 5d.**	**£292 2s. 2d.**	**8s. 11d.**	**11.4**

* Not including 'Number of Persons Relieved, not being Parishioners'

~ England only

All quarter and half pennies rounded up or down

Sources: *National Census, 1801*; BPP, 1803-4, XIII, *Abstract of Answers and Returns... relative to the Expenses and Maintenance of the Poor in England*; Karel Williams, *From Pauperism to Poverty* (London, 1981), pp. 148–150; Digby, *Pauper Palaces*, p. 84; Sokoll, *Essex Pauper Letters*, p. 29.

cent) were paupers in this sample of Norfolk parishes. Unsurprisingly, this meant that the amounts of money spent on poor relief were much higher in the thirty-four parishes that have surviving pauper inventories. On average, £380 11s. 9d. was spent on poor relief between 1802–3, compared to £292 2s. 2d. at a national level. This meant that most ratepayers had to pay much more than most to maintain local systems of relief in their parishes. The most accurate trends can be determined by examining the pauper inventories that are dated within a few years of this parliamentary report. These too show that parishes which inventoried the goods of their parishioners tended to have much higher poor rates and greater proportions of their populations on poor relief than wider Norfolk or England and Wales. In Besthorpe, Brockdish, and West Harling, for example, where inventories can be found for 1803 and 1804, average per capita expenditure between them was 15s. 10d. in 1802–3 and a combined total of 29.9 per cent of their populations were on poor relief between the same dates. In comparison, expenditure at a national level was nearly half this at 8s. 11d. per head of the population, and 11.4 per cent of the population in England and Wales were paupers between 1802–3.

There are, of course, considerable differences at an individual level across the sample. In Loddon, for example, only one per cent of the population were classed as paupers in 1802–3, resulting in an expenditure of 4s. 7d. per head of the local population. In West Harling, on the other hand, 72.1 per cent of the population were claiming poor relief in 1802–3, meaning that £1 1s. 9d. was spent per head of the population on relief. Despite local variation, the results show that overall in the southern and central parts of Norfolk, dependence and expenditure on poor relief were generally higher than in the rest of Norfolk. Although the extent to which these figures can be applied to the long eighteenth century is highly questionable, it is possible that people in these areas had a history of being more dependent on poor relief than others, since the stiff loams and clay lands there would have meant that it was difficult to farm profitably for long periods of time. This could help to explain why most pauper inventories were made in southern and central Norfolk. It indicates that parishes which had high poor rates and elevated rates of expenditure felt that it was necessary to inventory the goods of its parishioners, to maintain the system and ensure that it was not just ratepayers that were contributing funds to the parish chest.[44] The fact that most inventories were made in relatively close proximity to one another is also interesting in other ways. It may suggest that local officials shared best practice and ideas with one another about inventorying pauper populations. As the recent work of Samantha

[44] This is further discussed in chapter 2.

Shave has shown, such connections could be highly influential and were forged through correspondence, word of mouth, and trips to other parishes.[45]

We now turn to the sizes and rural-urban structures of the settlements which have surviving inventories. Table 3.3 has been constructed to give the reader some insight into the socio-economic and geographical characteristics of the settlements which made pauper inventories. A few notes of caution are needed before analysing the data. The population figures for 1676 are taken from the Compton census, which was created to survey people's religious affiliation and determine whether non-conformist religions were a credible threat to the dominance of the Anglican church. The source captures people aged 16 years and above or counts the numbers of families in parishes.[46] They have been used by historical demographers such as E. A. Wrigley and R. S. Schofield to calculate estimates of population by multiplying counts of individuals or numbers of families by 1.5 or 4 respectively. This obviously leads to all sorts of problems as the multiplier of 1.5 is built on estimates that around one-third of parish populations were aged under 16 years old, and the multiplier 4 relies on estimates of how large families were on average.[47] This is particularly problematic when the multipliers are applied to hamlets, villages, towns, and cities, which inevitably varied and had different demographic characteristics to one another.[48] The reliability of the Compton census itself is also open to question, as some of the local surveyors misunderstood their instructions and only returned the number of adult males or householders in their parish. Some surveyors may have also included children in their returns.[49] Even the figures from the national censuses, especially from 1801, 1811, and 1821, are problematic. For example, questions asked by census enumerators could be misunderstood, resulting in mistakes and inconsistent answers.[50] Children are also underrepresented on some returns and men in the armed forces or on merchant shipping are omitted.[51] Consequently, it must be stressed that the figures in Table 3.3 are crude and open to further debate. Nevertheless, for the purpose of determining the nature and approximate size

[45] Shave, *Pauper Policies*, pp. 150–196.

[46] Anne White and Mary Clapinson, eds., *The Compton Census of 1676: A critical edition* (Oxford, 1986), pp. xxiii–lxxxii.

[47] On why these multipliers are used and the potential problems with them, see: ibid., pp. lix–lxxvi; E. A. Wrigley and R. S. Schofield, *The Population History of England 1541–1871* (London, 1981), pp. 33–37.

[48] For further information on different types of settlements and how they can vary, see the chapters in Clark, *Cambridge Urban History*.

[49] Wrigley and Schofield, *Population History*, p. 34.

[50] J. A. Banks, 'The Social Structure of Nineteenth century England as seen through the Census', in Richard Lawton, ed., *The Census and Social Structure: An interpretation guide to nineteenth century censuses for England and Wales* (London, 1978), p. 183.

[51] Wrigley and Schofield, *Population History*, pp. 122–126, 588–596.

Table 3.3 Approximate populations of settlements that made pauper inventories, 1676–1831

Parish	No. p. invents	Dates	Compton census, 1676	National census 1801	1811	1821	1831
Ashwellthorpe	6	1695–1754	198	314	343	418	471
Besthorpe	2	1776–1803	92	391	430	519	542
Bressingham	13	1693–1814, n.d.	225	650	635	702	655
Brockdish	1	1804	150	370	367	385	482
Bunwell	1	1771	402	602	587	774	947
Carbrooke	1	1787	353	536	615	771	789
Cawston	19	1699	810	840	811	929	1,110
Forncett St. Peter	2	1784	573	538	590	638	727
Gissing	3	c.1720–1756	180	444	456	544	598
Hapton	2	1796, n.d.	111	172	148	186	200
East Harling	4	1821–1825	270	674	754	867	1,031
West Harling	2	1779–1803	156	122	112	116	107
Hilgay	1	1805	410	759	833	968	1,176
Hingham	9	1710–1731	810	1,203	1,263	1,442	1,539
Holme-next-the-Sea	3	1752–1770	146	165	185	219	268
Hopton	1	1731	–	202	225	274	260
Horningtoft	3	1771–1773	138	197	224	254	293
Ingworth	2	1769–1774	140	181	143	161	191
Letton	3	1759–1769	225 [inc. Cranworth]	131	144	127	133
Loddon	1	1751	600	799	937	1,038	1,175
Martham	12	1758–1772	309	639	679	845	895
Gr./Lt. Moulton	30	1693– c.1760s	90 [x 1.5]; 240 [x 4]	354	406	417	447
Norwich, St. Mary	2	1734–1772	573	1,018	1,097	1,521	1,361
Norwich	–	–	20,186	35,944	36,338	50,288	61,110

Table 3.3 *continued.*

Parish	No. p. invents	Dates	Compton census, 1676	National census 1801	1811	1821	1831
Redenhall with Harleston and Wortwell	44	1708–1828	Total: 893 Redenhall/Harleston: 780; Wortwell: 113	1845. R/H: 1459; W: 386	1953. R/H: 1,516; W: 437	2127. R/H: 1,641; W: 486	2321. R/H: 1,784; W: 537
Shelton	22	1692–1762	183	220	207	236	253
Shimpling	1	1785	95	169	170	179	227
Shipdham	23	1720	750	1,250	1,412	1,642	1,889
Stratton St. Mary	5	1774–1822	365	549	558	636	721
Surlingham	3	1747–1762	189	308	318	403	399
Tharston	1	c.1780–1793	225	372	369	369	392
Trowse (with Newton)	3	1694–1750	288 [inc. Newton/ Carrow]	428	488	549	583
Wighton	1	1819	327	446	433	507	542
Winfarthing	1	1816	216	565	588	683	703
Yelverton with Alpington	3	1738–1742	135 [Yelverton only]	163	165	169	197

Sources: White and Clapinson, *Census*, pp. cxix–cxx, 188-241; *National Census, 1801–1831*.

of the settlements which inventoried the goods of their parishioners, the figures are sufficient.

There are a number of different ways in which to define an area as urban or rural. These include population numbers, how nucleated the settlement was, the local economy, the numbers of people who were employed inside and outside of agriculture, the possession of a market, and whether the area had administrative and legal powers.[52] Population has most commonly been used by scholars to identify urban and rural areas as it offers researchers a systematic way in which to categorise settlements which can be applied across large areas of land. This is, however, fraught with difficulties since writers have employed a wide range of population limits to define towns. Some contemporaries saw places with only 200–300 inhabitants as towns.[53] Gregory King, Lorna Weatherill, and Ken Sneath defined a town as anywhere which had around 500 people in it.[54] Penelope Corfield and C. M. Law defined an eighteenth-century urban area as possessing 2,500 people or more.[55] E. A. Wrigley used 5,000 people as a limit and Jan de Vries excluded any areas which had fewer than 10,000 people in his study on European urbanisation from 1500 to 1800.[56] As such, there is no conclusive definition of what constituted an urban or rural settlement. Nevertheless, no matter what criteria researchers use Table 3.3 strongly suggests that most pauper inventories were made in rural settlements. Only seven parishes in the sample contained approximately 500 or more people in them in 1676. The populations of nearly all the parishes increased by 1801; however according to the data just over half of the parishes still had fewer than 500 people in them. No reliable estimates of population could be found for the eighteenth century, yet it stands to reason that the population of most settlements would have been somewhere in between the statistics from the 1676 and 1801 censuses. With this in mind, settlements such as Shelton and Ashwellthorpe, for example,

[52] Rosemary Sweet, *The English Town: Government, society and culture* (Harlow, 1999), pp. 7–10; Patten, *English Towns*, pp. 16–17, 21–28; Penelope J. Corfield, *The Impact of English Towns 1700–1800* (Oxford, 1982), pp. 4–6; Peter Borsay, *The English Urban Renaissance: Culture and society in the provincial town 1660–1770* (Oxford, 1989), pp. 3–5; Peter Clark and Paul Slack, *English Towns in Transition 1500–1700* (Oxford, 1976), pp. 2–7; C. M. Law, 'Some notes on the Urban Population of England and Wales in the Eighteenth century', *The Local Historian*, 10 (1972), p. 16.

[53] Sweet, *English Town*, p. 7.

[54] Corfield, *Impact of English Towns*, pp. 7–9; Joyce Ellis, *The Georgian Town 1680–1840* (Basingstoke, 2001), pp. 11–12, 14; Weatherill, *Consumer Behaviour*, p. 73–74; Sneath, 'Consumption, Wealth', pp. 58–61.

[55] Corfield, *Impact of English Towns*, pp. 4–7; Law, 'Urban Population', p. 16.

[56] E. A. Wrigley, 'Urban Growth and Agricultural Change: England and the continent in the early modern period', *Journal of Interdisciplinary History*, 15 (1985), p. 684; Jan de Vries, *European Urbanization 1500–1800* (London, 1984), pp. 18–19.

probably contained roughly 200 and 250 inhabitants respectively when the pauper inventories in this sample were created.

The largest urban centre in the sample was Norwich, which was England's second largest city before it was overtaken by Bristol around the mid-eighteenth century.[57] The second biggest settlement in this sample was the market town of Redenhall with Harleston (and Wortwell), for which there are the most pauper inventories in this volume. The extent to which this settlement was 'urban' in the sense that Norwich was, however, is debateable. It was described as a 'respectable market-town' in a trade directory from 1830. It had a population of nearly 1,800 people in 1831 (excluding Wortwell) and the town contained a wide range of shops and services, including general shopkeepers, clock/watch makers, and tea and china dealers, as well as a number of other retailers who were engaged in the selling of clothing, food, and drink. However, the town only contained two manufactories in bombazine and worsted, which were 'both of small importance' to the place, and it was mainly reliant on supplying and receiving the produce of the surrounding areas which was engaged in a mixture of arable and pastoral activities.[58] Some pauper inventories were made of people who had settlement in a rural parish but lived in an urban centre. John Dunnett's home parish, for example, was Besthorpe which had a population of 391 in 1801. Yet he was living in Wymondham, which had a total population of around 3,567 people, when a pauper inventory of his goods was taken in July 1801 **(8)**.[59] Esther Turner had an inventory made of her possessions in July 1803 and was removed from Norwich back to her rural home parish of West Harling around the same time **(56)**.

The reasons why pauper inventories tended to be made in rural settlements more often than urban ones are not clear, but a few tentative comments can be made. In rural parishes, the numbers of people claiming or requesting poor relief would have generally been smaller compared to urban populations. Thus, in a system that depended upon local officials keeping an eye on parishioners and their goods, the policy would have been easier to apply when the size of the population was relatively small and static and when everybody knew each other. In larger towns and cities such as Norwich, Great Yarmouth, or King's Lynn, it would have been much more difficult to keep track of paupers, as population was denser and parishioners could potentially move home without detection.

[57] Angus McInnes, *The English Town, 1660–1760* (London, 1980), pp. 4–6; Martins, *History of Norfolk*, p. 74.
[58] *Pigot and Co.'s*, pp. 544–545; *Census, 1831*; Patten, *English Towns*, pp. 244–296.
[59] *Census, 1801*.

Table 3.4 Chronological distribution of the pauper inventories by parish, c.1690–1834

Parish	No. p. invents	Chronological spread of pauper inventories					
		1690–1719	1720–1749	1750–1779	1780–1809	1810–1834	Undated
Ashwellthorpe	6	1695, 1711	1720	1754			
Besthorpe	2			1776	1803		
Bressingham	13	1693, 1718–19	1724, 1727	1759, 1773		1814	1
Brockdish	1				1804		
Bunwell	1			1771			
Carbrooke	1				1787		
Cawston	19	1699					
Forncett St. Peter	2				1784		
Gissing	3			1756			2
Hapton	2				1796		1
East Harling	4					1821, 1825	
West Harling	2			1779	1803		
Hilgay	1				1805		
Hingham	9	1710	1724–5, 1728, 1731				3
Holme-next-the-Sea	3			1752, 1766, 1770			
Hopton	1		1731				
Horningtoft	3			1771–3			
Ingworth	2			1769, 1774			
Letton	3			1759, 1762, 1769			
Loddon	1			1751			
Martham	12			1758, 1764, 1768, 1771–2			
Great Moulton with Little Moulton	30	1693, 1699, 1702, 1710	1722, 1735, 1737–8, 1748	1754, 1756, 1762, 1764, 1767			4

Table 3.4 *continued.*

Parish	No. p. invents	Chronological spread of pauper inventories 1690–1719	1720–1749	1750–1779	1780–1809	1810–1834	Undated
Norwich, St. Mary	2		1734	1772			
Redenhall w/ Harleston and Wortwell	44	1708, 1710, 1714	1731, 1733–4, 1737–46	1752, 1762		1828	
Shelton	22	1692, 1694, 1696, 1700, 1709, 1712–13, 1719	1723–4, 1729, 1741–3, 1746, 1748	1751, 1753, 1762			
Shimpling	1				1785		
Shipdham	23		1720				
Stratton St. Mary	5			1774	1793	1816, 1822	
Surlingham	3		1747	1762			
Tharston	1						1
Trowse (w/Newton)	3	1694	1749	1750			
Wighton	1					1819	
Winfarthing	1					1816	
Yelverton w/ Alpington	3		1738–9, 1742				
Total no. p. inventories	**230**	**45**	**91**	**63**	**9**	**10**	**12**

Chronological distribution of pauper inventories

Having considered the geographical distribution of pauper inventories, this section examines the chronological spread of the sources to further understand the practice of appraising and inventorying the goods of parishioners. Table 3.4 shows that most of the pauper inventories were made between 1720 and 1779 (also see Figure 2.2).[60] In total, 154 of the 230 pauper inventories were made between these dates across twenty-three of the thirty-four settlements. It was argued in chapter 2 that this may indicate that the inventorying of the goods of paupers was for benevolent reasons as well as financial purposes, since these were the years when parishes were generally more supportive to the poor. Their possessions gave the poor some agency which they could use to negotiate support. Once the inventories were made many claimants received relief until they died.

From 1690 to 1719, forty-five inventories can be found for eight different settlements, but most of these came from Cawston, for which there are nineteen inventories all made on 14 December 1699 **(25–43)**. Between the 1780s and 1830s, pauper inventories have been located for fourteen parishes, yet the overall number of inventories significantly declines to a total of no more than nineteen. In general, overseers' accounts, pauper letters, vestry minutes, and other parish-related sources tend to survive in much greater numbers from the late eighteenth century, due in part to the passing of Sturges Bourne's Acts of 1818 and 1819 which required parishes to preserve their records better.[61] With pauper inventories surviving in much smaller numbers from the 1780s, this suggests that overall parishes used the policy less frequently in the final decades of the old poor law. Due to the vagaries of record survival and because the inventories in this sample are not exhaustive, this observation is far from certain; however in other counties such as Dorset, Kent, Leicestershire, and Rutland, where virtually complete collections of pauper inventories have been found, the same trends can be seen.[62] The latest inventory in the sample is dated 1828 **(167)** and no pauper inventories have been found in Norfolk Record Office that were made in the period after 1834 when the Poor Law Amendment Act was passed. This is not to say that pauper inventories were not made during the new poor law. The focus of this volume is on the old poor law and so research has not been conducted to determine whether any unions used this discretionary policy.[63]

[60] See Appendix 3 for a list of the pauper inventories sorted by date.

[61] Sokoll, *Essex Pauper Letters*, pp. 19–24; Pamela Sharpe, '"The bowels of compation": A labouring family and the law, c. 1790–1834', in Hitchcock, King, and Sharpe, *Chronicling Poverty*, p. 89. For further information on the Acts, see: Shave, *Pauper Policies*, pp. 111–149.

[62] Harley, 'Pauper Inventories, Social Relations'.

[63] The latest pauper inventory I have found is for Widow Water of Otford, Kent dated 1835.

The distribution of pauper inventories is not equal across the thirty-four parishes in this sample. For most settlements, fewer than five inventories were found, and the numbers are particularly bolstered by the survival of inventories from Bressingham, Cawston, Hingham, Martham, Great Moulton with Little Moulton, Redenhall with Harleston and Wortwell, Shelton, and Shipdham. It would be tempting to read into this that some places applied the practice more often than others. Whilst this is probably true to some extent, there is evidence to suggest that parishes such as Bressingham, Martham, and others appraised and inventoried parishioners' goods much more commonly and for longer periods of time than survival rates suggest. The overseers' accounts of Bressingham and Martham, for example, mention the names of numerous paupers whose possessions were inventoried, yet there are only thirteen and twelve surviving inventories respectively for the parishes. Moreover, the only reason that there are large numbers of inventories for some places such as Cawston and Shipdham is because a number of inventories were made on the same date and have fortunately survived. In most parishes, inventories were written on loose pieces of paper and were thrown away or written over after the parish had taken the pauper's goods.[64] Many of the inventories that are transcribed in this volume may only survive because they were written or copied into overseers' accounts or vestry minutes. In Redenhall with Harleston and Wortwell, for example, the overseer spent 2s. 6d. making fifteen inventories in June 1731 and paid out a further 2s. 6d. 'for Entring the Same [inventories] into ye Town book', suggesting that they were copied over.[65] The volume that these inventories were reproduced in was devoted almost entirely to recording parishioners' goods between 1708 and 1743.[66] In total, eighty-two (36 per cent) of the inventories in this sample were written on loose pieces of paper,[67] while 148 (64 per cent) were copied or initially written in volumes such as overseers' accounts and vestry minutes. Collectively, this indicates that the policy was applied more frequently than surviving examples suggest.

From: KHLC P279/8/2, Otford public vestry book, 1820–1838. This is, however, from the old system as it took several years for unions to be set up and workhouses to be built after the new poor law was passed in 1834.

[64] For instance, the inventory of James Hunt of Lenham, Kent was cut up and used for notes and rough calculations. It is found among the pages of KHLC P224/12/2, Lenham overseers' assessments and disbursements, 1748–1760.

[65] NRO PD 295/94 Redenhall with Harleston and Wortwell overseers' accounts, 1721–1751. It is possible that some of these inventories that were copied are **127–137**.

[66] NRO PD 295/102, Redenhall with Harleston and Wortwell overseers' order book, 1708–1743.

[67] Moreover, sixty-four of the eighty-two pauper inventories written on loose pieces of paper came from only four parishes (Bressingham, Cawston, Hingham, and Shipdham).

Types of paupers whose goods were inventoried

Over the long eighteenth century, around two-fifths to half of the contemporary population received poor relief at one point or more in their lives, stemming from reasons such as unemployment, sickness, and the breakdown of the nuclear household.[68] Tim Wales's research, for instance, found that approximately two-fifths of the population in a small number of seventeenth-century Norfolk communities received poor relief at least one point in their lives.[69] Henry French found that in Essex at least 55 per cent of Terling's population recorded in the 1801 census received some sort of relief over time.[70] The pauper inventories thus potentially represent a considerable number of 'typical' poor people, as many individuals would have been in receipt of some form of poor relief at one point or more in their lives over the long eighteenth century. Before one makes such a claim, however, it is essential to assess the extent to which the people captured in the inventories are representative of the pauper population as a whole. It is important to do this as parishes rarely appraised the goods of everybody who received relief. Instead, officials tended to choose which parishioners they inventoried based on factors such as gender, age, and cost.

It is difficult to assess pauper inventories from one county as a single collection, as systems of poor relief varied from parish to parish and local practice was dependent upon the economic, legal, and cultural features of the respective settlements. This means that there is a limit to how far one can claim that pauper inventories are representative of all pauper populations across the old poor law.[71] Despite these problems, most of the pauper inventories record the belongings of comparable *types* of paupers. The bulk of the secondary literature on poverty in the south and east of England has found that before 1780 most paupers were women.[72] The Norfolk pauper inventories

[68] This figure could arguably be higher in some areas. Tim Hitchcock and Robert Shoemaker, for instance, contended that up to 60 per cent of the eighteenth-century population experienced 'significant poverty' during their lifetimes. Hitchcock and Shoemaker, *London Lives*, p. 5. More generally, the literature on the life-cycle of poverty is considerable and includes: Tim Wales, 'Poverty, Poor Relief and Life-cycle: Some evidence from seventeenth century Norfolk' in Richard M. Smith, ed., *Land, Kinship and Life-cycle* (Cambridge, 1984), pp. 351–404; Barry Stapleton, 'Inherited Poverty and Life-cycle Poverty: Odiham, Hampshire, 1650–1850', *Social History*, 18 (1993), pp. 339–355; B. Seebohm Rowntree, *Poverty: A study of town life*, 3rd edn. (London, 1902); Shave, 'The Dependent Poor?', pp. 67–97; Williams, *Poverty, Gender*, pp. 101–130; Healey, *First Century of Welfare*, pp. 171–211.

[69] Wales, 'Poverty, Poor Relief'; King, *Poverty and Welfare*, p. 80.

[70] Henry French, 'How Dependent were the "Dependent Poor"? Poor relief and the life-course in Terling, Essex, 1752–1834', *Continuity and Change*, 30 (2015), p. 201.

[71] These issues are explored above.

[72] King, *Poverty and Welfare*, pp. 164–167.

broadly mirror this trend as women's pauper inventories were in the majority from the late seventeenth century to the 1770s (Figure 3.2). Greater numbers of inventories were made of the possessions of women probably because they tended to earn less money than men and were viewed as more vulnerable and 'deserving' of support by authorities.[73] From the 1780s, however, this trend was reversed as men's pauper inventories became more common. The poor law had reached its 'crisis' years and men became more dependent on relief, owing to the decline in cottage industry and widespread enclosure of commons and open fields. Coupled with severe agricultural and manufacturing depressions and an over-stocked labour market particularly after the Napoleonic Wars in 1815, men further struggled to remain independent and provide for their families.[74] The proportions of men and women who received support inevitably varied from parish to parish, but the results in Figure 3.2 nevertheless broadly reinforce other studies which show that men were increasingly given help by overseers during the final decades of the old poor law.[75]

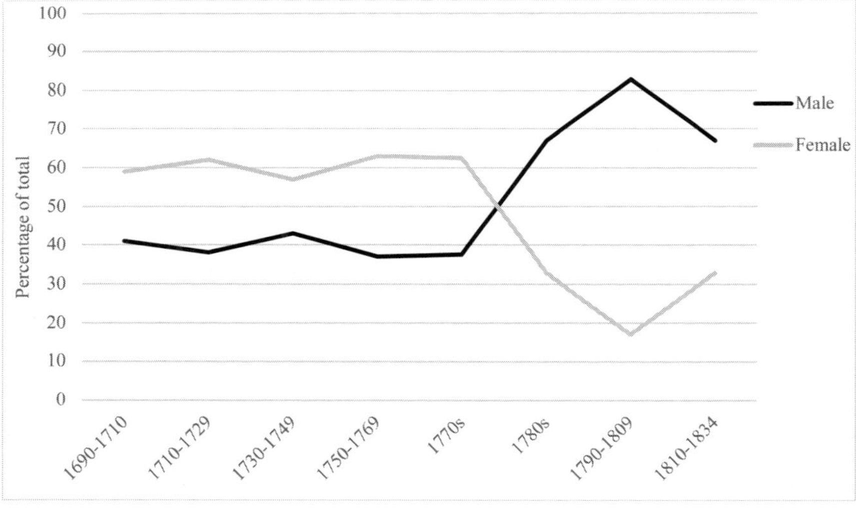

Figure 3.2 Distribution of Norfolk pauper inventories by gender over time, c.1690–1834

[73] Ibid., pp. 164–167; Williams, *Poverty, Gender*, pp. 101–130.

[74] King, *Poverty and Welfare*, pp. 164–167; Snell, *Annals*, pp. 108–114; Dunkley, *Crisis of the Old Poor Law*; Williams, *Poverty, Gender*, pp. 101–159; Brundage, *English Poor Laws*, pp. 25–69; Poynter, *Society and Pauperism*, passim.

[75] King, *Poverty and Welfare*, pp. 164–167; Henry French, 'An Irrevocable Shift: Detailing the dynamics of rural poverty in southern England, 1762–1834', *Economic History Review*, 68 (2015), pp. 782–784, 786–787, 797–805; Williams, *Poverty, Gender*, pp. 101–130.

At least 84 per cent of the women in the sample were widows or spinsters. Around 2 per cent were married and it is likely that the remaining 14 per cent of women were widows or spinsters.[76] Unfortunately, the marital status of 51 per cent of the men in the sample could not be determined, since parish officials tended not to describe men in this way. Where marital status could be ascertained, 15 per cent were widowers or bachelors and 85 per cent were married. At least 26 per cent of the men and women from the pauper inventories lived with children.[77] This figure is likely to be a considerable under-representation since it came from assessing wider overseers' papers where children were not always mentioned. Nevertheless, around 62 per cent of households which had children were headed by a female and 38 per cent by a male. The structures within these households could vary considerably. Sometimes these children lived with a single or widowed mother or father, and sometimes they resided with both of their parents. Occasionally they lived with one or more of their grandparents. The livelihoods of the people from the inventories are very difficult to find; however, when known this information suggests that most paupers came from labouring backgrounds. The occupations of six paupers in the sample have been established. Four were described as weavers, one was a husbandman, and one was a carpenter **(10, 17, 48, 53, 123, 217)**.

Figure 3.3 records the types of relief that men and women from the pauper inventories received. Regular relief is defined here as a pension paid to a parishioner in weekly, fortnightly, or monthly instalments.[78] Casual relief, such as the giving of small sums of money and relief in kind, was infrequent and mostly only used for short periods of time. It was not possible to discern whether people were on regular or casual assistance in around one-quarter of the pauper inventories. For example, sometimes the overseers' accounts were poorly kept, and it was not possible to tell if the support that people received was regular or casual.[79] Nonetheless, based on the inventories that could be accurately tracked alongside other sources, 85 per cent of women from the pauper inventories received regular relief and 15 per cent received casual relief between 1670 and 1729. From 1730 to the end of the old poor law, this gap had widened and nearly every woman in the sample (96 per cent) was on regular assistance. The results from the male-headed inventories equally indicate that more pauper inventories were made of the goods of men who

[76] Usually relief to married couples was in the husband's name. See the inventories numbered **51** and **224** for exceptions.
[77] Children are defined as 15 years old or younger.
[78] Most people on regular relief also received some sort of casual relief, such as clothing and rent payments.
[79] It is important to note that if there were any doubts over whether the person in the inventory was on relief the source has not been categorised as a pauper inventory.

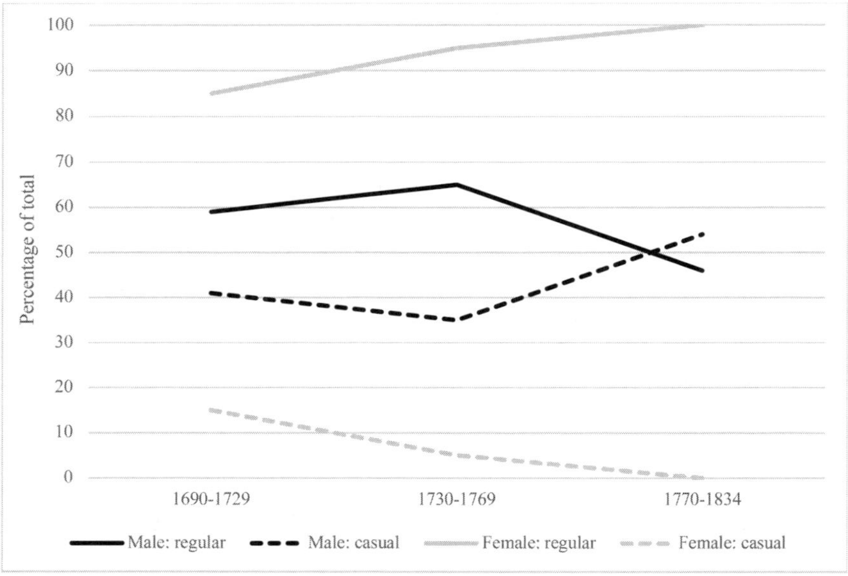

Figure 3.3 Types of poor relief that inventoried men and women received, c.1690–1834

Table 3.5 Average weekly pensions given to paupers on regular relief, c.1690–1834

	c.1690–1769	c.1770–1834	All years
Men	1s. 8d.	3s. 1d.	1s. 11d.
Women	1s. 6d.	3s. 2d.	1s. 9d.
Both	**1s. 7d.**	**3s. 1d.**	**1s. 10d.**

received regular relief. The gap, however, is much narrower and over the long eighteenth century 60 per cent of men from the pauper inventories received a pension and 40 per cent received casual relief.

As most pauper inventories were made of the belongings of people who received regular relief, this strongly suggests that parishes tended to inventory the goods of paupers who cost the most money. On average, male pensioners whose goods were appraised received 1s. 8d per week between c. 1690 and 1769, and 3s. 1d. per week between c. 1770 and 1834. Female pensioners received a mean of 1s. 6d. per week between c. 1690–1769 and 3s. 2d. per week between c. 1770–1834 (Table 3.5). These weekly payments could amount to sizeable sums of money over a period of time, since most of these paupers received pensions for many years before their goods were appraised by parochial authorities. There was overall little point in inventorying the goods of people on casual relief, since the amounts of money that they claimed from the parish were generally relatively small and only short term. Rather, overseers would have mostly targeted paupers who they thought were taking more from the parish fund and would need support until they died, when the parish could then claim their goods. Men who received casual relief were probably more likely to have their possessions inventoried than women in the same position as they were generally seen as less deserving by officials, meaning that the authorities felt more justified listing men's belongings with the aim of later taking them to compensate the parish.

The majority of paupers whose possessions were inventoried received support from the parish owing to life-cycle related problems, such as the death of a partner and sickness. The sample appears to represent a large number of paupers who were towards the end of their working lives and on regular relief due to old age and infirmity. Occasionally pauper inventories were made of the goods of people in their twenties or thirties; however most of the time there was little point in appraising the belongings of young people, since it could potentially be decades until they died (unless they were unwell) and their belongings reverted to the parish. At this point their possessions might have also become too old and worn to be sold or recycled around the community. As such, although the ages of only three people in the sample have been ascertained, the ages are relatively high at 57, 70, and 78 years old **(86, 216, 227)**. The ages of fourteen more people for whom pauper inventories were made have been found for Dorset, Essex, and Kent. In all, including the findings from Norfolk, the average age is 61, suggesting that the elderly were more likely to have their goods inventoried by parochial officials.[80] Moreover, four of these people with a recorded age were in their 80s and ten were aged between 60 and 86 years old.

People who lacked adequate wages or employment and received allowances from the parish through Speenhamland, the roundsman system, and labour rate generally did not have inventories made of their possessions. These forms of parish assistance became increasingly common from the late eighteenth century in the south of England and meant that in many areas huge proportions of the population were receiving some form of help from the parish.[81]

[80] These ages were found through analysis of a small number of parish registers and poor law records which mention ages.

[81] The Speenhamland system was a form of relief in which parishes subsidised people's incomes according to the price of bread and the number of children that people had. The system appears to have been most common during the French/Napoleonic Wars and was intended to be used during temporary crises until wage rates increased or people's employment prospects improved. The roundsman system involved sending people to work for ratepayers at reduced wages that were topped up by the poor rate. Under the labour rate, ratepayers could hire people to work for them at a wage set by the parish or choose to pay a labour rate tax to the parish. On allowance

Pauper inventories were made less frequently by overseers from the 1780s (Figure 2.2; Table 3.4) when these systems of help were most commonly used by parishes. This may mean that these types of parishioners are simply not captured in the pauper inventories owing to sampling issues. However, the same trends can be seen in pauper inventories from Dorset, Kent, Lancashire, Leicestershire, and Rutland, suggesting that people who received this type of relief had hitherto had their goods inventoried.[82] Perhaps more importantly, these parishioners generally did not have their goods appraised by parishes since officials saw little point in doing so, because allowances were only intended to be used by the recipients as a temporary measure. Moreover, these allowances were generally only used by younger and middle-aged able-bodied men who struggled to find regular and adequately paid employment. If parishes appraised the goods of these people, then they would generally have had to wait a long time before the person died to collect their possessions. This means that there is a limit to how far one can claim that pauper inventories are representative of *all* pauper populations across the length of the old poor law, but it does mean that the sample of claimants transcribed in this volume is largely consistent.

As a final means to assess how representative pauper inventories are, one can check whether the people from the inventories had paid poor rates earlier in their lifetimes and whether these amounts were significant sums of money. In the village of Martham, twelve pauper inventories survive between 1758 and 1772 **(80–91)**. Of these twelve inventories, only four or five were made of the goods of people who had previously paid rates or had partners who had done so.[83] The amounts that they had paid were mostly small and sometimes irregular. For example, in the twenty-five years before Roger Riches had his goods appraised in 1772, he had only paid 9d. for half a year of rates between 1753 and 1754. The other people from the sample tended to pay no more than around 2s. or 3s. in rates for the year. Each person had stopped paying rates

systems and for further context on why parishes used them, see: George R. Boyer, *An Economic History of the English Poor Law 1750–1850* (Cambridge, 1990), pp. 9–50; Mark Neuman, *The Speenhamland County: Poverty and the poor laws in Berkshire 1782–1834* (London, 1982); Mark Blaug, 'The Myth of the Old Poor Law and the making of the New', *Journal of Economic History*, 23 (1963), pp. 151–184; Blaug, 'Poor Law Report reexamined', pp. 229–245; Oxley, *Poor Relief*, pp. 109–119; Dunkley, *Crisis of the Old Poor Law*; Daniel A. Baugh, 'The costs of Poor Relief in South-east England, 1790–1834', *Economic History Review*, 28 (1975), pp. 50–68; John D. Marshall, *The Old Poor Law 1795–1834* (London, 1968); Eden, *State of the Poor*, 3 vols.; Williams, *Poverty, Gender*, pp. 9–10; Poynter, *Society and Pauperism*, passim; Brundage, *English Poor Laws*, pp. 27–29.

[82] For further information on these counties, see: Harley, 'Pauper Inventories, Social Relations'; idem, 'Material Lives of the English poor: A regional perspective'.

[83] One person could not be firmly identified as there were two people in the records with the same name.

for a number of years before their goods were inventoried.[84] Although this is only one example of a parish, these results nevertheless suggest that the people from the pauper inventories were not from affluent backgrounds and were thus not atypical of the conditions from which most paupers came.

Conclusion

This chapter has shown that there is a considerable range of inventories in parish archives which have much potential for future research. Goods-given inventories, for example, can be used to examine parish generosity and the economy of makeshifts, while poorhouse/workhouse-related inventories can be used to study old poor law institutions. Most notably, Norfolk represents the largest collection of pauper inventories ever assembled for a single county. Most pauper inventories were created between 1720 and 1779 in rural agricultural areas of southern and central Norfolk, where there were arduous farming conditions and a much higher dependence on poor relief than in other parts of the county and England and Wales. Although poor relief could be organised in numerous ways and many parishes experimented with different forms of assistance throughout the old poor law, officials appear to have generally inventoried the belongings of similar types of paupers. Between the seventeenth and late eighteenth century, women were most likely to have had an inventory made of their belongings, but after this date inventories were increasingly made of goods in male-headed households. In particular, parishes tended to appraise the goods of claimants who were generally more expensive to maintain and received parish assistance owing to life-cycle-related problems such as old age, infirmity, and sickness. Thus, the inventories are potentially representative of millions of other paupers whose goods were not appraised by poor law authorities.

These findings help us to clarify what it meant to be viewed as 'deserving' of relief by parochial authorities, as women, the sick, and elderly were typically seen as respectable members of the community as long as they were industrious, moral, and civil individuals.[85] However, in other ways it muddies the water since men were often viewed with suspicion by parish officers and the wider population, especially during the final decades of the old poor law.[86] In either instance, with the practice of appraising parishioners' possessions, it

[84] NRO PD 710/68; Cornford, 'Inventories of the poor', pp. 118–125. The last time that these paupers paid rates was 4, 8, 10, and 18 years before their goods were inventoried.

[85] Hindle, *On the Parish*, pp. 379–398; Shave, *Pauper Policies*, pp. 127–130.

[86] Brundage, *English Poor Laws*, pp. 25–69; Snell, *Annals*, pp. 108–114; Dunkley, *Crisis of the Old Poor Law*; Williams, *Poverty, Gender*, pp. 101–159; Poynter, *Society and Pauperism*, passim.

was clearly not only people's character or familial background that were assessed to qualify for relief, but also their belongings. This is not to say that people were denied relief because they owned very little. Rather, as the next chapter argues, pauper inventories capture claimants who owned a wide range of possessions.

Chapter 4

The structure and content of pauper inventories

It could be argued that because pauper inventories were made at a local level at the discretion and initiative of parochial officials, the sources are too disparate to be analysed as a complete collection. This supposition is, however, largely erroneous. As the previous chapters have shown, the system of appraising parishioners' goods appears to have been more thought-through and consistent than it first appears. This chapter develops this argument by focusing on the possessions that are listed in the sources. It starts by analysing four different pauper inventories to illustrate how they were formatted and laid out by appraisers. The items listed in the inventories and the representativeness of the goods are then analysed. It is argued that although there is some variation in how pauper inventories are laid out, the vast majority capture comparable information and use similar phraseologies. Most inventories enumerate a wide range of possessions and can be used to study a number of important aspects of domestic culture, such as consumption, domestic production, and household management.

Layout and format

The process of creating pauper inventories generally started when the overseer decided to appraise the goods of parishioner(s) who were on poor relief. The decision was generally taken after some communication with other parish officials and members of the vestry,[1] but on occasion some overseers probably took the initiative themselves. Appraisers then entered paupers' homes, invited or not, and went through their possessions writing down items as they

[1] For example, vestry minutes from Ightham, Kent, in 1783 show 'That the Overseers [are to] take an Inventry of all goods and Cloaths of the persons relievd By the parish and bring an Account of the same to the Vestry'. KHLC P202/8/1. In Fyfield, Essex, on 14 April 1707 'It is ordered by a Vestry this day ... that all Persons that receive Alms shall Take an Inventory of there goods & y^{t} no persons Shall be releived by a weakley rate before there be an Inventory of ye Goods taken by ye Officers of ye Parrish' in ERO D/P 144/8/1 Fyfield Parish Book, 1648–1732. It is also not unusual to have other people such as churchwardens listed as appraisers or witnesses alongside overseers in the inventories. This indicates that they knew about the policy and that the overseer had discussed the practice with others to some extent.

went. In most instances, the inventories were made by overseers and/or churchwardens and only occasionally did parishes hire people to do this.[2] Sometimes the goods were written directly into account books or vestry minutes, but at other times duplicate inventories were made when they were copied from loose sheets of paper into more lasting records such as hard-bound account books. The extent to which multiple copies of inventories were made, however, is difficult to determine since few reliable sets of duplicates have been located for Norfolk or other counties. Moreover, the making of copies is not noted in account books unless it led to an exchange of money.[3] Nevertheless, there is no reason to suspect that where this happened one copy would be significantly inferior to another, other than the odd omission of adjectives which describe the items and the occasional shortening of sentences.

Some inventories only very briefly list the objects and the names of the people involved in the inventory, whereas others describe the goods in intricate detail, outlining which rooms they were found in, how much they were worth, and what condition the items were in. The majority of inventories fall somewhere between these two extremes. Most start with an introduction that identifies to whom the goods in the inventory belonged, where it was made, when it was made, and who appraised the goods.

Figure 4.1 is an example of the most common type of pauper inventory found among parish collections **(156)**. The opening lines outline the date that

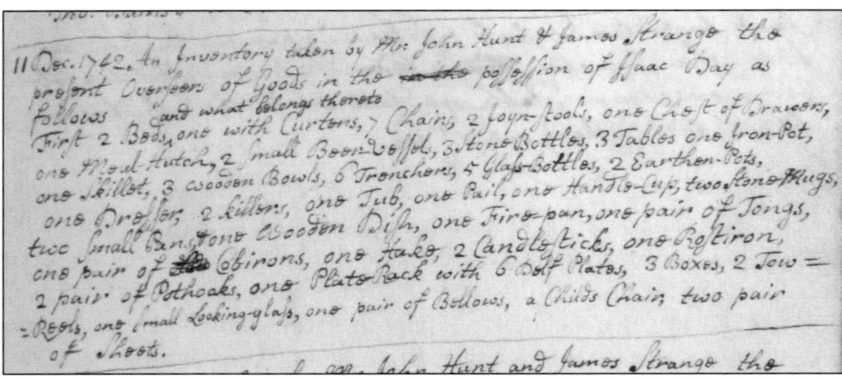
11 Dec. 1742. An Inventory taken by Mr. John Hunt & James Strange the present Overseers of Goods in the possession of Isaac Day as follows and what belongs thereto
First 2 Beds, one with Curtens, 7 Chairs, 2 Joyn-stools, one Chest of Drawers, one Meal-Hutch, 2 small Beer-Vessels, 3 Stone-Bottles, 3 Tables one Iron-Pot, one Skillet, 3 wooden Bowls, 6 Trenchers, 5 Glass-Bottles, 2 Earthen-Pots, one Dresser, 2 Killers, one Tub, one Pail, one Handle-Cup, two Stone Mugs, two small Pans, one Wooden Dish, one Fire-pan, one pair of Tongs, one pair of Cobirons, one Hake, 2 Candlesticks, one Rostiron, 2 pair of Pothooks, one Plate Rack with 6 Delf Plates, 3 Boxes, 2 Tow-Reels, one small Looking-glass, one pair of Bellows, a Childs Chair, two pair of Sheets.
John Hunt and James Strange the

Figure 4.1 Pauper inventory of Isaac Day's goods, Redenhall with Harleston and Wortwell, 1742 **(156)**

[2] For example, East Harling parish hired John Ellis, an 'Auctioneer & Appraiser', to inventory the possessions of paupers **(51, 52, 54)**.

[3] For instance, the accounts of Redenhall with Harleston and Wortwell show expenses at various times 'for Entring the Same [inventories] into y^{e} Town book'. NRO PD 295/94; NRO 295/102. Adrian Green and F. G. Emmison also found similiar trends, in Green, 'Heartless and Unhomely?', p. 81; Emmison, *Relief of the Poor*, p. 33.

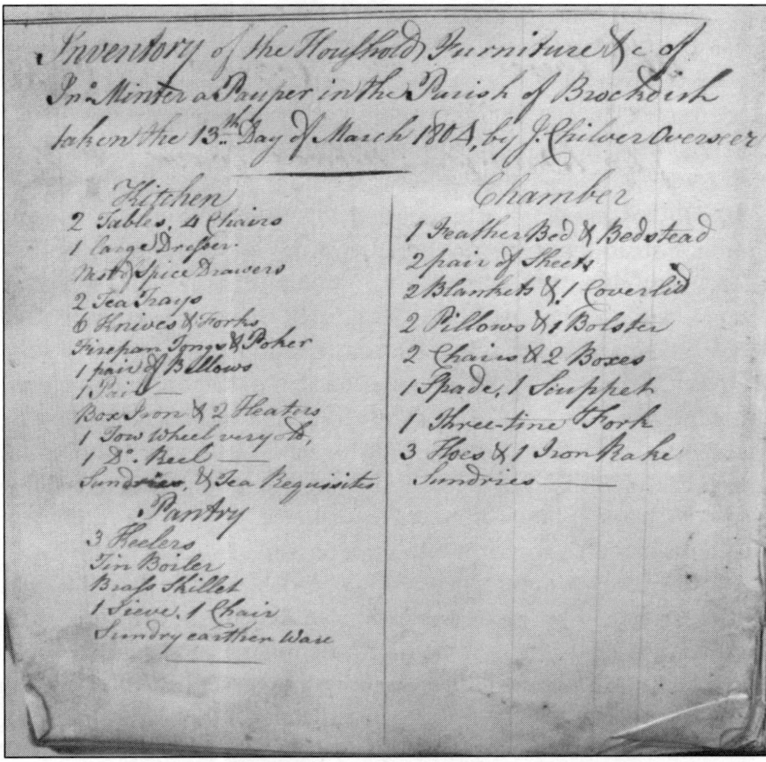

Inventory of the Household Furniture &c of
Jno. Minter a Pauper in the Parish of Brockdish
taken the 13th Day of March 1804, by J. Chilver Overseer

Kitchen
2 Tables, 4 Chairs
1 Large Dresser
Nest of Spice Drawers
2 Tea Trays
6 Knives & Forks
Firepan Tongs & Poker
1 pair of Bellows
1 Pail
Box Iron & 2 Heaters
1 Tow Wheel very old,
1 Do. Reel
Sundries, & Tea Requisites

Pantry
3 Keelers
Tin Boiler
Brass Skillet
1 Sieve, 1 Chair
Sundry earthen Ware

Chamber
1 Feather Bed & Bedstead
2 pair of Sheets
2 Blankets & 1 Coverlid
2 Pillows & 1 Bolster
2 Chairs & 2 Boxes
1 Spade, 1 Scuppet
1 Three-tine Fork
3 Hoes & 1 Iron Rake
Sundries

Figure 4.2 Pauper inventory of John Minter's goods, Brockdish, 1742 **(22)**

the source was created (11 December 1742); who took the inventory (overseers John Hunt and James Strange); and whose goods are listed in the source (Isaac Day). Most pauper inventories give little indication as to whether the subject of the inventory was on poor relief and why it was taken, meaning that additional research using poor law records is needed on all suspected pauper inventories. The possessions of the pauper are then recorded after these opening lines. Objects are often grouped together by appraisers. In this inventory, for instance, the overseers listed '7 chairs', '3 Stone Bottles', and '2 Candlesticks'. It is possible that these items were grouped together as they were identical, but the appraiser may have also listed the objects together for ease, meaning that little information can be inferred as to the shape, size, materials, and conditions of some of the items in the inventory.

In a similar manner, the pauper inventory of John Minter's goods (Figure 4.2; **22**) outlines the date that the document was made (13 March 1804), whose goods were appraised, and who took the inventory (J. Chilver, the overseer). The opening lines also disclose which parish made the inventory and describe John Minter as a 'Pauper'. The belongings of John Minter are listed line by line and the rooms in which the items were found are noted, thereby providing evidence of how particular objects may have been organised and used. One can examine room function and how this may have changed over time, by assessing how frequently particular objects were found in specific rooms. Unfortunately, only forty-four of the 230 inventories (19 per cent) provide this kind of detail and this information can be vague or misleading. For example, the inventory of Andrew Allen notes goods 'in ye other Roome' **(42)**, but the appraiser did not name the room or mention any other spaces in the house. Mary Shearling's inventory records '2 Beds *upstairs'*,[4] showing that her home had more than one floor and a staircase **(226)**. However, no other rooms are mentioned and the goods on each level of the house are generally not distinguished from one another.

The pauper inventories may not have generally recorded rooms simply because some claimants lived in one-room dwellings, or only occupied a single room as a lodger in a larger home.[5] For instance, in 1693 an inventory was made of Sara Hubert's goods by Moulton parish, while she was living in the home of John Brown due to her old age and blindness **(92)**. The pauper inventory of Widow Flattman's possessions in Redenhall with Harleston and Wortwell records items 'in ye Same Room Belonging to Hen: Branch' **(137)**. Sometimes landlords divided larger dwellings into several smaller lodgings to maximise profits. For several decades John Clare's family lived in a 'roomy and confortable' home with a garden for 40s. per year. However, the landlord decided to raise the rent to three guineas (63s.) a year and divided the house into four tenements, 'leaving us a corner of one room on a floor ... and a little slip of the garden which was divided into 4 parts'.[6] Most paupers in the sample, however, appear to have lived in homes with more than one room, despite not having their goods described on a room by room basis. Appraisers simply did not need to note rooms as most items were easily distinguishable from one another without this additional information.

A few notes of caution are needed when using inventories which list rooms. Just because certain rooms are not mentioned in inventories it does not mean that they did not exist. Junk rooms or empty rooms and corridors or hallways may have been omitted by appraisers, since there were few objects in these spaces that were worth noting. The shapes and sizes of the rooms and how they were connected are rarely noted by inventory takers. Nor are fixtures

[4] My italics.
[5] Lodging became more common over the long eighteenth century, especially among the elderly and mobile population. See: David Hussey and Margaret Ponsonby, *The Single Homemaker and Material Culture in the long Eighteenth century* (Farnham, 2012), pp. 151–160; King, 'Pauper Inventories', pp. 160–161.
[6] Robinson, *Clare's Autobiographical Writings*, pp. 114–115.

such as staircases, hearths, doors, and windows. The locations of the items in the rooms are rarely noted. In order to understand, for example, what items might be placed on mantlepieces, whether beds tended to be placed against walls, or where looking glasses might be positioned, it would be necessary to refer to other qualitative sources such as pictures of domestic interiors or autobiographies. Moreover, items such as candlesticks were intended to be moved and possessions including plates and dishes may have been put into storage rooms or storage units when not in use. Consequently, any meanings inferred from the location of objects in the inventories may be erroneous. The room names were written down by appraisers and their views on the names/functions of the rooms may have been very different to the owner's opinions. If lodgers were living in a pauper's dwelling their goods and rooms may have been omitted since the parish had no need to inventory these possessions. The analysis of room use and function is thus problematic and should be approached carefully by researchers.[7]

The third type of pauper inventory under scrutiny are those which put a monetary value on pauper possessions (Figure 4.3; **170**). Basic information such as the claimant's name (Widow Hatton), the date that it was created (22 May 1696), and the names of the appraisers are noted (Robert Futter and William Pearse), but monetary values are also assigned to the possessions. Sometimes the items are valued individually and on occasion they are grouped together with an overall valuation for the collection of goods. These types of inventories are unfortunately relatively uncommon. Out of the 230 pauper inventories in this volume, sixty-one provide valuations of one or more items (27 per cent). Of these, fifty-eight (25 per cent) record the total value of the pauper's *entire* possessions. Most of these inventories with valuations are dated before 1750 and only one inventory from the nineteenth century records monetary figures, meaning that it is difficult to accurately measure household value over time. Nevertheless, when compared to other counties it appears that Norfolk has an unusually high number of pauper inventories which record item prices. By contrast, only 2 and 8 per cent of the pauper inventories from Dorset and Kent include a total valuation of pauper goods.[8]

It is difficult to determine the extent to which the valuations of appraisers are accurate. Value, for example, could change according to the conditions,

[7] For further information and examples on using inventories to assess rooms and room use, see: Lena Cowen Orlin, 'Fictions of the Early Modern English Probate Inventory', in Henry S. Turner, ed., *The Culture of Capital* (London, 2002), esp. pp. 57–73; Overton et al., *Production and Consumption*, pp. 121–136; Muldrew, *Food*, pp. 177–182; Sneath, 'Consumption, Wealth', pp. 205–230; Ursula Priestly and Penelope J. Corfield, 'Rooms and Room use in Norwich Housing, 1580–1730', *Post-Medieval Archaeology*, 16 (1982), pp. 93–123; Anthony Buxton, *Domestic Culture in Early Modern England* (Woodbridge, 2015), pp. 208–242.

[8] Harley, 'Material Lives of the English poor: A regional perspective', pp. 80–82.

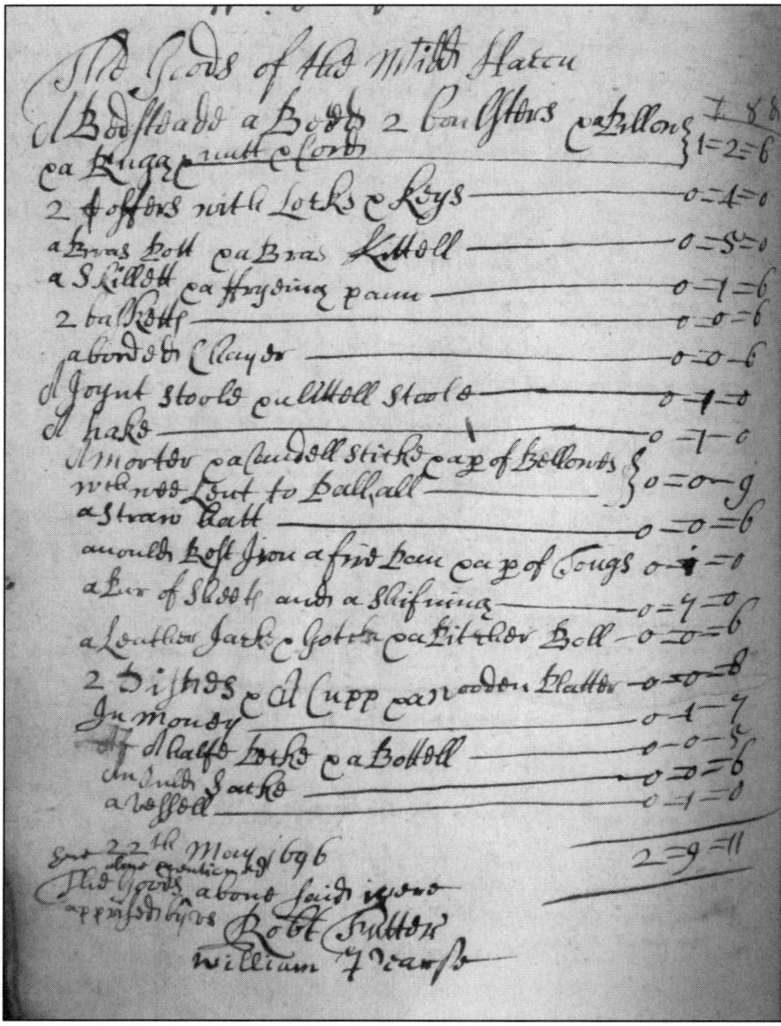
The Goods of the Widdow Hatton

A Bedsteade a Bedd 2 boulsters & a pillow & a Rugg a blankett & cords	£ s d 1=2=6
2 Coffers with Locks & Keys	0=4=0
a Brass pott & a Brass Kettell	0=5=0
a Skillett & a ffrying pann	0=1=6
2 baskets	0=0=6
a bordd & Chayre	0=0=6
A Joynt stoole & a little stoole	0=1=0
A hake	0=1=0
A morter & a candell sticke & a pair of bellows with some Lint to ball all	0=0=9
a Straw hatt	0=0=6
an ould Rost Iron a fire pann & a pair of Tongs	0=1=0
a pair of Sheets and a Shifting	0=7=0
a Leather Jack & Gotch & a Pitcher Boll	0=0=6
2 Dishes & a Cupp & a wooden platter	0=0=8
In money	0=1=7
A halfe Bushell & a Bottell	0=0=5
An ould Sacke	0=0=6
a vessell	0=1=0
	2=9=11

Ent 22th May 1696
The Goods above said were apprised by us
Robt Sutton
William Pearse

Figure 4.3 Pauper inventory of Widow Hatton's goods, Shelton, 1696 **(170)**

ages, and appearances of items, and prices may differ depending upon whether the source records the views of middling parish officials or poor claimants. The assessment of goods could also vary over time depending upon issues such as inflation and how saturated the market was with certain products. Further complicating the issue, the estimates may be based on what the parish expected to receive for the goods second-hand, or what the owner may have initially paid for the items.[9] Looking at the possessions from a purely quantitative perspective also neglects the emotional values bestowed on objects.[10] In spite of these issues, the reasons for appraisers generally not valuing parishioners' goods are relatively straightforward. Pauper inventories were made as a record of ownership with the idea of taking the goods at a later date, meaning that it was often pointless to value the possessions as their condition and value could change over time. Additionally, items could be taken from paupers to amass a stock of goods that could be given to other claimants or be used in the workhouse, further ensuring that there was little use in valuing them.

The final inventories considered here are those which include written agreements outlining that the parish was entitled to the claimant's possessions because they had given them relief. They are the rarest form of pauper inventory as most parishes did not go to this trouble and instead made informal agreements with parishioners to take their goods when they died. Figure 4.4 shows an example of one of these inventories taken in St. Mary in the Marsh in Norwich of the goods of Samuel Hunt in 1772 **(123)**. In a similar manner to the other three examples, the inventory records information such as the pauper's name, his possessions, the date that it was made, where it was made, and the names of the appraisers. Samuel Hunt's occupation is also rather unusually given. An agreement is included which affirms that the 'Goods Furniture and Things are in my [Samuel Hunt's] Possession and ... are the property of the Officers of ye Parish of St Mary in ye Marsh'. The pledge was undoubtedly written by the appraiser despite it being written in the first person, since the handwriting is the same throughout and Samuel Hunt's name is signed with an unsteady cross. This appears to have been a device that some authorities used to take parishioners' goods legally and avoid prosecution, since the parish lacked the requisite powers to inventory and take parishioners' goods. If the pauper agreed to give the parish their belongings and there was written proof of it, then there was theoretically little that paupers, families, or justices of the peace could do to stop the parish from taking the items.[11]

[9] In all likelihood it was the former, but it is nevertheless important to keep this in mind. On the value of goods in inventories, see: Mark Overton, 'Prices from Probate Inventories', in Tom Arkell, Nesta Evans, and Nigel Goose, eds., *When Death do us Part: Understanding and interpreting the probate records of early modern England* (Oxford, 2000), pp. 120–141; de Vries, *The Industrious Revolution: Consumer behaviour*, pp. 144–148; Muldrew, *Food*, pp. 182–187.

[10] Weatherill, *Consumer Behaviour*, pp. 16–19; Giorgio Riello, '"Things Seen and Unseen": The material culture of early modern inventories and their representation of domestic interiors', in Paula Findlen, ed., *Early Modern Things: Objects and their histories, 1500–1800* (London, 2013), pp. 142–143.

[11] The legality of taking pauper inventories is discussed further in chapter 2.

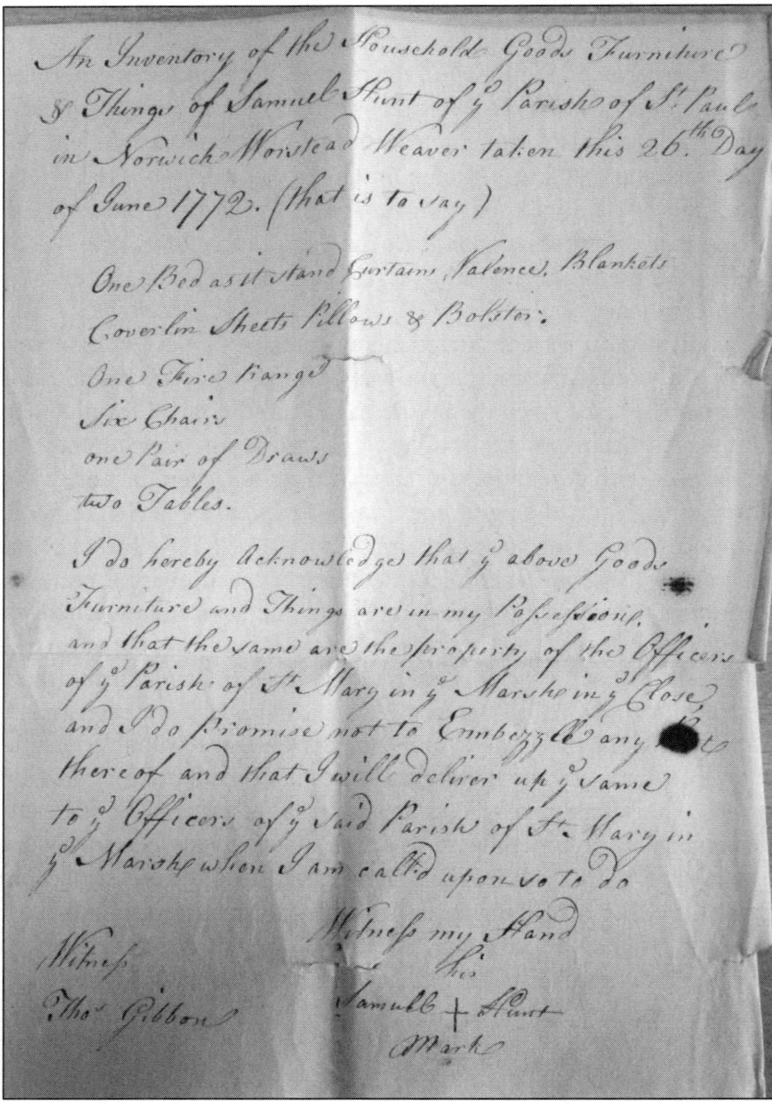

An Inventory of the Household Goods Furniture & Things of Samuel Hunt of ye Parish of St Paul in Norwich Worstead Weaver taken this 26th Day of June 1772. (that is to say)

One Bed as it stand Curtains, Valence, Blankets Coverlin Sheets Pillows & Bolster.

One Fire Range

Six Chairs

one Pair of Draws

two Tables.

I do hereby Acknowledge that ye above Goods Furniture and Things are in my Possession, and that the same are the property of the Officers of ye Parish of St Mary in ye Marsh in ye Close and I do Promise not to Embezzle any Part thereof and that I will deliver up ye same to ye Officers of ye said Parish of St Mary in ye Marsh when I am call'd upon so to do

Witness my Hand

Witness

Thos Gibbon

his
Samuell + Hunt
Mark

Figure 4.4 Pauper inventory of Samuel Hunt's goods, Norwich, St. Mary in the Marsh, 1772 **(123)**

Representativeness of items recorded in pauper inventories

This section will analyse the representativeness of the items in the pauper inventories. This is important to do as it is possible that parishes prioritised inventorying the goods of paupers who were materially richer than most, such as those who were previously of the middling sort before they became pauperised. This would mean that any samples of pauper inventories would be biased towards atypical claimants.

Despite these potential problems, there are a number of reasons to suggest that parishes appraised the goods of a wide spectrum of paupers and did not focus on those who owned a wide array of possessions. First, while some pauper inventories listed hundreds of objects, only a quarter of them list fifty or more items. Moreover, over half of them list no more than thirty items. Of course, these numbers are not precise and inevitably under-represent the goods that claimants owned; however, if materially rich paupers were a priority then one would expect the inventories to record many more items. Second, the estates recorded in the Norfolk pauper inventories were worth an average of £2 6s. 4d. between 1692 and 1825. This figure is based on only fifty-eight pauper inventories across a long period of time and so is tentative, but nonetheless suggests that more affluent parishioners were not a priority as the amount is relatively low. Labourers' probate inventories from Norfolk used in Craig Muldrew's research, on the other hand, record estates with an average value of £8.08. This amount is over three times higher than the Norfolk pauper inventories, despite the fact that the majority of probate inventories Muldrew used for Norfolk came from the first half of the seventeenth century, while the majority of pauper inventories were made in the eighteenth century.[12] Likewise, if one compares pauper inventories with valuations dated between 1692 and 1727 to the probate inventories used in Lorna Weatherill's research on the middling sort between 1675 and 1725, the data demonstrates that Weatherill's sample owned goods worth approximately 11 to 12 times more than paupers in this volume. Even when the results are only compared to husbandmen and labourers, the goods of paupers in Norfolk were worth less than half of those of the former.[13]

Third, one would expect animal ownership to be much higher if pauper inventories represented the materially richest of the dependent poor, particularly given the rural nature of the inventories. These were valuable assets worth several pounds which could be sold for profit by the parish or be used in the parish poorhouse/workhouse. Despite this, only two pauper inventories in the sample recorded pigs **(63, 68)**; two listed a cow **(68, 89)**; three noted an

[12] Muldrew, *Food*, pp. 172–173.
[13] Weatherill, *Consumer Behaviour*, p. 168.

ass (donkey) **(8, 68, 69)**; and none recorded sheep. These numbers are probably an underrepresentation since some inventories note items connected to animal ownership such as pig troughs and meat stools, yet it is still likely that animal ownership was low since animals or items connected to livestock are only recorded in around one in ten inventories. In Muldrew's and Ken Sneath's work on labourers' probate inventories, on the other hand, around half of labourers owned cows and high numbers also owned other types of livestock.[14] Recent comparisons of pauper inventories and labourers' probate inventories from Kent equally show that around 8 per cent of pauper inventories recorded animals, while 51 per cent of Kent labourers' probate inventories recorded livestock.[15] The probate inventories of the Kent middling sort also suggest that around half of people owned animals between 1600 and 1750.[16]

Overall then, it would be unfair to argue that appraisers prioritised inventorying the goods of materially rich paupers. Rather, pauper inventories represent the goods of people at the point when they turned to poor relief. A minority of paupers had been able to retain a considerable range of possessions, probably stemming from longer periods of earlier prosperity or prompt intervention by parish authorities, whereas a small number of paupers owned very few goods when their belongings were appraised by the parish. More typically, the majority of pauper inventories record the possessions of individuals that fell somewhere between these two extremes. With regular or casual relief rarely being enough to live off,[17] most people would have gone through periods of selling and pawning their goods before and during the time that they received poor relief, as well as extensively using other makeshift

[14] Muldrew, *Food*, p. 250; Sneath, 'Consumption, Wealth', pp. 143–144.

[15] Harley, 'Consumption and Poverty', p. 91. Sometimes select vestries would make people sell off animals before they were entitled to relief. See: Samantha A. Shave, 'The Impact of Sturges Bourne's Poor Law reforms in Rural England', *The Historical Journal*, 56 (2013), pp. 419–420. However, no records of this practice have been found with the paupers in this sample, suggesting that claimants generally did not own animals or owned them long before they received relief from the parish. Contemporary comments and secondary evidence also suggests that ownership of livestock was low among the poor during the long eighteenth century. See: Snell, *Annals*, 174–179; Leigh Shaw-Taylor, 'Labourers, Cows, Common rights and Parliamentary Enclosure: The evidence of contemporary comment c. 1760–1810', *Past and Present*, 171 (2001), pp. 95–126; Nathaniel Kent, *Hints to Gentlemen of Landed Property* (London, 1775), pp. 236–237; Eden, *State of the Poor*, vol. 1, esp. pp. 531–532; David Davies, *The Case of Labourers in Husbandry* (London, 1795), pp. 37–38.

[16] Overton et al. did not precisely say what percentage of probate inventories recorded animals. However, based on their tables which show activities such as butchering, dairy production, and combined arable/pastoral production, it is likely that around half of the inventories recorded animals. Overton et al., *Production and Consumption*, pp. 33–86.

[17] King, *Poverty and Welfare*, p. 258; Williams, *Poverty, Gender*, p. 65; Hindle, *On the Parish*, pp. 276–278; Healey, *First Century of Welfare*, pp. 136–137 . Also see Table 3.5 above.

economies including neighbourly charity and ad-hoc work such as nursing to make do.[18] Pauper inventories consequently represent the goods that people kept after a number of their possessions from more prosperous times had been sold.[19]

Usefulness of pauper inventories for studying material life

Although we have a sample which appears to be representative of paupers who did not have their goods appraised, the items recorded in the inventories are nonetheless difficult to assess for many reasons which are familiar to researchers of probate inventories.[20] Pauper inventories should be viewed as a representation of the home rather than a comprehensive record of its contents.[21] They are almost never complete and should not be used to claim that a particular item is not present because it is not recorded.[22] This is made obvious when the terms 'sundries' or 'lumber' are used, as they are in the example of John Minter above (Figure 4.2; **22**). Some appraisers simply noted 'some' earthenware or 'a few' plates and would use umbrella terms such as 'fire irons' and 'bedding' which lack specificity. Only moveable property is listed and details about gardens, lands, and the house are rarely given. Some items such as household linen, eating and drinking utensils, and clothing appear to be under-recorded in the inventories. The goods of lodgers are omitted in most cases. Equally, the inventories of paupers who were themselves lodgers only note the items that they owned and not the items that they had access to. Widow Allcock and Widow Reeves, for example, lived with one another in Shipdham in 1720 **(194, 195)**. Their goods were appraised separately by poor law officials, but since the two lived together it is possible that they shared items such as cooking pots, seating, and fire irons. Had the appraiser not

[18] Steven King and Alannah Tomkins, eds., *The Poor in England 1700–1850: An economy of makeshifts* (Manchester, 2003); Harley, 'Material Lives of the Poor and their Strategic use of the Workhouse', esp. pp. 81–85, 93–95; Hindle, *On the Parish*, pp. 15–95, 361–449; Williams, *Poverty, Gender*, pp. 131–159; Healey, *First Century of Welfare*, pp. 127–168; Richard Dyson, 'Welfare Provision in Oxford during the latter stages of the Old Poor Law', *Historical Journal*, 52 (2009), pp. 943–962. Also see: Broad, 'Parish Economies of Welfare', pp. 985–1006.

[19] This is explored further in Harley, 'Consumption and Poverty', esp. pp. 101–103.

[20] The following critiques of probate inventories are especially useful and can be used to inform the use of other types of inventories. Evans, 'Enlivening the Archive', pp. 40–72; Orlin, 'Fictions', pp. 51–83; John Bedell, 'Archaeology and Probate Inventories in the Study of Eighteenth-century Life', *Journal of Interdisciplinary History*, 31 (2000), pp. 223–245; Overton et al., *Production and Consumption*, pp. 13–32; and the various chapters in Arkell, Evans, and Goose, *When Death do us Part*.

[21] Riello, 'Things Seen', p. 127 makes the same point regarding probate inventories. Also see: Evans, 'Enlivening the Archive', pp. 40–72.

[22] Overton et al., *Production and Consumption*, p. 18.

made two inventories and noted that the two lived together, this aspect of domestic culture would have been missed.

Because pauper goods would inevitably be sold, end up in the poorhouse/workhouse, or be given to another pauper, some appraisers may have prioritised writing down items which could be sold or recycled around the community. This means that small items of little value such as love tokens and children's toys are generally not recorded in the inventories.[23] The inventory of Godfrey Goodrum included 'old Rubbish' **(145)**. This may have included items that were highly important to the pauper, but not deemed of sufficient value to be listed by the overseer of Redenhall with Harleston and Wortwell. Just because something was described as 'old' or 'broken' does not mean that it was worthless or had no utilitarian or sentimental value to its owners.[24] Items related to activities such as sewing are rarely found despite the fact that we know that it was ubiquitous.[25] Many small items such as thimbles and needles may have been hidden away in people's pockets when the inventory was made.[26] Only animals such as cows and pigs are listed by appraisers since they had financial or utilitarian value, whereas cats and dogs are not mentioned.[27] As such, we cannot use inventories to study sentimental objects and pets which probably meant more to their owners than any of the other goods in the inventory.

Occasionally pauper inventories may under-record possessions since the parish had taken some of them at a previous date. Swanage (Dorset) vestry minutes in 1773 noted that the parish should make inventories of parishioners' goods and take any items which it deemed superfluous. Parish officers were to:

[23] Bedell, 'Archaeology and Probate Inventories', pp. 224, 240; Jennine Hurl-Eamon, 'Love Tokens: Objects as memory for plebeian women in early modern England', *Early Modern Women: An Interdisciplinary Journal*, 6 (2011), pp. 181–186.

[24] Sara Pennell, '"For a crack or flaw despis'd": Thinking about ceramic durability and the "everyday" in late seventeenth- and early eighteenth-century England', in Tara Hamling and Catherine Richardson, eds., *Everyday Objects: Medieval and early modern material culture and its meanings* (Farnham, 2010), pp. 31–39; Jon Stobart and Mark Rothery, 'Fashion, Inheritance and Family', *Cultural and Social History*, 11 (2014), pp. 385–406.

[25] Bedell, 'Archaeology and Probate Inventories', pp. 224, 229, 240; Jenny McKenney, 'The "Bossy Shield": Money, sex, sentiment, and the thimble', *Lumen*, 34 (2015), pp. 1–23; Maureen Daly Goggin and Beth Fowkes Tobin, eds., *Women and the Material Culture of Needlework and Textiles, 1750–1950* (Farnham, 2009); Mary C. Beaudry, *Findings: The material culture of needlework and sewing* (New Haven, 2006).

[26] Barbara Burman and Jonathan White, 'Fanny's Pockets: Cotton, consumption and domestic economy, 1780–1850', in Jennie Batchelor and Cora Kaplan, eds., *Women and Material Culture, 1660–1830* (Basingstoke, 2007), pp. 31–51; McKenney, 'Bossy Shield', pp. 1–23.

[27] An exception to this might be hunting dogs. However, unsurprisingly, none of the pauper inventories recorded any since people needed game licenses to hunt.

> Go to the Dwelling House of the said Pauper and Take Possession of the Goods belonging to the Pauper And particularly Enter in the Parish Poor Book an Inventory of the goods to the Intent that the said Goods Shall be keept for the use of the Pauper as far as they are necessary to Him, & that What Goods do not appear necessary be disposed off, or keept in the hands of the said Officers & their successors for the use of the Parish ~~unless~~ till such times as the said Pauper, or those nearest ackind to Him or Her shall Reimpurst the Parish all such Moneys as shall have been Expended on account of the said Pauper & Family.[28]

It is unclear what the parish deemed as not necessary and whether these superfluous goods were still noted down in the pauper inventories, but this example helps to further demonstrate that we should be mindful of how pauper inventories may under-record a person's belongings. Likewise, examples of this can be seen in this sample. Upon inventorying Henry Wells' goods in 1717/18, the parish of Bressingham took a form from the claimant and left him with the rest of his goods **(10)**. Parishes may have also sometimes made paupers sell off their belongings and live off that money for a time before they were allowed relief, resulting in their corresponding inventories recording only a few basic items. When parishes applied this policy, however, they generally appear not to have made inventories since the parish had already saved money by making the pauper sell their possessions.[29] This policy of making paupers offload their goods before they were entitled to relief also appears to have been more widespread in the north than in the south and east of England.[30]

Some paupers may have hidden their goods or asked friends and relatives to look after them if they knew that somebody was coming to appraise their belongings. It is impossible to know the extent of this clandestine activity since it inevitably left little trace in the written record; however, it is likely that most paupers would have had difficulty in concealing their belongings without the parish knowing or suspecting something. The frequency and types of visits that parochial officials made on paupers could vary considerably. Some parishes would regularly visit pauper homes on a monthly basis, whereas others would rarely visit people or would only make special visitations when the pauper wanted something.[31] It is difficult to know whether these visits

[28] DHC PE-SW/OV/1/5, Swanage overseers' accounts, 1752–1780.

[29] CCAL U3/269/16/1.

[30] Harley, 'Pauper Inventories, Social Relations'.

[31] For instance, in Cranbrook, Kent visits to paupers were made monthly, however the parish would also make 'special visitations both within and without the parish as may be required by the overseers'. Melling, *Kentish Sources*, p. 185. Meanwhile other parishes went to claimants' homes when they wanted goods off the parish. See the example of the Adams family and Thomas Peat, in: Cirket, *Samuel Whitbread's Notebooks*, p. 52, 100. Other overseers neglected their duty and did not visit paupers as often as they should have. See the example of John Crowder and his

tended to be pre-arranged and thus whether people knew when they had to conceal their goods. Most of the pauper inventories were made in small rural parishes where many people knew or recognised one another and so there may have been little need to arrange visiting times. It would have been very difficult to hide belongings or move them to somebody else's home every time that somebody from the parish came to visit, without officials or ratepayers noticing and reporting it. Moreover, if the pauper had been visited in the past when the home had been more fully furnished, then the overseer would have probably noticed if the pauper suddenly had few possessions when it came to appraising the goods. Overall, the evidence appears to suggest that when visits were made to paupers with the intention of appraising goods, the parish foresaw that claimants might hide or sell their possessions and thus made surprise visits. Though relating to admission to a workhouse, the following example taken from Dartford, Kent, in 1733 suggests that visits were designed to catch people off guard and uncover what people and their homes were like on a normal day. It also suggests that if the parish thought that people were concealing their goods they would investigate it.

> I was calld upon to visit the Widow Brown as being extraordinary ill and between 3 and 4 this afternoon I visited her and surprized her and her daughter at dinner upon eels and I understand about noon she and her son, James and her daughter and the Widow Preston were at dinner upon hot mutton. When I came she attempted to throw herself in her clothes upon the bed, but I got in before she could be coverd. She spoke very heartily to me and did not seem near so ill as I expected. Her daughter desired me to take her into the workhouse for she had nothing to support her, nor any friends able to do it for her. I told her it was not in the power of any Visiting Governor to take her into the workhouse of his own accord, but to take care of her when she was regularly brought there. I understand she has sold her bed and goods but to whom and for what money it is proper for the parish officers to inquire. I believe it is a mock sale to prevent the parish having them towards her support, if any fraud can be discovered the parish will have them nevertheless, and she has goods worth having, especially her bed. I hear she has sold her new stock of coals, so that she is resolved to come here soon. But I think her daughter should first complain to a justice of her poverty and thereupon have an order to the overseers to take care of her and the overseers at the same time to complain of her fraudulent making away of her goods and have an order to restore them paying the money she received for them, before the Visiting Governors can take her in.[32]

daughter in: Cirket, *Samuel Whitbread's Notebooks*, p. 94. Also see: Hindle, *On the Parish*, pp. 258–259; Jeremy Boulton, 'Going on the Parish: The parish pension and its meaning in the London suburbs, 1640–1724', in Hitchcock, King, and Sharpe, *Chronicling Poverty*, pp. 33–34; Lees, *Solidarities of Strangers*, pp. 30–41; Healey, *First Century of Welfare*, pp. 90–91.

[32] Melling, *Kentish Sources*, p. 104.

Though most claimants would have been unable to conceal more than a few items, it should never be assumed that pauper inventories are complete. Wherever possible, the sources should be cross referenced against other sources and secondary literature to assess the extent to which inventories under-record items or how ownership may have changed over the life course.

The terms that appraisers used can be difficult to decipher and certain terms had distinct regional variations in meaning. A crock, for instance, in the south east was a metal cooking pot, but in the north it was a small earthenware pan.[33] Some of the words that appraisers used may even reflect local/regional accents, especially when they are written in a particular way by various enumerators. For example, keelers and andirons are often spelt 'killers' and 'handirons' respectively by appraisers across numerous parishes. A glossary is included at the back of this volume to address these issues; however, it is not always possible to find what every term means. Most inventories were written by overseers and churchwardens who had relatively high levels of literacy;[34] however there are numerous examples of appraisers in the sample who failed to follow basic rules of grammar and spelled words arbitrarily, archaically, or phonetically.[35] Dubious terms are defined in the footnotes to the inventories, but these terms are often open to further interpretation. Typically the inventories simply enumerate possessions without any qualitative description, let alone any indication of the values that owners invested in them. Other sources such as pauper letters and autobiographies can be used to circumvent these problems and understand how people may have felt about their belongings. Additionally, qualitative and linguistic analyses can be used on the pauper inventories to further understand what pauper possessions were like. First used by Mary C. Beaudry in 1988, qualitative and linguistic analysis uses the adjectives in the inventories to uncover the sizes, functions, colours, shapes, contents, conditions, ages, and compositions of items described in the documents.[36] By analysing terms such as 'new', 'old', 'joined', 'wooden', 'broken', 'blue', and so on, one can acquire a further glimpse into domestic life. For example, current research suggests that pauper items such

[33] *Oxford English Dictionary online* (http://www.oed.com); John S. Moore, *The Goods and Chattels of our Forefathers: Frampton Cotterell and district probate inventories, 1539–1804* (London, 1976), p. 302.

[34] See, for instance, the inventories of Martham parish **(80–91)**.

[35] For example, see Cawston parish **(25–43)**.

[36] Beaudry, 'Words for Things', pp. 43–50. For other studies which have used this methodology, see: Overton et al., *Production and Consumption*, pp. 114–116; Muldrew, *Food*, p. 200; Harley, 'Material Lives of the English Poor: A regional perspective', pp. 210–216. Also see: Evans, 'Enlivening the Archive', pp. 49–54.

as furniture became more colourful and that 'old' goods became less common by the late eighteenth century.[37]

Inventories are 'static' documents as they offer a representation of somebody's home at a fixed point in time. Consequently, they do not detail how people acquired their goods or how their material lives altered in response to the seasons, to life-cycle change, and to challenges such as worsening poverty. Generally speaking, besides odd breakages and losses of items, the goods that were recorded in the inventories would have gone to the parish and any additional items that were acquired after the inventory was made presumably went to officials too. For example, Elizabeth Trew of Redenhall with Harleston and Wortwell was looked after by Robert Quantrell while on poor relief. Underneath the inventory an agreement was made declaring that 'I [Robert Quantrell] Do promise that whenever she Happon To Dye... Every of them [items] shall be Accounted for or Return'd to the said parish' **(160)**. Disparate evidence shows what happened to the goods once they were taken by officials. The inventory of Jane Branch of Redenhall with Harleston and Wortwell is annotated to record which items were 'Gone' **(130)**, and the inventory of Jeremy Nudds' possessions was made 'for the benifitt of Town Stocke' **(173)**. Robert Websdale's inventory is marked up to show that a frying pan was given to or bought by Goody Parish and that three boxes, tongs, and a chest were sold by the parish **(102)**. Occasionally, goods-taken inventories record what happened to the goods once the pauper died. For instance, on the back of the pauper inventory of Widow Osburn's goods there is a goods-taken inventory which notes to whom the goods were sold and what they fetched in Hingham **(59)**. In the same parish, a pauper inventory was made of Widow Norton's goods in 1731. Besides the inventory, there is a goods-taken inventory which notes what the items were sold for **(66)**. An inventory of John Andrews' belongings taken several weeks after his death records which goods 'Remains' and notes that 'the Rest of the things are Dispos^{d} of by Town order' **(139)**. Sometimes items were not taken by the parish in the end. For example, in the inventory of Widow Townsend's goods from 1737, she bought a kettle back from the parish **(99)**. Overseers' accounts from Martham reveal that because the children of Priscilla Myhill paid for her funeral in March 1768, her possessions went to them instead of the parish **(85)**. In this sense, this pauper inventory may have been made to encourage children to support their elderly parents rather than leaving them to the support of the parish.

[37] Harley, 'Material Lives of the English Poor: A regional perspective', esp. pp. 97–98, 210–216.

Conclusion

We must be vigilant in our use of pauper inventories and analyse them with caution. Items may be missing from the inventories for myriad reasons and parishioners' belongings are mostly listed without any qualitative description by appraisers. Despite this, pauper inventories are very important sources for early modern and modern historians. Evidence suggests that they are representative of the goods of a wide spectrum of paupers and that appraisers did not focus on those that owned a wide variety of goods. Most pauper inventories offer a relatively complete picture of a claimant's home, as they list a range of mundane items such as fire irons and bedding, as well as more expensive goods such as furniture and non-essential items including clocks, looking glasses, and printed material. This allows readers to study people's household goods at one moment in time, when people were receiving poor relief and using the items.

Herein lies one of the main strengths of pauper inventories as a historical source. Other extant records such as pauper letters and contemporary comments often reveal highly impressionistic accounts and tend to emphasise the more unfortunate facets of the poor's material circumstances. For example, in a pauper letter written by the 65-year-old William James to the overseer of Chelmsford, Essex, he stated that he had 'only our Bed, & a few things brought in for us, by a friend or two'.[38] In March 1830 William King pleaded his case to the overseers of Braintree, Essex, claiming that 'I Cannot Do without Soume Help. Every thing of My Wearing apparell and Even My wifes Ring is Put of [pawned] to Procure food'.[39] The social commentator David Davies found that because of the rising costs of a number of basic necessities during the 1790s, the labouring poor predominantly ate bread day-to-day and had relatively little meat, beer, and milk.[40] He bemoaned that labourers were 'indifferently fed; badly clothed; some children without shoes and stockings ... In short, there was scarcely any appearance of comfort about their dwellings'.[41] In contrast, pauper inventories help to redress this imbalance and show that the poor were able to retain a number of their belongings over the long eighteenth century, despite often lacking sufficient food or fuel and being in continuous need of parochial assistance.

[38] Sokoll, *Essex Pauper Letters*, p. 390.
[39] Ibid., pp. 121–122.
[40] Davies, *Case of Labourers*, esp. pp. 31–40, 71–126.
[41] Ibid., p. 6.

Transcription conventions and editorial principles

Original text, spellings, and layout are retained wherever possible. Crossed out words are included with a strikethrough, but deleted words which are illegible have been omitted. Monetary figures are written in pounds (£/l/li), shillings (s.), and pence (d.). The inventories are dated according to the Old-Style calendar before 1752 (in which the new year began on 25 March) and New Style thereafter (new year on 1 January). Where the text is damaged, illegible, or ambiguous, and further information on the source can be ascertained, the following conventions are used:

Transcription conventions (used within the text of the inventory)

[ ] Insertions of editorial text (square brackets).

< > Conjectured readings of text which is illegible or has been damaged from holes, mice bites, burns, rips, and so on (pointed brackets).

< ? > Illegible words which cannot be deciphered (pointed brackets with a question mark).

Editorial conventions (located under the inventory)

RELIEF Details of the relief and help that the pauper received from the parish. Most of the time this information is not given in the inventory and has been found through examination of a wide range of sources such as overseers' accounts, vestry minutes, overseers' bills and receipts, and workhouse accounts. Regular relief (a pension) could be given to paupers in weekly, fortnightly, or monthly instalments. However, because many overseers' accounts record regular relief in quarterly or half-yearly sums, it is generally not possible to uncover how often people received their pension. Thus, for ease and to allow readers to compare claimants, all regular relief is noted in weekly payments.

FURTHER INFORMATION Where additional information on the pauper is found, such as familial status and age, it is stated here. While poor law accounts have been examined extensively, it is important to stress that this research is not exhaustive and there is potential for further work. Parish registers, for example, have only been used briefly and more comprehensive reconstitution of familial backgrounds is possible. Miscellaneous notes and information on other people mentioned in the inventory, such as overseers and appraisers, is also briefly noted.

CIRCUMTEXT This refers to written matter which is found on the source but is not regarded as part of the inventory. When there are jottings such as rough calculations or random marks, this has not been recorded.

DUBIOUS TERMS Where there are terms which are partially illegible, difficult to decipher, or are open to several interpretations, they are noted here.

EDITORIAL CHANGES This notes all changes that have been made to the transcription by the editor. Alterations to the inventories, however, are made very sparingly to present the inventories as accurately as possible.

DAMAGE Where parts of the text or document is damaged, such as through rips and holes, this is briefly noted here.

Pauper inventories

Ashwellthorpe pauper inventories

Three of the Ashwellthorpe pauper inventories survive in various places in a 'Town book', which contains the parish churchwardens' and overseers' accounts from 1693 and 1798 (NRO PC 88/1). The remainder of inventories can be found at the back of a set of overseers' accounts dated 1741–1775 (NRO PC 88/2). Also included in the volumes are goods-taken, goods-given, and debt-related inventories, as well as several other inventories which could not be categorised.

1. Ann Turner, 16 July 1695

NRO PC 88/1 Ashwellthorpe Town Book, 1693–1798.

AshwelThorpe july 16: 1695
An account of ye goods of Ann Turner wid: apprised & taken into ye towne book

		li d s
Imp^{r}	one flock bed & two bolsters a coverlet two sheets mat & cord & bedstead	0 – 10 – 0
Itm	one other bed as it stand	0 – 2 – 0
	two cubbards & a chest	0 – 10 – 0
	one table	0 – 2 – 6
	7 chaires	0 – 3 – 0
	one iron pot	0 – 3 – 0
	one warming pann & a Smoothing iron	2 – 0
	one rack 4 porringers & pewter dish one Speet & a hake 2 and irons	0 – 2 – 6
	fire pan & tongs roast iron	0 – 2 – 0
	one Skillet	0 – 1 – 0
	for Lumber	0 – 1 – 0
	for an old Kettle & a paile	0 – 2 – 0
		2 – 1 – 0

Apprised by { Edm: Lincolne, Sam: Potter }

John Burten, Robt: Shursten } overseers

RELIEF: Poor relief sources for the late seventeenth century lack detail. Extant records, however, show that Ann Turner was helped by the parish, as they paid £1 5s. for her rent around Spring 1695 (NRO PC 88/1).

FURTHER INFORMATION: The inventory and poor relief records show that Ann Turner was a widow. It is unknown what position (if any) Edmund Lincoln and Samuel Potter held in the parish (NRO PC 88/1).

DAMAGE: Ink smudge between lines 15–17, partially covering the first letters on the first words of the lines.

2. Widow Hill, 26 January 1710/11

NRO PC 88/1 Ashwellthorpe Town Book, 1693–1798

Jen^{y} ye 26: 1710

An enventory of the Goods of ye Wido Hill		li d s
Imp^{r}	A Bed As it Stand	02 – 10 – 00
	2 Brase Cetteles	00 – 10 – 00
	an Iorn Cettell	00 – 04 – 00
	A scilit & killer	00 – 01 – 00
	A Cubart	00 – 07 – 00
	2 Chaiers	00 – 01 – 00
	A Cofer and Box	00 – 02 – 00
	A warmnig pan	00 – 01 – 00
	A Trunk & littell tub	00 – 01 – 00
	A Littell table	00 – 04 – 00
		04 – 01 – 00

Petter George
Crist Marton } Aprisers
James Dufen

RELIEF: Widow Hill started to receive 6d. per week from the parish soon after this inventory was made (NRO PC 88/1).

FURTHER INFORMATION: It is not known whether Mary Hill, whose goods are noted in inventory number **3**, was the same person as Widow Hill. This is because the accounts between 1714 and 1723 are very inconsistent and lack detail. During the 1690s regular and casual relief was also given to Phillip Hill; however, it is unknown if he was any relation of Widow Hill. Crist (Christopher) Marton and James Dufen were overseers of the poor in Ashwellthorpe. It is unknown what position (if any) Peter George held (NRO PC 88/1).

3. Mary Hill, 2 November 1720

NRO PC 88/1 Ashwellthorpe Town Book, 1693–1798.

November 2: 1720
An Inventory of the Goods of Mary hill wid: Taken by us whoses names are hereunder written

Imp^{is} one Table 2 Joynt Stools one Rack one ~~Cubbard~~ one small Table one Iron Pott one Dressor one Large Brass Pott one Speet one Loome one Tubb: 4 Chairs one Box Iron & heets ~~Andorns~~ fire pan & tongs one hake one p of bellows 3 wheels one Tubb one killer & one boll one Alestool one Chest one Joynt Stool & box one Trunk & form one Cubbard 2 vessels & Alestool one Bed as it stand in the parlor one warming pan < ? > Chaire one Looking Glass & Dripping pan < ? > Beds one ye Chamber 3 Boxes Little vessels one paile one Joynt stool one killer more

RELIEF: Mary Hill is noted as a pauper in poor relief records, but no information could be found as to when relief started or what form it took (NRO PC 88/1).

FURTHER INFORMATION: The names of the appraisers are not noted beneath the inventory as the opening lines indicate. It is unknown if Mary Hill was the same person as Widow Hill in the inventory above **(2)**. This is because the accounts for the parish between 1714 and 1723 are of an inconsistent standard. During the 1690s regular and casual relief was also given to Phillip Hill; however, it is unknown if he was any relation of Mary Hill (NRO PC 88/1).

DAMAGE: Ink smudge on lines 10–11 making parts of the text illegible.

4. Edward Rushbrook, 1 October 1754

NRO PC 88/2 Ashwellthorpe Overseers' Accounts, 1741–1775.

Ashwellthorp
An Inventory of the Goods of Edward Rushbrook a Collectioner taken this first October 1754:

One Bed wth the Furniture
2 Boxes
one Stool:
warming pan
2 Tables
one Letch
2 Wheels & a Reel
one Biler & one pail
one Frying pan

P^{r}: Andirons
Tonges Hake
Smoothing Iron & Rest
one Candle Stick
one Tub – 3 Bottles
one Bowle 3 Chairs:
one Spade

RELIEF: Edward Rushbrook was on 1s. 6d. per week when this inventory was made. He had been receiving regular relief since 24 June 1753 and received casual relief at various times in the form of money, rent payments, and firewood (NRO PC 88/1–2). The inventory also notes that he was a 'Collectioner'.

FURTHER INFORMATION: Around mid–1752, 'Eliz. Risebrook' and 'Goody Rushbrook' are mentioned in poor law accounts, but it is unknown whether these people were relations of Edward Rushbrook. Edward is also colloquially referred to as 'Ned' on several occasions in poor law records (NRO PC 88/1–2). There is a later inventory of Edward Rushbrook's goods taken 30 September 1742. It is unclear why it was made, as Edward Rushbrook does not appear to have been on relief in 1742. The inventory is as follows (NRO PC 88/1):

The Goods of Edward Rushbrook
The Bebb [bed] and Furinerer [furniture] .. 2 . 0 . 0
Boyler fryan Pan & warman Pain .... 0 . 7 . 0
A Table.. 0 . 0 . 9
for Lumber of all sortes .... 1 .10. 0
Taking the 30th of September 1742......... 3 : 17.9

5. Constance Huggin, 1 October 1754

NRO PC 88/2 Ashwellthorpe Overseers' Accounts, 1741–1775.

The Goods of Constance Huggin [taken] the same time [as the inventory of Edward Rushbrook's goods, 1 October 1754]
2 Beds as they Stand
one Chist
one Table
one pail one Killer
2 wheels

RELIEF: Constance Huggin was on 2s. per week when this inventory was taken and was occasionally provided with firewood and rent payments from the parish. Poor law authorities also paid for a doctor to see her around August-September 1747 (NRO PC 88/1–2).

FURTHER INFORMATION: Overseers' papers show that Constance Huggin was a widow. Sometime between 2 August and 8 October 1752, the parish of Ashwellthorpe paid 14s. for 'removing Constance Huggin W:^{dw}'. It is, however, unknown which parish she left. Elizabeth and Benjamin Huggin also appear in poor relief accounts for the parish, but it is not known whether these people were relations of Constance Huggin (NRO PC 88/1–2).

6. Widow Cooper, 1 October 1754

NRO PC 88/2 Ashwellthorpe Overseers' Accounts, 1741–1775.

The Goods of wid Cooper Senr [taken] the Same Time [as the inventory of Edward Rushbrook's goods, 1 October 1754]

one Bed as it Stand
one Cubbard
2 Boxes

RELIEF: Widow Cooper was on 1s. per week when this inventory was made. She had received a pension from the parish for at least a decade prior to her goods being inventoried, but it is difficult to determine with certainty how much she received during this period. Widow Cooper rarely received relief in kind, but when she did she was generally given firewood or faggots (NRO PC 88/1–2).

FURTHER INFORMATION: An Edward Cooper also appears in poor law records for the parish from February 1753, but it is unknown if he was any relation of Widow Cooper (NRO PC 88/1–2).

Besthorpe pauper inventories

The pauper inventories from Besthorpe were written in the hands of the incumbent overseers on two small loose pieces of paper (NRO PD 309/52–53).

7. Widow Stephenson, 10 October 1776

NRO PD 309/52 Besthorpe Inventory of Widow Stephenson's goods, 1776.

october ye 10th 1776 an inventory of the widow Stephensons goods one Curtin bed a Chest of Drawes Two Tables Joynt Stool and Slip a Cubbard 2 porrage pots firepan Tongs Cobirons hake hanks and Speet a frying pan a Sive a par of Bellows Teakittle and iron fondo Box Iron and heters a warming pan Scales and Lead weights 7lb a hammar 1 Chair 3 Stools one Lye Leech a pail 2 Tubs 3 tharn chers Sum arthen ware a tow weel and Reel a pouter Rack and mantel pece and Shelf

RELIEF: Widow Stephenson was in receipt of 1s. per week and had been a pensioner for several years prior to her goods being inventoried by the parish. She also received occasional relief in the form of cash payments and flags. The parish paid her rent on several occasions. For instance, overseers' accounts show that the parish provided £1 2s. 10d. for 'a years [rent] for widow Stephenson apples Deducted' around the time that this inventory was taken (NRO PD 309/12).

FURTHER INFORMATION: The circumtext and overseers' accounts for the parish indicate that Widow Stephenson may have been living with Widow Kittle. For example, between Easter and Michaelmas 1777 the parish paid 15s. for a year's rent 'for widow Kittle and widow Stephenson'. Widow Stephenson had at least one son under her care when this inventory was made. There was also a girl and boy Stephenson who received 1s. and 1s. 6d. per week respectively when this inventory was made and were frequently given various items of clothing from the parish. These may have been Widow Stephenson's children, but they could also have been the children of Sarah and/or John Stephenson, who appear infrequently in poor law accounts for Besthorpe (NRO PD 309/12).

CIRCUMTEXT: Below the inventory the following was written:

paid mr Dunham for Rent 1 – 8 . 0
and Debt to Do .... 0 . 3 . 4
Recd of mr Dunham for apples gartherd of John Stephensons Trees
Recd out widow Kittles Rent
By John Lee .... 1 . 12 . 0

DUBIOUS TERMS: Line 4: 'fondo' – possibly fender.

8. John Dunnett, 10 July 1803

NRO PD 309/53 Besthorpe Inventory of John Dunnett's goods, 1803.

July 10, 1803 } Invetary of John Dunnett in Wymondham
Besthorp } Taking by John Johnson Overseer
And Abraham Howes Constable

Kitchen

one hake and hank a pear of Cobirions a pear of Tongs Two fire Irions a peair of Bullers one Chair three Stowels Irion pot a tea Kittle Coffer and tees and Dutppan Cart Saddle and Cart and A hoes Ass a pear of Hampers. A portmentur irion hoop pail frienpan turnip how and Iron toth Rake a peair of Candlesticks a bowl & Basket A Hoock A Gardingpot A Steel A fork & how and flagspade A Basket and Sunders

Bedroom

A Fether bed Cilvering a peair of Blankits a peair Sheets A Boutster and thre pullers Bedsted and hanings A Clock And Case a warming pan hammer and Sors Larnton Hatchet and Sholvel A waish killer And fork And all this Waring appearil And Sundears

RELIEF: John Dunnett received 2s. 6d. per week for several years from the parish, but started to receive an additional 6d. when this inventory of his goods was taken (totalling 3s. a week). He also received casual relief at various times in the form of rent payments, cash, tools, and flags. Up until mid–1802, his son John Dunnett junior received 1s. 6d. per week and his two boys sometimes received clothing (such as shirts and stockings) from poor law officials. The family were frequently sick during the 1800s. John Dunnett senior and his wife, for example, received cash payments for 'illness' and for being 'Sick' and 'lame' on numerous occasions (NRO PD 309/12).

FURTHER INFORMATION: John Dunnett was living in Wymondham (Norfolk), but had settlement in Besthorpe. He was married and had at least two sons called John and Edward living with him (NRO PD 309/12).

DUBIOUS TERMS: Line 14: 'Sors' – possibly saw.

Bressingham pauper inventories

The thirteen pauper inventories from Bressingham were all written on loose pieces of paper and can be found bundled together in NRO PD 111/114 and PD 111/170. Also included in the collection are two goods-given inventories and one inventory which records the goods that a pauper took into the workhouse with them. Several of the inventories are in a poor condition as parts have been eaten by rodents or are torn and heavily creased. There are also numerous ink smudges and the text is heavily faded in some areas.

9. Widow Tiller, 27 December 1693

NRO PD 111/170 Bressingham Inventories, 1693–1773.

An Inventory of the goodes of the wid: Tiler. Taken by Fra: Tilney minist^{r} of the parrish Brissingha in Norfoc & Tho: Cooke Churchwarden of the sd parrish & Robt Horner Gent an inhabitant of the sd parrish: ~~taken~~ this 27th day of Decembe 1693: as followeth.

Inprim A Bedstead wth Curtains as it stands ~~and a flock bed under it.~~
One feather bed upon it & flock bed under it.
One Chest 2 chaires 1 Trunck:
One Joint stoole & a desk.
One Cubbord one forme one Table upon Trussells. 3 chaires. 2 old stooles.
A paire of Cobirons fire pan & tonges
2 hakes 3 Brasse killer One warming pan
One skillel: A paire of Bellows
One Beere vessell & an Ale stoolle
One Tub & one skillel & a heck
A boulting hutch. A spining wheele
A Creame pot & One paile. A Crab Harrow wth wooden teeth: A two bushell sack
2 popling boards.
Taken by us as above sd
Fra: Tilney < ? >
Robert: Horner:
Tho: Cooke Churchwarden:

RELIEF: Widow Tiller was in receipt of 1s. 6d. per week when this inventory was made. The parish also gave her rent and firewood. For example, between 1694 and 1695, 12s. 6d. and 5s. was paid out by the parish for half a year's rent and firewood respectively (NRO PD 111/89).

10. Henry Wells, 17 February 1717/18

NRO PD 111/170 Bressingham Inventories, 1693–1773.

To all faithfull people to whome This p^{r}sent wrighting shall Come Henry wells of Brisingham In ye County of Norff: Linnin waver doe send greeting and soe forth: Know ye that I ye said Henry wells for and in Considderation of the sume of one pound and seventenn shillings & six pence paid by Thomas fullcher & Edmund Briant Churchwarden and Overseer of ye pa^{r}h of Brisingham to my Landlord weaxd for me ye said Henry wells of Brisingham and for and in Consideration of a sartaine Rent to be paid for me ye said Henry wells heath Bargained and solde and by this p^{r}sent writing doth grant Bargaine and sell unto ye said Thomas fullcher and Edm^{t} Briant of Brisingham and to there sucksessors all and singuler ye goods hosehold stuff and implements of house hold what soe ever spesified or contained in a sartaine writing here to Annexed to have ant to hold the said goods Household stuff and Implements of household what ever unto ye said Thomas fullsher and Edm^{t} Briant of Brisingham and to there sucksessor To ye only use and Behoofe of the Said Thomas fullsher and Edm^{t} Briant and to there suxseeders as Over seers and gardians for ye Church In wittness

Where of I Have Sett my hand & Seal his mark this 17 Day of February Anno ....Henry X wells

feb: ye 17th 1717 Sealed and delivered & ye said henry wells Hath put ye said Thomas fullsher and Edm^{t} Briant In possesstion of the p^{r}immises in delivering to them one forme being p^{r}t of ye primises on the other seide written there by putting them In posesstion of the whole

In ye p^{r}sents of.................................

his mark

Jonathan X Hart

Roger Back

A Shdwell of Shuch goods & Chattles as doe pas by ye deed of seale on ye other seid is as followeth ....

Imp^{r}ms one Lume
one Coule
one Cubberd table
one forme
one bed bed stead
matt & Line
one Brass pott
one pair of Cobbirons
one Slice
one paire of tongs
one Rosiron

RELIEF: The parish paid Henry Wells' rent (£1 17s. 6d.) when this inventory was made. The overseer was also paid 6d. 'for my trouble aboute hen wells' and 4s. was spent making the inventory. Prior to this, he and his wife received occasional cash payments from the parish for unknown reasons. The family continued to receive money from poor law officials after the inventory was taken. For example, in 1719 the parish spent 14s. on clothes for Henry's son and gave Henry money on several occasions for 'being sick' between 1720 and 1722 (NRO PD 111/89; NRO PD 111/170).

FURTHER INFORMATION: Because this agreement was between the parish and Henry Wells and did not involve the landlord, this is not a rent-arrears inventory. Sources show that only a form went to the parish, meaning that the items were not taken from Henry Wells even though the source mentions the 'sale' of his goods. Rather, he was able to keep his goods until called upon by the parish, meaning that this is a pauper inventory. Henry Wells was a linen weaver. Overseers' accounts for the parish indicate that he was married and that the couple had at least one boy living with them when the inventory was made. His wife was probably called Elizabeth (née Lane) and married him on 5 October 1707 in Bressingham. Henry Wells was buried on 3 October 1722 at a cost of 15s. 6d. to the parish. Accounts also mention that the officers went to Diss (Norfolk) to arrange this, indicating that he and his family lived there. It is, however, unknown whether he was living in Diss when this inventory of his possessions was taken, or whether he had moved there after the document was written (NRO PD 111/1; NRO PD 111/89; NRO PD 111/170).

CIRCUMTEXT: Note on back:

The Deed of Sale	}	To the < ? >
from Henry Wells		ofs<ers> of Bres<singham>

DUBIOUS TERMS: Line 9: 'heath' – he hath.

11. Ann Route, 25 May 1719

NRO PD 111/114 Bressingham Inventories, 1719–1815.

The 25 of May 1719
an account of ye Goods of Ann Rou<te> widdow In Bressingham taken of by ye Church wardens overseers and other ye Cheeif Inhabitents in the said parish:

Imp^{r}mis one feather bed and ye bedstad & Coverlet:
one flocke bed and bedstade all and belonging to it Except the mat
one warman pan
one Chest and A Cubbart
one Pottage pot and a kittle and 2 Skillets
one payar of dogirons and heak firepan and Tongs and bellows
Two beer < vessels > and A fryin pan
one putter < ? > A Candle Stick:
on<e> Tow w<ee>le and Chopenknife
one Spoyce box and A Salt box

RELIEF: Ann Route was in receipt of casual relief when this inventory was taken. She received cash for 'her sickness' on several occasions and the parish paid £1 for a nurse to look after her between Easter and Michaelmas 1719. She was also provided with firewood, turf, and rent payments from the parish. Ann Route had received support from poor law authorities for at least five years prior to this inventory being taken (NRO PD 111/89).

FURTHER INFORMATION: Ann Route was widowed. Sam and Elizabeth Route are also mentioned in the overseers' accounts during the 1710s, but it is unknown whether these people were any relations of Ann Route (NRO PD 111/89).

DAMAGE: Line 2: Text faded where 'Rou<te> is written. Poor law records indicate that Ann's surname was 'Route', but sometimes the name 'Rough' was used (NRO PD 111/89). There are holes in the source lines 12–14 and an ink spill on the first word on line 14.

12. Thomas Surgon, 16 September 1719

NRO PD 111/170 Bressingham Inventories, 1693–1773.

Septembr ye 16th 1719
An Invitory Made of ye goods of Thomas Surgon by Robt Kent Churchwarden of ye pa^{rsh} of Brisingham as followeth ....

Imp^{r}ims one Table
one Cubberd and a Chaire

one pair of Cobbirons
one paire of toings and fire pann
2 kittels & 2 Iron potts
one fring pann
one tubb and a box
and a Spining wheel
The Beds as they stand
and a warmeing pann

RELIEF: Thomas Surgon started to receive a pension of 2s. per week when this inventory was taken and was given a further 10s. 'by ye towns order'. In the subsequent months after September 1719, he received firewood and occasional cash payments for sickness and being in need. His children also received clothing from the parish, such as shifts, shoes, and stockings (NRO PD 111/89).

FURTHER INFORMATION: Thomas Surgon was married and had children. When clothing was provided for the couple's children, they were given two of everything, which may indicate that they had two children. The inventory cost the parish 6d. to make (NRO PD 111/89).

13. Ann Hart, 22 October 1724

NRO PD 111/114 Bressingham Inventories, 1719–1815.

October ye 22th – 1724

Bressingham

An acount of the Goods of Ann Hart taken By Jeremiah Smith and Robt Kentt present ofisers for the parish A fouresd
Imprimis
Itt on Beed as it stand with on bolster on pillo<w> and three payers of sheets Belongin to ye same
Itt on Larg Chest on Desk Box
Itt on ~~spining~~ tow wheel two tow Reels
on Chayer on Cushin and all her wearing Aparrill Lining and woolling

RELIEF: Ann Hart was in receipt of 1s. per week when this inventory was taken. She became a pensioner sometime between Michaelmas 1723 and Easter 1724 and also received stockings and shifts from the parish. From Easter 1725, Ann Hart appears to have looked after an orphaned boy. The parish paid 1s. 6d. per week for this initially, which presumably went to Ann Hart alongside her weekly pay. The boy also received clothing from the parish (NRO PD 111/89).

FURTHER INFORMATION: Ann Hart was probably a spinster since she was referred to by her Christian name and never as 'Widow'. Thomas Hart was also mentioned in poor law accounts, but it is unknown whether Ann Hart was any relation to him. Ann Hart was buried in Bressingham on 21 January 1726. Jeremiah Smith was a churchwarden and Robert Kent was an overseer of the poor (NRO PD 111/1; NRO PD 111/89).

DAMAGE: Right side of inventory ripped/worn away.

14. William Car, 14 December 1727

NRO PD 111/170 Bressingham Inventories, 1693–1773.

Bressingham December ye: 14th – 1727

Mrd An a Count of ye Goods of Wm Car taken By ye Officers of ye parish a foor sd for ye pmt of monyes for ye Reliefe of himselfe and his famelye ...

Itt in ye Lodgen Room on fether beed valluabl att on pound tenn shillings more on frieng pann trunk 1 box on stool valluabl at thre shillings

In y^{e} Roome they laey in 1 Cubbard 2 tow whells 2 wool whells 1 keler 1 scillet 1 wool Reel 2 tow Reels vallabl att twelve shillings

4 Chayers att two shillings } li d s
02 = 07 = 00

The <Ex>ool of y^{e} Goods A bove named ear taken and aprised By Jer Smith and Wm Houchen

Whear of I the sd Wm Car have Delivred to y^{e} sd Officers on scillet part and passel of y^{e} Goods a Bove named in y^{e} presence of

Jer Smith Wm Car X his
Wm Howchin marke

RELIEF: William Car did not receive any poor relief in the ten years or so before this inventory was made. He started to receive help from the parish for burying his child when this inventory was taken and sometimes received casual relief 'in time of need' (NRO PD 111/89). The inventory also notes that it was made 'for ye Reliefe of himselfe and his famelye'.

FURTHER INFORMATION: William Car was married (possibly to somebody called Elizabeth) and his child was buried around when this inventory was taken. Jeremiah Smith was a churchwarden and William Houchen/Howchin appears to have been a member of the vestry who acted as a witness to the appraising of these goods (NRO PD 111/1; NRO PD 111/89).

DUBIOUS TERMS: Line 2: 'Mrd' – unknown term. Line 10: '<Ex>ool' – possibly schedule.

15. Widow Brister, 7 February 1759

NRO PD 111/114 Bressingham Inventories, 1719–1815.

Bresingham

The Account of the Goods of the Widow Brister taken ye 7th of february 1759 by John Silven and William Kent Churchwardens Also ye Said John Silven Overseer ....

One Bed as it Stand with the firniture three Chairs four Kellers one Iron pott one table one old Couch a pair of Andrions and tongs & fire-pan one woolweel one Warming pan one Scillet one Vessel and Stone Bottle one Chist of Drawers

RELIEF: Widow Brister is noted as a pauper in various poor relief records, but no information could be found as to when relief started or what the exact nature of it was (NRO PD 111/93; NRO PD 111/111; NRO PD 111/117).

16. Ann Burrows, 7 February 1759

NRO PD 111/114 Bressingham Inventories, 1719–1815.

Bresingham

An Account of y^{e} Goods of y^{e} Widow Ann Burrows taken y^{e} 7.th February 1759 by John Silven and William Kent Churchwardens. also y^{e} afore=Said John Silvea Overseer ....

One Bed as it Stand with y^{e} firniture
One old Cubbard one Small Cubbard
one warmingpan two Chairs
three Earthen plates a pair of Andryons
a pair of tongs and potiron one hake
one Woolweel one table one Scillet
one Dale Box one Candlestick one Earthon dish
one hammer one Buffett Stool three Square threnchers and one Slip for a Stool

RELIEF: Ann Burrows is noted as a pauper in various poor relief records, but no information could be found as to when relief started or what form it took (NRO PD 111/93; NRO PD 111/111; NRO PD 111/117).

FURTHER INFORMATION: Ann Burrows was probably a spinster since she was referred to by her Christian name and never as 'Widow' (NRO PD 111/93; NRO PD 111/111; NRO PD 111/117).

17. William Adkins, 11 March 1773

NRO PD 111/170 Bressingham Inventories, 1693–1773.

An Inventory of the Goods & Effects of William Adkins late of Roydon in the County of Norfolk ~~weav~~ weaver, taken this 11th. Day of March 1773 by us ....

Robt Martin & Richd Ellis ~~one of the~~ Church Wardens and overseers of the Parish of Bressingham in the County afores^{d} as follows

In the Chamber

one Bed & Bedstead with blue Hangings
Two Blanketts
~~Four~~ Three Sheets
one Bolster
one other Bed & Bedstead with the Hangings
one Table
one Chair
two Boxes
one Cradle

In the Kitchen

one Bolting Hutch
one Table
one Buffett Stool
five Chairs
two tow spinning Wheels
one Coal Grate with Cheeks
one Gridiron
one pair of Bellows
one poker
two Stools
one pair of Tongs
Two ~~one~~ Iron pottage potts
two Skilletts
three candlesticks
one keeler
one funnell
one Hand Cup
a parcell of Earthen Ware
six Trenchers
one leech
one deal shelf
one Tea kettel

Robt Martin Church Warden
Richard Ellis Overseer

RELIEF: William Adkins is noted as a pauper in various poor law records, but no information could be found as to when relief started or what the exact nature of it was (NRO PD 111/93; NRO PD 111/111; NRO PD 111/117).

FURTHER INFORMATION: William Adkins appears to have lived in nearby Roydon, Norfolk, but had settlement in Bressingham. He was a weaver and was referred to as 'late' suggesting that he had recently died (NRO PD 111/93; NRO PD 111/111; NRO PD 111/117; NRO PD 111/170).

DAMAGE: Ink smudges lines 21–22, 24, and 26, making the text difficult to decipher.

18. Henry Fisher/Harrison, 16 October 1773

NRO PD 111/170 Bressingham Inventories, 1693–1773.

An Inventory of the Goods of Henry Fisher other wise Harrison taken by me Robt. Martin Church Warden of the parish Bressingham this 16th Day of October 1773 /
In the Chamber one Bed & Bedsted one Bolster, one Coverlin 6 Plates. Earthen, one Box In the low Room / one Table 3 Keelers One Leather Chair ~~one~~ two Wood Bottom Chair one Cowl one Lye Leech one wool wheel one winding wheel & two flyers one Box one Cubboard. a Parcell of old earthen ware one pottage pot one Cradle
Robt. Martin

RELIEF: Henry Fisher/Harrison is noted as a pauper in various records, but no information could be found as to when relief started or what form it took (NRO PD 111/93; NRO PD 111/111; NRO PD 111/117).

FURTHER INFORMATION: It is unknown why Henry was called Fisher and Harrison. Harrison may have been a nickname (NRO PD 111/93; NRO PD 111/111; NRO PD 111/117).

19. Mary Bravenett, 5 November 1773

NRO PD 111/170 Bressingham Inventories, 1693–1773.

An Inventory of the Goods of Mary Bravenett taken by me Robert Martin Churchwarden of the parish of Bressingham this fifth Day of November 1773 as follow
In the Low Room
One Chest of Drawers

one Corner Cupboard
Two Tables
Three Tow Wheels
Two Chairs
one pair of Bellows
one Tea Kettle
one pair of CobIrons
one fire pan
one pair of Tongs
one Hake
Three stools
one Box Iron
one Spitt
one GridIron
one Peal
Two Boylers
~~one vessell~~
In the Buttery
One Buffett stool
Two keelers
In the Chamber
Two Beds ~~as the~~ and Bedsteds

RELIEF: Mary Bravenett is noted as a pauper in various poor law records, but no information could be found as to when relief started or what the exact nature of it was (NRO PD 111/93; NRO PD 111/111; NRO PD 111/117).

FURTHER INFORMATION: Mary Bravenett was probably a spinster since she was referred to by her Christian name and never as 'Widow' (NRO PD 111/93; NRO PD 111/111; NRO PD 111/117).

20. William Arnold, 8 October 1814

NRO PD 111/114 Bressingham Inventories, 1719–1815.

An Inventory of W[m] Arnolds goods Oct 8/. 1814.
Two Bedsteads. 2 feather Beds 4 sheets 2 covertins – Bolsters &c
8 Chairs 3 small Tables 1 pail – Two keelers –

RELIEF: William Arnold was in receipt of 2s. 6d. per week from June 1813, but stopped receiving this around October-November 1813. The pension was resumed from early October 1814 at 1s. 6d. per week. William Arnold also received occasional cash payments from the parish. For example, on 22 February 1814 he was given £4 2s.

9 ½ d. from the parish; on 20 May 1814 he received £1 when he was 'at need'; and on 10 November 1814 his wife received 1s. when she was in need (NRO PD 111/90).

FURTHER INFORMATION: William Arnold was married and may have had children. On 30 December 1814, for example, 2s. per week was given to 'M<r> Arnolds boy' for 13 weeks. Mary Arnold also appears in the overseers' accounts, but it is unknown if she was William Arnold's wife, daughter, or no relation at all (NRO PD 111/90).

DUBIOUS TERMS: Line 2: 'covertins' – probably coverlets, but also possibly curtains (bed hangings).

21. — Hernwell, no date

NRO PD 111/114 Bressingham Inventories, 1719–1815.

List of Hernwells Furniture ....
2 – Bedsted's
6 – Chair's –
3. Table's
1. Wash keller
2. Baskest's
2 – Stools –
1 – Hake
1 – Gridiron
2 – Boxe's –
1. Spining Weel
2 – Bed's ....

RELIEF: It has not been possible to track Hernwell in poor relief records and determine their gender, since their forename is not noted and the inventory was not dated by the author. However, on the back of the inventory 'Pauper' is written, showing that Hernwell received relief.

CIRCUMTEXT: 'Pauper' written on the back.

Brockdish pauper inventory

Only one pauper inventory has been located for Brockdish from a set of overseers' accounts dated 1772–1811 (NRO PD 477/43). Located next to the pauper inventory there is an inventory of William Welton's goods in Brockdish parish house in 1799, which was taken while his family were on the parish and Welton was a cavalryman fighting in the French Wars.

22. John Minter, 13 March 1804

NRO PD 477/43 Brockdish Overseers' Accounts, 1772–1811.

Inventory of the Houshold Furniture &c of Jn° Minter a Pauper in the Parish of Brockdish taken the 13th Day of March 1804, by J. Chilver Overseer

Kitchen
2 Tables, 4 Chairs
1 large Dresser
Nest of Spice Drawers
2 Tea Trays
6 Knives & Forks
Firepan Tongs & Poker
1 pair of Bellows
1 Pail
Box Iron & 2 Heaters
1 Tow Wheel very old,
1 D°. Reel .....
Sundries & Tea Requisites
Pantry
3 Keelers
Tin Boiler
Brass Skillet
1 Sieve, 1 Chair
Sundry earthen Ware
....

Chamber
1 Feather Bed & Bedstead
2 pair of Sheets
2 Blankets & 1 Coverlid
2 Pillows & 1 Bolster
2 Chairs & 2 Boxes
1 Spade, 1 Scuppet
1 three-tine Fork
3 Hoes & 1 Iron Rake
Sundries .....

RELIEF: John Minter was in receipt of relief before this inventory was taken. This changed month to month from regular relief (generally around 1s. or 1s. 6d. per week) to casual relief (around 6d. or 1s. given each time for being 'in need'). In October 1803, the parish also paid 6s. towards his rent. When this inventory was taken, John Minter was on 6d. per week and was also given a total of 14s. in casual relief in March 1804. From April 1804, he was on the 'Weekly Collection' list and received 1s. per week (NRO PD 477/43).

DAMAGE: Line 15: 'Sundries' smudged.

Bunwell pauper inventory

The pauper inventory from Bunwell can be found at the back of a set of overseers' accounts for the parish (NRO PD 712/49). There is also an account of items given to Franc Shurman next to the pauper inventory.

23. Mary Coleman, 15 April 1771

NRO PD 712/49 Bunwell Overseers' Accounts, 1756–1776.

April 15th: 1771 The acount of mary Colemans Things
one Bed and Beddsted one Blankitt 2 Sheets one Coverlin Bedd
matt one Bolster and Cord one Jacket 2 Shifts 2 pete Coats one p^{r}
of Stays one apron. Delivered to Mr Ben Beatman
By Me Willm Parson overseer

RELIEF: Mary Coleman had been in receipt of 1s. 6d. per week for a number of years when this inventory of her goods was taken. She also received infrequent help from the parish when she was 'in need', and the authorities helped her with rent payments and infrequently purchased clothing for her. The parish provided 19s. 6d. 'for Mary Colemans funeral and Expences' when she died around mid-April 1771. Prior to this, the parish paid somebody to nurse and care for her while she was ill (NRO PD 712/49).

FURTHER INFORMATION: It is not known who Ben Beatman was. The goods were delivered to him several weeks after the inventory was made, meaning that it is not a 'goods-taken' inventory (NRO PD 712/49).

DAMAGE: Line 1: Hole in the document on the word 'Colemans'.

Carbrooke pauper inventory

Only one pauper inventory has been located for Carbrooke parish. It can be found at the back of a set of overseers' accounts, alongside a possible duplicate and two inventories which record the contents of the parish workhouse. The volume is scorched and currently marked as unfit for production in Norfolk Record Office (NRO MC 2941/2, 1025X2).

24. John Daniels, 4 September 1787

NRO MC 2941/2, 1025X2 Carbrooke Overseers' Accounts, 1776–1803.

Sept ye 4: 1787 Inventory of the Goods and Chattels of John Daniels Deleverd up to the parish offerses of Carbrook For there property And the Benefit of the parish

Two Beds Two Iron potts One pail one wash Killer One Chest Three Chears One Vessell One Table One Bowl a pair Bellows A pair of Tongs A Tea Kittle

RELIEF: John Daniels was in receipt of casual relief when this inventory was taken. He and his wife had received this for several years on an infrequent basis during times of 'Illness' and when 'In Want'. In May 1787, John Daniels is described as sick (possibly with smallpox) and received 6s. in total from the parish during this month (NRO MC 2941/2, 1025X2).

FURTHER INFORMATION: John Daniels was married and his 'family' are mentioned in overseers' accounts, which may suggest that he had children living with him when this inventory was taken. Records show that the goods were not literally 'Deleverd up to the parish offerses' and that John Daniels continued to own and use these items (NRO MC 2941/2, 1025X2). There is also another inventory of his goods dated 4 September 1788. This may be a goods-taken inventory or a duplicate which is dated incorrectly by a slip of the pen (NRO MC 2941/2, 1025X2):

Septr. 4th: 1788 An Inventory of the Goods and Chattels of Jno Daniels 2 Beds 2 Iron potts 1 pail 1 Wash Killer 1 Chest 3 Chairs 1 Vessell 1 Table 1 Bowl a pair of Bellows a pair of Tongs a Tea Kittle

Cawston pauper inventories

The nineteen pauper inventories for Cawston parish were all written in sequence on two large sheets of paper on 14 December 1699 (NRO PD 193/93). Inventories **25–35** were written by one hand and numbers **36–43** were written by another, suggesting that the task was split between two parish officials. On the opening page the first enumerator wrote that the inventories were made 'of All the poore that Recve Colecttion'. The appraisers' writing is particularly difficult to decipher as their spelling is erratic and the size of their lettering varies considerably. The sheets are also heavily creased with numerous tears in them.

25. Widow Penell, 14 December 1699

NRO PD 193/93 Cawston Inventories, 1699, 1826.

Dec the 14.th 1699
An inventorey Tacking by the Townsmen of Cawston of All the poore that Recve Colecttion as foloweth ....
The wido Penell
one Bad as it stan with on Bolster
on par of blanikett on sheett on covrin on form

RELIEF: No relevant poor relief records survive from 1699. However, these documents from Cawston are pauper inventories as they clearly state that they were made of 'All the poore that Recve Colecttion' (NRO PD 193/93).

CIRCUMTEXT: On the reverse: 'Inventory of Goods of Several Persons'.

26. Widow Garby, 14 December 1699

NRO PD 193/93 Cawston Inventories, 1699, 1826.

[Opening lines to the inventories] Dec the 14.th 1699
An inventorey Tacking by the Townsmen of Cawston of All the poore that Recve Colecttion as foloweth ....

[Inventory]
wido Garby
on Bad as it stan with 2 Blancketts 2 Boulsters on < shet > on < ? > tongs & fire pann < ? > on Pilow on Covren 2 Iron pott on Couberd on Cettell on Bed

Stould on chare 2 Bocks on Coufer on fri<e> pann on skillett on soule on buule on old stoule on < ? >

RELIEF: No relevant poor relief records survive from 1699. However, these documents from Cawston are pauper inventories as they clearly state that they were made of 'All the poore that Recve Colecttion' (NRO PD 193/93).

CIRCUMTEXT: On the reverse: 'Inventory of Goods of Several Persons'.

DUBIOUS TERMS: The inventory is very difficult to read meaning that several terms are difficult to decipher. Line 8: 'soule' – unknown term. Line 9: 'buule' – possibly bowl.

27. Widow Paten and Ann Clayton, 14 December 1699

NRO PD 193/93 Cawston Inventories, 1699, 1826.

[Opening lines to the inventories] Dec the 14.th 1699

An inventorey Tacking by the Townsmen of Cawston of All the poore that Recve Colecttion as foloweth ....

[Inventory]

wido: platen and Ann Clayton

on Bad as it stan with: ~~a~~ Cortens & vallans an par of Shett 2 Boulsters: on Rudge on Blanckett: on < ? > Soule on Coufer 2 Bockses on warmin pann: on skillett on Iron pott on Chest at Rob Gills with 2 Gowns on petacot on par of Stays on Bocks

RELIEF: No relevant poor relief records survive from 1699. However, these documents from Cawston are pauper inventories as they clearly state that they were made of 'All the poore that Recve Colecttion' (NRO PD 193/93).

FURTHER INFORMATION: Ann Clayton was probably a spinster since she was referred to by her Christian name and not as 'Widow'.

CIRCUMTEXT: On the reverse: 'Inventory of Goods of Several Persons'.

DUBIOUS TERMS: Line 7: 'Soule' – possibly stool.

28. Widow Woods, 14 December 1699

NRO PD 193/93 Cawston Inventories, 1699, 1826.

[Opening lines to the inventories] Dec the 14.th 1699

An inventorey Tacking by the Townsmen of Cawston of All the poore that Recve Colecttion as foloweth ....

[Inventory]

wido Woods

one Bad as it stands with on ~~Rudge~~ covrin on shett on couberd on bedstand on tabell 2 kitell on Iron ketell on <?>rd vesell on pouter desh on wod Bottell on cofer

RELIEF: No relevant poor relief records survive from 1699. However, these documents from Cawston are pauper inventories as they clearly state that they were made of 'All the poore that Recve Colecttion' (NRO PD 193/93).

CIRCUMTEXT: On the reverse: 'Inventory of Goods of Several Persons'.

29. Widow Reed, 14 December 1699

NRO PD 193/93 Cawston Inventories, 1699, 1826.

[Opening lines to the inventories] Dec the 14.th 1699

An inventorey Tacking by the Townsmen of Cawston of All the poore that Recve Colecttion as foloweth ....

[Inventory]

wido Reed

on Bad as it stann with on cevrin on Rudg on Blanckett on Chest on < ? > on dreser on kitall on fryi pann

RELIEF: No relevant poor relief records survive from 1699. However, these documents from Cawston are pauper inventories as they clearly state that they were made of 'All the poore that Recve Colecttion' (NRO PD 193/93).

CIRCUMTEXT: On the reverse: 'Inventory of Goods of Several Persons'.

30. Richard Ladrken, 14 December 1699

NRO PD 193/93 Cawston Inventories, 1699, 1826.

[Opening lines to the inventories] Dec the 14.th 1699

An inventorey Tacking by the Townsmen of Cawston of All the poore that Recve Colecttion as foloweth ....

[Inventory]

Rich Ladrken

on Bad as it stan w<i>th an covrin on shit on Blancket on Tabell on cofer a Bear vessel on ~~fryen pann~~ on kettell on ion pot 2 Bed Stould

RELIEF: No relevant poor relief records survive from 1699. However, these documents from Cawston are pauper inventories as they clearly state that they were made of 'All the poore that Recve Colecttion' (NRO PD 193/93).

CIRCUMTEXT: On the reverse: 'Inventory of Goods of Several Persons'.

DAMAGE: Line 6: Tear in the source where 'w<i>th' is written.

31. Robert Land, 14 December 1699

NRO PD 193/93 Cawston Inventories, 1699, 1826.

[Opening lines to the inventories] Dec the 14.th 1699
An inventorey Tacking by the Townsmen of Cawston of All the poore that Recve Colecttion as foloweth ....

[Inventory]
Robert Land
on Bad as it stann with covrin ~~Blancket~~ on Chest on coubert on ketell on chare on tabell

RELIEF: No relevant poor relief records survive from 1699. However, these documents from Cawston are pauper inventories as they clearly state that they were made of 'All the poore that Recve Colecttion' (NRO PD 193/93).

CIRCUMTEXT: On the reverse: 'Inventory of Goods of Several Persons'.

32. Widow Bloume, 14 December 1699

NRO PD 193/93 Cawston Inventories, 1699, 1826.

[Opening lines to the inventories] Dec the 14.th 1699
An inventorey Tacking by the Townsmen of Cawston of All the poore that Recve Colecttion as foloweth ....

[Inventory]
wido Bloume
on Bad as it stan with covrin & blanckett on fether Bad on Coufer on Bocks

RELIEF: No relevant poor relief records survive from 1699. However, these documents from Cawston are pauper inventories as they clearly state that they were made of 'All the poore that Recve Colecttion' (NRO PD 193/93).

CIRCUMTEXT: On the reverse: 'Inventory of Goods of Several Persons'.

33. Dorothy Ridge, 14 December 1699

NRO PD 193/93 Cawston Inventories, 1699, 1826.

[Opening lines to the inventories] Dec the 14.th 1699

An inventorey Tacking by the Townsmen of Cawston of All the poore that Recve Colecttion as foloweth ....

[Inventory]

Dorethy Ridge

on Bad as it stan with 2 Boulsters 2 Blanckets on covrin on coufer on Bocks

RELIEF: No relevant poor relief records survive from 1699. However, these documents from Cawston are pauper inventories as they clearly state that they were made of 'All the poore that Recve Colecttion' (NRO PD 193/93).

FURTHER INFORMATION: Dorothy Ridge was probably a spinster since she was referred to by her Christian name and not as 'Widow'.

CIRCUMTEXT: On the reverse: 'Inventory of Goods of Several Persons'.

34. Matthew Matthews, 14 December 1699

NRO PD 193/93 Cawston Inventories, 1699, 1826.

[Opening lines to the inventories] Dec the 14.th 1699

An inventorey Tacking by the Townsmen of Cawston of All the poore that Recve Colecttion as foloweth ....

[Inventory]

Math: Mathe<ws>

on Bad as it stan with on fether bed <o>n Blanckett on Sheett on covrin on chest on tabell on cobert on iron pot 2 tab<?> on

RELIEF: No relevant poor relief records survive from 1699. However, these documents from Cawston are pauper inventories as they clearly state that they were made of 'All the poore that Recve Colecttion' (NRO PD 193/93).

CIRCUMTEXT: On the reverse: 'Inventory of Goods of Several Persons'.

DUBIOUS TERMS: Line 7: '2 tab<?>' – possibly tables or tubs.

DAMAGE: Line 5: Tear in the source where the name is written. Line 6: Ink smudge by '<o>n Blanckett'.

35. Richard Barker/Barber, 14 December 1699

NRO PD 193/93 Cawston Inventories, 1699, 1826.

[Opening lines to the inventories] Dec the 14.th 1699

An inventorey Tacking by the Townsmen of Cawston of All the poore that Recve Colecttion as foloweth ....

[Inventory]

Richard <Barkar/Barbar>

on Bad as it stan with on shett on covrin on tabell on irn pott on skellett on stett on par of tong<s>

RELIEF: No relevant poor relief records survive from 1699. However, these documents from Cawston are pauper inventories as they clearly state that they were made of 'All the poore that Recve Colecttion' (NRO PD 193/93).

FURTHER INFORMATION: It is unknown whether Richard Barker/Barber was related to Thomas Barker/Barber, whose goods were also appraised in 1699 **(39)**.

CIRCUMTEXT: On the reverse: 'Inventory of Goods of Several Persons'.

DUBIOUS TERMS: Line 5: 'Barkar' – also possibly 'Barbar'. The b/k in the middle of the word more closely resembles other uses of the letter k than b in the document. This is, however, open to interpretation. Line 7: 'stett' – unknown/illegible term.

36. Widow Greenwood, 14 December 1699

NRO PD 193/93 Cawston Inventories, 1699, 1826.

[Opening lines to the inventories] Dec the 14.th 1699

An inventorey Tacking by the Townsmen of Cawston of All the poore that Recve Colecttion as foloweth ....

[Inventory]

Dec <y^{e}> 14th 1699 An Inventory of the Goods of Wid Grenwood as followeth
It on Bedd as it stands
It on Cubard & 2 Tables
It on Iron pott & a fringpan
It 4 plates puter & a skillett
It on Box & a Truncke
It on Killer & a Beere vesill
It on Reelle & a sive
It on Chayr & 2 strooles
It on smotheing Iron

RELIEF: No relevant poor relief records survive from 1699. However, these documents from Cawston are pauper inventories as they clearly state that they were made of 'All the poore that Recve Colecttion' (NRO PD 193/93).

CIRCUMTEXT: On the reverse: 'Inventory of Goods of Several Persons'.

37. John Kenen, 14 December 1699

NRO PD 193/93 Cawston Inventories, 1699, 1826.

[Opening lines to the inventories] Dec the 14.th 1699
An inventorey Tacking by the Townsmen of Cawston of All the poore that Recve Colecttion as foloweth ....

[Inventory]
John Kenen
It on Bedd as it stand
It on Iron pott & a skillett
And 2 peuter plates & a Fring pan
on Bere vesille & on spete and
on matacoke & 4 houghs & a hachett
and a hooke on Cubbard & on Chayr
and 3 stooles and a ~~Box Iron~~ pillen Iron
And a Table & 2 old Coofers & a sive
It on payr of Bellowes & a payr of tonnges

RELIEF: No relevant poor relief records survive from 1699. However, these documents from Cawston are pauper inventories as they clearly state that they were made of 'All the poore that Recve Colecttion' (NRO PD 193/93).

CIRCUMTEXT: On the reverse: 'Inventory of Goods of Several Persons'.

DUBIOUS TERMS: Line 12: 'pillen Iron' – clothes iron of some sort.

38. Henry Blackburn, 14 December 1699

NRO PD 193/93 Cawston Inventories, 1699, 1826.

[Opening lines to the inventories] Dec the 14.th 1699
An inventorey Tacking by the Townsmen of Cawston of All the poore that Recve Colecttion as foloweth ....

[Inventory]
Hen Blackborn on Bedd & an old Rugg And An old Coofer

RELIEF: No relevant poor relief records survive from 1699. However, these documents from Cawston are pauper inventories as they clearly state that they were made of 'All the poore that Recve Colecttion' (NRO PD 193/93).

CIRCUMTEXT: On the reverse: 'Inventory of Goods of Several Persons'.

39. Thomas Barker/Barber, 14 December 1699

NRO PD 193/93 Cawston Inventories, 1699, 1826.

[Opening lines to the inventories] Dec the 14.th 1699

An inventorey Tacking by the Townsmen of Cawston of All the poore that Recve Colecttion as foloweth ....

[Inventory]

Tho <Barker/Barber>
It on Bedd as it stands
It on old Cubard & 2 Tabell
It on Iron pott & a flag spade
& a hooke & Two Tubbs on Chayr
and on payr of Bellows on Joynt
stoole on Rost Iron & a payr of Tonngs
and an old Coofer

RELIEF: No relevant poor relief records survive from 1699. However, these documents from Cawston are pauper inventories as they clearly state that they were made of 'All the poore that Recve Colecttion' (NRO PD 193/93).

FURTHER INFORMATION: It is unknown whether Thomas Barker/Barber was related to Richard Barker/Barber, whose goods were also appraised in 1699 **(35)**.

CIRCUMTEXT: On the reverse: 'Inventory of Goods of Several Persons'.

DUBIOUS TERMS: Line 5: 'Barker' – also possibly 'Barber'. The b/k in the middle of the word more closely resembles other uses of the letter k than b in the document. This is, however, open to interpretation.

40. Edward Martin, 14 December 1699

NRO PD 193/93 Cawston Inventories, 1699, 1826.

[Opening lines to the inventories] Dec the 14.th 1699

An inventorey Tacking by the Townsmen of Cawston of All the poore that Recve Colecttion as foloweth ....

[Inventory]

Edw martins
It on Bed as it stands
It on Iron pott & a fring pan
It on skillet & a fier pan & A
payr of Tonges
It on Cubard & a meale sickell
and 3 stooles & a Chayer

RELIEF: No relevant poor relief records survive from 1699. However, these documents from Cawston are pauper inventories as they clearly state that they were made of 'All the poore that Recve Colecttion' (NRO PD 193/93).

CIRCUMTEXT: On the reverse: 'Inventory of Goods of Several Persons'.

41. William Bridge, 14 December 1699

NRO PD 193/93 Cawston Inventories, 1699, 1826.

[Opening lines to the inventories] Dec the 14.th 1699
An inventorey Tacking by the Townsmen of Cawston of All the poore that Recve Colecttion as foloweth ....

[Inventory]

Will Bridg 2 Beds as they stand with a New Blancket 2 old Coverings & 2 shets
It on Bed stoole & on Iron pott on payr of Tonngs Two ould Cubords & on spete

RELIEF: No relevant poor relief records survive from 1699. However, these documents from Cawston are pauper inventories as they clearly state that they were made of 'All the poore that Recve Colecttion' (NRO PD 193/93).

CIRCUMTEXT: On the reverse: 'Inventory of Goods of Several Persons'.

42. Andrew Allen, 14 December 1699

NRO PD 193/93 Cawston Inventories, 1699, 1826.

[Opening lines to the inventories] Dec the 14.th 1699
An inventorey Tacking by the Townsmen of Cawston of All the poore that Recve Colecttion as foloweth ....

[Inventory]

Andrew Allen

It on Bedd as it stands with Curtins and vallens a feather Bedd & feather Boulster 3 Blanckets 2 sheets & 2 Cover<leens> 2 pillows & pillow Bears

It on Jent stoole & a Bedstoole & 2 Chayers & a Cushon on Chest mor & a warming pan on Truncke on press Cuberd

It on sacke

It in ye other Roome on frame Table ~~Kittell~~ on Bras pott on skillet on puter Dish on payr of Toungs with fier pann & Bellows on payr of Gridg Irons Two Killers & a small Tabell & a payle on stand and a hooke & a hamer

It mor on hough a meale poke & a Chiver

It 2 Chayers & a Reele & a Boule

It on Fring pann and a Beere vesill and a forke

RELIEF: No relevant poor relief records survive from 1699. However, these documents from Cawston are pauper inventories as they clearly state that they were made of 'All the poore that Recve Colecttion' (NRO PD 193/93).

CIRCUMTEXT: On the reverse: 'Inventory of Goods of Several Persons'.

DAMAGE: Line 7: 'Coverl<eens>' smudged.

43. Widow Willson, 14 December 1699

NRO PD 193/93 Cawston Inventories, 1699, 1826.

[Opening lines to the inventories] Dec the 14.th 1699

An inventorey Tacking by the Townsmen of Cawston of All the poore that Recve Colecttion as foloweth ....

[Inventory]

wid willson

on fether Bed & 2 Blanckets & Bed stead on sheet & a Cuerling & a Boulster & pillow

It on Box & a Bed stoole & an old Chayr on sk<il>let and A pale

RELIEF: No relevant poor relief records survive from 1699. However, these documents from Cawston are pauper inventories as they clearly state that they were made of 'All the poore that Recve Colecttion' (NRO PD 193/93).

CIRCUMTEXT: On the reverse: 'Inventory of Goods of Several Persons'.

DAMAGE: Line 6: Hole between '2' and 'Blanckets'. Line 8: 'sk<il>let' smudged.

Forncett St. Peter pauper inventories

The two pauper inventories for Forncett St. Peter are found on the same page at the front of a set of overseers' accounts for the parish dated 1778–1791 (NRO PD 421/133).

44. Thomas Cullam, 12 January 1784

NRO PD 421/133 Forncett St. Peter Overseers' Accounts, 1778–1791.

An Inventory of Thomas Cullams Goods Chattles and Effects Valued & Apprized this 12 Day of January 1784 by me James Doe Overseer for Forncett S^{t} peter for Collection to the parish of Forncett S^{t} peter

On the Chamber

a Lomb furniture Trundle Lyelach Long Stool Spining Weel tub Sive

In the Kitching

a Large Kettle & Lid Reel 3 Earth pots Cup 2 Wood Dishes puter Cold pail Boiler & Lid french Oven Warming pan Hoe Hatchet Hook Stool Spade 4 Curtons Bed & Bedstead 2 Blankits 2 Sheets 2 pillers and 2 Cases Rug 2 puter Dishes 6 plates a Neast of Drawers trunk Looking Glass 2 Baskits a Cubboard Dresser Earthing whear 2 Bowles a 3 footed Stand & Top Killer funnal a Coffer teakittle a Boil Skillit frying pan 4 trunchers 3 Wood Spoons Ladle Joint Stool Stone Bottle 2 Gochis Ovel table Squear table 6 Small Chairs One Elbow D^{o} a Small Cole Range Gridiron fire pan tongs Speet teakittle Iron 2 Candle Stands Skillit Boxiron 2 Heeters a pair of Andirons 12 Knives & forks 2 Sheets 2 Shirts 3 Shifts 3 towels 2 piller Casses 4 Glass Bottles Sack 2 pokes for flower 2 Basons a Baker Glass a Waiter 2 teapots 4 Chinea Cups 6 Saussers a Bason a pair of Stais Hand Bason 2 Aprons, – I Thomas Cullam do Sell the within Goods Chattles & Effects to the parish Officers of Forncett S^{t} peter for Rent and Collection as Witness my Hand

Witness his	his
James X Doe	Thos X Cullam
mark	Mark

RELIEF: Thomas Cullam was in receipt of 2s. per week and the parish paid his rent (£1 17s. 6d.) when this inventory was taken of his goods. He occasionally received cash payments when he was in 'Need' (NRO PD 421/133). The inventory also notes that he was receiving 'Collection' and that the parish paid his rent.

FURTHER INFORMATION: There are numerous other people with the surname Cullam in the overseers' accounts, such as Benjamin, Michael, William, and James Cullam. It is unknown whether these people were any relation of Thomas Cullam. The belongings were only figuratively sold to the parish and Thomas Cullam was able to retain his possessions (NRO PD 421/133).

DUBIOUS TERMS: Line 7: 'Cold' – unknown term; possibly a coule/cowle.

45. Martha Smith, no date (c.1784)

NRO PD 421/133 Forncett St. Peter Overseers' Accounts, 1778–1791.

An Invitory of Martha Smiths Goods Chattles and Affects
Bed and bed steads Civerling and 2 Sheets Lie leech dresser dale box wash keller table an oak Chest chane hake spinning wheel and reel porrage pot box iron and heet ~~pail~~ three Chairs and pail

Witness his   Martha
James X Doe   The mark X of
mark   Smith

RELIEF: Martha Smith was in receipt of 2s. per week when the inventory was taken. She had received a pension for several years from the parish and appears to have received little additional relief other than this (NRO PD 421/133).

FURTHER INFORMATION: The year 1784 is based on where the inventory is located in the overseers' accounts. Martha Smith was probably living on her own as a widow or spinster when this inventory was made. James Doe was the overseer of the poor for Forncett St. Peter in 1784 (NRO PD 421/133).

Gissing pauper inventories

The pauper inventories for Gissing parish are spread across two volumes and loose sheets of paper. This suggests that the parish applied the policy for several decades and used various forms of record keeping to note down parishioners' goods (NRO PD 50/71; NRO PD 50/44; NRO PD 50/45). Among these records, there are also goods-taken and debt-related inventories, as well as numerous other inventories which could not be categorised.

46. Widow Watling, no date (c.1720–1750s; probably 1720s)

NRO PD 50/71 Gissing Inventories, 1726–1742.

An Enventory of the Widdow Watling Goods
2 Beds 3 Bedsteads 4 Boxes 3 Tables 1 Chest 1 Rele 7 Chaires 1 Cubbard 6 Stooles 1 morter 1 houre glass 1 Boyler 1 Iron pot 2 Skillets 2 Killers 1 Bole 1 paile 10 Trenchers 8 wooding Dishes 2 hooks 1 forke, Spet 1 peele 1 Chefindish 1 Box Iron 1 Candle Box 2 Cobirons 1 paire of Tongs 1 Fire pan 1 Brass Kittle 1 Tub 2 Beere Vessels 4 Coups 1 Puter Dish 1 Childs basket 1 Wooding Chamber pot 1 funel 1 Sive 3 Alestoole 1 pair of Scoles 1 Frying pan 1 Rutter 1 Turn 6 tooles 3 Shelves and Sum Lumber

RELIEF: Because the inventory could not be precisely dated it is not possible to establish what the exact nature of Widow Watling's relief was when the inventory was taken. Nonetheless, overseers' accounts show that Widow Watling was continually on regular relief between the 1720s and 1750s. In 1722, for example, she received 2s. 6d. per week and during most of the 1750s she received 1s. per week. She had several children who frequently received clothing from the parish during the 1720s and 1730s, such as shoes, shirts, stockings, caps, coats, petticoats, and breeches. The parish also paid Widow Watling's rent and gave her fuel on numerous occasions (NRO PD 50/44; NRO PD 50/45; NRO PD 50/47).

FURTHER INFORMATION: Widow Watling had at least two children living with her during the 1720s and 1730s (a son and a daughter) (NRO PD 50/44; NRO PD 50/45; NRO PD 50/47).

EDITORIAL CHANGES: Line 4: 'wooding' – written across two lines in the original as 'wood, ing'.

DAMAGE: The bottom of the page is ripped.

47. Widow Tutell, no date (c.1720–1740s)

NRO PD 50/44 Gissing Town Book, 1688–1741.

the Goods ~~for~~ of the wedou Tutell
won Beed and beed sted on Coverlet 2 Porreg Poots on Sceillet on hake won Par of Toungs 6 chares ~~3~~ 4 Tabeels won Cubbod on Rell on frienpan 11 Tranchers 4 mugs on Lockin Glase 2 Par of sheets on Putoo a Beed and Beedsteed a Roog and 2 Pellers 1 Boouster 1 vessel and 1 Cooffer on alle Stoulse 1 hook on hattchet 1 sasepan on Pornger 4 Speen Weles 1 Seuese 1 wodden Platter 1 Pail 2 bushels of weate

RELIEF: Widow Tutell was continually noted as a pauper between the 1720s and 1740s, but because the inventory could not be precisely dated it is not possible to establish what the exact nature of relief was when the inventory was taken. Nonetheless, she frequently received regular relief and clothing, fuel, and cash from the parish during times of sickness. For example, in 1732 she received 1s. or 6d. per week and received money for her ill health. Parochial authorities also gave her children clothing such as shifts, gowns, shirts, and stockings (NRO PD 50/44; NRO PD 50/45; NRO PD 50/47).

FURTHER INFORMATION: Widow Tutell had two young children living with her during the 1730s, named John and Hannah/Anna (NRO PD 50/44; NRO PD 50/45; NRO PD 50/47).

DUBIOUS TERMS: Line 4: 'Putoo' – unknown term. Line 6: 'Seuese' – unknown term.

48. John Smith, 4 November 1756

NRO PD 50/45 Gissing Overseers' Accounts, 1741–1759.

The Inventory of the Goods & Chattles of John Smith of Burston in ye County of Norfolk Carpenter taken by Mr Wi^{ll} Miller & Willm Sutton the 4th Day of Nov^{br} 1756

In the Kitchen

one hake, a fire pan, a pair of Ballows & a pair of Cobirons
a Gridiron, a Spit & a pair of Tongues
a Square Table & a minging huck
an oval table & five Chairs
Two Brass skellets & a vessell
a nest of drawer ....
a box iron & heats ....

In the Parlour

One feather bed with the bedstead & furniture as it Stands
a vessell one rush bottom Chair & an old trunk
an old Cradle with a pillow ....

a Small Brass Boyler with the Cov<er>
In the Shop
A Brass warming pan & an iron pottage pott wth ye hooks

RELIEF: John Smith was in receipt of casual relief when this inventory was taken. He received help such as clothing for his son and money for being 'in need'. The parish also paid £2 7s. 4d. for John Smith's rent between October 1756 and Easter 1757 (NRO PD 50/45).

FURTHER INFORMATION: John Smith was a carpenter and had settlement in Gissing, but was living in the village of Burston, Norfolk. He probably had several children, but only a 'boy' was specifically mentioned by overseers. Records note 'Expences... after Dumb Smith' on 27 May 1757 in Diss, Norfolk, which was only a short distance from Burston where John Smith lived. It is, however, unknown if 'Dumb' Smith was one of John Smith's children. William Miller was a churchwarden and William Sutton was an overseer of the poor for Gissing (NRO PD 50/45).

DAMAGE: Line 16: Ink smudged on the word 'Boyler' and 'Cov<er>'.

Hapton pauper inventories

The two pauper inventories for Hapton were written on loose sheets of paper (NRO PD 236/51).

49. William Read (junior), 15 April 1796

NRO PD 236/51 Hapton Inventories, 1796–1831.

An Inventory taken this 15th day of April 1796 of the Effects of Wm Read J^{n} A pauper. Belonging to the parish of Hapton, in the County of Norfolk – By Isaac Gardiner & Charles Hart, Overs^{rs} & James Funnell Churchwarden & Constable

Viz. In Kitchen
Two Tables & 9 Chairs
& a Tea Table 2 Killers & a Lye Leech
a pail a pair of Bellows a pair of
andirons, a hake & a2 Iron pots
fire shovel, tongs & horse & 2 brushes
Box iron 3 heaters, Lamp & CandleStick
2 wood Dishes, meal & flour sieves
Tea kettle frying pann 2 Earthen pots 5 pans
3 Stone Bottles & 5 Glass Bottles –
4 knives & forks Earthen ware 8 plates & 2 Oval
Dishes. & 2 pewter Plates, Corner Cupboard
& Tea Tackling, Iron Rake, 2 Scupets, 2
Hooks & a madhook & a spade –
a Bed as it stand & Bedstead, Box
tow weel & tow reel – a Hammer –

RELIEF: There are no surviving poor relief records from Hapton to fully contextualise this inventory. Nonetheless, this is a pauper inventory and William Read was in receipt of relief as he is described as 'A pauper' in the inventory.

50. Mary Huson, no date

NRO PD 236/51 Hapton Inventories, 1796–1831.

An Inventory of the Goods of mary Huson going to Tib^{m}

<A> Bed. as it stand Compleat 3 Chairs. A Table, a spinig weel & reel a warming pan. Coal grate. Spit. Tongs. Bellows Iron pot. Tea Kettle. Cup & Dish. frying pan. 2 Earthen pots. Chest drawers. a Box Killer & pail ....

3 Hat Boxes ....

RELIEF: It is not possible to fully contextualise this inventory since it is not dated. Nonetheless, this is a pauper inventory and Mary Huson was in receipt of relief as she is noted as a 'Collectioner' on the back of the document.

FURTHER INFORMATION: The inventory indicates that Mary Huson had settlement in Hapton but was living in the nearby village of Tibenham, Norfolk.

CIRCUMTEXT: On the reverse 'Collectioner'.

DAMAGE: Line 2: The word 'A' is smudged. The edges of the inventory are worn and there are some tears.

East Harling pauper inventories

The four pauper inventories from East Harling were all written on loose pieces of paper and can be found assembled in NRO PD 219/114. Among the collection, there is also an inventory of Thomas Harbour's goods taken 'in Distress for Rent'.

51. Rhoda Wretham, 9 April 1821

NRO PD 219/114 East Harling Inventories, 1821–1825.

An Inventory of the Household Furniture of Rhoda the Wife of Edward Wretham of East Harling in the County of Norfolk Taken this ninth Day of April 1821.

Wainscot Table with Drawer
Walnuttree D° with D°
½ Doz Hollow seat'd Chairs
Swinging Dressing Glass
Round Table
Childs armed Chair
D° wicker D°, pad lock & Key,
Painted Clothes Hutch, pr Sheets,
Stump Bedstead matt & Cord
Feather Bed, Bolster and Pillow
pr Blanketts, Patch Work Coverlid
Tow Wheel, Copper Tea Kettle,
1 pr Bellows, Stool, hearth Bar
Wash Keeler, Copper Boiler
1 pr pictures, pr flat Irons,
Coffee pot, Tin Roaster, Tea Caddy
Mock Silver Tea pot, Toasting fork
1 pr Iron Candlesticks, 1 pr Tongs,
Small Baskett, Small Linen Baskett,
Pail Bail and Hoops, firepan handle
Iron pot & pot Hooks } belong to Parish
Peel fork and oven hoe }

Taken on the abovementioned Day by me and branded EHP. in my Presence
John Ellis

RELIEF: Rhoda Wretham was in receipt of 7s. per week when this inventory was taken. Her husband, Edward, had been committed to Norfolk lunatic asylum in October 1820 and the parish paid 8s. 6d. per week to maintain him while he was in there. From 14 July 1821, the parish gave 8s. per week to the asylum. The institution was located in Thorpe St. Andrew (Norfolk) and was first opened in 1814. On 6 October 1821, the parish paid a final sum of £5 10s. 6d. to the asylum for 'Edward Wrethams Maintanance and Finural [funeral] at Lunitic Ayslum'. Rhoda and Edward Wretham also received a considerable amount of casual relief from the parish at various times for rent and children's clothing, as well as money when they were both 'in Illness' and 'in need' (NRO PD 219/94; Steven Cherry, *Mental Health Care in Modern England: The Norfolk Lunatic Asylum/St. Andrew's Hospital, 1810–1998* (Woodbridge, 2003)).

FURTHER INFORMATION: Under the law, the parish could legally distrain the goods of parishioners that needed to be maintained by the parish because of lunacy (see chapter 2). However, because the inventory was taken six months after Edward Wretham was committed to the asylum and since there are other pauper inventories from East Harling during the 1820s, this inventory has been categorised as a pauper inventory. Inventories of married women's belongings were normally made in the husband's name, but because Edward Wretham was not living at home and was sick this inventory was in Rhoda Wretham's name. Rhoda (née James) married Edward Wretham in East Harling on 30 October 1815. The couple had several children, but it is unknown how many they had. See chapter 2 for further information on the practice of branding paupers' goods to signify parish ownership. According to the overseers' accounts, John Ellis did not hold a position in the parish such as overseer of the poor. John Ellis is described as an 'Auctioneer & Appraiser' in the inventory of Parker's goods below **(54)** and overseers' accounts often note the payment of bills to him, suggesting that he was a paid associate of the parish. For example, in October 1820 the parish paid a bill of £2 17s. 8d. to John Ellis and March 1821 the parish paid a bill of £1 12s. to him (NRO PD 219/9; NRO PD 219/94; NRO PD 219/114).

52. Widow Whitehead, 9 April 1821

NRO PD 219/114 East Harling Inventories, 1821–1825.

An Inventory of the Household Furniture of the Widow of Henry Whitehead of East Harling Norfolk taken April the ninth 1821.

Stump Bedstead matt and Cord
Oat flight Bed & Bolster
1 Blankett, Green Coverlid, pr Sheets,
Leaf Table, Square Deal Table,
two Chairs, pail, Keeler, Iron pot
Tin Tea Kettle, Iron Candlestick
6 or 7 Articles of Earthenware
2 Boxes and Stool.
Hoe and Brush

Taken on the abovementioned Day by me and branded EHP.
John Ellis

RELIEF: Henry Whitehead was sick and received casual relief for a number of months before this inventory was taken. This was initially given to him sporadically but became more frequent as he grew more unwell. For example, in April 1820 he was provided with 10s. in total from the parish; in December 1820 he was paid £1; and in February 1821 he was given £1 2s. in total and also received wine, rum, and beer from the parish. Henry Whitehead died around February-March 1821 and his wife was subsequently given casual relief from the parish. On 6 April 1821 she started to receive a pension of 2s. per week (NRO PD 219/4; NRO PD 219/94).

FURTHER INFORMATION: Henry Whitehead was buried in East Harling on 9 March 1821 at the age of 35. See chapter 2 for further information on the practice of branding paupers' goods to signify parish ownership. According to the overseers' accounts, John Ellis did not hold a position in the parish such as overseer of the poor. John Ellis is described as an 'Auctioneer & Appraiser' in the inventory of Parker's goods below **(54)** and overseers' accounts often note the payment of bills to him, suggesting that he was contracted by the parish to make the inventory. For example, in October 1820 the parish paid a bill of £2 17s. 8d. to John Ellis and in March 1821 the parish paid a bill of £1 12s. (NRO PD 219/94; NRO PD 219/114).

53. George Orsborne, 12 October 1821

NRO PD 219/114 East Harling Inventories, 1821–1825.

An Inventorey of the Housel Furniture of Geo Orsborne of East Harling in the County of Norfolk taking this 12 day of Octr 1821

Fether Bed & Bolster
Straw Bed
1 p^{r} of Brankets
2 p^{r} of Sheets
2 Coverlits
2 p^{r} of Beds Steds

Oak dining table tea table half a Dozen of Elm Chares low chare three dale Boxes p^{r} of Bullows, firepan and Tongs p^{r} of flats two stone Bottles Cole Range, Painted Box, Lye Leech, copper waming pan, corner Cubbord Large copper Boiler, Large oak cloth chest, hake and hanks, wood cool shoot, small linnen horse, Iron fender & sifter, lot of Erthenware, Linnen Bausket, wash killor

RELIEF: George Orsborne was in receipt of casual relief and had received this for over 18 months before this inventory was taken. Money was generally given to him when he was 'in need' and 'in Illness'. For example, in December 1820 he was given a total of £1 1s. by the parish; in April 1821 he was paid £1 9s.; and in October 1821 he was provided with 9s. in total but also had his rent of £2 12s. 6d. paid by the parish (NRO PD 219/94).

FURTHER INFORMATION: George Orsborne is described as a weaver in the overseers' accounts and was living in the nearby village of Garboldisham (Norfolk) when this inventory was taken. It is possible that he was removed back to East Harling soon after his goods were appraised. He was probably living on his own as a bachelor or widower when this inventory was made (NRO PD 219/94; NRO PD 219/114).

DUBIOUS TERMS: Line 12: 'wood cool shoot' – a coal scuttle or coal chute made from wood.

54. — Parker, 16 November 1825

NRO PD 219/114 East Harling Inventories, 1821–1825.

An Inventory of the Household Furniture &c of   Parker as taken by me on the 16th Day of November 1825.

Round leaf Table
Square Oak D°
Buffett Stool & Slip
Old Oak Chest of Drawers
Minging Hutch
½ Doz wood seated Chairs
Arm'd Chair
Old Arm'd & low Chairs
2 Stools 2 Boxes Linen Stand & Baskett
4 Post Bedstead & ordinary hangings
Girt Web D° with half Tester & D°
Feather Bed Bolster pr pillows
Oat flight Bed Matt
one Blankett two Coverlids
3 Keelers Pail Iron pot Copper frying pan
Tin Tea Kettle Small tin Saucepan
Coal grate hake pr Tongs pr Bellows
fender 2 Stone Bottles some Earthenware
3 or 4 knives and forks. Cynder Sifter
two Looms two Winding Wheels

£ : s : D
Valued together at the sum of – 7 : 4 : 8
by me John Ellis
Auctioneer & Appraiser

RELIEF: There are two people in the overseers' accounts with the surname Parker: 'Woman' Parker and James Parker. It is not known whose goods were appraised in this inventory. Nonetheless, both had been in receipt of casual relief for several years when this inventory was taken. Money was given to both recipients on a frequent basis when they were 'in need' and 'in Illness'. Additionally, on 14 August 1824, the parish paid 8s. to bury James Parker's child and on 22 January 1825 the parish paid 6s. to bury the child of Woman Parker (NRO PD 219/94).

FURTHER INFORMATION: It is unknown if James and Woman Parker had any additional children other than the ones that were buried in August 1824 and January 1825. The overseers' accounts indicate that John Ellis did not hold a position in East Harling such as overseer and was only hired by the parish to take this inventory (NRO PD 219/94; NRO PD 219/114).

West Harling pauper inventories

Two pauper inventories have been located for West Harling in a set of overseers' accounts, written in the hands of the incumbent overseers (NRO PD 27/21). There is also an inventory of John Lancaster's belongings in the volume, which appears to have been taken after he abandoned his children and left them chargeable to the parish.

55. Widow Doe, 23 January 1779

NRO PD 27/21 West Harling Overseers' Accounts, 1771–1828.

Janry 23 1779 An Account Taken this day of the Houshould Effects of Widow Doe by

R Kitton & Abram Ayton

1: 4 Post Bedseat with hangings
1 feather Bed Bolster & Piller 1 Piller case
2 Blankets 1 Green Rug
1 Chest of Drawers 6[s.] 6[d.] 1 Double
Cupboard 1[s.]: 6[d.] .... } 9[s.]: 0[d.]
Sold 1 Brown Ovel Table with 2 Leaves
1 Dresser & Coule 2 White Rush Bottom^{d}
Chaires 2 Black D^{o} Rush Bottom^{d} Sold } 2[s.]: 0[d.]
1 Grill Iron 1 Pair of Tongs 1 fire Pan
1 Hank 1 Iron Porridge Pot
1 Box Iron & heeters 1 Pair of Bellows
1 Copper Tea Kettle 1 Tea Pot 1 Cup & Saucer
1 Tea Cannester 1 Pint Glass Bottle
1 Hour Glass 1 Iron Candlestick Lost
1 Tow wheele Rack & Reele s : d
1 Brass Skillett .... 0 : 3

RELIEF: Widow Doe was in receipt of 2s. 6d. per week when this inventory was taken. She first became a pensioner in April 1778 and was also provided with rent payments (10s. each time) and fuel from the parish (NRO PD 27/21).

FURTHER INFORMATION: Widow Doe died sometime between October 1779 and March 1780 and the parish paid £1 7s. towards her funeral. The overseers' accounts indicate that Widow Doe's goods were sold around March 1780 and that the parish raised £2 15s. 3d. for them and 'Lanchasters' belongings. The words 'Sold' and

'Lost' on lines 9 and 17 and sums of money on lines 7, 8, and 19 were probably not written when the inventory was initially taken and were added in March 1780 when the goods were sold by the parish. R. (Richard) Kitton was overseer of the poor when this inventory was taken. Abraham Ayton does not appear to have held a position in the parish when this inventory was made, but was overseer of the poor from April 1779 (NRO PD 27/21).

56. Esther Turner, 4 July 1803

NRO PD 27/21 West Harling Overseers' Accounts, 1771–1828.

July 4th 1803 An Acco^{t}: of the Goods beloning to Easter Turner. Sent home from Norwich By orders from Justicis to this Parish

1803 A Nicolson
By Overseer & Curh Warden
& A Nicolson. Constable

one Good Four Posted Bedstead with Green Cheney Hanings & Valants &^{c} Compleat
Good Fether Bed Boulster & Pillow and two Pillow Casses
Two Blankets <Half Twilt> & Cover
one pair Pretty Good sheets one D<o> ordenry ones
two pretty Good shifts two very ordenry ones
two Pitticoast old one Brown Cloack & one Reed Cloak one very old great Coat

RELIEF: Ester Turner started to receive a pension of 4s. per week when this inventory was taken. She does not appear to have received any casual relief in addition to this (NRO PD 27/21).

FURTHER INFORMATION: Overseers' accounts mention the death of somebody called Thomas in Ester Turner's home, but it is unknown what his surname was and thus whether he was any relation to Ester Turner. This inventory was taken just before or soon after Ester Turner was removed from Norwich at a cost of £3 15s. to West Harling parish (NRO PD 27/21).

DUBIOUS TERMS: Line 9: '<Half Twilt>' – possibly a woven quilt of some sort.

Hilgay pauper inventory

Only one pauper inventory has been located for Hilgay. It is found among a bundle of loose miscellaneous overseers' vouchers dated 1804–1805 (NRO PD 382/45).

57. William Johnson, 27 March 1805

NRO PD 382/45 Hilgay Overseers' Vouchers, 1804–1805.

An Inventory of Goods & Chattels of William Johnsons taken the 27th Day of March 1805

Kitchen – Round Table Sq Oak D^{o} Two Arm rush Bottom Chairs, three small Rush Bottom Chairs Two Wood Bottom Chaires, A Bedstead, Feather-Bed, Bolster, one Pillow, a Sheet & Coverlid, Matt & half Hangings. A Dresser with Drawers, A Knife Box A pail, pair of Bellows, An Iron Horse. Grate. fore Iron, and a p^{r} of Tongs. An Iron Box & rest, a Gridiron, & Iron pot –

In the Shop –

A wash Keeler, A Linnen Horse, A paire of Yokes A Frying-pan. A Tea Kettle, Two Stools, A pail, &c meat pot Six Augurs Seven planes; Tenor Saw, Hand-Saw. Axe. 12 Chissels Shave, A p^{r} of pinsers, 2 Hammers, Adze – Bout or Larger Hammer Squares, Gauges &c –

In the Chamber –

A Bedstead, Feather Bed, Bolster, Two Pillows, two Sheets, Blankett and Coverlid with Hangings and a Chair

Memorandum, on the Day above Written it was agreed to pay the sum of Two Pounds ten shillings Rentt & Charges One Pound, twelve shillings, & sixpence which was paid by W: Crist – On acct of the said W. Johnson –

RELIEF: William Johnson was in receipt of 9s. per week when this inventory was taken. The amount changed from month to month and sometimes his wife and son were mentioned, suggesting that the pension was intended to support the entire family. The overseers' accounts and inventory also show that the parish paid £4 2s. 6d. in total to cover William Johnson's rent and expenses. It is probable that the parish made this inventory to indemnify themselves of some of these costs when they later repossessed and sold the goods (NRO PD 382/41; NRO PD 382/45).

FURTHER INFORMATION: William Johnson was married and had at least one son when the inventory was taken. He and his wife and son are often noted as sick by the overseers, however no specific details about their illnesses are mentioned. W. Crist was one of the overseers of the poor for Hilgay in 1805 (NRO PD 382/41; NRO PD 382/45).

CIRCUMTEXT: 'An Inventory of Will: Johnson's Goods & Chattels' written on the back.

EDITORIAL CHANGES: Line 6: 'Drawers' – originally spelt Draw-ers' as it was written across two lines.

Hingham pauper inventories

The nine pauper inventories from Hingham were all written on loose pieces of paper and can be found bundled together in NRO PD 575/128. Eleven further inventories are found in the collection, which were made for unknown reasons or show the parish selling and/or taking the goods of paupers.

58. Robert Coper, 26 September 1710

NRO PD 575/128 Hingham Inventories, 1706–1731.

Hinghm Septm 26 – 1710
An Aco^{t}: Taken of Robb Coper Goods by will: Rock Churchwarden
2 Beeds & Bedin
3 Chayers & a Setle
A Cubbord
2 Coffers
2 Boxis
1 Table
1 fring pann
1 warming pann
1 potag pott

RELIEF: Robert Coper's wife was in receipt of 1s. 6d. per week when this inventory was taken. Poor relief sources are inconsistent and lack detail for the early eighteenth century meaning that it is not possible to determine when she became a pensioner and assess the exact nature of her poverty. Robert Coper and his wife also received small amounts of casual relief in the form of cash from the parish. For example, between January and March 1711 Robert Coper received 2s. 6d. in total and his wife received 5s. 6d. from the parish (NRO PD 575/124; NRO PD 575/126).

FURTHER INFORMATION: Poor law records also mention a Guy, Matt, Widow, Joseph, Sam, and Ann Coper during the first half of the eighteenth century, but it is unknown whether these people were any relation of Robert Coper such as his children (NRO PD 575/124; NRO PD 575/126).

59. Widow Osburn, no date (c.1723–1727)

NRO PD 575/128 Hingham Inventories, 1706–1731.

An Account of ye Wido Osburns things

Bed Chamber £ S D

1 Bed case & Matt 1 Feather Bed 1 bolster
3 Pillows 2 Blanketts 1 Coverlet ~~2 Sheets~~ } 3 – 0 – 0

Buttery 2 Kittles 2 Skillets A frying pan A Keep
1 Vessel A wash Killer A Wash Bowl 1 pail
1 Tub 2 Ale Stools 2 wood dishs 1 pewter plate
& poringer 2 Eathern pans & 2 pitchers
& smoothing Irons & Heets .... }

Chamber

1 Trickle Bed 1 bolster 1 Tick 2 blankets
1 Coverlet 1 Coffer & Form 2 Woolen Shifts
1 p^{r} Stays & Stomacher 1 old Gown
4 old Petticoats A Tartin Apron & Gown }

Kitchen

1 Table & Chest 1 Box 2 Stools 5 Chairs
1 Spitt 1 Gridiron 1 Hake 1 Hank 2 Candles^{ks}
1 firepan 1 p^{r} Tongs & bellows }

RELIEF: Widow Osburn was in receipt of 1s. 6d. per week from the parish between 1723 and 1727. The parish also occasionally paid her rent (15s.) and provided her with people to care for her during times of sickness (NRO PD 575/124; NRO PD 575/126).

FURTHER INFORMATION: The inventory was probably made sometime between 1723 and 1727 based on evidence of poor relief payments paid to Widow Osburn (NRO PD 575/124; NRO PD 575/126).

CIRCUMTEXT: On the back of the inventory is a list which records the selling of Widow Osburn's possessions (goods-taken inventory). It is undated but was almost certainly taken after the above inventory and probably after Widow Osburn's death (NRO PD 575/128): S D

Sold Goody Godfrey Gown Stays Stomachers pettycoats......5 = 0
Mrs Buck Table & Chair ....2 = 3
Box & Wash Bowl ....2 = 1
A Seive ....0 = 6
Goody Marsh frying pan & Skilet ....3 = 3
A wash Killer ....1 = 0
A Hake & Hank ....1 = 0
Gridiron & Candlestick ....1 – 0
2 Chairs ....1 – 2
2 Stools ....0 – 5

Gace Barns Smoothing Iron & Heets Linnen	2 = 6
Jno Skeepor y^{e} Keep & ale Stool	2 = 6
Recced Mrs Alden for Bedd	1 = 11 = 6
Good ficklen old Gown	1 = 6
	3 = 2 = 2
Reced of Wm Cooper for 1 Bed	2 = 10
	5 = 12 = 2

60. Widow Little, 8 June 1724

NRO PD 575/128 Hingham Inventories, 1706–1731.

June y^{e} 8. 1724.

An Inventory of y^{e} Goods of y^{e} Widow Little yn Seized for y^{e} use of y^{e} Town by Reason She was fon'd to be Reliev'd by the Parish

In the Kitchin one Bedd as it Stands Two Tables, one Cubbard, & Cubbard Draws Two Boxes, a p^{r}. Brass Scales four Chairs one joynted Stool, & Scrine, a p^{r}. Bellows Three Lattin Panns, one Cullender, & Beam one Warming Pann one pewter quart & pt three pewter porringers & Chamber Pott Ditt: two Gowns & one Petty-Coat, one Ridinghood & Seven Lining Sheats & Spining wheel A p^{r}. of Cobb-Irons one fire pann & tongs a pr one Gridg-Iron, three hakes one Basse Ladle

In ye Buttery one Boiler & Brass Lead & two Scillets, & one Little meat fickle 6 thran:

On the Chamber two flock Bedds Standing

In the out house three Tubbs & one tunle & two Pails, & Leach, a pr. mustard quarns, & ale Stool & two vessels & two Hogs Trows

RELIEF: Widow Little started to receive 1s. per week from the parish when this inventory was made. In addition, the parish gave Widow Little occasional cash payments and paid another parishioner, Elizabeth Godfry, 4s. for looking after Widow Little for five weeks (NRO PD 575/124; NRO PD 575/126; NRO PD 575/128). The inventory also notes that Widow Little was a pauper as the goods were 'Seized for ye use of ye Town by Reason She was fon'd to be Reliev'd by the Parish'.

FURTHER INFORMATION: Overseers' accounts indicate that the goods were not literally 'Seized' by the parish and that Widow Little continued to keep and use her belongings. Somebody called Sue Little is also mentioned in extant records, but it is unknown whether this was Widow Little or if this person was any relation of Widow Little. In March 1727/28, the overseer notes the payment of 6d. 'for Looking aft. ye wid. Little & her Daug'. It is probable that the daughter was living with Widow Little when this inventory was made. A young boy called Martin Little is also mentioned in poor law records sometime between 1712–1732, but it is unknown if this was Widow Little's son (NRO PD 575/124; NRO PD 575/126; NRO PD 575/128).

DUBIOUS TERMS: Line 11: 'fickle' – possibly firkin; Line 12: 'thran:' – unknown term; used as an abbreviation for something.

61. Widow Man, 23 March 1724/25

NRO PD 575/128 Hingham Inventories, 1706–1731.

March ye 23 1724
taken an acount of the widdow mans goods by the church worden and overseer
one bed and bed stead three Shets one blanket one coverled three chairs one tabel two Stools one box one bowl one pail two tubs one hook one hammar one Smothen iorn and hets one Reel one wood botel one pair of bellows one greg iorn fyphorn and tongs one fryen pan one basket one Skelet one iorn poreg pot four earthen pans two goches one sive four trenches two dishes two pots thre botels two pokes and a pair of bags

RELIEF: Widow Man was in receipt of 1s. per week when this inventory was taken. She had received a pension from the parish since June 1724 and received occasional relief in the form of cash and rent payments (NRO PD 575/124; NRO PD 575/126).

FURTHER INFORMATION: In 1730 clothing was given to Widow Man's sons on several occasions, but it is unknown how many children she had. In September 1724, the parish paid 2s. 6d. for removing Widow Man, however it is not known which parish she came from. The names of the overseer and churchwarden that took this inventory could not be discerned (NRO PD 575/124; NRO PD 575/126).

62. Widow Flowars, 16 November 1725

NRO PD 575/128 Hingham Inventories, 1706–1731.

16th Novem^{b} 1725 Dasesed

The account of ye howsell Goods Late ye wid flowars
one bed one bouster one <Certyen> one p<?> one bedstad one Cubard one Chest 2 tables one Peuter Rack one forham a Cettle 2 Chares

RELIEF: Widow Flowars was in receipt of 1s. per week when this inventory was taken. She started to receive this pension from mid- to late-1719. The parish also paid for clothing for her son and 14s. 8d. towards her funeral. Widow Flowar's son was subsequently given 6d. per week by the parish after his mother died (NRO PD 575/124; NRO PD 575/126).

FURTHER INFORMATION: Widow Flowars died in October or November 1725 (NRO PD 575/124; NRO PD 575/126).

DUBIOUS TERMS: Line 3: '<Certyen>' – possibly curtains (bed hangings). Line 4 – 'forham' – form.

DAMAGE: Text faded and some parts smudged, making it difficult to read.

63. William Burgany, no date (c.1726–1728)

NRO PD 575/128 Hingham Inventories, 1706–1731.

An Account of W$^{\underline{m}}$ Burganys things
1 Bed as it stands 2 bolsters ~~2 pillows~~ two Blankets 1 rug his waring appar'll 2 pigs a Kittle a pot Iron 2 Skillet 1 gridgion 1 Hake 1 frying pan bellows 1 Table 1 Dreser 2 Coffers ~~2~~ 1 box 1 pail 1 Killer 1 Vessel 1 joynt Stool 7 Chairs 1 Spitt fire pan & Tongs 2 Spice Drawes A Shelf & Case 1 pewter Dish 5 Earthen plates 12 potts & pans half Anker 2 half firkins 1 p^{r} Scales & weights 3 wood Dishes 6 trenchers an Hatchet Chamber 1 Bed Entire as it Stands 6 Bunches rush old killer a powdering Tub 2 brushes a CulleDer 2 old Shirts

RELIEF: William Burgany was on 2s. per week between 1726 and 1728. He also received casual relief in the form of cash and clothing from the parish. For example, in mid–1724 the parish gave William Burgany a pair of sheets worth 4s. In March 1728, William Burgany died and his wife subsequently received 1s. 6d. per week from the parish (NRO PD 575/2; NRO PD 575/124; NRO PD 575/126).

FURTHER INFORMATION: The inventory is probably datable to c.1726–1728 based on additional research on William Burgany's poor relief and death. He was married and it is probable that the couple had children as the overseer notes the payment of 2s. 10d. for hose and shoes for 'Burgney Child'. William Burgany was buried in Hingham on 26 March 1728 (NRO PD 575/2; NRO PD 575/124; NRO PD 575/126).

EDITORIAL CHANGES: Line 8: 'CulleDer' – written across two lines in the original as 'Culle=Der'.

64. Widow Dawson, no date (c.1727–1732)

NRO PD 575/128 Hingham Inventories, 1706–1731.

An Account of y^{e} Wid^{o} Dawson things
1 Bed & bolster 2 pillows 2 Blanketts 1 Coverlett 4 Sheets 1 Table c<lo>th 3 Towels 1 pewter Chamber pot 1 Skillet 1 Kittle 1 Gridiron 1 Coff<e>r & Box 1 Keep ....

RELIEF: Widow Dawson was in receipt of regular relief between 1727 and 1732. She initially started on 6d. per week in 1727 but this gradually increased to 1s. 6d. per week by 1731. The parish also frequently paid people to look after her during times of sickness and gave her additional money and clothing occasionally (NRO PD 575/124; NRO PD 575/126).

FURTHER INFORMATION: The inventory probably dates from c.1726–1728, based on additional research on Widow Dawson's poor relief. Hingham parish registers note the burial of the widow Rose Dawson 2 May 1732. This was almost certainly Widow Dawson as her name stops appearing in overseers' papers around this time (NRO PD 575/2; NRO PD 575/124; NRO PD 575/126).

DAMAGE: Lines 2–3: Writing faded on 'c<lo>th' and 'Coff<e>r'.

65. John Larthman (junior), no date (c.29 March 1728)

NRO PD 575/128 Hingham Inventories, 1706–1731.

An account of Jno Larthman's Things Junier.

One Webing-Coat & westcoat one Pair of Sheeps Leather-Breeches, one Hatt, Two Shert's, a New Pair of Shooes, one Looking-Glass, one old Skillet one Dale-Box

RELIEF: The overseers did not always distinguish between 'Old' John Larthman and John Larthman 'junior', so it is not possible to fully reconstruct John Larthman junior's experience of the poor law. Nevertheless, records show that John Larthman junior was in receipt of 1s. 3d. per week when this inventory was taken and received additional money from the parish when he was sick (NRO PD 575/124; NRO PD 575/126).

FURTHER INFORMATION: This inventory is probably datable to 29 March 1728, as there is a goods-given inventory written below it in the same hand dated 29 March 1728. The overseers' papers note relief being given to John Larthman's wife and son, as well as Goody and Elizabeth Larthman during the 1720s, but it is unknown whether they were related to John Larthman junior (NRO PD 575/124; NRO PD 575/126).

66. Widow Norton, 30 August 1731

NRO PD 575/128 Hingham Inventories, 1706–1731.

Wido Nortons Goods prized by Mr Wm Cooper & Jno Kirby August 30 = 1731

	£ S D
one Bed as it stand	1 = 10 = 0
one porridge pot	0 = 3 = 0
one warming pan	0 = 4 = 0
one frying pan	0 = 2 = 0
one Gridiron	0 = 1 = 6
Spite Hake & Hank	0 = 1 = 8
1 p^{r} Tongs	0 = 1 = 0
Iron Scures fire pan & Candlesticks	0 = 0 = 9
Smoothing Iron & Heats	0 = 1 = 6
two Tables	0 = 1 = 6
A Chest & Coffer	0 = 3 = 0
one p^{r} Bellows & [4] Stools	0 = 2 = 6
pewter Quart & pint & Dish	0 = 2 = 0
a Lanthorn 6^{d} Kittle 1^{s}	0 = 1 = 6
Six Trenchers	0 = 1 = 0
Bowl & Cup	0 = 0 = 9

A Reel	0 = 1 = 0
Hammer & Hatchet pail	0 = 1 = 0
3 Chairs	0 = 1 = 0
Earthen pans	0 = 1 = 0
3 Killers	0 = 3 = 0
Ironing <B>oard	0 = 1 = 0
Broom & Stand	0 = 0 = 4
3 Sheets	0 = 3 = 0
Wood & Corn	0 = 3 = 0
two forms	0 = 1 = 0
Deal Board	0 = 0 = 6
	£3 : 13 = 6

RELIEF: Widow Norton was receiving a pension of 1s. 3d. per week when this inventory was taken. In addition, the parish sometimes gave her extra money, clothing, and helped her during times of sickness. For example, between July–September 1732 the parish paid Widow King £1 12s. to look after Widow Norton for four weeks when she had smallpox (NRO PD 575/124; NRO PD 575/126).

FURTHER INFORMATION: Parish registers note the burial of Bridget Norton 28 August 1731, two days before this inventory was taken. It is, however, unknown whether this was Widow Norton as the overseers' accounts note a payment to Widow King for looking after Widow Norton a year after this burial. It is possible that this was a back-dated payment. Two people called Sarah and James Norton also received relief from the parish during the 1720s–1730s, but it is not known who they were in relation to Widow Norton. William Cooper and John Kirby were probably hired by the parish to inventory and sell Widow Norton's goods (NRO PD 575/2; NRO PD 575/124; NRO PD 575/126).

CIRCUMTEXT: Alongside the pauper inventory of Widow Norton's possessions, there is an inventory of the same goods being sold by the parish (goods-taken inventory) (NRO PD 575/128):

An Account of what they were Sold for y^{e} Same Day [30 August 1731] by y^{e} Same persons [William Cooper and John Kirby]

	£ S D
Porridge pot & two Earthen Dishes	0 = 3 = 6
Pot 1^{d} Gridiron Six Trunchers & broom	0 = 2 = 7
Lanthorn & Candlestick	0 = 0 = 8
Chair & Stool	0 = 0 = 7½
Bed as it Stand	1 = 9 = 0
Table & Ironing board	0 = 2 = 3
Pail & Killer & Bottles	0 = 1 = 7
Leech & pan	0 = 0 = 3
Tubs 2^{s}:6^{d} pewter pint 6^{d}	0 = 3 = 0
3 Sheets & warming pan	0 = 6 = 6
The Reel	0 = 1 = 0
Chest	0 = 2 = 0
Table & two Chairs	0 = 1 = 5
Wood & Corn	0 = 3 = 0

Coffer & Funnel	0 = 1 = 6
Smoothing Iron & Heets	0 = 1 = 6
Pail 2^{d} Stool 6^{d} Stand 2^{d}	0 = 0 = 10
Hank & Kittle	0 = 1 = 0
Stool 2^{d} Hammer 3^{d}	0 = 0 = 5
firepan & Tongs	0 = 0 = 11
frying pan	0 = 2 = 6
Spitt & Hake	0 = 1 = 6
Deal board & Stool	0 = 1 = 0
Pr Bellows	0 = 1 = 9
Pewter Dish & Quart	0 = 1 = 5½
Hatchet	0 = 0 = 3
	£3 : 13 = 6

DUBIOUS TERMS: Line 11: 'Scures' – unknown term.

EDITORIAL CHANGES: Line 15: Widow Norton probably owned four stools as there were four on the 'goods-taken' inventory of her possessions (see circumtext).

DAMAGE: Lines 25–26: Hole in the page obscuring the word '<B>oard'.

Holme-next-the-Sea pauper inventories

All three pauper inventories from Holme-next-the-Sea are written in the hands of the incumbent overseers and are found scattered in a set of overseers' accounts from the period 1704–1783 (NRO PD 629/50).

67. Susan Greves, 7 June 1752

NRO PD 629/50 Holme-next-the-Sea Overseers' Accounts, 1704–1783.

June ye 7 1752 an acount of Susan Greveses things
a Bed & bed Stead too Sheets too Blanckets and a Boulster and Coverlin too tables ~~tables~~ a Cofer and a box a trunck one char a fryingpan a bear tub and a byler

RELIEF: Susan Greves was in receipt of 1s. per week when her goods were inventoried by the parish. It is possible that she also received casual relief but due to inconsistencies in poor law accounts with her name this could not be confirmed (NRO PD 629/50).

FURTHER INFORMATION: Overseers' accounts note the giving of relief to Susan Greves, but also record help being given to Widow Greves and Elizabeth/Betty Greves. It is possible that Widow Greves was Susan Greves. It is unknown whether Elizabeth/Betty Greves was any relation to Susan Greves (NRO PD 629/50).

DAMAGE: Lines 1–4: Bleed-through from writing on the other side of the page, making the source difficult to transcribe.

68. Thomas Trips, 29 November 1766

NRO PD 629/50 Holme-next-the-Sea Overseers' Accounts, 1704–1783.

Novr 29 1766
the a Count of Thos Trips things the Bad 2 Sheets a Blanket a Ruge & hangins 3 Tabels a Ming trouth a dreser a Chist half a Dosen Chars and a Chist of Draws a large Chist a Laking Glase a Iorn ~~Porrdge~~ Poredge pott & a pair Belowrs & one Iorn box 2 heters the hors and par Cotcradel upon the Charmber a bed 2 blankets one Sheet and Ruge a Small Bare Tube a Spad hack & hachett Sith Sekel and all belonging Till for Euse a hogstule & Trow a Line pigg worth 14^{s} Shillings a Stowl the ass and pad he rid on and a Cow and 2 Stone ~~botels~~ Bottels

RELIEF: Thomas Trips was in receipt of casual relief when this inventory was taken. The parish gave him coal every Easter and occasionally paid him money. For example, in April 1766 Thomas Trips was provided with 11 bushels of coal from the parish and in October 1766 he was given a total of 4s. relief (NRO PD 629/50).

FURTHER INFORMATION: Thomas Trips was probably living on his own as a bachelor or widower when this inventory was made (NRO PD 629/50).

DUBIOUS TERMS: Line 8: 'the ass and pad he rid on' – the ass and pad [possibly saddle] that he rode on'.

69. Widow Holybrad, 7 May 1770

NRO PD 629/50 Holme-next-the-Sea Overseers' Accounts, 1704–1783.

may ye 7 – 1770 an Acount of Wd Holybrads things two beds & bedsteds two Coverlines five Sheets a warming 3 pillows a Bolstr two porigepots a <?>bill a Chist of Drawers a pick bill a bear tub two larg handrakes a small hand Rake two Larg meat pots a two cardtub and Eard wash kiler five stonebottles one sack a Bushil poke a spade a painted Cupbord 3 Chairs two Iron Candlesticks two tales a pair of Tongues a pair of Bellowes a Cole Range a p<?> a Cinderpan five Tranchers a Saw a Lanthorn a Link pan; Ironbox & 2 heaters a gun a Small Lookinglass an howerglass a pail a Larg hammer a fork a Small Brass Kittle a Copper Teakitle a pigsrack two sycthes & staves tacks fit forise two Steell traps an ass

RELIEF: The parish paid 13s. in total for burying Henry Holybrad in May 1770 and Widow Holybrad subsequently started to receive a pension of 4s. 6d. per week from the parish. Henry Holybrad was almost certainly Widow Holybrad's husband. Prior to this, they received occasional casual relief from the parish during periods of sickness and for rent and coal. For example, between Easter 1768 and Easter 1769 the parish paid the Holybrad's rent, contributed 7s. towards coal, and £1 7s. for 'HolleyBroad in Ilness' (NRO PD 629/1; NRO PD 629/50).

FURTHER INFORMATION: Widow Holybrad appears to have only recently been widowed when this inventory was taken. The burial of her presumed husband, Henry Holybrad, took place on 6 May 1770 (NRO PD 629/1; NRO PD 629/50).

DUBIOUS TERMS: Line 4: 'Eard' – unknown term. Lines 7–8: 'Link pan' – unknown term; possibly a latch pan. Line 9: 'pigsrack' – unknown term. Line 10: 'staves tacks fit forise' – unknown terms. Last two words possibly 'fit for use'.

EDITORIAL CHANGES: Line 10: Comma removed between 'an ass'.

Hopton pauper inventory

The pauper inventory from Hopton is found next to the disbursements of the overseer from 1731 in a volume of overseers' accounts (NRO PD 563/49). Hopton was part of Suffolk before 1974 and is included in this volume as historically it was located only around a mile from the Norfolk border. Today the settlement is known as Hopton-on-Sea.

70. Robert Pycrass, 1 May 1731

NRO PD 563/49 Hopton Overseers' Accounts, 1718–1842.

1 Day May 1731

RoBert Pycrass Goods

2 Bednats Bed and Bedstead and hangings and 1 pair of Sheets and 1 pair of Blanket<s> one TaBele and 2 Chairs and a Jointed Stoil a ~~Chist~~ a Chist a spinin Wheel and reel a frien pan and a pot a Worming pan

RELIEF: Robert Pycrass was in receipt of 2s. 6d. per week when this inventory was taken. Poor relief sources are inconsistent and lack detail before 1731 so it is difficult to establish when he became a pensioner. The parish also gave Robert Pycrass flags and paid his rent on an annual basis (NRO PD 563/49).

DAMAGE: Line 4: 'Blanket<s> – s crossed out or smudged; 'a ~~Chist~~' – crossed out or smudged.

Horningtoft pauper inventories

Three pauper inventories survive from Horningtoft in a set of overseers' accounts for the parish (NRO PD 642/35). The volume is in a poor condition and each of the pauper inventories is damaged in some way, such as with rips, faded text, and smudges. Two goods-taken and one bastardy-related inventory can also be found in the account book.

71. Widow Pratt, 2 December 1771

NRO PD 642/35 Horningtoft Overseers' Accounts, 1689–1775.

An Accou<nt> <of> the <Goods> <?> of The Widow Pratt this 2nd of December 1771

One Bed as it stand with Hangings
Two Boxe's
5 Chairs
1 Oak Table
1 Deal D°
Minging Trow
One Iron Pott
One Skillet
Tea Kittle
Two Plats Racks 2 Plates
Dresser
One Meat Pott
Half a Dozen Trenchers
Wooden Mortar & Pestle
One Earthen Cullender
Lanthorn
Warming Pan
Toast Pott
Real
Larg Bowl
Looking Glass
Stone Bottle
Wash Killer
Dresser and long stool

RELIEF: Widow Pratt was in receipt of 1s. 6d. per week when this inventory was taken. The overseers' accounts for the parish are patchy in the years before this inventory was made, meaning that it is unknown whether she had been a pensioner for a long period of time or whether she had started relief recently (NRO PD 642/35).

FURTHER INFORMATION: There is a Girl Pratt in the overseers' accounts who received 1s. per week during the early 1770s. This may have been Widow Pratt's daughter. There is also an inventory of Widow Pratt's belongings being sold by the parish around 10 October 1777 (goods-taken inventory) (NRO PD 642/35):

Sold of the Wido Pratts Goods	L	S	D
} Eliz Crow Box Table Tea Kittle &c	0	4	0
} Lanthorn Plates Bowl	0	1	3
Prose Smith Rack	0	1	0
Mr Raven Skewers Pott Toast	0	0	7
Goodman Stool	0	0	3
John Reeve 2 Chairs skillit Warming Pan Keeler Bottle & dishes }	0	4	0
James Pratt Teable	0	2	0
Candle Stick Earthen Dish	0	0	6
Box	0	0	3
Panns	0	0	2½
Pott Porrage	0	1	6
Minging Trough	0	1	0
Bed	1	6	0
Chairs	0	0	6
Stool	0	0	3
Rack Trenchers Mortar &c	0	1	0

DAMAGE: Line 1: Top line ripped and text faded.

72. Martha Ralph, 9 December 1772

NRO PD 642/35 Horningtoft Overseers' Accounts, 1689–1775.

A True Inventory of the Goods and Houselfurniture of Martha Ralph taken by Mr Thos Raven & J Moy Henry Reade & Wm Shekell officers of the Parish of Horning<toft> this 9th of December 1772

In the Kitchen

Two Tables One Minging Trough
Five Chairs Four Stools 1 Salt Box
a Cubberd Plate Rack with Four Plates
Bellows Tongs Fender 1 Hake, Two Eard=Tub
Close Basket and Pail Looking Glas<s>
an Hour Glass Candle Sticks Two
2 Canesters Gridiron <&> Lamp

Pantry
Frying Pan 2 Beer Tubbs Latch Pan &
Pail Iron Porish Pott and Tea Kittle
Earthing Potts 5,
Buttery
An Iron Pott Two Milk sives
On the Chamber Feather Beds
One Bed with Hangings D^{o} 1 without Hang
One Chest One Coffer 2 Chairs a Tub and Cive
Brass Bake Pan
In the yard
One Linen Horse 4 Long stools 2 ale stooles
Hogs Trough

RELIEF: The parish started to give Martha Ralph 5s. per week from Michaelmas 1772 and she was sometimes also given faggots (NRO PD 642/35).

FURTHER INFORMATION: Martha Ralph is frequently referred to as Widow Ralph by the overseers. Just before Martha Ralph started to receive poor relief, parish registers note the burial of William Ralph on 14 June 1772. This was probably her husband as the date of burial correlates closely to when Martha Ralph started to receive poor relief from the parish. The couple also probably had young children. Overseers' accounts reveal that Thomas Raven and J. Moy were the overseers of the poor for Horningtoft. It is probable that Henry Reade and William Shekell did not hold positions in the parish and were paid associates or members of the vestry (NRO PD 642/2; NRO PD 642/35).

DUBIOUS TERMS: Line 8: 'Eard' – unknown term. Line 14: 'Porish' – porridge.

DAMAGE: Line 3: 'Horning<toft>' – page torn. Line 9: 'Glas<s>' – page torn. Line 11: '<&> Lamp' – page torn

73. Frances Smith, 24 May 1773

NRO PD 642/35 Horningtoft Overseers' Accounts, 1689–1775.

A True Inventory of the Housellfurniture of Frances Smith Widow taken by Thos Raven & J Moy the 24th of May 1773

1.st One Bed as it stand with a Bolster 2 Pillows 2 Blankits Coverlin and Hangings, Two Tables 3 Chairs, 2 Stools, Pewter Rack, Porage Pott, Tea Kittle, Bellows, Tongs, 1 Hake, Warming Pan, 5 Earthing Potts, 6 Earthing Pans, Reel, Handle cup small Boler 1 trencher 2 Sileeling Dishes, Candle Stick, Iron Box with heaters Looking Glass, Spice Draws, Lyelatch, Pails, Wort Sive, 2 small Tubs, for Beer, a Chest Containing Bord & Bed linning &c a Deal Box with a Lock, 1 Chamber Pott, Close Basket

RELIEF: Frances Smith started to receive 1s. per week when this inventory was taken of her goods. The parish also gave her coal and paid her rent on occasion. For example, in October 1773 the parish paid £1 10s. for her rent (NRO PD 642/35).

FURTHER INFORMATION: The overseers' accounts and inventory indicate that Frances Smith was a widow and had a daughter living with her when the inventory was made. Frances Smith was buried on 6 December 1774 in Horningtoft and her daughter was subsequently given 1s. per week by the parish. Thomas Raven and J. Moy were overseers of the poor for Horningtoft (NRO PD 642/2; NRO PD 642/35).

DAMAGE: Line 10: 'Baskett' smudged.

Ingworth pauper inventories

The two pauper inventories from Ingworth were written by the incumbent overseers and can be found in the parish 'Town book' of 1768–1798 (NRO 521/26).

74. Dan Heagon, 25 December 1769

NRO PD 521/26 Ingworth Town Book, 1768–1798.

Decem^{r} 25 1769 Dan Heagon Guds ancerd By The Oversayers of Ingworth
A Bead as it stan with Coferlin 2 Blankets 2 Sheets 2 pilers: 3 Chars 2 Tabils a Wormin pan a Hi<?> <?>
witnes Ben Culley his mark BC
A Tea Kitell BC

RELIEF: Dan Heagon was in receipt of casual relief when this inventory was taken. The overseer wrote that Dan Heagon was 'several times in Need' in the late months of 1769, receiving £2 14s. 6d. in total (NRO PD 521/26).

FURTHER INFORMATION: There is also a 'Girl Hagon' mentioned in the poor law records from January 1770, who frequently received clothing from the parish. It is unknown if this was Dan Heagon's daughter. Ben Culley may have been hired by the parish to take this inventory, as the overseers of Ingworth at this point were John Crow and John Clark (NRO PD 521/26).

DUBIOUS TERMS: Line 1: 'ancerd' – possibly entered or answered.

DAMAGE: Line 3: 'Hi<?> <?>' – words smudged.

75. Tom Storey, 14 November 1774

NRO PD 521/26 Ingworth Town Book, 1768–1798.

By the overSers
November 14 1774 taken acount of Tom Storey Things
One Bed two Cowvering One Blankett 1 Bolster 1 Piller, Bedstead & hanglings, a Round Table half 6 fiddle Back Char Cofer & great Char, Warning pan two porrage pots A frying pan A Brass Boller a Brass Kittle A tee Kittle tongs & Ballis a Reel three Beear tubs fender & Speet a larg ioron Crow, & Bouter Dish two dgiron, & Catten Rod, two Candle Siks a Maid & Brackets a Squear Table a Skillet two ale stols

X X

witness To<m> Goos TG Jeremy Mash J M

X

RELIEF: Tom Storey was in receipt of casual relief when this inventory was taken, such as clothing for his son and daughter and fuel. He also sometimes received regular relief for short periods of time. For example, around February 1774 Tom Storey was given 3s. per week for ten weeks and on 14 June 1774 the parish paid out 5s. for four weeks relief and for 'Fetching his Firing' (NRO PD 521/26).

FURTHER INFORMATION: Parish records indicate that Tom Storey had at least one son and daughter. Their names may have been Phoebe and Charles. The overseers of Ingworth were John Clarke and William Randall. It is unknown who 'To<m> Goos' and Jeremy Mash were (NRO PD 521/26).

DUBIOUS TERMS: Line 6: 'Bouter' – possibly pewter. Line 7: 'dgiron' – gridiron; 'Catten' – possibly curtain.

DAMAGE: Line 10: 'To<m>' – pen smudge.

Letton pauper inventories

The overseers' accounts of Letton parish cover 1744–1791 and contain the three pauper inventories that survive for the settlement. Also included in the volume are two goods-given inventories and one inventory relating to arrears of rent (NRO MC 76/50, 534X10).

76. Widow Wix [Wise], 20 September 1759

NRO MC 76/50, 534X10 Letton Overseers' Accounts, 1744–1791.

September the 20: 1759 Toock an account of the Widow wix is Things
1 Bed 1 pair of Draws 1 Cubbard 2 Tables an Iron Pott Worming pan 7 Chairs 1 Jointed Stool Firepan & Tongs 1 Gril Iron 1 Spit 1 pair of Bellows 1 Brass Kittle 1 Skillet 1 vessull hak 1 Reele 1 Chest 1 frying pan 2 Iron Candle Sticks

RELIEF: Widow Wix was in receipt of a pension of 1s. 6d. per week when this inventory was made and was also given firewood from the parish on occasion. She probably first became a pensioner around Easter 1759 (NRO MC 76/50, 534X10).

FURTHER INFORMATION: It is possible that Widow Wix was the widow of the pauper Thomas Wix senior who died around September 1759. Thomas Wix junior and William Wix also appear in the overseers' accounts, but it is unknown whether they were any relation of Widow Wix (NRO MC 76/50, 534X10; NRO PD 359/3).

77. Widow Bannett, 1762 (day and month unknown)

NRO MC 76/50, 534X10 Letton Overseers' Accounts, 1744–1791.

1762 Took Account of the Widow Bannetts Things
one Bed 2 Tables 4 Chairs one Chest one Par of Bellows Fire pan & Tongs one ~~Ros~~ Gril Iron one Hake a Iron Bott Frying Pan one Pail 2 Vessells one Reele 3 Ston Bottls 5 Trenchers a Wash Stowl 2 Killers 2 Skilletts

RELIEF: Widow Bannett was in receipt of 2s. 6d. from Michaelmas 1762. The parish also paid out 18s. for her rent between Easter and Michaelmas 1762 (NRO MC 76/50, 534X10).

FURTHER INFORMATION: The precise date of the inventory is unknown; however, it is probably datable to around Michaelmas 1762 as Widow Bannett started to receive relief from the parish around then. The parish registers record the burial of William Bannett on 12 August 1762. This may have been Widow Bannett's husband as it closely correlates to when Widow Bannett started to receive relief (NRO MC 76/50, 534X10; NRO PD 359/3).

78. Widow Elvey, 14 April 1769

NRO MC 76/50, 534X10 Letton Overseers' Accounts, 1744–1791.

April 14: 1769 Took account of Widow Elveys Things

Kitchin

One Ovel Table one round Table one Square Do one neast of Draws 5 Chairs firepan & Tongs Hake & Grill Iron Tea Kittle spice Draws Bellows Warming Pan Bake Pan 2 Skilletts

Bed Rume

2 Beds as thay Stands Kitchin Chamber 2 mattocks & Flag Spad 2 Hatchads one peel & matt 2 Hooks & 2 D<e>rlers

Scullery

3 Vessells & one Chest 2 Dog Irons frying pan one Iron Pott

RELIEF: Widow Elvey started to receive 3s. per week when this inventory was made. The parish also paid her rent every year and gave her money and firewood on occasion (NRO MC 76/50, 534X10).

FURTHER INFORMATION: Widow Elvey may have been living with somebody else soon after this inventory was made, as the overseers' accounts note the payment of rent for 'Wixes & the Wid Elveys Rent' on several occasions. It is unknown if this is Widow Wix above **(76)** or somebody else. Widow Elvey was probably not living in Letton when this inventory was taken, as the accounts note the removal of her from another unknown parish sometime between Easter 1769 and Easter 1770 (NRO MC 76/50, 534X10).

DUBIOUS TERMS: Line 8: 'D<e>rlers' – unknown term.

Loddon pauper inventory

Only one inventory survives for Loddon, in the form of a note in a volume of overseers' accounts, 1720–1752 (NRO PD 595/22).

79. Alexander Wade, 26 November 1751

NRO PD 595/22 Loddon Overseers' Accounts, 1720–1752.

An Inventory of Allexan^{dr} Wades Goods
Nov 26 A Bed & Bedstead
1751 A Cupboard
a Warming Pan
4 Chairs & a frying Pan a Hock
2 Tables fyar Pan Tongs Bellows
a Sm^{l} Killer tee Cup a Kettle & Looking Glass
a Trencher Lanthorn & Morter
a Bocks & a Stool and 2 Brushes
a CandlesBocks 4 Iron Rods
a Quart Pot A Candle Stick and W^{d} Pint
3 P^{r}. Pincers 7 Awls 3 Knives
Long Sticks & a Bocks with a Hammer
a Working Seat & a Skreen

RELIEF: Alexander Wade started to receive poor relief from the parish on 10 November 1751. He is described as 'at need' each time he is noted in the overseers' accounts and received 1s. 6d. every week. The parish also paid out 10s. towards his rent on 26 November 1751 (NRO PD 595/22).

FURTHER INFORMATION: Alexander Wade was probably living on his own as a bachelor or widower when this inventory was made (NRO PD 595/22).

DUBIOUS TERMS: Line 11: 'W^{d} Pint' – unknown term. Perhaps a wooden drinking vessel.

Martham pauper inventories

The pauper inventories from Martham come from a set of overseers' accounts dated 1744 to 1785 (NRO PD 710/68). They are the same inventories used in Barbara Cornford's study on the possessions of the poor (Barbara Cornford, 'Inventories of the Poor', *Norfolk Archaeology*, 35 (1970–1973), pp. 118–125); however, two of the inventories that Cornford used have been omitted here. This is because one records the possessions of somebody who did not receive poor relief from authorities, and the other lists the possessions of a parishioner who had abandoned his family and left them chargeable to the parish. All the inventories are found at the back of the volume and were written by the churchwardens and overseers of the parish.

80. Elizabeth Bland (the younger), 14 October 1758

NRO PD 710/68 Martham Overseers' Accounts, 1744–1785.

Ann Account of the Goods & Chattles of Eliz^{a}. Bland the Younger taken this 14.th Day of Octo^{b} 1758 by the Church Warden and Overseer of Martham as Under

To a Bed as it Stand with Curtains Blue
with one Coverlid a Blanket & 2 pair of Sheets
To one Oak Table 2 Small ones
To Six Segging Bottom Chairs
To 1 Leather Bottom D^{o}. one Cupboard
To one Chest of Draws one Reel
To one Copper tea Kettle tea pot & Dishes
To one pair of Small Brass Scales & beam
two brass half pound Weights & 1:2 OZ D^{o}.
One OZ. half ounce & ¼ Brass D^{o}.
1 two pound & 2 Single pounds 1 Lead D^{o}.
one Speet. one Hake 1 Hank. one Iron Colerange
fire pan tongs poker Bellows & fore Iron
one toast Iron. three Iron Candlesticks
one Small Hammer 1 Hour Glass one Double levil Sail
one pewter half pint & one half qu D^{o}.
one frying pan one Iron pot & one
Saucepan & Skillet both brass one Iron Frame
a pair of Spice Draws & one Small box two Table Cloths

one buffet Stool three Stone bottles & Nine Glass D^{o}.
three Earthen pots one D^{o}. Gotch & other Earthen ware
half peck & qu Measures one hand Brush
two Bibles & one prayer book two Small Washing Killers

RELIEF: There are two people called Elizabeth Bland (the younger and elder) living in Martham at this time **(84)**. As a result, it is not possible to precisely determine how Elizabeth Bland the younger was relieved. Nonetheless, overseers' accounts show that both parishioners received 1s. per week when their goods were inventoried and that they had been receiving this amount of money for a number of years. They were also both given coal and rent payments from the parish (NRO PD 710/68).

FURTHER INFORMATION: The overseers often distinguish between the two Elizabeth Blands by calling them Widow Bland and Mrs Bland, but it is unknown which one is which. Both were, however, in all likelihood widowed. The names of the overseer and churchwarden are not noted under the inventory as the author states. Nonetheless, poor law records show that William Rieve and William Sutfield were overseers of the poor in October 1758, but the name(s) of the churchwarden(s) are unknown (NRO PD 710/68).

DUBIOUS TERMS: Line 18: 'Double levil Sail' – unknown term.

81. Mary Crosshold, 14 October 1758

NRO PD 710/68 Martham Overseers' Accounts, 1744–1785.

Ann Account of Mary Crossholds Goods taken at the Same Time [as Elizabeth Bland the younger's inventory]

To a Green bed with Curtains one Coverlid
one Blankit ~~two~~ one Sheet~~s~~ & three Old Chairs
One Iron pot a pair of tongs one Small deal Table
One Trunk One Box one Frying pan
one pair of Bellows a Washing Killer
Iron Colerange & poker one hand Brush
2 Shiffts, 2 old Gounds, 1 yillow
Quilted Pettey Coat 2 under
Petty Coats a 2 old Quilted Petty Coats
a Blue Mentle 2 Cotten aprons
1 Reele 3 Capps 2 Blue<?> Hand^{s}.
3 Capps more & Hood 2 W^{t} Hand <?>
1 Bket D^{o} Double <?>ffeett 2 Capps
more a p^{r} of Shoes Baskett
& Iron <Pattery>
2 Sausers. 2 pans & old Capp Red Gotch

RELIEF: Mary Crosshold was in receipt of 9d. per week when this inventory was taken. She had received a pension from the parish since around Michaelmas 1756 and was also given coal and flags from the parish at various times (NRO PD 710/68).

FURTHER INFORMATION: Lines 1–8 are written in a different hand to lines 9–17. Line 18 is written vertically on the left-hand side of the original. Mary Crosshold is also referred to as Mary Crosswell in poor law records. After Mary Crosshold's death between Michaelmas 1759 and Easter 1760, the parish sold some of her goods. Her bed, for example, was sold for £1 1s. Mary Crosshold was not referred to as a widow by the overseers, so may have been a single woman. The overseers' accounts note the removal of Mary Crosshold from an unknown parish between Michaelmas 1758 and Easter 1759 (costing 1s.), suggesting that she was not living in Martham when this inventory was made. Mary Crosshold died sometime between Michaelmas 1759 and Easter 1760 and was buried at the ratepayers' expense (NRO PD 710/68).

DAMAGE: Parts of lines 13–17 are illegible as the ink is smudged.

82. Mary Wright, 14 October 1758

NRO PD 710/68 Martham Overseers' Accounts, 1744–1785.

Ann Account of the Goods of Mary Wright Wid Taken by the Church Warden & Overseer of Martham as Under this 14.th of Octo^{B}. 1758

To one Bed as it Stand with one Coverlid
two Blankets & two Sheets
to a pair of Draws one table one Chest
three old Chairs one Reel one Iron pot
one pair of tongs & bellows
one Oak Chest & Killer a pail
one Iron Candlestick

RELIEF: Mary Wright was in receipt of 1s. per week when this inventory was made. She had received this for a number of years and was also given rent payments, additional money during times of sickness, coal, and flags by the parish. Around July 1763 Mary Wright was buried by the parish at a total cost of 17s. (NRO PD 710/68).

FURTHER INFORMATION: Mary Wright was widowed and often referred to as Widow Wright in poor relief sources. The goods of Mary Wright raised 19s. 1d. when they were sold by the parish at her death in 1763. William Rieve and William Sutfield were overseers of the poor in October 1758, but the name(s) of the churchwarden(s) are unknown (NRO PD 710/68).

83. Widow Conyard, 14 October 1758

NRO PD 710/68 Martham Overseers' Accounts, 1744–1785.

Att the Same Time [as Mary Wright's inventory] Taken An Account of the Widow Conyards Goods as Under
To one Bed & beding & it Stand
four Old Chairs one Iron pot one pail
two Stone bottles <o>ne deal Table
one Wooden bowl & handcup
one Deal & one Oak Dressers
one Speet one pair of tongs & bellows
one pail one Reel & one Iron Candlestick

RELIEF: Widow Conyard was in receipt of 1s. 6d. per week when this inventory was made. She had received a pension from Martham parish since Easter 1750 and was also regularly given rent payments, coal, and flags. Widow Conyard died between Michaelmas 1759 and Easter 1760 and the parish paid 10s. towards her funeral (NRO PD 710/68).

FURTHER INFORMATION: Widow Conyard had one or more adult children who had left home by the time that this inventory was taken. Between Easter 1752 and Easter 1753, for example, overseers' accounts for the parish note the payment of 1s. 3d. 'To Mrs. Cobb for her mother Conyard'. After Widow Conyard died some of her goods were sold by the parish for an unrecorded sum (NRO PD 710/68).

DAMAGE: Line 5: Ink stain between 'bottles' and '<o>ne'.

84. Elizabeth Bland (the elder), 14 October 1758

NRO PD 710/68 Martham Overseers' Accounts, 1744–1785.

Att the Same Time [as Mary Wright's inventory] Taken ths Account of Eliz^{a}. Blands the Elder as Under
One bed & bedding as it Stand
one pair of Draws one Oak Chest
one large tub one deal table one frying pan
one Iron pot one Washing Killer
one Hake Iron. a pair of tongs one Speet
one Iron Candlestick one flag Spade
two Wooden Dishes one brass skimer
one Reel & ~~two~~ Three Chairs

RELIEF: There are two people called Elizabeth Bland (the younger and elder) living in Martham at this time **(80)**. As a result, it is not possible to precisely determine how Elizabeth Bland the younger was relieved. Nonetheless, overseers' accounts show that both parishioners received 1s. per week when their goods were inventoried and that they had been receiving this amount of money for a number of years. They were also both given coal and rent payments from the parish (NRO PD 710/68).

FURTHER INFORMATION: The overseers often distinguish between the two Elizabeth Blands by calling them Widow Bland and Mrs Bland, but it is unknown which one is which. Both were, however, in all likelihood widowed (NRO PD 710/68).

85. Priscilla/Widow Myhill, 18 December 1764

NRO PD 710/68 Martham Overseers' Accounts, 1744–1785.

Ann Account of the Goods & Effects of the Wid. Myhill Taken by the Church Wardens & Overseer of the Parish of Martham this 18.th Day of December 1764

one Cupboard Bed a<s> tit Stand with Coverlid Blankit
and two Sheets a Chest of Drawers late Mary Cobb
1 Chest of Draws Wid. Myhill<s>
1 Iron Stove tongs & poker & Dust pan 1 pair bellows
1 Small trunk 1 Oak Standard 1 Copper t<e>a kittle
1 Warming pan 1 Washing Killer 1. Water pail
2 tea pots 4 Stone Cups & Saucers 1 Oak Table
1 Oak Chair & 3 D^{o} Seg Bottoms
2 yellow earth Dishes & 2 plates

RELIEF: Widow Myhill was in receipt of 1s. per week when this inventory was taken. She had received casual relief from the parish, including rent payments, coal, and flags since Easter 1755, and first became a pensioner in Easter 1758 (NRO PD 710/68).

FURTHER INFORMATION: Overseers' accounts reveal that Widow Myhill's forename was Priscilla. Edward Myhill was given £1 1s. in rent payments every year from Easter 1748 to Easter 1755. This was probably Widow Myhill's husband as the date when Edward disappears from the overseers' accounts and presumably died correlates closely to when Widow Myhill started to receive poor relief from the parish. Boy, Susan, and Mary Myhill are mentioned in the overseers' accounts occasionally, but it is unknown whether they were Widow Myhill's children. Records show that Widow Myhill was buried on 27 March 1768 and that her children paid for the funeral. In exchange for this, the parish did not take her goods and let the children keep them. William Rieve and William Sutfield were overseers of the poor in October 1758, but the name(s) of the churchwarden(s) are not known (NRO PD 710/68).

CIRCUMTEXT: Below the inventory, the following was written: 'March 28. 1768. Wid Myhill was Buried at the Expence of her Children and took ye abovementioned Goods for ye Same'.

DAMAGE: Line 4: 'a<s>' smudged. Line 6: 'Myhill<s>' smudged. Line 8: 't<e>a' smudged.

86. John Brunson, 18 December 1764

NRO PD 710/68 Martham Overseers' Accounts, 1744–1785.

An Account of th<e> G<oods> and Effects of Jn°. Brun<s>on Taken by the Church Wardens & Overseer of the Parish of Martham this 18th of December 1764

1 Bed & Bedstead as it Stand with Curtains Blue
a Coverlid 2 Blankits 4 Sheets 1 Bowlster
2 Chest of Drawers 2 White Tables & 1 Small one
1 Oak Cupboard Six pewter plates
2 Dishes blue & White with 6 D°. plates
2 Iron pots & pot hooks a frying pan a Warming pan
a fire Range poker tongs & fire pan a Grid Iron
& toasting Iron 1 Iron Hake & 1 hank two Speets
1 Smoothing Iron & heaters 3 Iron Candlesticks
2 Brackets 1 Small looking Glass 5 Black Chairs with
Segg Bottons & 4 Other 1 Water pail 1 peek Measure
& Long Brush 1 Copper Tea kittle 2 beer tubs
1 tin Coffee pot 6 Cups Stone & Saucers 1 tea pot
& 1 Bason red
Upon the Chamber 1 bed & bedstead 1 Coverlid
& 5 Old Chairs 1 Table & Old deal box

RELIEF: John Brunson was in receipt of 1s. per week when this inventory was made. He had been given flags, furze, and coal by the parish since Easter 1761 and had been a pensioner since Easter 1762 (NRO PD 710/68).

FURTHER INFORMATION: John Brunson was married and was approximately 78 years old when this inventory was taken. He died around 1772–1773 at the age of 89. Boy Brunson and Mary Brunson also appear in the accounts, but it is not known if they were any relation to John Brunson. Between Easter 1744 and Easter 1756, John Brunson was a small ratepayer and paid between 1s. 6d. and 3s. 6d. every 12 months to the parish. William Read was overseer of the poor in December 1764, but the name(s) of the churchwarden(s) are unknown (NRO PD 710/68; Cornford, 'Inventories of the Poor', p. 118).

DAMAGE: Line 1: Ink smudges on 'th<e>', 'G<oods>', and 'Brun<s>on'.

87. Mary/Widow Piercon, 18 December 1764

NRO PD 710/68 Martham Overseers' Accounts, 1744–1785.

Ann Account of the Goods and Effects of the Wid. Piercon Taken by the Churchwardens & Overseer of the Parish of Martham this 18th. day of December 1764

In the Low Room one Blue Bed as it Stand with Curtains
with Coverlid two Blankits three Sheets Bowlster & pillow bears
a Chest of Drawers and Oaken box
two four footed Tables
2 Leather Chairs & 4 Other Chairs & one Great Chair
1 fire Range tongs & poker a pair of Bellows
a toasting Iron
a Dresser & one Oval Table
Six earthen Blue & white Plates 1 yellow earthen dish
1 Water pail 1 Iron pot & Iron Cover & pot hooks
1 Iron hake & a hank. 1 Smoothing Iron & heater
1 Reel. 1 Brass Tea kittle 1 Long helved Brush
2 Iron Candlesticks a Beam & Scales Weights a
2 pound & pound Lead 1 Washing killer

RELIEF: Widow Piercon was in receipt of 1s. 3d. per week when this inventory was made. She started to receive a pension from Michaelmas 1764 after the death of her husband John and was also given rent payments from the parish. John Piercon had received regular relief from the parish since around June/July 1760 (1s. to 1s. 6d. per week) and was also provided with flags and coal (NRO PD 710/68).

FURTHER INFORMATION: Poor law records for the parish reveal that Widow Piercon's forename was Mary and indicate that Widow Piercon died sometime between Easter and Michaelmas 1766. William Read was overseer of the poor in December 1764, but the name(s) of the churchwarden(s) are unknown (NRO PD 710/68).

DUBIOUS TERMS: Line 15: 'helved' – handled.

88. Robert Howell (the elder), 18 December 1764

NRO PD 710/68 Martham Overseers' Accounts, 1744–1785.

Ann Account of Robt. Howell the Elder taken at the Same time as above [Widow Piercon's inventory] ye 18.th of December 1764
a Blue Bed & Bedstead with Coverlid 2 Blankits & 3 Sheets
a Bolster & 2 pillows & 1 deal table on the Chamber
In the Kitchen 2 deal tables & 1 Small one on the Stool
Six Ashen Chairs & 3 Peggin Chairs
1 Oak Chest 1 Leather Trunk 5 earthen plates & 1 dish
a Warming pan. firepan. tongs & bellows 1 Hake Iron
& 2 Hanks 4 Iron Scu<e>rs. 1 Iron pot & Iron Led & pot hooks
1 Water pail a Washing killer 1 Meal Chest
3 Small beer tubs 6 Glass Bottles

RELIEF: Robert Howell started to receive 1s. 6d. per week in the weeks after Michaelmas 1764. This was soon increased to 2s. per week and he was also occasionally given flags from the parish (NRO PD 710/68).

FURTHER INFORMATION: Robert Howell was married. Between the 1740s and 1770s, somebody called Robert Howell is listed as a small ratepayer, paying between 1s. 8d. to 4s. 8d. every 6–12 months. The accounts, however, do not mention whether this is Robert Howell junior or senior. William Howell and his wife are also mentioned in poor law records, but it is unknown whether they were any relation of Robert Howell. William Read was overseer of the poor in December 1764, but the name(s) of the churchwarden(s) are not known (NRO PD 710/68).

DUBIOUS TERMS: Line 9: 'Scu<e>rs' – Unknown term. Possibly scissors or skewers.

89. Edward Knights, 16 March 1768

NRO PD 710/68 Martham Overseers' Accounts, 1744–1785.

March y[e] 16; 1768
an a Count of Edw[d] Knights Goods and Caettels: Takeing By the Churchwardens and Overseers of the Pore of The said Parish of Martham:

To one Co<w>e To 2 Beds and Bed close Bedstandes and other Emplements Their Belongeing too; one Chist of Drawers and five Chaiers: Porrige pot and hake fier-pan and Tongs; Small Kittle Pail and Table Worming pan and bellowers and one Coofer and 2 Stooles ....

In the Middle Room — To one Pair of Spice Drawes one Churn 2 Butter farkins and five Berstubs ale stoole and one Marsh tub one Swilltub 2 Killers and wheel Burrow and 3 Trunchers one Quarter of a Peck one Box and flower Kid ....

In the Back Room — one Old Coofer and Childs Chaier ....

One the Chamber — One Brass Brooing Kittle one Flower tub one Spade 2 hatchets and Mattock one Garden Rake 3 Sythes and Flagg spade one Tur<f> Spade and fork and Short Lether ....

To one Boat and Quant an one Haystack

RELIEF: Edward Knights was in receipt of occasional casual relief when this inventory was made. For example, between Michaelmas 1767 and Easter 1768, Edward Knights was given '2 Bushels of Wheat In Illness' worth 11s.; between Easter and Michaelmas 1768 he was provided with flags, turf, and furze; and between Michaelmas 1771 and Easter 1772 he was paid 3s. because he had 'no Work' (NRO PD 710/68).

FURTHER INFORMATION: Edward Knights was married and probably had children living with him. Boy Knights is occasionally mentioned in overseers' accounts for the parish and this may have been his son. For instance, between Easter and Michaelmas 1768, the parish allowed Francis Proctor £1 'w^n took the Boy Knights'. Edward Knights was previously a ratepayer between Michaelmas 1762 and Easter 1764, paying 3s. 9d. to 4s. 6d. to the parish every six months. Edward Knights died sometime between Easter and Michaelmas 1773. The parish paid 13s. towards his funeral and subsequently gave his wife 2s. 6d. per week. Thomas Francis was one of the overseers of the poor in March 1768, but the name(s) of the churchwarden(s) are unknown (NRO PD 710/68).

DUBIOUS TERMS: Line 18: 'Lether' – possibly ladder.

DAMAGE: Line 17: 'Tur<f>' – smudged making the word partially illegible.

90. Elizabeth/Widow Smith, 16 December 1771

NRO PD 710/68 Martham Overseers' Accounts, 1744–1785.

Ann Acount of ye Goods and Effects of Robt Smiths Wid^o Taken by ye Church Wardens & Overseer of ye Parish of martham ye 16 Day of December 1771 As Under

one Bed as it Stands with Green hangins a Pair of Blanketts & a Pair of Sheets & a Green Rugg & a Bouster & one Pillow & one Pillow Case one Goun 3 Quilted Pettey Coats & one Skirt & a Under Coat & a Hooded Cloak & 3 Shifts & 2 Black hatts 4 Chairs & a Dubil lafeed Table a 4 footed Table & a Jointed stool & a Chest of Draws & a Looking Glass 7 Earthen Plates a Pudding Pan & 2 Yellow dishes 3 Red Pans & 4 Glass Bottes & 2 Stone Bottles a Tea Kettle and a half Peck pot & a Pail a Tea Kettle 3 Tea Pots 4 Cups & 3 Saursers a Small Box & 2 Tea Cannesters a Coffe mug & a vinnegar Bottle 2 Pint pots & a half Pint a Pair of Bellows & a Poker & 2 Potirons a Ironing Box & 2 heets a for Iron & 2 Sauspans a Pair of Shoes & Clogs & a Pair of Iron Pattens 5 Caps & 2 White Aprons 3 Colourd Hankerchiefs & a Pair of Black Gloves 2 more Blue & White hankerchiefs & 2 Colourd Aprons one Bord Cloth & one Napkin one Candle stick a Long hake & one Speet one Shovel one Long Brush & one Baskett & 2 Spoons & a Reel

RELIEF: Widow Smith was in receipt of 1s. 9d. per week when this inventory was taken. She had received a pension from the parish for a number of years prior to having her goods inventoried and was provided with clothing, rent payments, and flags. Prior to this, her husband Robert received a pension from the parish (2s. per week) and was given additional money during times of sickness, flags, and coal before his death in c.1762 (NRO PD 710/68).

FURTHER INFORMATION: Overseers' accounts for the parish show that Widow Smith's forename was Elizabeth. She died between Michaelmas 1771 and Easter 1772 and her goods were subsequently cleaned and raised £1 15s. when they were sold by poor law authorities. In exchange the parish paid 13s. towards her funeral. Widow Smith's husband used to be a small ratepayer between the 1740s and Easter 1761, contributing between 1s. 1½d. to 7s. every 6–12 months. He first received relief around November 1761 and appears to have died between Easter and Michaelmas 1762. John Carrier was one of the overseers of the poor in December 1771, but the name(s) of the churchwarden(s) are unknown (NRO PD 710/68).

91. Roger Riches, 14 February 1772

NRO PD 710/68 Martham Overseers' Accounts, 1744–1785.

Ann Acount of ye Goods & Efects of Roger Riches Taken by ye Church Wardens & Overseer of ye Parrish of martham ye 14th Day of Feb. 1772 as under

One Bed with Green Hangins one Pair of Sheets and a Coverling an old Standing Chest Cubord one Large Chest of oak 2 fower footed Tables and 5 Chairs a Jointed stool with a Runner a worming Pan & a Looking Glass 4 Tea Pots & 2 Cups & Sausers & an Ironing Box & a Pair of heets one Speet & a Lafe of a Table for a Skreen 8 Plates & 2 White Basons one Red dish 4 Glass Bottles and a 3 Pint stone Bottle & a Blew and White gotch 3 Beer Tubs 3 Killers one Iron Pot one Pail & a hand Cup a Large Pigs stool & a Small Pigs Stool one Spade one mattock and one hook a Flouer tub a Pudding Cup & a Butter half Firkin one Long brush one Plate Rack Scyth & Staff & Sickell a Fiergrate and a Pair of Tongs and one Skeep; one ye Chamber a Bedstead & a Pair of Sheets & Civerlin

RELIEF: Roger Riches was in receipt of casual relief when this inventory was made. He started to receive this from 1769 and was provided with coal and furze from the parish. From Michaelmas 1771, he and his wife were regularly given money due to sickness and the parish also paid 14s. 4d. for 'Cloathing Roger Richeses Boy' (NRO PD 710/68).

FURTHER INFORMATION: Roger Riches was married and had at least one child (a son) when this inventory was made. Sarah Riches frequently appears in the overseers' accounts, but it is not known whether Roger Riches was related to her. Roger Riches was a small ratepayer between Easter 1753 and Easter 1754, paying 9d. for half a year of rates. John Carrier was one of the overseers of the poor in March 1772, but the name(s) of the churchwarden(s) are unknown (NRO PD 710/68).

Great Moulton with Little Moulton pauper inventories

One of the inventories in this collection was written on a loose sheet of paper (NRO PD 489/51); the other twenty-nine inventories were noted in three sets of overseers' accounts which cover 1695–1764. They were written in the accounts at various intervals and may have been derived from other copies. Also included in the volumes are debt-related, goods-taken, and goods-given inventories, as well as a handful of other inventories which could not be categorised (NRO PD 489/29–31).

92. Sara Hubert, 3 July 1693

NRO PD 489/29 Great Moulton with Little Moulton Overseers' Accounts, 1695–1738.

July ye 3. 1693 An Inventory then made and taken of all the Goods and Chattells of Sara Hubert Collectioner now dwelling with John Browne in the Town of Moulton in Norf by us the Officers and other Inhabitants of y^{e} said Town whose Names are here-underwritten

	li s
Imp^{r}imis A Bedstead and feather Bed Matt and Cord one Bolster two feather Pillows one Cover cloth .... }	01 – 05 – 00
It one Kettle one Skillett one Chest one Box and a smal Table	00 = 10 = 00

Ben wisman	Church-warden
Solomon Sharpe	Overseer
John y^{e} X Mark of Sheppard	Constable
Ri. Wilson	Rector
Nath Howard	
Tho: Brighting	

RELIEF: Sara Hubert was in receipt of 1s. 6d. per week when this inventory was made. She was blind and living with John Brown who was paid 6d. per week to look after her. She had been a pensioner for at least a year before this inventory was taken, and also received rent payments, firewood, clothing, and linen from the parish (NRO PD 489/29). The inventory also notes that Sara Hubert was a 'Collectioner'.

FURTHER INFORMATION: Sara Hubert was probably a spinster since she was referred to by her Christian name and not as 'Widow'. The overseers' accounts for the parish indicate that she died around Easter 1700 and that her goods were added to the town stock and sold by the parish. It is probable that Nathaniel Howard and Thomas Brighting were vestrymen and not parish officers (NRO PD 489/29).

93. Margaret Smith, 3 July 1693

NRO PD 489/29 Great Moulton with Little Moulton Overseers' Accounts, 1695–1738.

July ye 3.^{d} 1693 An Inventory then made and taken of all the Goods and Chattells of Marg<aret> Smith Widow and Collectioner in the Town of Moulton in Norf by us the Officers ~~of~~ and other Inhabitants of the said Town whose names are here underwritten.

Imp^{r}imis A Bedstead and feather-bed Matt and Cord two feather Bolsters & one straw bolster one Cover-cloth & one Blankett and Curtains	li s <?> 01 <?> <?>
It. one Kettle one Skillett and a table Cupboard and one armed Chair	00 12 <?>

In witness whereof we have hereunto set our hands

Ben wisiman	Church-warden
Solomon Sharpe	Overseer
ye X Mark of John Sheppard	Constable
Ri. Wilson	Rect^{r}
Nath: Howard	
Tho: Brighting	

RELIEF: Margaret Smith was in receipt of 1s. per week when this inventory was made and was first given regular relief by the parish in early 1693. She was also provided with faggots, firewood, and occasional cash payments from the parish (NRO PD 489/29). The inventory also notes that Margaret Smith was a 'Collectioner'.

FURTHER INFORMATION: Records for the parish show that Margaret Smith was widowed. It is probable that Nathaniel Howard and Thomas Brighting were vestrymen and not parish officers (NRO PD 489/29).

DAMAGE: Right side of page partially cut off by volume binding, making parts illegible. Line 9: 'Cupboard' partially smudged.

94. Widow Tackling, 24 July 1699

NRO PD 489/29 Great Moulton with Little Moulton Overseers' Accounts, 1695–1738.

An Count of the Goods of the wido Tackling taken by ye Church warding oversers for ye pore for the towne of moulton in ye moth of Jyly the 24 <u>1699</u>

on Beed and Bedstead on bouler and Coverleit
on porege pot on Cheist on Cheyer
on Skelit <child> polew on Greate doore

RELIEF: Widow Tackling was in receipt of around 1s. 4d. per week when this inventory was made. She had received a pension from the parish for several years and was also given firewood and clothing. From Easter 1699, she appears to have become increasingly unwell and several different people were paid by the parish to look after her (NRO PD 489/29).

FURTHER INFORMATION: Between Easter 1699 and Easter 1700, Widow Tackling was buried at the expense of the parish, at a cost of 14s. 6d. in total. Her goods were then taken and sold for £1. The overseers of Moulton in June 1699 were Benjamin Wiseman and Charles Beak. The churchwardens were Thomas Marjerum and Benjamin Wiseman (NRO PD 489/29).

DAMAGE: Smudges on line 1 where 'Goods of the' is written.

95. Henry and Susan Barret, 7 January 1701/2

NRO PD 489/29 Great Moulton with Little Moulton Overseers' Accounts, 1695–1738.

January ye 7: 1701

An Inventory then made And taken of all ye Goods And Chattels of Henry Barret And Susen his wife in ye Towne of Moulton Collectionors Norfolke by us ye officers And others Inhabitents ye s^{d} Towne of Moulton ~~in Norfolk~~ whose Names are hereunder written

	l s d
Imp: in ye bed Chamber 3 feather beds. 2 bedsteads. 3 blanckets 2 knavs 2 Coverlets & 2 bedsteads	04 – 10 – 00
in ye Same Room. one C Chest	00 – 10 – 00
one Joynt Stoole & 1 Chayer: 2 boxes 2 bere vessels at	00 – 10 – 00
in ye Chamber it 3 Tubbs at	00 – 05 – 00
one bedstead at 5^{s}	00 – 05 – 00
In ye hall: 4 Chayers	00 – 04 – 00
one Keepe	00 – 04 – 00
one Table one Joynt Stoole and other Lumber at	00 – 05 – 00
More in ye Chamber it 2 brass Kittles – 1 Iron pott	00 – 18 – 00

This Inventorye of thees Goods was taken by us

Bartholomew Buxton
And John Gilbert

RELIEF: The parish paid half a year's rent for the Barrets, totalling 12s., around when this inventory was made. From Easter 1702, Henry Barret received 1s. per week for six weeks and from 18 May 1702 this increased to 1s. 6d. a week. The parish continued to pay Henry Barret's rent, paid to repair his shoes, and gave him firewood. The Barrets appear to have been living outside Moulton when this inventory was taken, as the overseers' accounts note the removal of Henry Barret from an unknown parish sometime between Easter and Michaelmas 1702 (NRO PD 489/29). The inventory also notes that Henry and Susan Barret were 'Collectionors'.

FURTHER INFORMATION: The total value of goods in the inventory is £7 11s. 0d. Bartholomew Buxton was an overseer of the poor, but it is unknown who John Gilbert was (NRO PD 489/29).

96. Josh Miller, 18 October 1710

NRO PD 489/29 Great Moulton with Little Moulton Overseers' Accounts, 1695–1738.

An Account of ye Goodes of Josh Miller taken by ye church wardens and overseers of ye towne of moulton ye 18th Day of october Anno Domo <u>1710</u>

Imp one Bed and Bedsted matt and corrd one Grate cubard one chest one Deske 2 Littell Tabels 4 ould chayers 2 coverd Stoules 2 ould Stoules one iorne pott 1 skillett 1 warmeing pan 1 fryng pan 4 Sheets 1 coverlett 2 Blanckets one Hake and 1 hanke 1 fire Shovell 1 payr of tongs 1 payr of Andiorns and other litt<le> nescerry Goods 1 Kettell and tub

RELIEF: Josh Miller was in receipt of 1s. or 1s. 6d. per week when this inventory was made and was removed from the neighbouring village of Aslacton to his home parish of Moulton. He was also given firewood and money from the parish for his rent and when he was sick (NRO PD 489/29).

FURTHER INFORMATION: Josh Miller was probably living on his own as a bachelor or widower when this inventory was made. Elizabeth Miller is mentioned in the overseers' accounts, but it is unknown if she was any relation. The churchwardens of Moulton were Mr Howard and Joseph Sheppard and the overseers were John Johnson and William Thrower (NRO PD 489/29).

DAMAGE: Line 7: Ink smudge/leak by 'litt<le>'

97. John Church, 6 August 1722

NRO PD 489/29 Great Moulton with Little Moulton Overseers' Accounts, 1695–1738.

August ye 6th 1722.

~~In y^{e}~~ An Inventory then taken of John Churches goods

a bed & boulster and a pair of sheets a blankett and a Quilt a pillow and pillow bear an ovill table an arm Chair and 4 small Chairs 2 litle tables a Chafeing dish a morter and a pestle #

2 vessells an ale stool one Chist a small Cheese press a paile a small skillett and a midlen skillett a fire shovell and tongs and Cobb irons a Speet and a Candlesick #

upon ye Chamber a bed and bed Stade ~~Sheets~~ a pair of sheets and a blanket and a boulster and Curtins a Coffer and a Trunke a desk 3 joynt stools a side sadle a long table 2 bibles 2 Common prayer Books a porridge pott a Small brass kitle a hake and 2 hanks #
3 pewter dishes and 4 pleats

RELIEF: John Church was in receipt of between 2s. 6d. to 5s. per week when this inventory was made. The amount of regular relief that he received changed every few weeks and it is unknown when he first started to receive a pension. The parish also paid for a doctor to see John Church when needed (NRO PD 489/29).

FURTHER INFORMATION: The author appears to have separated out rooms and different spaces using a '#' in the inventory. In Easter 1727 the parish notes a payment 'to John Church 55 weeks 2^{s} & 6^{d} a week for ye 2 Childen', suggesting that he had children. The handwriting that the inventory was written in matches that of Edward Aldis or Robert Shearing, who were the overseers of the poor in 1722. It is unknown if this is the same John Church that had his goods appraised by the parish of Moulton in the 1760s **(121)** (NRO PD 489/29).

DUBIOUS TERMS: Line 7: 'midlen skillett' – probably a middling or medium-sized skillet.

98. Widow Blake, 15 September 1735

NRO PD 489/29 Great Moulton with Little Moulton Overseers' Accounts, 1695–1738.

Sep ye 15: 1735 An account then taken of ye goods

of ye widow Blake	li s d
one Bed as It Stand	01 01 00
one Brass Pott one Iron pott	
two Tables four Chaires	00 07 06
two Coffers one Box	
one Skillett one paier of androns	
on Gridiron one Hak	00 05 00
one fire shovel	Miles Bux<ton>
	01 13 00
	Wm Chamberlayne

RELIEF: Widow Blake started to receive a pension of 9d. per week when this inventory was made (NRO PD 489/29).

FURTHER INFORMATION: The total is incorrect and should add up to £1 13s. 6d. William Chamberlayne was probably a churchwarden of Moulton. It is unknown whether Widow Blake was related to John Blake, whose goods were appraised in 1764 by the parish of Moulton **(117)** (NRO PD 489/29).

99. Widow Townsend, 29 August 1737

NRO PD 489/29 Great Moulton with Little Moulton Overseers' Accounts, 1695–1738.

August ye 29th: 1737
An account of the Wido^{w} Townsends Goods taken By Wm Chamberlayne and Edwd Moore Church Warden and Overseer ....

3 Beds as they Stand	4 : 0 : 0
Linnen and Drawrs	1 : 0 : 0
one Small Boyler	0 : 5 : 0
a frying Pann	0 : 1 : 0
a payle..	0 : 1 : 6
a payer of Bellows	0 : 1 : 0
a Gridiron	0 : 1 : 6
one Hake Speets Candle Stick	0 : 2 : 6
one fire Shovel Tongs Androns	0 : 3 : 6
a warming Pann	0 : 5 : 0
7 Small Chaiers an armed Chaier	0 : 4 : 0
one ovel Table and a Small Table	0 : 4 : 6
a wash Killer	0 : 2 : 0
3 Small vessells	0 : 2 : 6
all the Earthing ware and Bottles	0 : 3 : 0
	6 : 17 : 0

a Large Brass Kittle – 1 : 1 : 0
the wido Townsend p^{d} for the kettle

RELIEF: Widow Townsend was given casual relief when this inventory was taken. Between Michaelmas 1737 and Easter 1738, for example, she was paid 3s. by the parish and was provided with 4s. by order of the justice. She was also sometimes sick, such as in June 1737, when Dame Foulger was given 3s. per week to nurse her for two weeks (NRO PD 489/29).

100. Widow Cock, 11 July 1738

NRO PD 489/29 Great Moulton with Little Moulton Overseers' Accounts, 1695–1738.

July ye 11:th 1738
An Inventory of the Goods of the Widow Cock
Deceased then taken and apprized

A Bed as It Stand	1 : 15 : 0
2 Payer of Sheets	0 : 07 : 6
a frying Pann	0 : 01 : 0
a Warming Pan	0 : 01 : 6

fire Shovell and Tongs a payer of andirns	0 : 03 : 0
a Skillett	0 : 01 : 6
an Iron Pott	0 : 02 : 6
an Armed Chaier	0 : 01 : 0
a Gowne an quilted Coat a Shift a Cloak an apron a payer of Stockings	0 : 4 : 0
a payer of Stayes	0 : 1 : 6
	2 : 18 : 6

RELIEF: Widow Cock was in receipt of 3s. per week when this inventory was taken. She had been a pensioner since Michaelmas 1737 and the parish also provided her with money towards her rent. Widow Cock had smallpox and the parish paid various people to look after her. For example, on 29 May 1737 officials gave 4s. to 'Dame Cat for 3 weeks lookeing after Widd Cock' and on 6 June 1737 6s. was paid to 'Dame Foulger for Nurseing at Widd Townshands 2 weeks' (NRO PD 489/29).

FURTHER INFORMATION: Overseers' accounts for the parish indicate that Widow Cock's husband was called Robert. She died around July 1738 as the inventory mentions that she was 'Deceased' (NRO PD 489/29).

101. James Hilling, 11 July 1738

NRO PD 489/29 Great Moulton with Little Moulton Overseers' Accounts, 1695–1738.

July: ye 11: 1738

An Inventory of the Goods of Ja: Hilling San^{o} Then Taken

In the Kitchen

a Long Tabele 2 Cubburds a Bed as It Stand a Pewter Dish 3 Pewter Plates a Small Table 2 Small Chayors a Grat Chayor an Iron Pott – a Skillett Earthing wheare and Bottles Stooles fire pan and Tongs and Heak – a – Large Iron pott.

In The Chamber

2 Beds as they Stand

RELIEF: James Hilling was in receipt of casual relief when this inventory was taken, such as clothing and money (NRO PD 489/29).

FURTHER INFORMATION: James Hilling was probably living on his own as a bachelor or widower when this inventory was made (NRO PD 489/29).

102. Robert Websdale, 28 September 1748

NRO PD 489/30 Great Moulton with Little Moulton Overseers' Accounts, 1747–1757.

Sep$^{<t>}$ 28: 1748 an account of Robt Websdales Goods Deceased

Sold +	a Bed as It Stand	1 : 0 : 0
	a Table	0 : 1 : 0
+	2 Chaiers	0 : 2 : 0
	2 Iron Pottage Potts	0 : 4 : 0
Goo^{d} Parish –	a frying pan	0 : 3 : 0
~~goo^{d} Parish~~ –	a wormeing pan	0 : 2 : 6
Tonges Sold	fire pan Tonges Gridgiron	0 : 3 : 0
	a wash Killer and Payle	0 : 1 : 6
	a mullock	0 : 0 : 6
	2 Spinning wheels a Reel	0 : 2 : 6
Chest Sold	a Hanging Cubbad a Chest	0 : 5 : 0
1 Sold	3 Boxes	0 : 2 : 0
	a Skillet	0 : 1 : 0

RELIEF: Overseers' accounts note that Robert Websdale was a pauper, but records are inconsistent for the mid-eighteenth century meaning that it is not possible to determine how long Robert Websdale received relief for and the exact nature of his poverty. After Robert Websdale died around September 1748, his son was placed under the care of Thomas Mendham at the expense of the parish (NRO PD 489/30).

FURTHER INFORMATION: The total value of goods is £2 8s. 0d. The inventory is annotated with what happened to the goods once they were taken by the parish (left-hand side of the page on lines 2, 4, 6–8, and 12–13). The addition of Goody Parish's name on line 6 indicates that she either bought or was given the frying pan from the parish. The inventory was probably edited with this text soon after it was first written as Robert Websdale is noted as 'Deceased'. Robert Websdale was presumably widowed since his son was looked after by Thomas Mendham after he died and not his wife. There is also a second inventory of Robert Websdale's goods, but it is not dated so it is not possible to determine why it was made (NRO PD 489/30):

Late Robt websdall on one ~~gridge iron~~ ...	00 : 00 : 06
~~one mathook~~ ~~one hake~~ one fire shovel ...	00 : 02 : 03
one wormen pan one ~~Iron < pot >~~	00 : 03 : 00
one table	00 : 01 : 00

103. Richard Pottel, no date (c.1740–1754)

NRO PD 489/30 Great Moulton with Little Moulton Overseers' Accounts, 1747–1757.

The account of the goods at Richard pottels

	£ s d
one Bed as it Stan	01 : 00 : 00
one Iron pot one wash killer	00 : 03 : 00
one wheel one Reel	00 : 03 : 00
Frying pan	00 : 01 : 00
two Chaires one box one Coofer one payer of tongs one Joynt Stool }	00 : 0<?> : 00
one hake one payer of bullers	00 : 01 : 00
one table one wash killer	00 : 02 : 00
one Letch two pailes	00 : 01 : 00

RELIEF: Richard Pottel was in receipt of 1s. 6d. per week from the parish when this inventory was made. He had been a pensioner for a number of years and was also given firewood on occasion. The parishioner was buried at a cost of 13s. 6d. in total to the parish in 1754. His wife was provided with casual relief and soon started to receive a pension of 6d. per week after his death (NRO PD 489/30).

FURTHER INFORMATION: The total value of goods is approximately £1 11s. 0d. The inventory could not be accurately dated but based on poor relief records and other inventories from the parish, it was probably made between the late 1740s and 1754. Richard Pottel died around April 1754. The parish also made an inventory of his wife's belongings on 14 October 1754 **(111)**. It is, however, unknown what happened to the goods in this inventory and the extent to which they were passed on to Widow Pottel (NRO PD 489/30).

DAMAGE: Line 7 – page damaged where the values are written.

104. Widow Moor, 14 October 1754

NRO PD 489/30 Great Moulton with Little Moulton Overseers' Accounts, 1747–1757.

Oct^{br} ye 14th 1754 [start of page]

[Inventory]

the Widd Moors things a Skillet	00 01 – 00
a Bed a Killer a Box	
an Iron pot table & Dresser.............	01 – 05 – 00
3 Wheels 2 Iron Potts Pyman...........	00 03 – 00

RELIEF: Widow Moor was in receipt of 9d. or 1s. per week when this inventory was made. She had received this since around Easter 1753 and was given money when she was 'In Need' and by order of the justice. Her children were also provided with clothing at various times from the parish (NRO PD 489/30).

FURTHER INFORMATION: The total value of goods is £1 9s. 0d. Records for the parish indicate that Widow Moor had at least two daughters living with her when this inventory was made. It is possible that the two iron pots on line 6 belonged to Widow Pyman, whose goods are appraised below **(106)**. There is also a pauper inventory of Widow Moor's goods dated 19 April 1762 **(114)**. This second inventory appears to have been made to update the parish records (NRO PD 489/30–31).

105. Widow Parish, 14 October 1754

NRO PD 489/30 Great Moulton with Little Moulton Overseers' Accounts, 1747–1757.

Oct^{br} ye 14th 1754 [start of page]

[Inventory]
at the Widd – Parish

a Bed an old Box a trunk	01 – 00 00
a Cupboard ~~an~~ 2 Iron pots a Killer a Vessell a Box frying & Warming pan 2 Wheels a pair of Tongs & Bellows a Reel and Jointed Stool	00 07 – 00

RELIEF: Widow Parish was in receipt of 1s. per week when this inventory was taken. She had been in receipt of a pension from the parish since Easter 1749 and was occasionally given firewood and clothing. She was also provided with additional money from the parish when she and her daughter were 'In Need', 'In Sickness', and by order of the justice (NRO PD 489/30).

FURTHER INFORMATION: The total value of goods is £1 7s. 0d. The overseers' accounts note that she had at least one daughter living with her when this inventory was made called Jemimah. There is an undated pauper inventory of Jemimah Parish's goods (mainly clothing) below **(119)**. There is a pauper inventory of Widow Parish's goods dated 19 April 1762 **(115)**. This second inventory appears to have been made to update the parish records (NRO PD 489/30–31). There is also a third undated inventory of Widow Parish's goods, but it is unknown when and why it was made. It is as follows (NRO PD 489/30):

The account of widow paris^{h}: goods	£ S d
one Bed one box	00 : 15 : 0
two Small Iron pots	00 : 03 : 0

106. Widow Pyman, 14 October 1754

NRO PD 489/30 Great Moulton with Little Moulton Overseers' Accounts, 1747–1757.

Oct^{br} ye 14th 1754 [start of page]

[Inventory]
at the Wid Pymans

a Bed a Hutch a Coffer a Box 2 Iron pots a Wheel .... }	01 – 05 – 00

RELIEF: Widow Pyman was in receipt of 1s. 6d. per week when this inventory was made. She had received a pension from the parish for a number of years before her goods were appraised and was also provided with clothing and linen on occasion. Widow Pyman appears to have become increasingly unwell from 1755, as overseers' accounts for the parish note a number of payments to her due to 'her Illness'. For example, almost every week in October 1755 she was given an extra 6d. from the parish and in November 1755 Widow Moor (**104**) was paid 4s. for looking after Widow Pyman (NRO PD 489/30).

107. Widow Porter, 14 October 1754

NRO PD 489/30 Great Moulton with Little Moulton Overseers' Accounts, 1747–1757.

Oct^{br} ye 14th 1754 [start of page]

[Inventory]

at the Widd Porters	
a Bed & Box a Reel	01 – 00 00
fire Shovel & tongs	
a Cupboard an Iron pot	
a Warming pan 4 Chairs Joint Stool & Table a hake & Tongs two Cups and sarsers and tearpot frying pan }	00 05 00
and hook....................	
2 Wheels Wash Killer	

RELIEF: Widow Porter was in receipt of 1s. 6d. per week when this inventory was made. She first became a pensioner around Easter 1753 and she and her daughter(s) were given clothing from the parish. Authorities also paid for a doctor to see her occasionally and she was provided with additional money during times of illness and when she was 'in Need' (NRO PD 489/30).

FURTHER INFORMATION: Widow Porter had at least one daughter called Elizabeth living with her when this inventory was made. She also probably had other children, possibly called Mary and Lydia. Poor law records show that Widow Porter was buried at the parish's expense around April 1762 (NRO PD 489/30–31). There is also a joint inventory of goods left by Widow Porter and Widow Pottle from 1762. It was probably made to record the items that the parish had taken from the paupers after they had died which were stored in the townhouse. There is also a pauper inventory of Widow Pottle's goods taken before this from 1754 **(111)**. The joint inventory is as follows (NRO PD 489/31):

April ye 19th: 1762 An Account of W^{t} things belong to ye Parish In the Townhouse Left by the Wid^{s} Porter & Pottle on ye highgreen

2 Coal grates 2 purrs 2 Iron horses A pair of Spice Drawars	00	10	00
A Shelf A Hake fire Shovell & Tongs Bellows 3 Chairs	00	08	04
A Brass Skillett Boxiron & heats	00	04	06
A Warming pan A Coop A Large Cupboard an old Cupboard	00	09	00
A Keller A frying pan	00	02	06
2 Iron potts ~~an Earthen pot~~	00	08	00
A half peck an earthen pot A Cup	00	02	00
[Total:	02	04	04]

108. Amy Hammond, 14 October 1754

NRO PD 489/30 Great Moulton with Little Moulton Overseers' Accounts, 1747–1757.

Oct^{br} ye 14th 1754 [on previous page]

[Inventory]

At Amey Hammonds	li	s.	d.
a Bed a Chest & Trunk			
a Killer & Chair	01 –	00	00
3 Chairs an Iron pot			
a Table a Kittle................................	00	02	00

RELIEF: Amy Hammond was in receipt of 6d. per week when this inventory was made. She had received a pension from the parish for a number of years and was occasionally given firewood and money when she was 'In Need', sick, and by order of the justice. Her children were also frequently provided with clothing from the parish (NRO PD 489/30).

FURTHER INFORMATION: The total value of goods is £1 2s. 0d. Amy Hammond had at least two daughters living with her when this inventory was made called Amy and Mary. She was probably removed from another unknown parish to Moulton around May 1754, as the overseers' accounts note the payment of 1s. 6d. for 'Removeing Trixon and Amey Hammond' (NRO PD 489/30–31). There are two other extant inventories related to Amy Hammond. The first appears to be a goods-given inventory but it is unknown who Edward Moor was and what he had to do with Amy Hammond. The second one may be a pauper inventory, but this could not be proven. The first inventory is as follows (from: NRO PD 489/30):

Novem 7th: 1755 Then Lent Amey Hammond the Goods under mentioned to Ramove from the Towne House to Edwd Moors

A Bed a Chest a Trunk a Killor a Chaier .... 1 : 0 : 0
3 Chaiers Iron pott a Table 2 Killor Kettle .... 0 : 2 : 0

I Acknowledg I have Burrowd the goods above mentioned wich I promise to account for to the Church Wardens or Succesers 2 Spening wheels a Reel

her
Witnes my Hand Amey X Hammond
Mark

The second inventory is as follows (NRO PD 489/30):

The Acount of Amey Hamond things
on Bedd tin Shillings a tabel 3 Chears 3 thrinshers two Shill A Chist two Shillings a payer of Bellors 6 pans on hake on Shill on Iornpot – a gridiorn 3 shillings a Ciller 2 Shillings A Spining Weel – 2s – 6d the holl of all ye Goods – 1l – 1s – 6d

109. Widow Hilling, 14 October 1754

NRO PD 489/30 Great Moulton with Little Moulton Overseers' Accounts, 1747–1757.

Oct^{br} ye 14th 1754 [on previous page]

[Inventory]
at ye Wid Hillings

a Bed a Coffer a Box
a Stool .... 01 – 10 00
a Warming pan &
frying pan a Table a Stool
a Cupboard 3 Chaire an
Iron pot fire Shovell & } 00 10 00
tongs a Gridge iron Candle
Stick a Speet A hake
another Iron Pott
Tea things 3 Wheels

RELIEF: Widow Hilling was in receipt of 9d. per week when this inventory was taken and was given 1s. 6d. per week for looking after Goody Trixon. She had been in receipt of a pension for several years prior to this inventory being taken. Widow Hilling was also occasionally paid money when she was 'In Need' and her children were frequently given clothing by the parish (NRO PD 489/30).

FURTHER INFORMATION: The total value of goods is £2. She had at least two daughters and one son living with her when this inventory was taken. Goody Trixon was the wife of Edmund Trixon whose goods are noted in **110**. Widow Hilling was probably caring for Goody Trixon as she was ill (NRO PD 489/30).

110. Edmund Trixon, 14 October 1754

NRO PD 489/30 Great Moulton with Little Moulton Overseers' Accounts, 1747–1757.

Oct^{br} ye 14th 1754 [on previous page]

[Inventory]

at Ed^{md} Trixons a Bed an Iron pot a Joint Stool	01 – 00 00

RELIEF: Edmund Trixon's wife was in receipt of casual relief when this inventory was taken. She appears to have been frequently sick and was given money when she was 'In Need' and by order of the justice. The parish paid Widow Hilling 1s. 6d. per week to look after her. Edmund Trixon also sometimes received firewood and the parish paid the couple's rent (NRO PD 489/30).

FURTHER INFORMATION: The Trixons may have been removed from another, unknown, parish to Moulton around May 1754, as overseers' accounts note the payment of 1s. 6d. for 'Removeing Trixon and Amey Hammond'. Widow Hilling, who cared for Goody Trixon, also had her goods appraised by the parish in 1754 **(109)** (NRO PD 489/30).

111. Widow Pottle, 14 October 1754

NRO PD 489/30 Great Moulton with Little Moulton Overseers' Accounts, 1747–1757.

Oct^{br} ye 14th 1754 [on previous page]

[Inventory]
at ye Widow Pottles

A Bed & Reel A Joint Stool A Table & Linnen Baskit A Cupboard A Coffer an Iron pot A wash Killer A Chair A frying pan & hake a Skillett	01 – 10 – 00

RELIEF: Widow Pottle was in receipt of 6d. per week when this inventory was made. She started to receive a pension soon after her husband, Richard Pottle, died in April 1754. Widow Pottle was also given additional money 'by Order' and when she was 'In Need' on numerous occasions soon after her husband died (NRO PD 489/30–31).

FURTHER INFORMATION: A pauper inventory was also made of the goods of Widow Pottle's husband, Richard, sometime between the 1740s and 1754 **(103)**. It is unknown what happened to those goods and how many of them passed to Widow Pottle. Overseers' accounts show that Widow Pottle died around August 1761 from an 'Ilness' of some sort (NRO PD 489/30–31). There is also a joint inventory of goods left by Widow Porter and Widow Pottle from 1762. It was probably made to record the items that the parish had taken from the paupers after they had died which were stored in the townhouse. The joint inventory is transcribed in the further information section of inventory **107**.

112. Sarah Harvey, 14 October 1754

NRO PD 489/30 Great Moulton with Little Moulton Overseers' Accounts, 1747–1757.

Oct^{br} ye 14th 1754 [on previous page]

[Inventory]
at Sarah Harveys
A Bed A Trunk & Wheel } 01 – 00 – 00
A Chair ....

RELIEF: Sarah Harvey was in receipt of 1s. per week when this inventory was taken. She appears to have become pregnant out of wedlock and so in December 1753 she married the putative father, John Harvey, at the parish's expense at a cost of £1 8s. 6d. in total. In January 1754, the parish outlined a method to support Sarah, stating that it is 'Then Agreed wth Edmund Trickson for the Beeing of Sarah the Reputed Wife of Jno Harvey At 4^{d} p^{r} week Till her Lying in: And for Twenty Shillings for one Month for her Maintainance at her Lying in: the Said Edmund Trickson to find her and the Child wth Victuals and Drink and Nursing for the Space of one Month as Above Said: The Officers Allowing him Tenn faggots of Wood'. It is probable that this is Edmund Trixon above **(110)**. Overseers' accounts also show that Sarah Harvey was given bed and board on occasion (NRO PD 489/30).

FURTHER INFORMATION: Somebody called Mary Harvey (and her child) is also frequently mentioned in the overseers' accounts in 1754, but it is unknown whether they were any relation of John and Sarah Harvey (NRO PD 489/30).

113. Robert Roberts, 1756 (c. April-May)

NRO PD 489/30 Great Moulton with Little Moulton Overseers' Accounts, 1747–1757.

An Account of the goods of Robart Robarts
A Cubbard a ston Bottle 2 puding Pans
a Coffer a Pitcher puding pan & Earthin dish
a Table a Colet Spining wheel a Reel 3 Earthin Plates
3 Chaiers a Joynt Stool a Small Stool a hand Saw
frying Pan Skillet fier pan Tongs a Paile
Grid iron Hake hour Glas 2 Glas Bottles Bed Bedsteat
Sheets Coverling and part of a Table
a Loom Tow and Engine ....

RELIEF: Robert Roberts was a pensioner when this inventory of his goods was taken. Around Easter 1756, Robert Roberts' pension increased from approximately 1s. to 2s. per week. The parish also paid for his rent on occasion (NRO PD 489/30).

FURTHER INFORMATION: The inventory is probably datable to April or May 1756 based on its position in the overseers' accounts. He was probably married, as 'old Robrts wife' is mentioned in poor law records for the parish. Robert Roberts appears to have been living approximately five miles away in Dickleburgh, Norfolk, when this inventory was taken, as the overseers' accounts mention journeys to Dickleburgh on his behalf and the removal of him to Moulton in March 1757 (NRO PD 489/30). There is also a later inventory of Robert Roberts' possessions taken soon before he was removed in February 1757. This one appears to be a rent-arrears inventory that was copied into the overseers' accounts. William Claveland was Robert Roberts' landlord and appears to have seized his belongings as he was owed rent. The inventory is as follows (from: NRO PD 489/30):

febry ye 21s 1757
An accntt of Robrt Robrts goods att Willm Clavelands
a Bed as it stand with one Civrlin & Boulster and pillow one Sheet one joynt Stool & old Cubbard two Chairs fire Shovel & tongs one Loom and the towe one small table one Cofer one powdering tub an old ~~lye leech~~ 2 hatchett and Brotch hook a glass keep one Cliver and pestol one skillet without a frame a reel & wheel 3 earthen plates one gotch hlf pint pott grid iron one Chair more a picking frame

114. Widow Moor, 19 April 1762

NRO PD 489/31 Great Moulton with Little Moulton Overseers' Accounts, 1757–1764.

April ye 19th: 1762 [start of page]

[Inventory]

The Wid ~~Parrish~~ Moor A Bed	1 –	00	00
A Shelf 2 Bowls 2 glass Bottles porrage Dish 2 Saucers		02	06
A Box & Shelf	0	02	00
An Iron Kittle & Brass Skillet	0	02	06
A Heak	0	01	00
Wid More Earthen Ware 2 pudding pans A Salt pot Saucer A pottager and 2 pipkins .... }		01	00
A Dresser A Spinning Wheell 4 Trenchers A Table	0	05	00
A Stoap Bottle A keller		01	03
A Chair A frying pan	0	02	04

RELIEF: Widow Moor was in receipt of 9d. per week when this inventory was taken. She was also given a shift in July 1762 (NRO PD 489/31).

FURTHER INFORMATION: The total value of goods is £1 17s. 7d. An earlier pauper inventory of Widow Moor's goods was taken on 14 October 1754 **(104)**. This inventory appears to have been made to update the earlier one. It is unknown whether Widow Moor's two daughters who were living with her in 1754 were still with her in 1762 (NRO PD 489/30–31).

115. Widow Parish, 19 April 1762

NRO PD 489/31 Great Moulton with Little Moulton Overseers' Accounts, 1757–1764.

April ye 19th: 1762 [start of page]

[Inventory]

Wid Parishs A Bed	1 – 00 00
2 Boxes A Shelf	0 – 03 06
A Cupboard A Coop an Iron pot	0 – 07 – 00
A frying pan A Large Iron pot A Warming pan .... }	0 – 10 00
A pair of Bellows an Old iron pot	10 – 06
2 Wheels 2 Chairs & A Reel 2 Joint Stools A Stoap Bottle }	05 00
~~A Shelf~~	

RELIEF: Widow Parish was in receipt of 1s. 6d. per week when this inventory was made. She had received a pension from the parish since Easter 1749 and was also provided with clothing at various times. From early 1762, Widow Parish was frequently given additional cash payments during her 'time of need'. She eventually died around December 1762 and was buried at the ratepayers' expense at a cost of 15s. 6d. (NRO PD 489/31).

FURTHER INFORMATION: The total value of goods is £2 16s. 0d. An earlier pauper inventory of Widow Parish's goods was taken on 14 October 1754 **(105)**. This inventory appears to have been made to update the earlier one. Overseers' accounts for the parish note that Widow Parish had at least one daughter called Jemimah, but it is unknown whether they were still living together when this inventory was made. There is an undated pauper inventory of Jemimah Parish's goods (mainly clothing) below **(119)** (NRO PD 489/30–31). There is also a third undated inventory of Widow Parish's goods, but it is not known why this one was made (see further information of **105**) (NRO PD 489/30).

116. Chris Collers, 19 April 1762

NRO PD 489/31 Great Moulton with Little Moulton Overseers' Accounts, 1757–1764.

April ye 19th: 1762 An Account of the Household goods at Town house on the High green

in Kitchen at Chriss Collers	
A Chest of Drawers A Box A fire Sheffle and Tongs A gridgeiron	00 – 06 – 06
A Brass Skillet a Small Iron pot 2 Candle Sticks A Warming pan	00 06 00
2 pails 2 Chairs A Tunal ~~A Chair~~	00 03 00
A Joint Stool A Cupboard A Hand Saw	00 05 06
Earthen Ware	00 02 00
A Bruss	00 00 10
A Jack	00 00 04
A pair of Bellows	00 01 00
A Bed & Bolster A piller A pair of Sheets A Coverlet 2 Blanketts & bedstead A Coffer A Streek A Beam and Scales Lead Waights 3^{lb} – 2	01 15 06

RELIEF: Chris Coller was in receipt of 1s. 6d. per week when this inventory was taken. He had been a pensioner for a number of years prior to his goods being appraised by parochial officials and had his rent paid on occasion up until August 1761, costing £1 3s. every six months. The parish also provided him with clothing and firewood, and sometimes gave his wife money when she was ill (NRO PD 489/31).

FURTHER INFORMATION: The total value of goods is £3 0s. 8d. The overseers' accounts show that the townhouse on the High Green was housing provided by the parish for its paupers and a place where parish stock was stored. Chris Coller was married but his wife's name is unknown. Poor law records note the removal of Chris Coller to Moulton from an unknown parish in August 1761 (NRO PD 489/31).

DUBIOUS TERMS: Line 16: 'Streek' – probably a strike.

117. John Blake, 7 May 1764

NRO PD 489/31 Great Moulton with Little Moulton Overseers' Accounts, 1757–1764.

May ye 7th: 1764

The account of Jn° Blakes things in the Townhouse

		li s. – d.
Parler	A Bed as it Stands	0 – 15 – 0
	A Trunk, A Box, A Table 2 Joint Stools A Coffer A half firkin an Old Tubb A Lye Leech an Nursing Candle Stick A hoe and Cleaver A Reell A Spinning Wheell	0 – 10 – 0

A Scyth and two Sickles A Beetle
and three Iron Wedges 2 ~~A~~ hatchetts
A hook ....

Kitching) A frying pans 2 Iron potts
A Mathook A peck A Table
A Great Chair 2 Small Chairs
A Cupboard ½ Dz Trenchers
three Wood Dishes A Sausepan
A Ladle A pewter Bason
2 <E>arthing Dishes A Quart — 0 – 10 – 0
pot and <A> Gotch, 2 ~~A~~ Stoap Bottles — 1 = 15 = 0
A <B>rass Skimmer 2 hammers
A Glass Bottle A pair of Bellows
a fire Shovell and tongs 2 Wood
Bowles A pipkin A Scieve A Linnen
poke A Sack an Iron Candle Stick

RELIEF: John Blake was in receipt of relief when this inventory was taken, but it is unknown if this was a pension or casual relief. In the months before this inventory was taken, he was given 1s. 6d. on a weekly basis due to being 'at Need'. The parish also occasionally paid for people to look after John Blake during times of sickness (NRO PD 489/31; NRO PD 489/38).

FURTHER INFORMATION: Overseers' accounts for the parish show that the townhouse was housing provided by the parish for its paupers and a place where parish stock was stored. John Blake started to live there from November 1763. Mary Blake is also mentioned in poor law records, but it is not known whether she was any relation of John Blake. Around April 1764, Goody Blake was buried at the parish's expense but it is unknown whether this was Mary Blake and/or a relation of John Blake. Nor is it known whether John Blake was related to Widow Blake, whose goods were appraised in 1735 by the parish of Moulton **(98)** (NRO PD 489/31; NRO PD 489/38).

DAMAGE: Line 20–22: Ink smudge/leak by '<E>arthing', <A>, and '<B>rass'.

118. Susan Buck, 21 October 1767

NRO PD 489/51 Great Moulton with Little Moulton Inventories, 1767–1770.

Oct^{br} the 21st: 1767: An Inventory of the Goods In the Townhouse where Susn Buck Lately Dwelt ....

A Table) A Groge iron) A Joint Stool) Two Iron Potts) Two Brass Skillits) one without a frame) A heak) a pair of Bellows) Three Spinning Wheels) A Cupboard) one Meal hutch) A hanging Cupboard) A pewter keep) an Old Chair) A frame of a Joint Stool) A Coal Great: and potiron an Old Sifter)

RELIEF: Susan Buck had received a pension for more than a decade prior to her goods being inventoried in 1767. She received 2s. 6d. per week from the parish during most years and was provided with firewood, food, and money from the parish on numerous occasions when 'in Need'. She was also sometimes given money and clothing to help maintain her children (NRO PD 489/30–31; NRO PD 489/38).

FURTHER INFORMATION: Overseers' accounts show that the townhouse was housing provided by the parish for its paupers and a place where parish stock was stored. Susan Buck lived there but was placed under the care of John Jermey along with her goods in 1767 (see circumtext). She had several children, but it is unknown how many were living with her when this inventory was taken (NRO PD 489/30–31; NRO PD 489/38).

CIRCUMTEXT: This pauper inventory is followed by an inventory of goods given to Susan Buck's carer John Jermey and a clause stating that the goods are the property of the parish (NRO PD 489/51):
Moulton Oct^{br} the 21st: 1767: An Account of All the Houshold Goods Belonging to the Said Parish and Now in the possession of John Jermey: one Bed as it Stands) A Box without A Lid) an Iron pot four Trenchers) one pewter Dish these things were Carryed to the Sd John Jermeys by Susan Buck ....
Be it known Unto all Men that I John Jermey Do hereby promise Unto the Church Wardens and Overseers of the poor of the Said Parish of Moulton aforesaid to Deliver Unto them or either of them all the above mentioned Goods Whensoever they or any of them Shall Demand the Same without any Demand whatsoever for the being of the Said Susan Buck: On the forfeiture of paying Unto the Said officers, or any one of them on Demand the Sum of five pounds of Lawfull mony As Witness my Hand

Witness	John Jermey
Thos Brighting	his X mark

119. Jemimah Parish, no date (c.1760s)

NRO PD 489/31 Great Moulton with Little Moulton Overseers' Accounts, 1757–1764.

The Account of w^{t} things Jemimah Parish Left at her Descease as Wearing Apparell

A Linnen handkerchief
2 pickling Aprons and a Tarting one
5 peticoats 2 Shifts 3 ~~Gounds~~
2 Straw hatts 2 pair of Shoes
A Spinning Wheel & Reel,
A Linnen Apron: A Stuff Gound
3 Courlerd handkerchiefs 3 White handkerchiefs
A pair of Sleeves 2 pair of Gloves
A pair of pocketts 5 Caps 3 pair <of St>ockings
A Cloke, A pair of Sheets and A Cloke at Bucks
2 pair of Stays 3 Stomachers A pockett A Lace

more 3 handkerchiefs ~~A~~ Caps 4) 5 Old Books
A pair of pottings

RELIEF: During the 1760s Jemimah Parish was in receipt of a pension of around 1s. every week. She was also given money on occasion when ‘at need’ (NRO PD 489/31; NRO PD 489/38).

FURTHER INFORMATION: Jemimah Parish was the daughter of Widow Parish who died in December 1762 and had two pauper inventories made of her possessions in 1754 and 1762 **(105, 115)**. The precise date of this inventory is not known, but it was taken when she died. This source is unusual compared to the other pauper inventories in the sample as it mainly lists clothing (NRO PD 489/31; NRO PD 489/38).

DAMAGE: Line 11: Pen leak on ‘<of St>ockings’.

120. John Nudds, no date (c.1760s)

NRO PD 489/31 Great Moulton with Little Moulton Overseers’ Accounts, 1757–1764.

the Houselgoods of John Nudds at ye upper Towne house

a Bed as it Stand	01 – 05 – 00
a Loom	02 – 10 – 00
part of a Loom and Stuff	00 – 10 – 00
2 Leather Boxes and a Wooden one 2 stools	00 – 03 – 00
a Parcel of Mowltraps:	00 – 01 – 00
Kitchen	
a Table, a Tub and a bowle Iron pot a Skillet	
a friing pan	00 – 07 – 00
2 Spining Wheels a Speet	00 – 03 – 00
Tongs Cobiaons	00 – 02 – <?>
a Shelf	00 – 00 – <6>
a hake & gridgiron	00 – 02 – <?>
a Worman pan & a Reel	00 – 02 – <?>
Chairs 3	00 – 03 – <?>
a pair of Bellows	00 – 01 – <?>
a Salt Box	00 – 00 – <?>
a Slip & a pail	00 – 01 – <?>
a Goose house	00 – 01 – <?>
pottage Dishes & arthen Ware	00 – 01 – <?>

RELIEF: John Nudds was continually noted as a pauper during the 1760s, but because the inventory could not be precisely dated it is not possible to establish what the exact nature of relief was when the inventory was taken. Nonetheless, extant records show that John Nudds was frequently given casual relief when he was ‘in

Need' and was given rent payments by the parish. His daughter was also provided with clothing on occasion (NRO PD 489/31; NRO PD 489/38).

FURTHER INFORMATION: The total value of goods is approximately £5 12s. 6d., however because the right-hand side of the page is damaged this figure is inaccurate and an underrepresentation. Overseers' accounts show that the townhouse was housing provided by the parish for its paupers and a place where parish stock was stored. John Nudds had at least one daughter living with him during the 1760s (NRO PD 489/31; NRO PD 489/38).

DAMAGE: Right side of page ripped and worn away, making some numbers illegible.

121. John Church, no date (c.1760s)

NRO PD 489/31 Great Moulton with Little Moulton Overseers' Accounts, 1757–1764.

The Houselgoods John Church brought with him to the High Green [Townhouse]

A Bed Steat bed and Curtains
A Blanket 2 Sheet & a Civerlin
and a pillow and a Bowlster
a Cofur
A Close Stool

RELIEF: John Church was continually noted as a pauper during the 1760s, but because the inventory could not be precisely dated it is not possible to establish what the exact nature of relief was when the inventory was taken. Nonetheless, extant records show that John Church was given a pension of 3s. to 3s. 6d. per week from March 1763. Records show that John Church was also frequently provided with cash during 'time of Need' and that the parish paid parishioners and doctors to look after him when he was sick (NRO PD 489/31; NRO PD 489/38).

FURTHER INFORMATION: Mary Church is mentioned in the overseers' accounts, but it is unknown whether she was a relation of John Church. Poor relief papers show that the townhouse was housing provided by the parish for its paupers and a place where parish stock was stored. It is unknown whether this is the same John Church who had his goods appraised by the parish of Moulton in 1722 **(97)** (NRO PD 489/31; NRO PD 489/38).

Norwich, St. Mary in the Marsh pauper inventories

The two pauper inventories from Norwich, St. Mary in the Marsh were all written on loose pieces of paper and can be found in a bundle of documents in NRO PD 499/79. Also included in the collection are four inventories that were made for arrears of rent.

122. Lady/Jemima Pleasant, 14 May 1734

NRO PD 499/79 Norwich, St. Mary in the Marsh Inventories, 1734–1772.

May the 14 Lady Pleasa<nt>
Bed Bolster Rug 2 Shettes Bed Stead table paile trunk 4 Chairs Bellows fier pan tongs Candel Stick four tost Iron Bares Bottel Sauspan Baskett 2 Dishes for frute 3 Small potts 2 tea Dishes 2 Milk prinegers Chamber pott 2 window Curtains puten pan and yellow Dish Irenpan parish pott a Broad

RELIEF: Lady Pleasant was in receipt of 1s. per week when this inventory was taken. The parish also sometimes provided her with additional money and clothing, and paid various expenses on her behalf when she gave birth to a child around August 1733 (NRO PD 499/45).

FURTHER INFORMATION: Overseers' accounts for the parish show that Lady Pleasant's forename was Jemima/Jem. It is probable that she had her child out of wedlock. Lady Pleasant was removed from another unknown parish to her home parish of Norwich St. Mary in the Marsh sometime between Easter 1732 and Easter 1733 (NRO PD 499/45).

CIRCUMTEXT: On the back 'Ann Inventory of Lady Pleasants goods May 1734'

DUBIOUS TERMS: Line 5: 'parish' – possibly porridge; 'Broad' – possibly a table board.

123. Samuel Hunt, 26 June 1772

NRO PD 499/79 Norwich, St. Mary in the Marsh Inventories, 1734–1772.

An Inventory of the Household Goods Furniture & Things of Samuel Hunt of ye Parish of S^{t}. Paul in Norwich Worstead Weaver taken this 26th. Day of June 1772. (that is to say)

One Bed as it stand Curtains, Valence, Blankets
Coverlin Sheets Pillows & Bolster.
One Fire Range
Six Chairs
one Pair of Draws
two Tables.

I do hereby Acknowledge that ye above Goods Furniture and Things are in my Possession and that the same are the property of the Officers of ye Parish of St Mary in ye Marsh in ye Close, and I do promise not to Embezzle any <Par>t there of and that I will deliver up ye same to ye Officers of ye said Parish of St Mary in ye Marsh when I am call'd upon so to do

Witness my Hand

Witness
Thos Gibbon

his
Samull X Hunt
Mark

RELIEF: Samuel Hunt started to receive casual relief when this inventory was made. The parish also provided him with additional money when he and his wife were 'in need', sometimes paid the couple's rent (costing £1 18s.), and paid expenses when his wife gave birth to a child in April 1772. The agreement at the bottom of the inventory and overseers' accounts show that Samuel Hunt had agreed to give the goods to the parish in exchange for relief, but continued to use his possessions until the parish required them (NRO PD 499/46).

FURTHER INFORMATION: Samuel Hunt was a worsted weaver and was married with at least one child. He appears to be living in Norwich St. Paul when this inventory was taken, despite having settlement in Norwich St. Mary in the Marsh. Thomas Gibson was one of the overseers of the poor for Norwich St. Mary in the Marsh (NRO PD 499/46; NRO PD 499/79).

DAMAGE: Line 13: Ink leak on '<Par>t'.

Redenhall with Harleston and Wortwell pauper inventories

The largest collection of pauper inventories in Norfolk is from Redenhall with Harleston and Wortwell. They can be found in a wide range of formats, such as on loose sheets of paper and account books. A number of the inventories appear to have been initially written on loose pieces of paper and were then copied into a bound book. The parish even had a volume that was devoted almost entirely to recording parishioners' belongings (NRO PD 295/102). Goods-given, debt-related, and workhouse-related inventories can also be found among records of the parish.

124. Susan Aldred, 8 May 1708

NRO PD 295/102 Redenhall with Harleston and Wortwell Overseers' Order Book, 1708–1743.

An Inventory of the goods w:^{ch} were belonging to Sus:^{n} Ald<red> and taken by M^{r}. W^{m}. Coates & M^{r}. W^{m}. Taylar Ov<erseers> of the Poor for the use of the Towne of Harle<ston> & Collection May the 8:th 1708 as followeth

One Table
One Box
One Bedd
Two old Coffers
One Frying pann
One forme
One p^{r}. of Bellowes
One pottage pott
Two Joynt Stooles
One large Washbowle
One hake & Grediron
One p^{r}. of Tongs &
Two Chaires

RELIEF: Susan Aldred started to receive a pension of 8d. per week several weeks before this inventory was made. She was also paid money from the parish during 'Sickness and at other needfull times' and was given 5s. every two quarters for her rent (NRO PD 295/93; NRO PD 295/102).

FURTHER INFORMATION: Thomas Aldred is also mentioned in extant records, but it is unknown if he was any relation of Susan Aldred (NRO PD 295/93; NRO PD 295/102).

DAMAGE: The left-hand side of the page is faded making some words illegible, including 'Ald<red>, 'Ov<erseers>', and 'Harle<ston>' (lines 1–3).

125. Robert Burton, 1710 (day and month unknown)

NRO PD 295/102 Redenhall with Harleston and Wortwell Overseers' Order Book, 1708–1743.

<Int> Robt. Burton what Goods he have
One Bed two p^{r}. Old Sheets. wth: Blank^{t} & Ruge

RELIEF: Robert Burton was continually noted as a pauper in 1710, receiving a mixture of regular and casual relief. For example, between Easter and Michaelmas 1710, he was paid 1s. per week for 11 weeks. In previous years he was occasionally given money when 'in Sickness and at other needfull times' (NRO PD 295/93; NRO PD 295/102).

FURTHER INFORMATION: This inventory probably dates from 1710 based on its position in the overseers' order book. Records also mention a George Burton, George Burton's wife, and Widow/Goody Burton, but it is unknown whether they were any relation of Robert Burton (NRO PD 295/93; NRO PD 295/102).

DUBIOUS TERMS: Line 1: '<Int>' – inventory.

126. Widow Bottwright, 23 March 1713/14

NRO PD 295/93 Redenhall with Harleston and Wortwell Overseers' Accounts, 1692–1721.

An Inventory of Wid^{w}: Bottwrights Goods who Dec^{d}. March ye 23th: 1713/14
As follows:
1 Bed & Bedstead & bolster & Coverlett
2 New sheetes / 4 Chaires
2 Old Coffers
1 old Hanging Coba<r>t
1 paire of Bellows
1 fire pan & paire of Tongs
1 Candle stick & 1 keepe
2 Trenchers & 1 wooden Cann
1 Frying pann & 1 Earthen pott
2 Spoons & 1 pipken
2 Shifinings & 3 old Caps

RELIEF: Widow Bottwright was in receipt of 1s. 6d. per week when this inventory was taken. She had received a pension from the parish for a number of years before her goods were appraised and was also given clothing and money from officials when 'in Sickness and at other needfull times' (NRO PD 295/93; NRO PD 295/102).

FURTHER INFORMATION: Records indicate that Widow Bottwright died around March 1713/14 from an unspecified illness and that the parish paid a total of 18s. to bury her (NRO PD 295/93; NRO PD 295/102).

DAMAGE: Line 6: 'Coba<r>t' – the 'r' is smudged.

127. Widow Reed, 20 June 1731

NRO PD 295/102 Redenhall with Harleston and Wortwell Overseers' Order Book, 1708–1743.

An Inventory of the Goods in ye Possession of Step Reeds Widdow: And taken by M^{r}: John Sawer & Mr John Jackson Church-Wardens & M^{r}: John Edwards Overseer of ye Poor; for the Use of the Town of Harleston and Collection: taken June 20th 1731. (which is as followeth.)

one Bed and Bedstead
two Pillows
one pare of Sheets
two Skillets
one Iron Kettle
one Cubbard
one Hake
one Spiningweel
one Pail
one Table
one Chest
four Chairs
three Stools
one Basket
one Old bed & bedsted
one Iron Candlestick
~~one Stool~~

RELIEF: Widow Reed was in receipt of 2s. 6d. per week when this inventory was made. The parish also frequently paid her rent, gave her money when 'in Sickness and Other Needfull times', and she was provided with clothing, firewood, and faggots. Her children were also given clothing by the parish on numerous occasions (NRO PD 295/94; NRO PD 295/102).

FURTHER INFORMATION: Widow Reed's husband, Stephen, was buried at the ratepayers' expense at a cost of 17s. 4d. sometime between Michaelmas 1729 and

Easter 1730. Poor law records indicate that Widow Reed and her children were removed from the parish of Framlingham (Suffolk) to Redenhall with Harleston and Wortwell soon after her husband died. It is probable that the couple had at least two children when the inventory was taken and that their names were Isaac and Ann (NRO PD 295/94; NRO PD 295/102).

128. Thomas Self, 26 June 1731

NRO PD 295/102 Redenhall with Harleston and Wortwell Overseers' Order Book, 1708–1743.

An Inventory of the Goods in the Possession of Tho: Self taken by Mr: John Edwards Overseer. June 26th 1731

one Bed and bedstead
two Bolsters
one Small Kettle
one Boyler
two Coffers, one old Chest
one Cubbart, one Little Table
five Chairs, one Candle Stick
one Hake, one Frying-pan
one pare of Tongs, one pare Bellows
one Black Goch, & one black Bottle Earthen
one Spade, one Turnup Crome, a hay fork
one old pail.
~~a Jack~~

RELIEF: Thomas Self was in receipt of 2s. per week when the inventory was made. He had been a pensioner for several years prior to his goods being appraised and was also given firewood and additional money when 'in Sickness and at Other Needfull times' from the parish (NRO PD 295/94; NRO PD 295/102).

FURTHER INFORMATION: Thomas Self was married (NRO PD 295/94; NRO PD 295/102).

129. Flegg Pettow, 26 June 1731

NRO PD 295/102 Redenhall with Harleston and Wortwell Overseers' Order Book, 1708–1743.

1731
June 26 Of the Goods in the Possession of Flegg Pettow; by Jn°: Edw

one Bed & Bedstead, a Spining-weel, and a Cradle one hake, one fire Shovel one Iron pot, & one frying-pan one Cloase Brush, one Kettle; 2 small Boxes one Chair, & one Stool.

RELIEF: Flegg Pettow's wife was in receipt of 1s. per week when this inventory was taken. She was also given money when 'in Sickness and Other Needfull times' and the parish paid various people to look after her while she was unwell (NRO PD 295/94; NRO PD 295/102).

FURTHER INFORMATION: All relief payments were made out to 'Flegg Pettow's wife'. Flegg Pettow is not directly mentioned in poor relief records for the parish, meaning that it is unknown whether he was still alive when this inventory was taken (NRO PD 295/94; NRO PD 295/102).

DAMAGE: Line 2: Text faded by 'Edw'.

130. Jane Branch, 26 June 1731

NRO PD 295/102 Redenhall with Harleston and Wortwell Overseers' Order Book, 1708–1743.

1731

June ye 26th: An Inventory of the Goods taken in the possession of Jane Branch. taken By M^{r}. John Edwards Overseer of ye Poor

Aug^{t} – 5th (viz) these Goods now in the possession of W^{m}: Anger

Gone

Two Beds & Bedsteads, one Coffer, five Chairs, two Tables two Tow-Weels,

Gone Gone

one Wool-Weel one Hake, two hand-Irons one fire-Shovel & tongs, two pott-hooks, one pestle one Gridiron one Brass-Skimer, one Looking-Glass, one spitt, one flesh-fork one Ironing-Box, a Sueit-Chopper, one Reel, two Iron potts one pare of Bellows, two Killers, one Pail, one Brush two Bowls, one Vessel, two Glasses, some Earthen-ware one Latten Pudding-pan, three Iron candle-sticks, one tinderbox one Small Baskett

RELIEF: Jane Branch was in receipt of 1s. per week when this inventory was taken. She had been a pensioner for a number of years prior to her goods being appraised and was also sometimes given firewood, clothing, and money when she was 'in Need' from the parish (NRO PD 295/94; NRO PD 295/102).

FURTHER INFORMATION: Lines 4, 5 and 8 are written in a different hand to the rest of the document. This suggests that the pauper inventory was annotated on 5 August (unknown year) to record which goods William Anger had taken from Jane Branch or which goods were missing. Jane Branch appears to have been living on her own without any children when this inventory was taken as a single woman or widow. Henry Branch also had his goods inventoried by the parish in 1731 **(137)**, but it is unknown whether he was any relation of Jane Branch (NRO PD 295/94; NRO PD 295/102).

131. Ann Green, 26 June 1731

NRO PD 295/102 Redenhall with Harleston and Wortwell Overseers' Order Book, 1708–1743.

Of the goods in the Possession of Ann Green Taken by M^{r}: John Edwards June ye 26th 1731

Two Beds & Bedsteds three Pewter-dishes, three porringers, & a Saucer three Large Earthen Dishes, two Gridirons, one Spitt two pot-Hooks, one Skimmer, one Box Iron & heaters. two hand irons, one fire-Shovel & tongs, & Bellows, one Salt-box two tables, five Chairs, two Candle-Sticks, a meat-Chopper one pail, one frying-pan, two Pottage-Potts, some Earthenware one Warming-pan, one Pestle & Morter, one Killer two boxes one Coffer-Cubbart, one Basket, one Sive, one Lanthorn, one Reel, one Spining weel, one Looking-Glass, one hook.

RELIEF: Ann Green was in receipt of 1s. per week when this inventory was taken. She had been a pensioner for a number of years prior to her goods being appraised and was given firewood on occasion. The parish also sometimes paid her rent and gave her children clothing (NRO PD 295/94; NRO PD 295/102).

FURTHER INFORMATION: Ann Green was widowed and she had two children (probably both girls) living with her when this inventory was made. John Edwards was an overseer of the poor for the parish (NRO PD 295/94; NRO PD 295/102).

132. William Afsey (senior), 26 June 1731

NRO PD 295/102 Redenhall with Harleston and Wortwell Overseers' Order Book, 1708–1743.

Of the Goods in the Possession of W^{m}: Afsey sen^{r} taken by Mr John Edwards Overseer June ye 26th. 1731

one old bed & bedstead one Boltster one Pillow, one Boyler one pot, one Kittle, one Cubbard one Coffer, one Joynt-stool 4 Chairs, two Spining-weels, one Reel, one Warning-pan one frying-pan, one hake & pot-hooks Bellows tongs & fire Shovel two hand-Irons, one Salt-box, one Gridiron, two Candle Sticks, one Table, one Ash Tub, one small Coffer, one Looking-Glass one

Lanthorn, 2 small Baskets, one Killer, one wooden-Bowl one Spade, one hammer, 2 pails, & some earthen-ware.

RELIEF: William Afsey senior and his wife received a pension of 2s. per week when this inventory was made. The couple had received a pension from the parish for a number of years prior to their goods being appraised and were also sometimes given clothing, firewood, and additional money when 'in Sickness and at Other Needfull times' (NRO PD 295/94; NRO PD 295/102).

FURTHER INFORMATION: William Afsey senior was married (NRO PD 295/94; NRO PD 295/102).

133. Ann Burton, 26 June 1731

NRO PD 295/102 Redenhall with Harleston and Wortwell Overseers' Order Book, 1708–1743.

Of the Goods In ye possession of Ann Burton Taken by M^{r}: John Edwards Overseer. June 26th 1731 (viz)

One Bed & Bedstead, 3 Chairs, one Spinning Weel one Cubbert, one hake, one Joynt stool, a pare of Bellows one Reel, one Kettle, one Coffer, one frying pan.

RELIEF: Ann Burton was in receipt of 9d. per week when this inventory was made. She had received a pension from the parish for several years, ranging from 6d. to 9d. per week (NRO PD 295/94; NRO PD 295/102).

FURTHER INFORMATION: Ann Burton was widowed. There is mention of John Burton's widow in overseers' accounts for the parish, but it is unknown if this was Ann Burton (NRO PD 295/94; NRO PD 295/102).

134. Elizabeth Trew, 26 June 1731

NRO PD 295/102 Redenhall with Harleston and Wortwell Overseers' Order Book, 1708–1743.

Of the Goods In the Possession of Eliz Trew taken by M^{r}. John Edwards Overseer June 26th. 1731 (viz)

One Bed and Bedstead, one Boltster, one Pillow, four Chairs, one Table, two Boxes, one Joynt stool, one Sive one Looking-Glass, one Cubbard, one Reel, one Spining-weel, two pots, 2 handirons one fire-Shovel & tongs pott-hooks, two Candle-sticks, one hake, two Larg stone Bottles, and some Earthen-ware, one warming pan, two skillets, three Killers, one Large wooden Bowl, two pails, and one Boxiron.

RELIEF: Elizabeth Trew was in receipt of 1s. per week when this inventory was taken and was given 1s. 3d. per week to look after the children of Reed. It is unknown if these were the children of Widow Reed, whose goods were inventoried by the parish of Redenhall with Harleston and Wortwell on 20 June 1731 **(127)**. Elizabeth Trew had been a pensioner since April 1728 and was also sometimes provided with clothing, firewood, and money when she was 'in Need' from the parish (NRO PD 295/94; NRO PD 295/102–103).

FURTHER INFORMATION: Elizabeth Trew was probably living on her own as a spinster since she was referred to by her Christian name and never as 'Widow' (NRO PD 295/94; NRO PD 295/102–103). There is a second pauper inventory of Elizabeth Trew's goods taken 15 April 1745 **(160)**. This inventory appears to have been made to update the parish records.

135. Widow Todd, 26 June 1731

NRO PD 295/102 Redenhall with Harleston and Wortwell Overseers' Order Book, 1708–1743.

Of the Goods in ye Possession of Geo Todds Wid^{w}: (viz) taken by M^{r}. John Edwards overseer June ye 26th 1731.

One old Bed & two Bedstead, two Boltsters, three Spining-weels, one Reel, one wash-Killer, one Pottage-pot Six old Chairs, two Tables, one Cubbard and Shelves for Dishes, and a hanging Shelf, one Box Iron, one Gridiron, two handirons, one hake, one Salt Box, one Pare of Bellows.

RELIEF: Widow Todd was in receipt of 2s. per week when this inventory was made. She had been a pensioner for a number of years prior to her goods being appraised by the parish and was given money when 'in Sickness', clothing, and rent payments on occasion (NRO PD 295/94; NRO PD 295/102).

FURTHER INFORMATION: Widow Todd had three children living with her when this inventory was made. Overseers' accounts and parish registers show that Widow Todd was buried at the ratepayers' expense on 14 March 1739 (NRO PD 295/3; NRO PD 295/94; NRO PD 295/102). There is a second pauper inventory of Widow Todd's goods taken 29 September 1738 **(144)**. This one appears to have been made to update the parish records.

136. Elizabeth/Widow Goldspink, 26 June 1731

NRO PD 295/102 Redenhall with Harleston and Wortwell Overseers' Order Book, 1708–1743.

Of the goods in ye Possession of Wid^{w}: Goldspink, taken by M^{r}. John Edwards Overseer, June ye 26th 1731. (viz)

One Bed & Bedstead, one Chair and some very old things

RELIEF: Widow Goldspink was in receipt of 1s. 6d. per week when this inventory was taken. She had been a pensioner for at least a decade prior to her goods being appraised and was also sometimes given clothing and firewood from the parish (NRO PD 295/3; NRO PD 295/94; NRO PD 295/102).

FURTHER INFORMATION: Widow Goldspink's forename was Elizabeth. Mary Goldspink is occasionally mentioned in poor relief records, but it is unknown if she was any relation of Widow Goldspink. Parish registers and overseers' accounts show that Widow Goldspink was buried in the parish on 19 November 1738 (NRO PD 295/3; NRO PD 295/94; NRO PD 295/102).

137. Lettice/Widow Flattman and Henry Branch, 26 June 1731

NRO PD 295/102 Redenhall with Harleston and Wortwell Overseers' Order Book, 1708–1743.

Of the goods in the Possession of Wid^{w}: Flattman; taken by M^{r}. John Edwards Overseer, June ye 26th. 1731. (viz)

another Inventory taken on ye 21 of Nov^{br} 1737

One Bed; Bedstead Boltster, and two Pillows, one Dresser, one Table one Coffer one Box, & a Lesser Box, one hake, one Gridiron two pott hooks, two pare of Bellows, one Skillett, one Hake, one Boxiron one Spitt, four Candlesticks, one Large Cubbard, one Pottage-pot one Wash Tub, one Tray, four pewter spoons, one Looking-Glass Six Chairs, a Rock-reel, a Curtain-Rod, two handirons, one fire Shovel, one pare of tongs, two Box-irons, one pare of Bellows and Some Earthen ware.

Also in ye Same Room Belonging to Hen: Branch (viz) one Bed & Bedstead under, and one Stool.

RELIEF: Widow Flattman was in receipt of 1s. per week when this inventory was taken. She had been a pensioner for around a year before her goods were appraised by the parish and was infrequently given additional money when 'in Sickness and Other Needfull times'. Henry Branch appears to have been living with Widow Flattman. He was in receipt of 6d. per week when this inventory was taken (NRO PD 295/94; NRO PD 295/102).

FURTHER INFORMATION: Overseers' accounts show that Widow Flattman's forename was Lettice. Henry Branch appears to have been widowed or single. Neither pauper appears to have had any children living with them when this inventory was made. Widow Flattman was buried on 10 November 1737. Jane Branch also had her goods inventoried by the parish in 1731 **(130)**, but it is unknown whether she was any relation of Henry Branch. The statement 'another Inventory taken on ye 21 of Nov^{br} 1737' on the left-hand side of the page (lines 3–7) is written in a different hand. The note was made when a second pauper inventory was taken of Lettice Flattman's goods in 1737 **(142)**. This second inventory appears to have been made to update the parish records (NRO PD 295/3; NRO PD 295/94; NRO PD 295/102).

138. Lionel Lawson, 10 November 1731

O PD 295/102 Redenhall with Harleston and Wortwell Overseers' Order Book, 1708–1743.

Of y^{e}. Goods in the possesion of Lina Lason taken by M^{r}: Thos: Mapes Overseer Nov^{br} ye 10th 1731 (viz)

one Bed Bedstead & Curtings one Rugg two Blanketts one Boulster one Pillow a Back Iron, fire Shovel & tongs two hand-Irons one Large Trunk one Chest one Table three Chairs one Baskett one Candle-stick one Large Bible & some other books one Little box a Little Trunk two Joynt-stools one Lanthorn one Pail one pewter Dish one pewter Chamber-pott a pair of Bellows a Small Boyler one Round-Gridiron one brush one Skillett a half-peck two Wooden Bowls one hammer some Bottles and Some other Little-odd things

RELIEF: Lionel Lawson was in receipt of 1s. 6d. per week when this inventory was made. He had received this since 1725 and was also given clothing and rent payments from the parish. The overseers paid Goody Mann 2d. per week for several months from October 1731 to look after Lionel Lawson as he became increasingly unwell. In October 1732, he died and the parish paid 16s. in total for the funeral (NRO PD 295/3; NRO PD 295/94; NRO PD 295/102).

FURTHER INFORMATION: Lionel Lawson appears to have been living on his own without any children as a bachelor or widower. The parish spent 1s. making this pauper inventory and 6d. 'for Entring them in ye Town book'. Lionel Lawson was buried on 30 October 1732 in Redenhall with Harleston and Wortwell. His goods were subsequently sold by the parish, raising £3 6s. 10d. (NRO PD 295/3; NRO PD 295/94; NRO PD 295/102).

139. John Andrews, 8 December 1731

NRO PD 295/102 Redenhall with Harleston and Wortwell Overseers' Order Book, 1708–1743.

of Goods in ye possesion of Jno Andrews taken by Mr Mapes Dec^{br}. ye 8th. [1731]

one bed and Bedsteed two Bolsters one Rugg three Sheets one Table one old Stool

RELIEF: John Andrews was in receipt of 2s. per week when this inventory was taken. He had been in receipt of a pension since around mid–1725 and was also given clothing on numerous occasions by the parish. From May 1731, Widow Medcalf was paid 3s. every four weeks to look after John Andrews during times of sickness (NRO PD 295/94; NRO PD 295/102).

FURTHER INFORMATION: This inventory is most likely datable to 1731 based on its position in the overseers' order book and the pauper's date of burial. John Andrews was probably widowed or single. Poor law records and parish registers show that John Andrews was buried on 6 July 1732 at a cost of 14s. 4d. to the town. The parish spent 6d. making this inventory (NRO PD 295/3; NRO PD 295/94; NRO PD 295/102). Under this source, there is a second inventory which records what happened to John Andrew's goods (NRO PD 295/102):

> July ye 24th. 1732.
> Remains of Jno. Andrews^{s} things a westcoate a pair of Shoes & Stockings & a new Shirt Left at Wid^{w}. Medcalfs the Rest of the things are Dispos^{d} of by Town order

140. Widow Chamberlaine, 29 December 1733

NRO PD 295/102 Redenhall with Harleston and Wortwell Overseers' Order Book, 1708–1743.

Decemb^{r}: the 29th. 1733

Of the Goods in the possesion of Wid^{w}: Chamberlaine taken by Order of Thos: Lincolne Overseer

one Table one hake one Gridiron an old Boxiron 2 Stools 4 Chairs one Cubbard one Killer one porridge pot one wooden Cup one Ladle a basket one Reel one Spining-weel one frying pan one bed Bedstead – Curtains &c one Chest one Looking-Glass a Sive one Bowle one old Iron pot.

RELIEF: Widow Chamberlaine was in receipt of between 1s. 6d. to 2s. per week when this inventory was made. She was also given 2s. per week for looking after an illegitimate child named Margaret Ellis. Widow Chamberlaine started to receive relief from the parish soon after her husband died around July 1732. The parish also gave her rent payments, clothing, and money when 'in Need' (NRO PD 295/94; NRO PD 295/102).

FURTHER INFORMATION: Widow Chamberlaine's husband, Robert, was buried on 1 August 1732 at a cost of 14s. 4d. to the parish. Poor law records note Henry Chamberlaine on occasion, but it is unknown whether he was any relation of Widow Chamberlaine (NRO PD 295/3; NRO PD 295/94; NRO PD 295/102).

141. Samuel Harman, 15 June 1734

NRO PD 295/102 Redenhall with Harleston and Wortwell Overseers' Order Book, 1708–1743.

An Inventory taken June ye 15th 1734 By M^{r}: Alex^{dr} Staples / the present Overseer of ye Poor; of ye Goods of Sam^{el}. Harman wch. where in ye house of Crashfield Revitt of Wortwell. (viz)

In the Kitchin a Wooden Cup & Spoon; a wooden ~~Table~~-Chair Table-fassion two Earthen Dishes & two Earthen Sausers & a Chair & one Candle-stick a Spade Mattock Hook hatchett a Scoupett Tip^{t} wth Iron a keep & a Low Stool a Large Iron pot wth. 3 Liggs
In the Chamber
A Bed Boltster Rugg a pair of Sheets & Bedsted a Small Box wth. some books a Small Table & a Small Iron-pot a hammer a Joynt Stool a Chest wth a pair of Sheets

RELIEF: Samuel Harman was in receipt of 1s. 6d. per week when this inventory was made. He first became a pensioner in 1730 and was also given rent payments and money on numerous occasions when he was 'in Sickness' and at 'Other Needfull times' from the parish (NRO PD 295/94; NRO PD 295/102).

FURTHER INFORMATION: Samuel Harman was probably living on his own as a widower or bachelor when this inventory was made. He was living in Wortwell and it cost the parish 1s. to go there and create this inventory. Samuel Harman was living in the home of Crashfield Revitt and the parish paid his lodging costs. Crashfield Revitt was not a pauper and appears to have been relatively wealthy as he is recorded as a voter in a poll book from Norfolk in 1734 (NRO PD 295/94; NRO PD 295/102; *A Copy of the Poll for the Knights of the Shire for the County of Norfolk* (Norwich, 1734), p. 191).

DUBIOUS TERMS: Line 4: 'Table-fassion' – possibly a table fasten.

142. Lettice Flattman, 21 November 1737

NRO PD 295/102 Redenhall with Harleston and Wortwell Overseers' Order Book, 1708–1743.

An Inventory taken by M^{r}. Jno: Smith the present Overseer this 21th. Day of Novem^{br} 1737 of ye Goods Late Lettice Flattmans. (viz)

One Bed Bedstead one Pillow, Boltster, two blanketts
A Coverlid, 3 Sheets Curtings &c .....
two Shifts and a Little Other Linnen one Cubbard a Large Earthen pot and Some other Earthen ware one Dresser one joynt Stool one Leaf Table two Chests one Box one Great Chair 4 Small

Chairs; a warming pan & a frying-pan a Small keep one Spitt two Candlesticks a peper-box & Dridging box a greater two Hakes one Gridiron a Porridge pot & hooks a Skillett a pair of Cobirons fire Shovel & tongs a pair of Bellows a Look'glass some Pictures a Cloase-brush 2 Boxes one Boxiron & Stand old a flesh fork a hook & one Iron skuze

RELIEF: Lettice Flattman was in receipt of 1s. 6d. per week when this inventory was made. She had been a pensioner since 1730 and was also given rent payments and money when 'in Sickness' and 'at other Needfull times' by the parish (NRO PD 295/94; NRO PD 295/102).

FURTHER INFORMATION: Lettice Flattman was widowed. Poor law records and parish registers indicate that she became increasingly unwell from 1737. She eventually died and was subsequently buried at the ratepayer's expense on 10 November 1737 at a cost of around 18s. in total. The parish paid 1s. for making this inventory of her possessions and for copying it into the overseers' accounts. An earlier pauper inventory of Lettice Flattman's goods was taken on 26 June 1731 **(137)**. This inventory appears to have been made to update the earlier one. The first inventory indicates that Lettice Flattman was living with another pauper, Henry Branch, but there is no evidence to suggest that the two were still living together in 1737 (NRO PD 295/3; NRO PD 295/94; NRO PD 295/102).

DUBIOUS TERMS: Lines 13: 'Iron skuze' – unknown term.

143. Nicholas Burley (junior), 29 September 1738

NRO PD 295/102 Redenhall with Harleston and Wortwell Overseers' Order Book, 1708–1743.

An Inventory taken by M^{r}. John Peck the present Overseer of ye Poor this 29th. Day of Sep^{t}. 1738. viz: – – – of the Goods in the Possesion of Nich^{a} Burley Jun

One Bed & Bedstead four Chairs one pair of Cobirons one Table one Stool one Desk one Hutch one Vessel one Hake one Iron-Pott one Pail one Gridiron one Warming pan one Frying pan

RELIEF: Nicholas Burley was in receipt of casual relief when this inventory was taken. He was given rent payments from the parish and his wife was provided with money when 'in Sickness or at other Needfull times' and by order of the justice. His son and daughter were also sometimes given clothing from the parish (NRO PD 295/94; NRO PD 295/102).

FURTHER INFORMATION: Nicholas Burley was married and they had at least one son and one daughter. An Alice Burley is mentioned in overseers' records, but it is unknown whether she was the wife, daughter, or another relation of Nicholas Burley (NRO PD 295/94; NRO PD 295/102).

144. Widow Todd, 29 September 1738

NRO PD 295/102 Redenhall with Harleston and Wortwell Overseers' Order Book, 1708–1743.

An Inventory taken of ye Goods belonging Wid^{w}: Todd by M^{r}. Jno. Peck Overseer the 29th day of Sep^{t}: 1738 viz

one Bed a Boltster & Bedstead one Cubburd one Weel & Reel a Candle-stick a Dresser & Cole a Shelf an Iron-porridg pot four old Chairs .... a Cover Lid & a new Sheet –

RELIEF: Widow Todd was in receipt of 2s. 6d. per week when this inventory was made. She had been a pensioner for a number of years prior to her goods being appraised and was given clothing, rent payments, and money when 'in Illness' (NRO PD 295/94; NRO PD 295/102).

FURTHER INFORMATION: Widow Todd's husband's name was George. She had three children living with her during the early 1730s and it is probable that they were still living with her when this inventory was taken. Overseers' accounts and parish registers show that Widow Todd was buried at the parish's expense on 14 March 1739. An Usilla Todd and Ruth Todd (with a child born out of wedlock) are also noted in poor law records for the late 1730s, but it is unknown if they were any relation of Widow Todd (NRO PD 295/3; NRO PD 295/94; NRO PD 295/102). An earlier pauper inventory of Widow Todd's goods was taken on 26 June 1731 **(135)**. This inventory appears to have been made to update the earlier one.

145. Godfrey Goodrum, 27 November 1738

NRO PD 295/102 Redenhall with Harleston and Wortwell Overseers' Order Book, 1708–1743.

Goods in ye Possesion of Godphry Goodrum

An Inventory taken by M^{r}. Hen Jay the present Overseer on ye 27th day of Nov^{br}: 1738.

In the Kitching

there is 23 Earthen plates & 3 earthen Dishes some pictures; a Dresser with Drawers two Tables 9 Chairs one Boyler & one pot one Hake a pair of hand Irons & tongs; a pair of Spice drawers, a Corner Cubbart wth Small Earthen wear; two Doz of Glass Bottles and old Cubbert two Brusshes, a Looking Glass ~~a~~ plate Shelfs a pair of Window Curtains a killer & pail & old Rubbish

In the Chamber

one Bed Bedsted &c – one pair of Sheets

RELIEF: Godfrey Goodrum was in receipt of 2s. 3d. per week when this inventory was taken. He started to receive a pension sometime between Michaelmas 1737 and Easter 1738 and was also given clothing, faggots, and money when ‘in Sickness’ and ‘at other Needfull times’ (NRO PD 295/94; NRO PD 295/102).

FURTHER INFORMATION: Godfrey Goodrum was married. It is possible that Hannah Goodrum, buried on 26 December 1738 in Redenhall, was his wife. The parish paid 6d. making this inventory and 6d. for copying it into the town book (NRO PD 295/3; NRO PD 295/94; NRO PD 295/102).

DAMAGE: Ink spill on line 9 by ‘Shelfs’.

146. Susan Burrows, 15 January 1738/39

NRO PD 295/102 Redenhall with Harleston and Wortwell Overseers’ Order Book, 1708–1743.

Goods in the Possession of Susan Burrows

An Inventory taken by M^{r}: Hen Jay the present Overseer on ye 15th day of Jan 1738–9

Two Beds one Bedstead and Matt & Coverlid one Chest one good Sheet a Gown petty-Coat one Wooden Bowl some wheat one Pewter dish in The s^{d} Chest with Several old things; one Hake 3 Trenchers one Wooden dish one Spining Wheel and reel 2 Chairs –

RELIEF: Susan Burrows started to receive a pension of 1s. per week when this inventory was made. An additional 2s. per week was given to Widow Mullinger for the care of her child. This was probably because they were both sick. Susan Burrows was also frequently given casual relief from the parish such as rent payments, money when she was ‘in Sickness or Other Needfull times’, and items such as clothing (NRO PD 295/94; NRO PD 295/102).

FURTHER INFORMATION: Susan Burrows appears to have been living on her own as a single woman. Her child is noted as ‘B C’ in poor law records, showing that they were born out of wedlock. Around 1738, Susan Burrows was removed from another, unknown, parish to Redenhall with Harleston and Wortwell. The parish spent 1s. making this inventory and copying it into the overseers’ accounts (NRO PD 295/94; NRO PD 295/102).

147. James Keely, 2 February 1738/39

NRO PD 295/102 Redenhall with Harleston and Wortwell Overseers’ Order Book, 1708–1743.

Feb^{r}. y^{e} 2^{d} 1738–9 An Inventory Taken by M^{r}. Hen Jay of y^{e} Goods in the possession of James Keely.

In y^{e} Lower Room

one Hake, 4 Chairs, 2 Tables, one Warming-pan, one Cradle, a Box-Iron & 2 heaters, 3 Candle Sticks, 4 Earthen plates, 8 Trenchers a fire=Shovel & tongs, a Small Boyling pot, a frying-pan, a Skillett a Boule Cup & dish all wood, 2 Earthen dishes, a pair of Bellows, 2 Pitchers & a Mugg 2 Window Curtains

in y^{e} Chambers

one flock bed a feather-Boltster bedstead Line, Matt Cover Lid &c 2 Coffers a Chamber pot one Feather-bed &c one Coffer one Chair 4 Curtains –

RELIEF: James Keely started to receive casual relief from Easter 1738. At various times the parish gave him and his family food and money when 'in Sickness or Other Needfull times' (NRO PD 295/94; NRO PD 295/102).

FURTHER INFORMATION: James Keely and his 'family' are noted in poor relief records several times, suggesting that he had a wife and children. The parish spent 1s. making this inventory and copying it into the overseers' accounts (NRO PD 295/94; NRO PD 295/102).

148. Widow Searls, 2 June 1739

NRO PD 295/102 Redenhall with Harleston and Wortwell Overseers' Order Book, 1708–1743.

An Inventory taken by Hen Jay Deputy Overseer for John Lord this 2^{d} Day of June 1739 of the Goods in the possession of Wid^{w}: Searls (as follows)

In the Kitching

One Hake one pair of tongs one pair of handirons one pair of Bellows one Small Kettle one Gridiron one frying pan one pewter Dish one Hour Glass one Skillett one pewter Porringer one pail one Joynt stool 3 Chairs a Looking-Glass-frame with a Drawer; three Earthen dishes two Spining weels one Table one Boxiron

In the Parler

one Iron pot, one Large Kettle one Reele one Vessel one Killer one Large Chest one Wooden box one Candle Stick –

one Bed Bedstead Rugg & Curtains one keep one Sive –

3 trenchers one Warming pan one Old Sithe one Hickle one Small Looking-Glass one fork and a Crop of Beans on ye Ground

RELIEF: Widow Searls was in receipt of 6d. per week when this inventory was taken. She first became a pensioner in mid–1737 and was also sometimes given money from the parish when 'in Sickness' and 'at other Needfull times' (NRO PD 295/94; NRO PD 295/102).

FURTHER INFORMATION: The parish spent 1s. making this pauper inventory and copying it into the overseers' accounts (NRO PD 295/94; NRO PD 295/102).

149. Ann/Widow Alexander, 6 May 1740

NRO PD 295/102 Redenhall with Harleston and Wortwell Overseers' Order Book, 1708–1743.

An Inventory taken by M^{r}. Samuel Mason Deputy for Jam^{s} Roberts this 6th day of May 1740. of ye Goods Left by Ew^{d}. Alexanders Wid^{w} as follows

sta<?>e away

a Bedstead & Bolster; a Small nest of Drawers; ~~a Deal Box no Lidd~~, a Blankett, a Real, a Large Ovel Table, a Square Table, a Great Chair; A Cushing Chair a Large Cubbard, an old Lanthorn, 2 Chairs without Bottoms, a Joint-Stool, a Candle-Stick, a Hake; & a pair of tongs.

RELIEF: Widow Alexander was in receipt of 5s. per week when this inventory was taken. She had been a pensioner since late–1737 when her husband died. In addition to a pension, Widow Alexander frequently received money when 'In Sickness or Other Needfull times' from the parish and her children were often provided with clothing. She was also sometimes given firewood (NRO PD 295/94; NRO PD 295/102).

FURTHER INFORMATION: Widow Alexander's name was Ann and her husband Edward was buried at the ratepayers' expense on 12 November 1737. She had at least two children living with her when this inventory was made. One of them was a boy (probably called Robert) and one was a girl. Widow Alexander was buried at the expense of Redenhall with Harleston and Wortwell on 5 May 1740, at a cost of £1 0s. 6d. in total. Her children were subsequently supported by the parish. Extant records show that James Roberts was an overseer of the poor and Samuel Mason was the deputy overseer (NRO PD 295/3; NRO PD 295/94; NRO PD 295/102).

DUBIOUS TERMS: Line 3: 'sta<?>e away' – this was written above '~~a Deal Box no Lidd~~' and may suggest that the box was taken away.

150. Mary Gower, 10 May 1740

NRO PD 295/102 Redenhall with Harleston and Wortwell Overseers' Order Book, 1708–1743.

An Inventory taken by M^{r}: Sam^{el} Mason deputy for Jam^{s} Roberts on ye 10th day of may 1740. of ye Goods Left by Mary Gower. (as follows)

One Bed & 2 Boltsters feathers one flock Boltster; a Rug & a Blankett one Pillow 3 Pillow Bears one Porridge-pot, 3 pair of Sheets, one Skillett a Long Earthen pot, a Cole; – a warming-pan a Sq^{r}. Table, a Sq^{r}. Box, a Baskett, a Wooden Pint 2 Candle Sticks, one fire pan – a pair of Tongs, and ~~a Hake~~, a

Gridiron, a pair of Cobirons, a Trunk with some Small Linnen one Large Chest wth a Lock with three pewter dishes 3 Porringers a Bason a Salt Sellar a Board Cloth in ye Same; a Frying-pan a pair of Pott-hooke, 2 Iron Curtain Rods 4 Chairs a Wooden Cup Small wth Salt, a pair of Stays, two Gowns and two petty-Coats and a Spitt at Kerrissons and a Hammer
Memorandum ye pewter sold

RELIEF: Mary Gower was in receipt of 2s. 6d. per week when this inventory was made. She had received a pension from the parish since around mid–1737 and was sometimes given clothing and money when 'in need' (NRO PD 295/94; NRO PD 295/102).

FURTHER INFORMATION: Mary Gower was probably widowed or a single woman. Poor law records for the parish suggest that she may have been living with somebody called Spark senior. Mary Gower was buried on 11 May 1740 at a cost of 11s. to the parish. Her goods were then washed and moved to the workhouse, or sold, or were given to other paupers, such as Kerrison, who is noted in the inventory on line 11. The parish spent 1s. making this pauper inventory and copying it into the overseers' accounts. Records show that James Roberts was an overseer of the poor and that Samuel Mason was the deputy overseer (NRO PD 195/3; NRO PD 295/94; NRO PD 295/102).

151. Widow Catchpool, 4 July 1740

NRO PD 295/102 Redenhall with Harleston and Wortwell Overseers' Order Book, 1708–1743.

An Inventory taken by M^{r}: Samuel Mason Deputy Overseer for M^{r}. Jam^{s}. Roberts, on the 4th. day July 1740. of the Goods in ye possession of Wid^{w} Catchpool as follows

Two Beds wth. what belongs to them, 4 Pewter Dishes, a Brass pot, 2 Skillets, 3 Tables, 5 Chairs, 2 Joynt-stools, 2 Cubbards, a Box-Iron wth Heaters, 2 Leather-Trunks, one Huck, a pair of Cobirons, a fire pan and Tongs, a pair of Bellows, 1 Hake, 1 Gridiron, one Warming-pan, 1 Frying-pan, 2 Killers, one pail, one Driping pan, 6 Trenchars, 1 Looking-Glass, one Hour-Glass, 1 Candle-stick, a Small Clever, with other Trifles.

RELIEF: Widow Catchpool and her daughter were in receipt of a joint pension of 2s. 3d. per week when this inventory was made. They had received regular relief since late–1737 and were also given firewood, rent payments, and money when they were 'in Need' or 'Sickness' (NRO PD 295/94; NRO PD 295/102–103).

FURTHER INFORMATION: Widow Catchpool's daughter was called Elizabeth and appears to have often been unwell. She was buried on 12 December 1745 at a cost of 18s. to the parish. Widow Catchpool died less than a year after this and officials spent 19s. 6d. to bury her in August 1746. It is possible that Widow Catchpool had another daughter called Mary Catchpool living with her. The parish spent 9d. making this pauper inventory of Widow Catchpool's possessions and copying it into the overseers' accounts. James Roberts was an overseer of the poor (NRO PD 295/3; NRO PD 295/94; NRO PD 295/102–103). There is a second pauper inventory of Widow Catchpool's goods taken 3 January 1745/46 **(162)**. That inventory appears to have been made to update this earlier one.

152. Robert Garrard, 4 July 1740

NRO PD 295/102 Redenhall with Harleston and Wortwell Overseers' Order Book, 1708–1743.

An Inventory taken by M^{r}: Samuel Mason Deputy Overseer for M^{r}: Jam^{s} Roberts, on ye 4th day of July 1740. ~~(as follows)~~ of ye Goods in ye Possession of Robt Garrard (as follows) –

One Bed and what belongs thereto, 1 Tubb, 2 Vessels, 1 Killer, 1 Table, 1 Joynt stool, 1 handle Brush, – 3 Chairs, a pair of Cobirons, a fire Shovel & Tongs, a pair of Bellows, 2 Candle-sticks, 1 Pail, a Gridiron 3 Spining-Weels & a Reel, a Warming-pan, a Looking-Glass, 1 Glass-Keep some Earthen-ware, 1 Spitt, 1 Hake a Frying-pan, 1 Cloths-Brush, one Iron Pott and one Brass pott.

RELIEF: Robert Garrard was in receipt of casual relief when this inventory was made. Between Michaelmas 1739 and Easter 1740, he appears to have been removed from another, unknown, parish to Redenhall and was subsequently given 10s. in rent payment and money from the parish occasionally (NRO PD 295/94; NRO PD 295/102).

FURTHER INFORMATION: Robert Garrard was probably married and had at least one child. The parish spent 9d. making this pauper inventory and copying it into the overseers' accounts. James Roberts was an overseer of the poor (NRO PD 295/94; NRO PD 295/102).

DAMAGE: 'Looking' and 'Cloths' smudged on lines 7–8.

153. Widow Salter, 4 July 1740

NRO PD 295/102 Redenhall with Harleston and Wortwell Overseers' Order Book, 1708–1743.

The Goods in the Possession of Wid^{w}: Salter taken by M^{r}: Samuel Mason Deputy Overseer for Jam^{s} Roberts on ye 4th. day of July 1740.

One Bed & Boltster &c, 1 Chair, & 1 Box, – –

RELIEF: Widow Salter was in receipt of 1s. per week when this inventory was made. She started to receive a pension from the parish sometime between Michaelmas 1739 and Easter 1740 and was also sometimes given money when 'in need' and 'by order' of the justice. The parish also frequently gave her clothing and firewood (NRO PD 295/94; NRO PD 295/102).

FURTHER INFORMATION: The parish spent 6d. making this pauper inventory and copying it into the overseers' accounts. James Roberts was an overseer of the poor (NRO PD 295/94; NRO PD 295/102).

154. John Cupper, 11 July 1740

NRO PD 295/102 Redenhall with Harleston and Wortwell Overseers' Order Book, 1708–1743.

July 11th. 1740

An Inventory taken of ye Goods of John Cupper in Waybread, on ye 11 Day of July 1740. By M^{r}: John Sawer and M^{r}: Sam^{el} Mason; (as follows)

One Bed & Bedstead &c; two pair of Sheets, a Sq^{r}: Table, a keep, a Deal Ovel Table, two Iron Pots, a Brass Skillett two Iron Hakes, a pair of Cobirons, a pair of Bellows – a Brass-basting-Ladle, one Iron Candlestick, a Warming pan one Chest, one Meal-huch, one Lei-Leach, two Killers, – one Tow-wheel, 5 Trenchers, four Chairs, an Old hair Sive one Spitt – –

RELIEF: The parish started to give John Cupper's wife a pension of 1s. 6d. per week when this inventory was taken. His wife was also given cash on occasion and the couple's rent (£1 2s. 6d.) was paid by the parish (NRO PD 295/94; NRO PD 295/102).

FURTHER INFORMATION: John Cupper was residing in Weybread, Suffolk, when this inventory was taken, but had settlement in Redenhall with Harleston and Wortwell. Weybread is only around one mile from the Norfolk border and 1.5 miles from Harleston. Overseers' accounts indicate that John Cupper and his wife were removed from Weybread back to Redenhall with Harleston and Wortwell around July 1740. The couple had children, but it is unknown how many they had. The parish spent 6d. making this pauper inventory and copying it into the overseers' accounts. Samuel Mason was the deputy overseer of the poor and John Sawer was probably a churchwarden (NRO PD 295/94; NRO PD 295/102).

155. Francis Semmons, 6 January 1740/41

NRO PD 295/102 Redenhall with Harleston and Wortwell Overseers' Order Book, 1708–1743.

Jan ye 6th 1740.

An Inventory taken by M^{r}. Sam^{el} Mason of the Town Goods in ye Possession of Fran^{s} Semmons (on ye Common)

In ye Low Room

one Porridge pot, 3 Glass Bottles 3 Trenchers one Ovel Table, one Square. Table. one Looking-Glass a Cubbard a keep, a Small Trunk one Spining Wheel, a Real – 3 old Chairs, Some Tea Earthen-ware, a Hake a Hock a Hatchett, a Sithe, an old Spade.

above Stairs

one Bed, Bedstead, Boltster, a Rugg one Blankett and Curtains, 3 pair of Sheets.

RELIEF: Francis Semmons was in receipt of casual relief when this inventory was taken. He had received this since around Michaelmas 1739 in the form of money by order of the justice and when he and his wife were 'in Need'. They were also sometimes given rent payments and clothing from the parish (NRO PD 295/94; NRO PD 295/102).

FURTHER INFORMATION: Francis Semmons was married to a woman named Susan and they had at least three children when this inventory was made. The parish spent 9d. making this pauper inventory and copying it into the overseers' accounts. Samuel Mason was the deputy overseer of the poor (NRO PD 295/3; NRO PD 295/94; NRO PD 295/102). There is also a 'goods-given' inventory relating to Francis Semmons, dated 20–22 December 1740 (from: NRO PD 295/94):

Goods Bought for Fran^{s} Semmons

Dec^{br}:	20 A bed & other things belonging to it..	1	5	0
	22 A Pott & Hooks of M^{r}. Sawer	0	6	2
	Expenses Hiring a place & Carrying things.......	0	0	6
		1	11	8

156. Isaac Day, 11 December 1742

NRO PD 295/102 Redenhall with Harleston and Wortwell Overseers' Order Book, 1708–1743.

11 Dec. 1742. An Inventory taken by Mr. John Hunt & James Strange the present Overseers of Goods in the ~~in the~~ possession of Isaac Day as follows

First 2 Beds and what belongs thereto one with Curtens, 7 Chairs, 2 Joyn-Stools, one Chest of Drawers, one Meal-Hutch, 2 Small Beer-Vessels, 3 Stone Bottles, 3 Tables one Iron-Pot, one Skillet, 3 wooden Bowls, 6 Trenchers, 5 Glass-Bottles, 2 Earthen-Pots, one Dresser, 2 killers, one Tub, one Pail, one Handle-Cup, two Stone Mugs, two Small Pans, & one Wooden Dish, one Fire-pan, one pair of Tongs, one pair of Cobirons, one Hake, 2 Candlesticks, one Rostiron, 2 pair of Pothooks, one Plate-Rack with 6 Delf Plates, 3 Boxes, 2 Tow=Reels, one Small Looking-glass, one pair of Bellows, a Childs Chair, two pair of Sheets.

RELIEF: Isaac Day was in receipt of 1s. 6d. per week and had received a pension intermittently from the parish for several years prior to his goods being appraised. He was also given money from the parish when he was 'lame', 'in Sickness', and 'in Need' (NRO PD 295/94; NRO PD 295/102–103).

FURTHER INFORMATION: Poor relief records show that Isaac Day was married and had children. John Day also appears in the overseers' accounts, but it is unknown whether he was any relation of Isaac Day (NRO PD 295/94; NRO PD 295/102–103).

157. Frances Metchels, 11 December 1742

NRO PD 295/102 Redenhall with Harleston and Wortwell Overseers' Order Book, 1708–1743.

An Inventory taken by Mr. John Hunt and James Strange the present Overseers on the 11th. day of Dec. 1742 of the Goods in the possession of Frances Metchels Widow as follows

One Bed and what belongs thereto, Seven Chairs, two Tables, one Cupboard, three Boxes, one Trunk, one Beer-Vessel, a pair of Bellows, a pair of Tongs, a Fire-pan, two Iron-Pots, two Small Killers, one Pail, one Hour-Glass, one Small Looking-Glass, eight Delf Plates, three Small wooden Dishes, one Earthen Dish, two Gotches, three Stone Pots, two pint Bottles, one Wool-Wheel, one Wool Reel, one Childs Basket, two pair of Sheets, a Box-iron.

RELIEF: Frances Metchels was in receipt of 1s. 6d. per week when this inventory was made. Along with her children, she was given additional money and had her rent paid by the parish several times (NRO PD 295/94; NRO PD 295/102–103).

FURTHER INFORMATION: Frances Metchels was widowed and had children living with her when this inventory was taken (NRO PD 295/94; NRO PD 295/102–103).

158. Elizabeth Twist, 17 June 1743

NRO PD 295/102 Redenhall with Harleston and Wortwell Overseers' Order Book, 1708–1743.

An Inventory taken of ye Goods in ye Possesion of Eliz: Twist by M^{r}. Charles Bennett ye present Overseer on ye 17th day of June 1743; Viz:

One bed in fashing of a Chest of Draws wth a Pillow, Boulster, Blankett, Coverlid & two pair of Sheets one pair of Handirons, a fire Shovel & tongs, a pair of Bellows a Small Salt box two Small Ovel Tables a Keep or Cubbard, one Looking-Glass, one Sq^{r}. Table Table wth a drawer one Warming pan, one Frying pan, two Small pott Bell mettle one pewter dish, one old Trunk, one

Sq^{r}. Wooden Box 3 or 4 Earthen plates 5 Small Chairs one Great Chair 3 Small Window Curtains ....

RELIEF: Elizabeth Twist was in receipt of casual relief when this inventory was made. Most notably, the parish paid 15s. towards her rent. This appears to have been the catalyst for the parish taking an inventory of her goods, as the overseer wrote that it was 'Order'd that Eliz: Twists Rent be paid by the Overseer & That an Inventory be taken of her Goods' in May 1743 (NRO PD 295/94; NRO PD 295/102–103).

FURTHER INFORMATION: Elizabeth Twist was probably living on her own as a spinster since she was referred to by her Christian name and never as 'Widow' (NRO PD 295/94; NRO PD 295/102).

DAMAGE: Line 6: 'drawer' smudged.

159. Ann Capon, 24 June 1744

NRO PD 295/117 Redenhall with Harleston and Wortwell Inventories, 1744–1762.

An Inventory taken by M^{r}: Jam^{s}: Wright overseer of the Poor on June ye 24th. 1744 of the Goods of Ann Capon (as follows)

a Chest of Drawers, & a Bible, a Large Ovel Table, a Small Skillett, a Small Boyler, a fire Shovel, 3 old Napkins, a Gridiron, a pair of Hand-Irons, 2 Small books, a Brush, a Small Ovel Table – a Small Trunk, 5 Chairs, a Frying pan; A Bed, bedstead, & Curtains &c a Boltster; Pillow, ~~for~~ 2 pair of Sheets 2 Blankets, an old Cover-Lid; also 4 old Chairs

RELIEF: Ann Capon was in receipt of 1s. 6d. per week when this inventory was taken. She started to receive a pension around six months before her goods were appraised and was also sometimes given clothing from the parish (NRO PD 295/94; NRO PD 295/103).

FURTHER INFORMATION: Ann Capon was probably living on her own as a spinster since she was referred to by her Christian name and never as 'Widow'. This inventory was made one day before Ann Capon moved in to the home of Thomas Dain, who was employed by the parish to look after vulnerable parishioners such as children and the elderly. The parish spent 1s. making this pauper inventory and copying it into the overseers' accounts (NRO PD 295/94; NRO PD 295/103).

160. Elizabeth Trew, 15 April 1745

NRO PD 295/117 Redenhall with Harleston and Wortwell Inventories, 1744–1762.

An Inventory taken on Aprill ye 15th 1745. of ye Goods belonging to Eliz Trew; by M^{r}: John Edwards, M^{r}. Wiseman and M^{r}. John Jackson: (viz.)

1 bed & bedstead, 1 Cubbard, 4 Chairs, 1 Coffer 1 Table & Stool 1 Desk, 1 Box-Iron, 1 pair of Cobirons, 1 pair of Tongs; 1 firepan, 1 hake & gridiron, 2 Candle sticks & a pair of Bellows, A Porrige pot & Kettle, 1 pail & Bowl, one pair of Old Sheets ....

....

May 17: 1745 the above Goods of Eliz Trew's Which I Recd With her I Do promise that whenever she Happon To Dye for be Sent for to the Said Parish again they Every of them shall be Accounted for or Return'd to the said parish

Witness officers the R Mark
Isaac Wales. of Robert Quantrell
Chris: Wiseman

RELIEF: Elizabeth Trew was in receipt of 1s. 6d. per week when this inventory was made. She had been a pensioner since April 1728 and was given clothing and money 'in time of Need' from the overseers. Additionally, the parish paid people to look after her when she was unwell (NRO PD 295/94; NRO PD 295/102–103).

FURTHER INFORMATION: Elizabeth Trew was probably living on her own as a widow or spinster when this inventory was made. The note below the inventory indicates that Elizabeth Trew was looked after and lived with Robert Quantrell soon after the inventory was taken. Robert Quantrell was not a pauper according to poor relief records. It is unknown what position (if any) Isaac Wales and Chris Wiseman held in the parish (NRO PD 295/94; NRO PD 295/102–103). An earlier pauper inventory of Elizabeth Trew's goods was taken on 26 June 1731 **(134)**. This inventory appears to have been made to update the earlier one.

161. Amey Gardner, 29 November 1745

NRO PD 295/117 Redenhall with Harleston and Wortwell Inventories, 1744–1762.

An Inventory of the Goods of Amey Gardner taken Nov 29 1745 By M^{r}: John Sawer Churchwarden And John Bond Overseer

A Bed, Bedstead, Curtains as it Stand.
A Chest of Drawer's A Deale Box.
A Warming pann A fire pan And Tongs
A freing pann A Roaster a hake
A Skillitt A Small Sauce pann
A pillion and Cloth 5 Chair's 2 Old Ones
One Sheet

RELIEF: Amey Gardner started to receive 6d. per week by town order when this inventory was taken, so that she could 'have proper Care taken of her'. She was also sometimes given additional money and cash towards her rent from the parish (NRO PD 295/94; NRO PD 295/103).

FURTHER INFORMATION: Amey Gardner was probably living on her own as a spinster since she was referred to by her Christian name and never as 'Widow' (NRO PD 295/94; NRO PD 295/103).

DUBIOUS TERMS: Line 8: 'pillion' – pillow or saddle.

162. Widow Catchpool, 3 January 1745/46

NRO PD 295/117 Redenhall with Harleston and Wortwell Inventories, 1744–1762.

An Inventory of the Goods of the W^{d}: Catchpoole Taken By M^{r}: John Hunt Churchwarden And John Bond Overseer January 3^{d}: 1745 –

A Bed And Bedstead Curtains and all things as it Stand = A Small Trundled Bed D^{o}: 2 Oak; Square Tables 1 Deale D^{o}: 2 Joint Stooles 6 Old Chairs 1 Oak Cheast 1 pair Cobirons A fire pan And Tong's 1 Large hanging Cubboard 1 Small D^{o}: – 1 pair Sheets a Grid=iron a Six Pint Bottle 2 Quart mogs 1 Box=iron And 2 heaters 1 hour glass A wooden Bowle 1 Earthen Dish &c:

RELIEF: Widow Catchpool was in receipt of 3s. per week when this inventory was made. She had received a pension since late–1737 and was also given firewood, rent payments, and money when she was occasionally 'in Need' or 'Sickness' from the parish. On 30 December 1745, the parish ordered that Widow Catchpool would live in the home of Thomas Dain, who was employed by the parish to look after vulnerable parishioners such as children and the elderly. This did not, however, last very long and on 12 January 1745/46 Widow Catchpool moved into the spare room of John Goldspink's house (NRO PD 295/94; NRO PD 295/102–103).

FURTHER INFORMATION: Widow Catchpool had a daughter called Elizabeth who was buried on 12 December 1745 at a cost of 18s. to the parish. Widow Catchpool died less than a year after this and officials spent 19s. 6d. to bury her in August 1746. It is possible that Widow Catchpool had another daughter called Mary Catchpool living with her (NRO PD 295/3; NRO PD 295/102–103; NRO PD 295/102). An earlier pauper inventory of Widow Catchpool's goods was taken on 4 July 1740 **(151)**. This inventory appears to have been made to update the earlier one and record what possessions Widow Catchpool had when she moved in with Thomas Dain.

163. Alexander Bazer, 8 April 1746

NRO PD 295/117 Redenhall with Harleston and Wortwell Inventories, 1744–1762.

An Inventory of Sand^{r}. Bazers Goods taken by Mr John Sawer & M^{r}. John Bond April 3^{d}. 1746

It^{m}. One Bed as it stand 2 pair of Sheets.
One trundle Bed as it Stand. A pair of Oak Drawers A Dale Table. A Dale Striking board 2 boxes One dale One Old Table. An Oak Stool. 7 Chairs. 1 Great Chair –
One Iron pott & hooks. firepan tongs Gridgiron & Andirons. A hake & speet. A pewter Cowl & 2 Dishes 1 plate 1 porringer 5 Earthen plates. A Looking Glass. A spice drawers. A Dale box 2 Spinning weels. A pail & 3 little killers. A Warming pan

RELIEF: Alexander Bazer was in receipt of 2s. per week when this inventory was taken. He had been a pensioner since around April/May 1740 and was also occasionally given rent payments and fuel from the parish (NRO PD 295/94; NRO PD 295/103).

FURTHER INFORMATION: Parish registers show that Alexander Bazer was married to Ester Bazer. The couple had at least one son named Robert when this inventory was made, who was baptised on 2 January 1744. The parish spent 6d. making this pauper inventory. John Sawer was a churchwarden and John Bond was an overseer of the poor (NRO PD 295/3; NRO PD 295/94; NRO PD 295/103).

164. John Brown, 6 October 1746

NRO PD 295/117 Redenhall with Harleston and Wortwell Inventories, 1744–1762.

An Inventory of Jno Browns Goods take by Mr Saml Barns October the 6th 1746

2 Tables 2 Stools A Large Cubbard 7 Chairs Andirons firepan & Tongs Gridgiron A hake Warming pan A pair of Bellows A boiler 2 Skillets A pail 2 Chest 2 Spining Wheels A bed

RELIEF: John Brown was in receipt of casual relief when this inventory was taken. He was given money on numerous occasions during times of sickness and was also provided with rent payments and faggots from the parish (NRO PD 295/94; NRO PD 295/103).

FURTHER INFORMATION: John Brown was probably living on his own as a widower or bachelor when this inventory was made. Records for the parish indicate that he was living in Darsham, Suffolk, in mid–1746 but had moved back to Harleston (Jay's Green) by the time that this inventory was taken. Samuel Barns is occasionally noted in overseers' accounts, but it is unknown if he held a position such as churchwarden (NRO PD 295/94; NRO PD 295/103).

165. Widow Meek, 18 February 1752

NRO PD 295/117 Redenhall with Harleston and Wortwell Inventories, 1744–1762.

1752 An Inventory of the Wid. Meeks Goods taken by me Saml Butcher Overseer Feb: 18: 1752

A Bed & Boulster & bed Sides two pieces of Sheets and a piece of a Coverling an Iron pott and two Broken Iron Potts, a hook or Bill an Hake an old Killer and pail without a bail an old fire pann and tongs an old Candel Stick and Cup ....

RELIEF: Widow Meek was in receipt of small amounts of casual relief such as rent payments (15s.) and clothing when this inventory was taken (NRO PD 295/94–95; NRO PD 295/103).

166. Phillip Knight, 3 March 1762

NRO PD 295/117 Redenhall with Harleston and Wortwell Inventories, 1744–1762.

An Inventory of the Houshold Goods of Philip Knight taken by Mr Robt Tricker and Mr Peter Wales Churchwarden & Overseer 3^{d} March 1762

In the Kitchen

5 Baskets, a Tub, a Lye Letch, a Pail, 2 Kettles, 3 small Kellers 2 Stools, 2 Chairs, a parcel of Earthen Ware, wooden Cups &c

In the Chamber

A large Bed, 2 Blankets, a Rug, Bolster Bedknat & Bedstea<d> a Bedstead, a Rug, 2 Chairs, a Stool, 2 Chairs, a Close stool

In small Chamber

A Firepan Tongs, a pair of Bellows, 5 Chairs, a Table a Jointstool, a Slip, a Brush, a Chest, a Cradle, a Childs Chair & a Warming Pan

RELIEF: Phillip Knight and his family started to receive 4s. per week from March 1762. He and his wife were also frequently given large amounts of casual relief in the form of cash and rent payments (NRO PD 295/95; NRO PD 295/103).

FURTHER INFORMATION: Phillip Knight's wife was buried in March 1762. The parish contributed 2s. 6d. towards the costs of her burial. He had at least two children living with him when this inventory was made. One of them was buried in June 1764 and the parish contributed 5s. 6d. towards the costs of this. Phillip Knight also had a son and in July 1762 the parish paid 1s. 6d. towards 'Ph Knights Expences to Halesworth abt his Son going Apprentice'. Mary Knight also appears in overseers' accounts for the parish, but it is unknown whether she was any relation of Phillip Knight (NRO PD 295/95; NRO PD 295/103).

DAMAGE: Page ripped on the left-hand side of the page.

167. Michael Aggus, 24 December 1828

NRO PD 295/106 Redenhall with Harleston and Wortwell Overseers' Order Book, 1828–1831.

An Inventory of Michael Aggus's Furniture taken by J Hill and J. Barber at Earsham Decr. 24. 1828

Eight Day Clock / makers name
Robt Goodwin
Mahogany Be~~a~~ureau with
four Drawers
Pembroke Table
Chamber D°
Breakfast D°
Old Deal D°
Five Elm hollow seat Chairs
Two Elbow to match D°
Corner Cupboard & Cradle
Three Brass Candlesticks
Two Iron D° and Snuffers
Two Box Irons Heaters & one rest
Italion Iron
Four Prints Glaz^{d}. & Framed
Meat Axe and Bird Cage
Iron Horse and Plate Iron
Sugar Clippers and Steel
Set very old Fire Irons
Copper fixed and Furnace
Mahogany waiter & Chees tray
one Beaker Glass two Wine D°
Tea Pot Caddy & Sundries
Six Knives and Forks
Pepper and Mustard Castors
Glass Salt Seller
Small Tea Pot & Nut Cracks
Hook and trowel
Scuppett Spade and Hoe
Mattock Pick and two Forks
Brass Frying Pan
Copper Tea Kettle
Two old Broken Chairs –
Large Copper Boiler
Small D° D°
Saucepan D°
Two D° Iron
Garden Pot and dibble
two Wash Keelers
Water Pail
Hand Keeler and Bason
Sundry Hods & Shelves
Large Meal Hutch
10 or 12 Pieces of Crockery
D° Glass Bottles
Bread Keeler & Lanthorn
Beer Cask and Ale Stool
Very old Meat safe
two Hammers. Old Cupboard
Copper Scales & Sundry weghts
Four Post Beadstead & Hangings
Mattrass Feather Bed Bolster
and two Pillows
Counterpane Blankets & Sheets
Stump Beadstead, Oat flight Bed
Feather Bolster one Blanket
Linen Chest & 4 old Chairs
Tent Bedstead and Hangings
Mattrass Blanket & Sheet
Stump Bedstead Oat flight Bed
two Sheets one old Blanket
Childs Crib D° Coach Cart
Chest with four Drawers
D° with Five D° & looking Glass
Large Oak Chest & hand Brush
Small Stool and Desk Stool
Large Easy Chair

RELIEF: Michael Aggus started to receive casual relief when this inventory was made. Most of the time the parish paid him money to help his unwell daughter. For example, in January 1829 2s. 6d. was given to the family almost on a weekly basis to help his daughter (NRO PD 295/101; NRO PD 295/106).

FURTHER INFORMATION: Michael Aggus appears to have been married and had at least one daughter and one son living with him when this inventory was taken. He had settlement in Redenhall with Harleston and Wortwell, but lived in the nearby village of Earsham, Norfolk. On 16 February 1829, the parish ordered that 'Michael Aggas be allowed ten shillings this week, and that on his next application for relief he and his family be removed home'. The family continued to receive relief after this date, but it is unknown whether the parish followed through with their threat to remove the family. J Hill and J. Barber's names are sometimes mentioned in poor law records, but it is unknown whether either of them held a position in the parish such as overseer of the poor or churchwarden (NRO PD 295/101; NRO PD 295/106).

DUBIOUS TERMS: Line 31: 'D° Coach cart' – possibly a child's pram of some sort.

Shelton pauper inventories

The pauper inventories for Shelton can be found in a range of account books which note the disbursements and expenses of overseers, churchwardens, and constables. Most of them were written at intermittent times and can be found scattered throughout the volumes. Also included in the collection are goods-taken and debt-related inventories.

168. Anne Roberts, 28 October 1692

NRO PD 358/41 Shelton Overseers' Accounts, 1670–1734.

An Inventory of ye Goods of Anne Roberts Widow. taken ye 28th. day of October. 1692

		li s. d.
Inp^{r}	an old bedstead	0 – 5 – 00
	Itm an old table	0 – 2 – 06
	Itm an old desk, & a coffer, & a chest	0 – 6 – 00
	Itm 2 chaires & one joint Stool	0 – 1 – 06
	Itm an iron pot, & pothooks	0 – 6 – 00
	Itm a brasse skillet, & a pail	0 – 1 – 00
	Itm an old hake, & an old cliver ...... } Itm a piece of a pair of fire tongs .... }	0 – 1 – 06
	Itm an old pair of bellowes, & a basket	0 – 1 – 00
	~~Itm a chair~~	
	Sum total	01 – 04 – 06.

apprized ye day above written
by
Thomas Flatman
Jonathan Vines.

These goods were by ye consent of ye Inhabitants of Shelton ye 28th. day October 1692. given to Anne Buck Widow upon condition y^{t} She Shall keep ye daughter of Anne Roberts widow two full yeares from ye day of ye date hereof ye Town of Shelton promiseing to pay for ye Schooling of ye Said girl two pence a week from this day till o^{r} Lady day next. & not to take her away from ye said Anne Buck Widow dureing ye said term of two yeares nor yet she long as she ye said Anne Buck will keep her. Witnesse o^{r} hands

S A Rand Rect: of Shelton
Tho Dawson overser
Stephen Gray church warden

To this bargain above written I Anne Buck Widow doe consent & agree Witnesse my hand this 28th. day of October 1692.

RELIEF: Anne Roberts was in receipt of casual relief when this inventory was made, including cash and rent payments. The parish also paid around 14s. 10d. towards her funeral and gave her daughter clothing on occasion (NRO PD 358/41).

FURTHER INFORMATION: Anne Roberts was widowed and had at least one daughter. She was buried on 15 July 1692. Poor law records show that this was a pauper inventory and not a goods-taken inventory as the source suggests. Anne Buck does not appear to have been a pauper and was employed by the parish to look after and teach Anne Roberts' daughter (NRO PD 358/1; NRO PD 358/41).

169. John Hatton (junior), 9 February 1693/94

NRO PD 358/41 Shelton Overseers' Accounts, 1670–1734.

An Inventory of the Goods of John Haton Jun taken by the Overseers & Churchwardens the 9th day of February 1693: As followeth: //

	li s d
Imprimis One Posted bed stead One bed Matt & Cord One p of Sheets One blankett One coverlett 2 bousters	1 = 10 = 0
One Other li<n>en bedstead Matt & cord & p of Sheets One feater boulster & a flocke boulster one Coverlett	1 = 05 = 00
2 Cobarts	0 = 07 = 00
3 Tabells	0 = 06 = 00
One Greate Cheste	0 = 05 = 00
2 Joynted stooles & a planke stoole .	0 = 1 = 06
One box	0 = 01 = 00
Eight Chayers	0 = 04 = 00
Two Long Spining wheeles & ~~wheele~~ a Reele	0 = 05 = 00
One Neaste of Drawers	0 = 01 = 00
A Bras wormeing pan & a Skillett & bras Candellsticke	0 = 03 = 06
One Iron Pott & hookes	0 = 05 = 00
a p of Cobirons a p of Tongs a firepan helve a fryeing pan a bras Posnett..........	0 = 05 = 00
3 pewter Poringers a pewter Chamber pott a pewt pott to drinkin a Candellsticke & salte seller of pewter..	0 = 2 = 0
a Looke-Glase & five Glase bottells a Gotch civer=red with pewter	0 = 01 = 00

a p of bellowes a salt box a smootheing Iron a Greate Tub a bedstead 2 beeds 2 Coffer a Joynt forme 2 Ould Chayers one Ould Stoole a Cobart Tabell a dresser a Joynt forme	0 = 10 = 0
2 basketts 2 payles And Other Lumber	0 = 02 = 00
	5 = 14 = 0

Thos Dawson oversears
Henry Knites
Steaven Gray Churchwarden
aprisers

RELIEF: John Hatton and his family were given 10s. in total 'by order' between February 1693/94 and April 1694. The family may have subsequently started to receive 1s. per week from the parish, which was changed to 6d. per week around May 1694. It is probable that John Hatton was also sometimes provided with cash and firewood from the parish (NRO PD 358/41).

FURTHER INFORMATION: The familial background of John Hatton junior is difficult to establish as the overseers did not often distinguish between John Hatton junior and senior. The accounts, however, mention that John Hatton had a family, suggesting that he was married with one or more children. Overseers' papers note the burial of 'Hatons wife', 'Hatons Child', 'Goody Haton', 'old Hacon', and 'Widow Hackon' between Easter 1692 and Easter 1697. It is, however, unknown whether these people were relations of John Hatton junior. Because of this, it is not known if John Hatton junior was related to Widow Hatton, who had her goods inventoried in 1696 **(170)** (NRO PD 358/41).

170. Widow Hatton, 22 May 1696

NRO PD 358/41 Shelton Overseers' Accounts, 1670–1734.

The Goods of the Widd Hacon	li s d
A Bedsteade a Beed 2 boulsters & a pillow & a Rugg & matt & Cord ...	1 = 2 = 6
2 coffers with Locks & keys	0 = 4 = 0
a Bras pott & a Bras Kittell	0 = 5 = 0
a Skillett & a fryeing pann	0 = 1 = 6
2 basketts	0 = 0 = 6
a borded Chayer	0 = 0 = 6
A Joynt stoole & a littell Stoole	0 = 1 = 0
A hake	0 = 1 – 0

A morter & a Candell sticke & a p of Bellowes wch wee Lent to Pall, all ...	0 = 0 – 9
a Straw hatt	0 = 0 = 6
an ould Rost Iron a fire pan & p of Tongs	0 = 1 = 0
a Par of Sheets and a Shifning	0 = 7 = 0
a Leather Jacke & Gotch & a Pitcher Boll	0 = 0 = 6
2 Dishes & A Cupp & a wooden Platter	0 = 0 = 8
In money	0 = 1 = 7
A halfe Pecke & a Bottell	0 = 0 = 5
an Ould Sacke	0 = 0 = 6
a Vessell	0 = 1 = 0
here 22th May 1696	2 = 9 = 11

above <exenticned>
The Goods above Said were
apprised by us Robt Futter
William Pearse

RELIEF: Widow Hatton was in receipt of 1s. per week when this inventory was made. She had received this since around 1694 and was sometimes given firewood. The parish also paid various people to look after her during times of illness (NRO PD 358/41).

FURTHER INFORMATION: The familial background of Widow Hatton is difficult to establish as the overseers generally did not distinguish between the different people with the surname Hatton. Widow Hatton, however, had probably been widowed since around 1694, as her name starts to appear in the accounts after the funeral of 'Old Hacon', who was probably her husband. The parish paid around £1 towards her funeral when she died around April/May 1696. Poor law records note the burial of 'Hatons wife', 'Hatons Child', and 'Goody Haton' between Easter 1692 and Easter 1693. It is, however, unknown whether these people were relations of Widow Hatton. Because of this, it is not known if Widow Hatton was related to John Hatton junior, whose goods were inventoried in 1692 **(169)**. The parish received £1 4s. 6d. from selling some of the goods of Widow Hatton to William Pearse between 1696–1697. It is unknown who 'Pall' was (line 12). Robert Futter and William Pearse were possibly churchwardens in the parish in 1696 (NRO PD 358/41).

171. Francis Karrington, 21 May 1700

NRO PD 358/41 Shelton Overseers' Accounts, 1670–1734.

The Goods of Francis Karrington upon his craweing collection of ye Town of Shelton & takeing ye patch upon himself & family were apprized by y^{e} <?>se of ye Town of Shelton upon ye 21th. day of May 1700. as ye Law requires.

	<u>In ye fire room. & closet by it</u>	
Inp^{r}	a bed as it stands wth a bedstead coverlet & two blankets a bolster & 2 pillows mat & line	04 – 00 – 00
Itm	5 stooles & 4 chaires	00 – 03 – 00
Itm	firepan & tongues, a payr of cobirons, a payr of bellows..	00 – 03 – 00
Itm	a brasse kettle, 2 brasse skillets <u>2</u>. powdering tubs & a pail	00 – 10 – 00
Itm	2 iron pots, an hake, a rostiron, a Spit & a payr of pothooks	00 – 07 – 06
Itm	2 dressers & a tub	00 – 01 – 06
	<u>In ye other room</u>	
Itm	a bed & bedstead 2 bolsters a pillow, a blancket coverlet mat & cord	01 – 00 – 00
Itm	a pewter bason, a pewter chamber pot, 2 porringers& two little sawcers	00 – 03 – 00
Itm	a brasse candlestick & 3 cups	00 – 01 – 00
Itm	a great wicker chayr & a cushion	00 – 06 – 00
Itm	7 earthen plates & earthen candlestick, & gally pot & a glass case	00 – 03 – 00
Itm	a warming pan	00 – 02 – 00
Itm	a stone gotch & a tin bake pan	00 – 01 – 00
Itm	a tub & a bowl	00 – 03 – 00
Itm	2 beer vessells	00 – 01 – 00
Itm	four payr of sheets 7 pillow beers, 1 towell napkins & other houshold linnen	02 – 00 – 00
Itm	a desk box as it stands	00 – 10 – 00
Itm	an old cupboard	00 – 02 – 00
	<u>In ye chamber</u>	
Itm	a table & two stooles	<u>00 – 02 – 00</u>
	<u>In all</u>	<u>09 – 19 – 00</u>

In prsance of us	apprized by
S A: Rand Rect: of Shelton	Stephen Gray
Tho Dawson	Samwell Bullyn
John Smyth	

RELIEF: Francis Karrington started to receive a pension of 2s. 6d. per week when this inventory was made. In addition, the parish sometimes gave him firewood, bushels of meal, and clothing, and helped his wife by giving her extra money and hiring people to look after her during times of sickness (NRO PD 358/41). The inventory also notes that Francis Karrington was 'craweing collection' from Shelton parish.

FURTHER INFORMATION: Francis Karrington was married and probably elderly, as he is sometimes described as 'old Carrington' in poor law records. He was buried on 27 January 1703/4 at a cost of around 17s. to the parish. Samuel Bullyn and John Symth were overseers of the poor and Thomas Dawson and Stephen Gray were churchwardens in Shelton (NRO PD 358/41). The source notes that the inventory was taken 'as ye Law requires', but it is important to note that there was no legal basis in making inventories of paupers' goods (see chapter 2). There is a later inventory of Francis Karrington's goods from 1703/4 in the same overseers' account book. It was probably made to record the taking of Francis Karrington's goods after his death (NRO PD 358/41):

Delivered Febr y^{e}. 7th. 1703[/4]. by John Bennet ye exectuto^{r} of his Grandfather John Bennet unto Stephen Grey Churchwarden & John Smyth Overseer of Shelton ye goods of Francis Carrington deceased as followeth

Inpr twenty & one pieces of linnen bundlid in an old linnen cloth

Itm. three baggs wth hops weighing (pokes & all) Sixteen pounds

Itm one cloth coat, one wastcoat, one payr of breeches, & one payr of lineings

Itm two payr of stockings, one payr of upperbodies, & stomacher, & two petticoats

Itm one Silver spoon.

Mem ye cloth coat above mentioned, was sold by Mr Smyth one of ye Overseers of Shelton for ten Shillings, as appears by his account

Mem y^{t} upon ye 14th day of september 1704. Mr Smith was discharged of all ye goods late Fr: Carringtons in ye p^{r}sence of ye Inhabitants of Shelton.

172. Barbara Jermyn, 31 July 1700

NRO PD 358/41 Shelton Overseers' Accounts, 1670–1734.

An Inventory made the 31th day of July 1700 of ye goods of Barbara Jermyn Widdow

Impremis one feather bed three boulsters & five pillows
Item two coverlets and three sheets
Item a flock bed in Thomas Francis his hand
Item a livery cubberd
Item a warming pan

Then agreed that she should have 2^{s} 6^{d} p weeke the paiement to begin on munday the 5th of August 1700 & is before that munday & that good: Baily have no more p weeke till Easter day next & so long if ye widdow live she is to keepe her for ye same money weekely.

witnesse William Pearse } Church wardens
Thos Dawson }
Sam: Bullin
the marke of
John O Roberts

RELIEF: Barbara Jermyn started to receive a pension of 2s. 6d. per week when this inventory was made. Prior to this she was paid 9d. per week to look after 'Robts child'. She was frequently provided with clothing such as an apron, petticoat, and shirts from the parish (NRO PD 358/41). The inventory also notes that she was given '2^{s} 6^{d} p weeke the paiement to begin on munday the 5th of August 1700'.

FURTHER INFORMATION: Barbara Jermyn was widowed and appears to have had adult children who had moved out by the time that the inventory was taken. She was buried on 18 December 1701. A Robert Jermyn is also noted in overseers' accounts for the parish, but it is unknown whether he was any relation of Barbara Jermyn. The circumtext (see below) reveals that the goods did not go to the parish when Barbara Jermyn died. Instead, an agreement was made between parochial officials and Thomas Jermyn (presumably her son), who agreed to pay the costs of Barbara Jermyn's funeral and received the possessions in exchange in April 1702. Goody Baily was another pensioner in Shelton parish. Sam Bullin and John Roberts were overseers of the poor for Shelton. There is also an inventory of unknown type of Richard Jermyn's goods from October 1701 and a pauper inventory of William Jermyn's goods from April 1712 **(174)**; however, it is unknown whether these people were relations of Barbara Jermyn (NRO PD 358/41).

CIRCUMTEXT: There is a note underneath the inventory dated 6 April 1702, stating that (NRO PD 358/41):

> The goods abovementioned were when Richard Mathis was Overseer of ye poor of Shelton by ye consent of ye Townsmen of Shelton given to Thomas Jermyn for burying of ye above mentioned Barbara Jermyn at his own cost & charge.

173. Jeremy Nudds, 15 November 1709

NRO PD 358/41 Shelton Overseers' Accounts, 1670–1734.

15th November 1709

An Inventory of the Goods now In the possession of Jeremy Nudds. now Entered unto Collection att the ~~value~~ Rate of 2^{s} 6^{d} p weecke now taken & apprised by the Church warden & Overseers for the Poore as Followeth for the benifitt of Town Stocke

Innprimis	a Cobart	00 = 03 = 00
	A Large Table & 2 little tables 2 Stooles	00 = 03 = 06
	Item 3 Spining wheels & a Reele	00 = 03 = 00
	3 Chayers & Ironpott a paile a Skillet	00 = 07 = 00
	A Smotheing Iron a hake & a Tub 2 vessells & coffer & a Draft hook	00 = 02 = 00
	Item a bed 3 bolsters & a pillow & Rug Matt & Cord as itt stands	01 = 00 = 00
	Item a Trunke a Cofer & a Deske & one Table & warmeing pan...........	00 = 10 = 00

Item 2 bedsteads 2 bulsters Matt Cord 00 = 04 = 00
2 = 12 = 6

Robt Futter Church wardens
Sam Bullyn } Overseers
James Boote }
Charles Pearse Cunstabls

RELIEF: Between Easter 1709 to Easter 1710, the parish gave £7 8s. 6d. 'upon the Account of Jeremy Nuds his familie'. This sum probably included a pension of 2s. 6d. per week, as the inventory states that he had 'now Entered unto Collection att the ~~value~~ Rate of 2^s 6^d p weeke'. Prior to this the parish sometimes paid his rent, costing 12s. 6d. each time for half a year's rent, and he was given money when 'In his necessitie' and 'by ye consent of ye town' (NRO PD 358/41).

FURTHER INFORMATION: Jeremy Nudds was married and had several children when this inventory was made. Part of the £7 8s. 6d. that was paid out 'upon the Account of Jeremy Nuds his familie' may have been used to bury him, particularly given that his name stops appearing in overseers' accounts for the parish and that of a Widow Nudds starts to appear (NRO PD 358/41).

174. William Jermyn, 16 April 1712

NRO PD 358/41 Shelton Overseers' Accounts, 1670–1734.

Aprel 16 – 1712
An Account then taken of the goods of William Jermyn by the overseers As follweth
Impremis one feather beed & bedstead & boulster & Sheets one brass pot one Large table And one Couberd –
one paile – one Lervera Cuberd & Spinen weele & Reele
more two Chairs

RELIEF: William Jermyn started receiving a pension of 1s. per week when this inventory was made. He received this for around ten weeks but was also provided with a lot of casual relief in addition to this, including firewood, coal, and clothing. William Jermyn, his wife, and daughter were also frequently given money during times of sickness and the parish sometimes paid people to look after them (NRO PD 358/41).

FURTHER INFORMATION: William Jermyn was married to Frances and had several children. Frances Jermyn was buried on 13 June 1713 at the ratepayers' expense, at a cost of around 17s. 6d. Poor law records note the expenditure of 1s. 6d. for the removal of William Jermyn from an unknown parish sometime between Easter 1711 and Easter 1712. Grace, Alice, and Thomas Jermyn are also mentioned in the overseers' accounts during the 1710s; however, it is unknown whether they were related to William Jermyn. There is also an inventory of unknown type of Richard Jermyn's goods from October 1701 and a pauper inventory of Barbara Jermyn's goods from

July 1700 **(172)**, but it is unknown whether these people were relations of William Jermyn (NRO PD 358/1; NRO PD 358/41).

DUBIOUS TERMS: Line 6: 'Lervera' – probably livery.

175. Goodman Dunnen, 6 August 1713

NRO PD 358/41 Shelton Overseers' Accounts, 1670–1734.

the Account of Goodman dunnen things things tacken this: 6: day of August 1713: by the ouffers of Shelton as followeth

Imprimas one fuer bed and bedstead and bouster and A brascittel ~~2 pots~~ and Ioyren pots and a chist 2 tables and 3 chers 2 vese<l>s and 2 cabbers 1 Spet and a pe<r>rer of Arnnes and a warminpan

RELIEF: Goodman Dunnen was in receipt of occasional casual relief when this source was made. Between Easter 1712 and Easter 1713, for example, he was given a quarter of firewood worth 4s. and had £2 house rent paid by the parish (NRO PD 358/41).

FURTHER INFORMATION: Goodman Dunnen was probably living on his own as a bachelor or widower when this inventory was made (NRO PD 358/1; NRO PD 358/41).

DUBIOUS TERMS: Line 4: 'cabbers' – possibly cupboards. Line 5: 'pe<r>rer of Arnnes' – unknown term; possibly a pair of andirons.

DAMAGE: Several ink spills/smudges on lines 4–5, making 'pe<r>rer' partially illegible.

176. Joseph Bateman, 3 February 1718/19

NRO PD 358/41 Shelton Overseers' Accounts, 1670–1734.

3d Feb: 1718

An Inventory of the Goods that weare Joseph Batemans before he tooke Collection & now were Delivered by the Overseers for pore to make use of

Imprimis 2 beds & bedsteads & 2 Coverletts
2 bousters Mats & Cords
A Livery Cobart
A Frieing pan
A porrige pott
A table
3 Chayers
A Cradell
A Spining whele & Reele

RELIEF: Joseph Bateman was in receipt of casual relief when this inventory was taken. Between Easter 1719 and Easter 1720, for example, the parish paid out numerous sums of money to Joseph Bateman 'in time of lamenes' and paid £1s 6s. 6d. towards his rent. On 18 April 1720, the accounts note the payment of 'fower pounds & tenn Shillings for healeing of Joseph Batemans Legges & Katerine Jexes' **(178)**. The problems with Joseph Bateman's legs, however, were not resolved from this, as the parish continued to pay Joseph Bateman during times of sickness and paid doctors several pounds to see him regarding his legs (NRO PD 358/41). The inventory also states that Joseph Bateman 'tooke Collection'.

FURTHER INFORMATION: Joseph Bateman was married to a woman called Christiana when this inventory was made. Poor law records mention 'Batemans Dore' between Easter 1720 and Easter 1721, which indicates that the couple had at least one daughter living with them. Between Easter 1719 and Easter 1720, the overseers' accounts note the payment of 1s. to remove Joseph Bateman from another, unknown, parish. The pauper inventory of Widow Bateman below dated 1728/29 **(180)** was Joseph Bateman's wife (NRO PD 358/1; NRO PD 358/41). Overseers' accounts for the parish indicate that the goods were not taken from Joseph Bateman as the inventory suggests. There is a second inventory of Joseph Bateman's goods taken several months later on 29 September 1719; however, it is unknown whether this was a new pauper inventory to mark his moving into the town house (parish-provided housing) or a goods-taken inventory (NRO 358/41):
29th Day of September 1719
An Inventory of the Goods of Joseph Bateman now taken Into the Town booke & now Entereding to Collection & Putt Into the Towne house & apprised by us the Officers of the said Towne of Shelton Ass Followeth

	li s d
Imprimis 2 beds & bedsteads as they stand	1 = 5 – 0
One Cubbard One Iron Pot one Tub one Table	0 – 8 – 0
One Reell One Little table 5 Chayers one Paile One Gridiron 3 beare Vessells	0 = 4 = 00
~~One Chest~~ One hake One Tub One warming Pan One Payer of Sheets a Speet	0 = 7 = 00
A Frieing pan	0 = 2 = 00
	2 = 6 = 00

177. Francis Baker, 12 October 1719

NRO PD 358/41 Shelton Overseers' Accounts, 1670–1734.

12th October 1719

An Inventory of the Goods of Francis Baker now taken Into the Towne booke of Shelton & Entering to Collecton & Putt Into the Towne house & apprised by us the officers of the said Town as Fo<lloweth>

	l s d
InPrimis One Table 3 Joynt Stools 6 Chayers	0 = 7 = 00
One Table 2 Cobarts a Dresser	0 = 4 = 00

One hake Tongs bellowes a forke a Spining wheel & a Reele 6 Stone bottells 2 hamer & a hooke & a hatchett	0 = 6 = 00
One bed & bedstead boulster as it stands ...	1 = 00 = 00
One Other bedstead & Chist	0 = 04 = 00
a Littell trunke & all other thing belong= ing to the house	0 = 05 00
There is a Chist of Frances Jermyns In the house with these goods at 2s	2 = 6 = 0

RELIEF: Francis Baker started to receive a pension from officials when this inventory was taken. Overseers' accounts for the parish, however, are poorly kept and so it is unknown how much Francis Baker received per week. Around Easter 1720, Francis Baker is noted as being in receipt of 1s. per week. In addition, Francis Baker was occasionally given firewood and money during times of sickness from the parish (NRO PD 358/41). The inventory also notes that Francis Baker was 'Entering to Collecton'.

FURTHER INFORMATION: Poor law records show that the townhouse was housing provided by the parish for its paupers and a place where parish stock was stored. Francis Baker was married and buried on 29 July 1721 in Shelton (NRO PD 358/1; NRO PD 358/41). It is unknown who Frances Jermyn (line 14) was and whether they were a relation of Barbara Jermyn **(172)** and William Jermyn **(174)**.

178. Katherine Jex, 3 February 1722/23

NRO PD 358/41 Shelton Overseers' Accounts, 1670–1734.

3d Febr 1722

A Inventory of the goods that wer taken by the Overseers of the poore of Katerine Jex widd upon her taken Collection as Foll

A bed & bedstead & 2 blankett
a boulster
A Cobart & Keepe a table
A spining wheele & Reele

RELIEF: Katherine Jex started to receive a pension of 1s. 6d. per week when this inventory was made. She was also given rent payments, faggots, and the parish paid out money for her 'lay in' when she gave birth to her child around April 1723. Katherine Jex was also sometimes unwell. On 18 April 1720, for example, the accounts note the payment of 'fower pounds & tenn Shillings for healeing of Joseph Batemans Legges [see **176**] & Katerine Jexes' (NRO PD 358/41). The source also notes that the inventory was made 'upon her taken Collection'.

FURTHER INFORMATION: Katherine Jex was widowed and her husband may have been named Thomas. Extant poor relief records for the parish indicate that she had at least one child soon after this inventory was made, as she is noted as 'lay in' in April 1723. The overseers of the poor for Shelton were Henry Tostecke[?] and John Chasten in February 1722/23 (NRO PD 358/1; NRO PD 358/41).

179. Mary/Widow Frances, 2 March 1723/24

NRO PD 358/41 Shelton Overseers' Accounts, 1670–1734.

March 2 1723
An invetory of the Goods of the Widdow frances^{es} then taken into the towne Book as followeth

on Bed with old Curtings on Iorn pot and Iorn Cittle 4 Chairs on table and a joynt Stool on powter dish wi<?> hake tonguse Severall Books and Other Small things

RELIEF: Widow Frances started to receive a pension from the parish when this inventory was made. The overseers' accounts for the parish, however, are inconsistently kept so it is unknown how much she received weekly. She was also occasionally given money during times of sickness (NRO PD 358/41).

FURTHER INFORMATION: Overseers' accounts and parish registers show that Widow Frances' forename was Mary. She was buried in Shelton on 14 May 1724 (NRO PD 358/1; NRO PD 358/41).

DUBIOUS TERMS: Line 5: 'wi<?>' – illegible term.

180. Christiana/Widow Bateman, 5 March 1728/29

NRO PD 358/41 Shelton Overseers' Accounts, 1670–1734.

An Inventorey of The Goods of ye Widdow Bateman Takin The 5th: day of march 1728/9
One Bed & Bedstade & bed matt
a Large Iron Pott a Table a Coffer
a Stool & Reele a whele & a paile
a pair of Sheetts a Hachitt Sould To Good^{w} Gibbs at 1^{s}

RELIEF: Widow Bateman was receiving a pension of around 10d. or 1s. per week when this inventory was made. She was also often given money and faggots, and her children were provided with clothing and medical help from the parish. Prior to her husband's death around February 1728/29, he was receiving a pension of 1s. per week from the parish and was frequently given additional cash, clothing, and medical help for his bad leg. Between Easter 1728 and Easter 1729, the parish also paid out 5s. for 'Curing Bateman Familey of ye Itch' (usually scabies) (NRO PD 358/1; NRO PD 358/41).

FURTHER INFORMATION: Overseers' accounts and parish registers indicate that Widow Bateman's forename was Christiana and that she was married to Joseph Bateman, who was buried at a cost of 10s. 11d. to the parish on 2 March 1728/29. Widow Bateman appears to have had several children living with her when this inventory was made. One of their daughters, Thomasin, was buried on 10 August 1727 in Shelton at the expense of the parish. There are two earlier inventories of Joseph Bateman's goods taken in 1719 **(176)**. It is unknown who Goodwin Gibbs (line 6) was (NRO PD 358/1; NRO PD 358/41).

181. Ann Milles, 26 October 1741

NRO PD 358/42 Shelton Various Accounts and Papers, 1735–1779.

The Accou<nt> of Ann Milles Goods Octo^{br}: 26: 1741
A Cubbord & Lock & key
A Small table
A forme with a Drawer
A Bed & furnuture as it Stand
A Pottage pott & frieing pan
2 Chaires & Reele a hake & paile
A Ciller a paire of Bellows & Bill hooke

RELIEF: Ann Milles' children started to receive a pension of 1s. to 1s. 6d. per week when this inventory was taken. They were also sometimes provided with clothing and shoes from overseers. Prior to this, Ann Milles was given small amounts of money irregularly from the parish (NRO PD 358/42).

FURTHER INFORMATION: Ann Milles was probably single as she is not referred to as 'Widow Milles' in poor law records and the baptism records of her children do not mention a father. She had one young boy called Henry and one young girl called Martha when this inventory was made. Ann Milles and her children were probably removed from Stratton (Norfolk) sometime between Easter 1738 and Easter 1740. She was buried in Shelton at a cost of 14s. to ratepayers on 28 August 1741 (NRO PD 358/1; NRO PD 358/42).

DAMAGE: Line 1: Parts of the text are faded making it difficult to decipher.

182. Widow Thrower, 28 September 1742

NRO PD 358/42 Shelton Various Accounts and Papers, 1735–1779.

An Accomp^{t} of Nicholas Thrower Widows Things: Sep^{t}: y^{e}: 28: 1742
A Bed as it Stand
A Coffer A Desk
Two Spining weels & Reele
A Hatchett A Spade & Tongs
A Great Bible :3: Sheets

RELIEF: Widow Thrower was in receipt of 1s. 6d. per week when this inventory was made. She had received a pension from the parish for a number of years before her goods were appraised by poor law authorities. In addition, she was occasionally provided with money, rent payments, and clothing from the parish. Her children were also frequently given clothing (NRO PD 358/42).

FURTHER INFORMATION: Widow Thrower probably lost her husband, Nicholas, in 1739, as overseers' accounts for the parish record the burial of somebody called 'Thrower' then. Widow Thrower had at least two children (a boy and a girl) living with her when this inventory was taken (NRO PD 358/1; NRO PD 358/42).

183. John Francis (junior), 28 September 1743

NRO PD 358/42 Shelton Various Accounts and Papers, 1735–1779.

An Accomp^{t} of John Francis Goods junor Sept: 28: 1743 By the Church wardens and overseers of the Parish of Shelton
A <B>ed & Bedstead & <?> pillows furniture as it Stan<ds>
A <?>inding weele & Spining weele
A S<p>ade & tow Whele – a litle deske & Chaire
23: wood hornings & Swift & moul Spade
A Table a little trunk & Chest an Iyron pot
A Tub a Cup and dish a long table a Reele
& four Chaires a pair Spise Boxes a Small
Desk a little hatchett and hour glass – –
A Hake & Andrions fire pan & tongs and
gridiron a Small Lanthorn and Candle Stick
A Chushing a Sive & Bellows a Spit

RELIEF: John Francis junior was in receipt of 1s. 6d. per week when this inventory was taken. Unfortunately, the overseers' accounts of Shelton do not often distinguish between John Francis junior and senior, meaning that it is difficult to tell what other relief John Francis junior received (NRO PD 358/42).

FURTHER INFORMATION: The marital status of John Francis junior is unknown as poor law records for the parish tend to not distinguish between him and John Francis senior. John Matthews and Matthew Rose were the overseers of Shelton when this inventory was made, but it is not known who the churchwardens were (NRO PD 358/42).

DUBIOUS TERMS: Line 4: '<?>inding weele' – winding or grinding wheel.

DAMAGE: Page is ripped and very creased making parts of the inventory difficult to read.

184. Widow Fulcher, 30 July 1746

NRO PD 358/42 Shelton Various Accounts and Papers, 1735–1779.

An Accomp^{t} of The Widow Fulchers Goods July: y^{e}: 30th: 1746 By the Churchwardens And Oversier of the Said Parish

A Bed & furniture as it Stand
A paire of Andrions & hake & fire pan
A warming pan Three Chairs a Cubbord a lock & key
Four Spining weels & Reel two Small tables
A pottage pott: a bowl & fring pan.

RELIEF: Widow Fulcher was in receipt of 1s. per week when this inventory was made. She had received this for a number of years prior to her goods being appraised by the churchwardens and overseers. She also had her rent regularly paid by the parish and her children were frequently given clothing such as breeches, shoes, and shirts (NRO PD 358/42).

FURTHER INFORMATION: Widow Fulcher was probably elderly as she was sometimes referred to as 'old' in poor law accounts. She had at least two children (boys) living with her when this inventory was taken. Between Easter and Michaelmas 1745, the parish had paid 2s. to remove her from another, unknown, parish. John Ward and John Buch were the overseers of Shelton when this inventory was made, but it is not known who the churchwardens were (NRO PD 358/42).

185. John Frances (senior), 18 January 1747/48

NRO PD 358/42 Shelton Various Accounts and Papers, 1735–1779.

The Account of John Frances's Goods Senior Takeon January the 18 1747. By the Churchwardens and overseers of the Parrish of Shelton

In the Kitchen

A Bed and Furniture a Large Cupbord a Dresser 2 Killers five Chairs three Stools three Pails a Poridge pot and hake a hank a Skillet an ale Stole one Vessle two Candlesticks a Worman pan

In the Butthre

one Vessle one Stoole two Tubs a frying pan and a wheel.

on the Chamber

three Killer two pots one wheel

RELIEF: John Frances was in receipt of casual relief, such as cash payments, when this inventory was taken. He was buried in Shelton at a cost of 19s. to the parish in January 1747/48. His wife was subsequently given money, clothing, and meat from the parish when 'in need'. Unfortunately, the overseers' accounts of Shelton do not often distinguish between John Frances junior and senior, meaning that it is difficult to tell what other relief John Frances senior received (NRO PD 358/2; NRO PD 358/42).

FURTHER INFORMATION: John Frances was married and was buried in late January 1748/49 in Shelton. William Tubby was the overseer of Shelton when this inventory was made, but it is unknown who the churchwardens were (NRO PD 358/2; NRO PD 358/42).

186. Henry Brown, 12 July 1748

NRO PD 358/42 Shelton Various Accounts and Papers, 1735–1779.

The account of Henry Browns things taken July the 12 1748 By the Churchwarden and overseers of the poor of the parrish of Shelton as fo<ll>oweth.

two Beds and furniture as they Stand and Brewing kottle two Boxes and a Trunk one Brew<ing> tub one Stool one Leech one Spade three Vessels one ale Stool one powdering tub one tunel two Dishes three Earthen pots three puding pans two Basons two Tables one Bultenhutch five Chairs one Joint Stool one Coule a wash Killer two Earthen Dishes Six threnchers a fire pan and Tongs a pair of Bellows Hake andirons two Candlesticks one Hour Glass one Keep and Spice Drawers a worman pan and frying pan two Iron pots a hatchet and hook one Spining wheel and Reel Box Iron and heats one peel one Rude<?>

RELIEF: Henry Brown was in receipt of 1s. 6d. per week for eight weeks between Easter and Michaelmas 1748. The parish also provided £1 4s. towards his rent and paid out £1 11s. 6d. for a doctor to treat his arm. Henry Brown's son was additionally given clothing by the authorities (NRO PD 358/42).

FURTHER INFORMATION: Henry Brown appears to have been married to somebody called Sarah and had a number of children when this inventory was made. Francis Richard and Robert Barrett were the overseers of Shelton, but it is unknown who the churchwarden was (NRO PD 358/2; NRO PD 358/42).

DUBIOUS TERMS: Line 12: 'Rude<?>' – unknown term.

DAMAGE: Lines 3, 5 and 7: Writing heavily faded on the words 'fo<ll>oweth', 'Brew<ing>', 'Tables', and 'Joint'. Line 12: Page torn by 'Rude<?>', making the term illegible.

187. Thomas Taylor (junior), 23/30 April 1751

NRO PD 358/42 Shelton Various Accounts and Papers, 1735–1779.

An Account of the Goods of Thos Taylor jun^{r} late of Banham in the County of Norfk Taken April ye 30th 1751 distraind by John Bale of Buckingham in the Sd County for Relif due to him and redeem'd by the Overseers & Churchwardens of the Parish of Shelton in ye County aforesaid whereby the

Goods were pledged to the Sd Officers for the Use of the said Parish for the Sum of twenty Shillings pd the Sd Landlord for Rent for the Charge of bringing the Sd Goods away to Shelton, And for the farther Sum of five Pounds one Shillings and six Pence disburs'd for the Sd Taylor to James Leslly by Robt Barret Overseer in the year 1748

Imp^{r} One Feather Bed Bolster Pillows Bedstead and Covering
One Chest of Drawers
5 Chairs 3 Vessels. One Tow-Wheele
2 Tables. 2 Stools one Trunk a Childs Chair
3 Killers. One Pewter Cold
4 Pewter Plates one Pewter Dish
2 Candle Sticks one Spit
One Pair of Bellows
A Fire-Pan and Tongs
One Frying P<a>n
One <B>ra<ss> <P>ot
One Brass <warm>ing Pan
one Look<ing> Glass

RELIEF: Thomas Taylor was provided with casual relief from the parish. The inventory was made for 'Relif due to him', totalling £6 1s. 6d. (£1 for rent and £5 1s. 6d. given to him between Michaelmas 1748 and Easter 1749) (NRO PD 358/42).

FURTHER INFORMATION: The inventory shows that Thomas Taylor lived in Banham, Norfolk, but had settlement in Shelton. He was referred to as 'late' showing that he had recently died. It is unknown who the churchwardens of Shelton were in April 1751. Records show that the landlord, John Bale/Bate, had tried to distrain the goods of Thomas Taylor as he was £1 in arrears. The parish stopped this from happening and in return made a pauper inventory of Thomas Taylor's goods soon after he died (NRO PD 358/42; NRO PD 358/61). An earlier inventory dated seven days before this one (23 April 1751) shows the landlord attempting to distrain Thomas Taylor's goods before the parish stepped in to help (NRO PD 358/61):

April ye 23^{d}. 1751
An Invitory of the Goods Chattles and Cattle of Thos Taylor Junior of Bandham Distrain by me John Bate for ½ years Rent Ending at a Lady Last the

Imp In The Kittching
one Bed as it stands. a chest of Drawers. 5 chairs 3 vesells a Tow weele 2 Tables 2 stooles one Trunk a childs chair 3 Killers A pewter Cold 4 plates a pewter Dish 2 Candle sticks one speet a pair of Bellows Firepan and Tongs a Frying pan a Brass pot a worming pan A Looking Glass

DUBIOUS TERMS: Line 14: 'Cold' – unknown term; possibly a coule/cowle.

DAMAGE: There are numerous holes in the document, making several terms partially illegible on lines 19–22. However, using the rent-arrears inventory of Thomas Taylor's possessions (see further information) it was possible to reconstitute what the terms were.

188. William Brett, 29 September 1753

NRO PD 358/42 Shelton Various Accounts and Papers, 1735–1779.

An Account of W^{m}. Bretts things taken by y^{e}. Parish officers take'n 29 of Sep^{t} 1753

1 Bed 3 Sheets 1 Iron pot 1 pail 4 Chairs 1 Dresser 1 Chest 1 firepan a pair of tongs 1 Skillett a pair of Bellows 1 fire pan 2 Kill<ers> 1 Table 1 Wheele 1 Reele 1 hook 1 Sieve 1 ham<mer> 1 pewter Dish 1 Eke

RELIEF: William Brett was in receipt of a small amount of casual relief such as money when this inventory was taken. He appears to have died around mid–1753 and his wife subsequently started to receive money from the parish during times of 'need', rent payments, and clothing. Between Easter and Michaelmas 1753, William Brett's wife received 1s. 6d. per week for several weeks, and by Easter 1754 this pension was given to her on a continuous basis (NRO PD 358/42).

FURTHER INFORMATION: William Brett was married and appears to have died around mid–1753 (NRO PD 358/42).

DUBIOUS TERMS: Line 5: 'Eke' – possibly hake.

DAMAGE: Lines 4–5: The words 'Kill<ers>' and 'ham<mer>' are cut off by the binding of the volume.

189. Mary Taylor, 8 February 1762

Duplicate copies in NRO PD 358/42 Shelton Various Accounts and Papers, 1735–1779 and NRO PD 358/61 Shelton Various Papers, 1704–1769.

Febuary ye 8 1762 an Envetory Made of Mary Taylers things
One feather Bed Bolster Pillows Bedstead and Coverling
one Chiste of Drawers
5 Chairs 1 Vessel
2 Teables and joint stule
3 Killers
1 Cubbard and 1 Iron pot
1 Skillet 1 puwter pleate
2 wooll weeles
1 Heake and two hanks
1 pair of Tonges and Andrions
a Box iron and heeters
a pair of Bellows and a warming pan
and one friing pan a Large trunk
two Candle Sticks

a fire pan and three Sheets
one water paile

her
Elizebeth X Smith
mark

Wm Radwill Witness

RELIEF: Mary Taylor was in receipt of a pension of 2s. per week when this inventory was taken. She also received medical help related to the birth of her daughter in 1760 and was given money when 'at need' from the parish. She died around January/ February 1762 and her daughter subsequently became dependent on parish support (NRO PD 358/42).

FURTHER INFORMATION: Mary Taylor appears to have been a single woman when this inventory was taken. She gave birth to her daughter, Sarah, around March/ April 1760 and who was baptised on 21 April 1760. In 1762 Sarah Taylor was described as a 'lame Girl' by the parish. Mary Taylor was buried in Shelton at the parish's expense on 2 February 1762. Her goods were sold around Easter 1762 and raised 13s. It is unknown who Elizabeth Smith and William Radwill were (NRO PD 358/2; NRO PD 358/42).

Shimpling pauper inventory

Only one pauper inventory has been located for Shimpling. It can be found in a set of churchwardens' accounts which have since been annotated with a modern hand (NRO PD 102/32).

190. Widow Long, 9 June 1785

NRO PD 102/32 Shimpling Churchwardens' Accounts, 1761–1810.

June 9. 1785 an Account of Widow Longs Furniture &c.

1. – – – Bed with Curtains &c
2. – – – a Napkin press & Drawers
3. – – – a Corner Cubbard
4. – – – a Looking Glass
5. – – – a Tea tray
6. – – – a Knife
7. – – – a Salt Box
8. – – – a Spit
9. – – – a Box Iron and heets   a warming pan
10. – – – a Candlestick   & frying D°
11. – – – a Minging huch
12. – – – 3 Iron pots
13. – – – a Back Iron
14. – – – a pair of Cobirons
15. – – – 2 hanging Cubbards
16. – – – 5 Chaire Small
17. – – – 2 Elbow D° –
18. – – – 2 Woolweels & reel
19. – – – a Skelitt & Tea Cittle
20. – – – an ale Stool
21. – – – 3 Small Vessels
22. – – – 2 Kellers
23. – – – a pair of Lye Tongs
24. – – – 8 Glass Bottle
25. – – – 1 Stone D° & Quantity of Arthenware

RELIEF: Widow Long started to receive 3s. per week when this inventory was made. Prior to this, her husband James Long received 7s. per week and was frequently given money when 'in need'. Presumably her husband died and then this inventory was made as relief switched to her. Clothing and materials were also provided to her daughters. On 14 October 1785, for example, the parish paid 2s. 11½d. 'for 2 ½ yrd of hemp Clooth for Wi^{d}. Long Girls & thread' (NRO PD 102/36).

FURTHER INFORMATION: Widow Long's husband, James, appears to have died around mid–1785 and the couple had several daughters (NRO PD 102/36).

CIRCUMTEXT: The original source has been annotated with a modern hand which defines and clarifies what some of the terms meant. These additions have been omitted in the transcription above.

Shipdham pauper inventories

The twenty-three pauper inventories for Shipdham were all written in sequence on several sides of a large sheet of paper on 24 May 1720 (NRO PD 337/158). The text is all written in the same hand and the enumerator wrote that the inventories were made of 'Colectioner[s] of the town'. The writing is heavily faded and the sheet is heavily creased in parts.

191. John Dorman, 24 May 1720

NRO PD 337/158 Shipdham Inventories, 1720.

An Inventory of all the Goods of John Dorman a Colectioner of the town of Shipdham in the County of Norfolke as they are valued by the Overseers of the town aforesaid whose hands are under named Done the 24 day of may Anno 1720

		li s d
in the Chamb =	one fether bedd and two Small bedds 2 Bedd Steads one Boulster and three pillows one Keverling and Blanketts Shets and 2 pillow bears on the beds ...	02 : 00 : 0
	a Chest with 3 Shetes 3 pillow-bears and Shirts & Shifts..........	00 : 05 : 0
	a Table 4 Iron wedges and a p^{r}: of Curtains without Lumber	00 : 05 : 0
in the Low Roomes =	one cofer one Boxx 2 forms 2 Small vesells a powdering Tubb 2 killers	00 : 05 : 6
	2 Kettells a brass pott a Skellett and worming pann................	00 : 15 : 0
	3 Tables 2 Cubbards a Large Chest a Trunke	00 : 06 : 0
	a Spete a p^{r}: Tongs a Gredgiron Cheafendish Smothing iron	02 <6>
	a heake 2 hanks a Spining whell and Reele a p^{r} bellows............	03 : 0
	3 Chayers three Stooles and Shomakers tooles	00 : 02 : 0

a flagg Spead a Turff Spead a hatchett and mattuck a Saw a Spead a Sheane a p^{r} Scalles and waights	00 : 04 : 0
Earthen whear wood Dishes and other Lumber	00 : 01 : 6
	04 09 : 6

RELIEF: No relevant poor relief records survive for Shipdham from 1720. However, these documents are pauper inventories as the appraiser stated that they were made of 'Colectioner[s]'.

DUBIOUS TERMS: Line 27: 'Sheane' – unknown term; possibly shears or a sherne (churn).

DAMAGE: Line 20: Writing faded and page damaged by '02 <6>'.

192. Ealles Platfoot, 24 May 1720

NRO PD 337/158 Shipdham Inventories, 1720.

Ealles Platfoots Things are as under written –	li s d
a Bedd with a Blankett and pr. Shetes a pillow a boulste with what belong to the bedd as it Stands	00 : 10 : 0
an Iron Kettle a Cofer a box	00 : 05 : 0
one Reelle one bow-Stooles a Small brass Kettle	00 : 01 : 0
	00 : 16 : 0

RELIEF: No relevant poor relief records survive for Shipdham from 1720. However, these documents are pauper inventories as the appraiser stated that they were made of 'Colectioner[s]'.

193. John Doughty, 24 May 1720

NRO PD 337/158 Shipdham Inventories, 1720.

John doughtys things are as under

a bed and bedstad a cofer and old cubbard and Small things a Small Kettle	00 : 10 : 0

RELIEF: No relevant poor relief records survive for Shipdham from 1720. However, these documents are pauper inventories as the appraiser stated that they were made of 'Colectioner[s]'.

194. Widow Allcock, 24 May 1720

NRO PD 337/158 Shipdham Inventories, 1720.

An Inventory of all the thi<ng>s of the wid Allcock as an<der>

~~2 B<edds> as they Stand with their bedsteads and Cur<tai>ns w<ith> <Cover>lins and 2 Boulsers and 2 pillows to they <?> <?> <?> 2 foorms~~

	li s
a Bedd and Bedstead Curtain 2 Blancketts a Boulsters 2 pillows a Rugg 6 Chayers a foorm 3 Tables	03 : 00 : 0
a hake a Joynt Stoole a Reele a Cofer an Iron pott	00 : 07 : 0
a Grediron 2 <Sm>oo<t>hing irons <a> whele other Small things	00 : 05 : 0
	03 : 12 : 0

RELIEF: No relevant poor relief records survive for Shipdham from 1720. However, these documents are pauper inventories as the appraiser stated that they were made of 'Colectioner[s]'.

FURTHER INFORMATION: Widow Allcock appears to have been living with Widow Reeves in 1720, whose goods are transcribed in **195**.

DAMAGE: Lines 1–3 and 9 heavily faded meaning that a number of words and letters are difficult to read.

195. Widow Reeves, 24 May 1720

NRO PD 337/158 Shipdham Inventories, 1720.

	li s d
the wid Reeves things a<t> the Wid: A<llc>ocks	
a bedd and Bedstead a Coverlin a Bowlster and Table a Cubbard and forme an ould ir<o>n pott and ould Things	00 : 10 : 0
a Small brass pott a hake a <p>^{r} Tongs	00 : 03 : 0
	00 : 13 : 0

RELIEF: No relevant poor relief records survive for Shipdham from 1720. However, these documents are pauper inventories as the appraiser stated that they were made of 'Colectioner[s]'.

FURTHER INFORMATION: This inventory indicates that Widow Reeves was living with Widow Allcock, whose goods were also appraised by Shipdham parish in 1720 **(194)**.

DAMAGE: The inventory is faded, making some parts of it difficult to decipher.

196. Widow Adkens, 24 May 1720

NRO PD 337/158 Shipdham Inventories, 1720.

Wid°: Adkens goods	li s d
a bedd and Bedstead a Coverlin a Boulster	00 : 9 : 0
a Trunke and Blanketts	

RELIEF: No relevant poor relief records survive for Shipdham from 1720. However, these documents are pauper inventories as the appraiser stated that they were made of 'Colectioner[s]'.

197. Widow Ouldham, 24 May 1720

NRO PD 337/158 Shipdham Inventories, 1720.

Wid°: Ouldmans Goods at Robt: Taylers	li s d
a bedd and Beadstead a Boulster coverlin Blankett a Box	00 : 10 : 0

RELIEF: No relevant poor relief records survive for Shipdham from 1720. However, these documents are pauper inventories as the appraiser stated that they were made of 'Colectioner[s]'.

FURTHER INFORMATION: The inventory indicates that Widow Ouldman was living with Robert Taylor. Because no poor relief accounts survive from Shipdham, however, it is unknown who Robert Taylor was. He may not have been a pauper since his goods were not appraised like those of other claimants in May 1720.

198. Sarah Tillets, 24 May 1720

NRO PD 337/158 Shipdham Inventories, 1720.

Sarah Tilletts Goods at John Rawlings	li s d
a bedd and Bedstead a p^{r} Shetes and 2 blankett	00 : 10 : 0

RELIEF: No relevant poor relief records survive for Shipdham from 1720. However, these documents are pauper inventories as the appraiser stated that they were made of 'Colectioner[s]'.

FURTHER INFORMATION: The inventory indicates that Sarah Tillets was living with John Rawlings. Because no poor relief accounts survive from Shipdham, it is unknown who John Rawlings was. He may not have been a pauper since his goods were not appraised like those of other claimants in May 1720.

199. Widow Simonds, 24 May 1720

NRO PD 337/158 Shipdham Inventories, 1720.

Wid^{o}: Simonds goods are as undr

a Bedd~~s~~ a Boulster two Shetes Coverlins 2 Blankets and Curtains	02 : 00 : <0>
a Table a Cubbard a firepan p^{r}: Towngs a hake and vessell and other things with a whell .... }	00 : 02 : 6
	02 : 2 : 6

RELIEF: No relevant poor relief records survive for Shipdham from 1720. However, these documents are pauper inventories as the appraiser stated that they were made of ‘Colectioner[s]’.

200. Widow Mallett, 24 May 1720

NRO PD 337/158 Shipdham Inventories, 1720.

<A>n Inv<en>tory <of> all the wid^{o}: malletts things a Colectioner of the town <o>f Shipdham as they are prized the 24 day of may 1720 as under

	li s d
2 Bedds and Bedsteads with all their furniture as they Stand	03 : 00 : <0>
a Chest a Cubbard a Box and Stoole 5 Chayers a Joynt Stole.......................................	00 : 15 : 0
2 Tables a hake a firepann a p^{r}: Tongs a p^{r} Cobirons	00 : 06 : 0
a p^{r}: bellows a Gredirен 2 Kettells an Iron pott a Reele a Skellett	00 : 12 : 0
a vesell Tubb and payll and other Small things	00 : 01 : 6
	04 : 14 : 6

RELIEF: No relevant poor relief records survive for Shipdham from 1720. However, these documents are pauper inventories as the appraiser stated that they were made of ‘Colectioner[s]’.

DAMAGE: Lines 1–2: The inventory is faded, making parts of it difficult to decipher.

201. Widow Fuller, 24 May 1720

NRO PD 337/158 Shipdham Inventories, 1720.

	li s d
the Wid^{o}: Fullers Things are as under	li s d
a Bedd and Bedstead Curtains 2 Blanketts Boulster and Coverlett 2 pillows a Cofer in the Rooms ...	03 : 00 : 0
a Cubbard a brass pott a Kettle 5 Chayers 2 Stoles	00 : 08 : 0
a firepan a p^{r} Tongs a hake and Spete a Skellet a p^{r} Cobions and other Small things	00 : 02 : 6
	01 : 19 : 6

RELIEF: No relevant poor relief records survive for Shipdham from 1720. However, these documents are pauper inventories as the appraiser stated that they were made of 'Colectioner[s]'.

202. — Rice, 24 May 1720

NRO PD 337/158 Shipdham Inventories, 1720.

An Account of Rices things <S>en^{d} as under	li s d
a bedd and Bedstead a Coverlit and Shete as they Stand...	01 : 10 : 0
a Chest an ould Cubbard a hake p^{r}: bellows Tongs Salt Box	00 : 03 : 0
a Kettle an Iron pott a Skellett a worming pann 3 Chayers	00 : 05 : 0
a Spade 2 Stoles and other Small things ...	00 : 01 : 6
	01 : 19 : 6

RELIEF: No relevant poor relief records survive for Shipdham from 1720. However, these documents are pauper inventories as the appraiser stated that they were made of 'Colectioner[s]'.

203. William Bright, 24 May 1720

NRO PD 337/158 Shipdham Inventories, 1720.

William Brights goods are as under	li s d
a bedd and Bedstead with Curtains 2 Boulsters a pillow 3 Shetes a Rugg a Sattle and Cushen one blankett and pillow bear	02 : 10 : 0

RELIEF: No relevant poor relief records survive for Shipdham from 1720. However, these documents are pauper inventories as the appraiser stated that they were made of 'Colectioner[s]'.

FURTHER INFORMATION: It is unknown if William Bright was any relation of Widow Bright, whose goods were also inventoried by Shipdham parish in May 1720 **(206)**.

204. Widow Fish, 24 May 1720

NRO PD 337/158 Shipdham Inventories, 1720.

Wid°: Fishes Things are as Followeth	li s d
a bedd one boulster one pillow a blanket a Shete Curtins and Curlet........................	01 : 15 : 0
a hutch a Scillett a Reele and a Stoole	00 : 04 : 0
	01 : 19 : 0

RELIEF: No relevant poor relief records survive for Shipdham from 1720. However, these documents are pauper inventories as the appraiser stated that they were made of 'Colectioner[s]'.

205. Widow Ranson, 24 May 1720

NRO PD 337/158 Shipdham Inventories, 1720.

An Inventory of all the goods of the Wid°: Ranson a Colectoner of the town of Shipdham are as under

	li s d
a Bedd and Bedstead a blankett a Chest 2 Boxes	00 : 15 : 0
a Kittle a Fryenpan a Reele a Stole a Table a wormenpan and other Small potts and panns	00 : 05 : 0
	01 : 00 : 0

RELIEF: No relevant poor relief records survive for Shipdham from 1720. However, these documents are pauper inventories as the appraiser stated that they were made of 'Colectoner[s]'.

206. Widow Bright, 24 May 1720

NRO PD 337/158 Shipdham Inventories, 1720.

Wid° Brights goods are as under

a box a form a fryenpan a nayll .... one Chayer a Tubb ad an Iron pott at Jo Franceses	00 : 05 : 0

a bedd and bedstead a boulster a blanket and Shete	00 : 12 : 6
	00 17 : 6

RELIEF: No relevant poor relief records survive for Shipdham from 1720. However, these documents are pauper inventories as the appraiser stated that they were made of 'Colectoner[s]'.

FURTHER INFORMATION: It is unknown if Widow Bright was any relation of William Bright, whose goods were also inventoried by Shipdham parish in May 1720 **(203)**. It is also not known who Jo Frances (line 3) was or why Widow Bright's iron pot was in his/her possession.

207. Widow Stagg, 24 May 1720

NRO PD 337/158 Shipdham Inventories, 1720.

an Account of the wid°: Staggs Goods	li s d
a bedd and Blankets beddstead a Table a Could a Box and Cofer a Cubbard.............	00 : 15 : 0
a fryen pann a hake a Gridiron an iron pott a Spete and Small things	: 05 : 0
	01 : 00 : 0

RELIEF: No relevant poor relief records survive for Shipdham from 1720. However, these documents are pauper inventories as the appraiser stated that they were made of 'Colectoner[s]'.

DUBIOUS TERMS: Line 2: 'Could' – unknown term; possibly a coule/cowle.

208. Margaret Bowl, 24 May 1720

NRO PD 337/158 Shipdham Inventories, 1720.

The Goods of margrett Bowl are as under	li s d
a bed and bedstead a boulster a Civ<erl>ip a pillow a Shet................................	00 : 10 : 0
a Cubbard an Iron Kettle a fryen pan a payr Tongs	00 : 06 : 0
2 Skelletts a vesell a form a Reele a wash Bowl a Cofer a box and Earthen whear and Small things .... }	00 : 05 : 0
	01 : 01 : 0

RELIEF: No relevant poor relief records survive for Shipdham from 1720. However, these documents are pauper inventories as the appraiser stated that they were made of 'Colectoner[s]'.

FURTHER INFORMATION: Margaret Bowl was probably a spinster since she was referred to by her Christian name and not as 'Widow'.

209. Widow Head, 24 May 1720

NRO PD 337/158 Shipdham Inventories, 1720.

	li s d
Wid^{o}: Heads goods are as under	
a bedd a bedstad a boulster 3 blankets a pillow a Cofer a box	01 : 12 : 0

RELIEF: No relevant poor relief records survive for Shipdham from 1720. However, these documents are pauper inventories as the appraiser stated that they were made of 'Colectoner[s]'.

210. Ann Wright, 24 May 1720

NRO PD 337/158 Shipdham Inventories, 1720.

	s d
Ann Wrights goods	
a bedd and bedstead a boyler and box =	06 : 0

RELIEF: No relevant poor relief records survive for Shipdham from 1720. However, these documents are pauper inventories as the appraiser stated that they were made of 'Colectoner[s]'.

FURTHER INFORMATION: Ann Wright was probably a spinster since she was referred to by her Christian name and not as 'Widow'.

211. Elizabeth Brett, 24 May 1720

NRO PD 337/158 Shipdham Inventories, 1720.

	li s d
Eliz Bretts goods are as under	
a bedd and beddstead a boulster a Civerlin one Blankett 2 Shetes 4 Chayers 2 Kettells	01 : 10 : 0
a worming pann a Skellett a p^{r} Tongs bellows firepan a Roster a heake	00 : 05 : 0
a Table a payll a p^{r}: bellows a Spete and other Small Things	00 : 05 : 0
	02 : 00 : 0

RELIEF: No relevant poor relief records survive for Shipdham from 1720. However, these documents are pauper inventories as the appraiser stated that they were made of 'Colectoner[s]'.

FURTHER INFORMATION: Elizabeth Brett was not referred to as 'Widow Brett' in this inventory as other women were in the parish, suggesting that she was a single woman.

212. Widow Gilldens, 24 May 1720

NRO PD 337/158 Shipdham Inventories, 1720.

the Wid° Gilldens Goods

a bed and bedstead whell and goods ...... 00 : 06 : 0

RELIEF: No relevant poor relief records survive for Shipdham from 1720. However, these documents are pauper inventories as the appraiser stated that they were made of 'Colectoner[s]'.

213. Widow Stimpson, 24 May 1720

NRO PD 337/158 Shipdham Inventories, 1720.

the Wid°: Stimpsons Goods

a cofer a Trunke 3 Shetes .... 00 : 03 : 0

RELIEF: No relevant poor relief records survive for Shipdham from 1720. However, these documents are pauper inventories as the appraiser stated that they were made of 'Colectoner[s]'.

Stratton St. Mary pauper inventories

The five pauper inventories from Stratton St. Mary were noted in overseers' accounts and vestry minutes (NRO PD 122/54; NRO PD 122/38–39). The inventories found in the back of NRO PD 122/39 are ripped and torn in parts. Also included in the volumes are goods-taken inventories, as well as several inventories which could not be classified.

214. Widow Booty, 27 January 1774

NRO PD 122/54 Stratton St. Mary Accounts of Weekly Collections of the Poor, 1770–1813.

An Account of the Widow Bootys Goods
Jany: An Old Bolster & pillow
27: 1774 A Bed; Bedstead Old Blue Curtain
Old Quilt Blankets 1 p^{r} old sheets
1 Chest Drawsser 2 old Chairs

RELIEF: Widow Booty was in receipt of a pension of 2s. per week when this inventory was taken. She had received this for a number of years prior to her goods being appraised by the parish. It is unknown whether she received additional support from officials, since the overseers' accounts for the settlement only note the distribution of pensions to parishioners (NRO PD 122/38).

FURTHER INFORMATION: Widow Booty died one day before her goods were appraised by the parish; she was buried in Stratton St. Mary on 30 January 1774 (NRO PD 122/2; NRO PD 122/38).

CIRCUMTEXT: Underneath the inventory the selling of Widow Booty's goods is noted (NRO PD 122/54):
Feby 11th: 1774 Sold all the above Goods
To Elizebeth Clark Servant To M^{r}. John Dix at Shalton for 3 : 12 : 0
Ric^{d}. Nicks^{s} Sum for the Us of the Towne
By Me Thomas Allen overseer

215. William Buck, 30 July 1774

NRO PD 122/54 Stratton St. Mary Accounts of Weekly Collections of the Poor, 1770–1813.

July 30th 1774 An Account W^{m}. Bucks Goods

In the Kitchen as Under

1 Jack 2 Speets 4 Iron Candle Sticks & a Lamp 2 Hakes 2 fire Pans 2 Pair Tongs 1 Poker 1 Horse 1 Pair Bellows a Gridiron a small Cubboard 8 small Chairs 1 Great Chair 1 Deal Table 1 Slip D^{o}. 1 Oak D^{o}. a Small looking Glass a small Dresser and Warming Pan

In ye Pantry

4 Casks 1 Ale stool a meal Hutch 3 Tubs a Small stool 1 Pottage Pott 1 Frying Pan & an Old Skillett

In ye Bed Room

1 Bed, Bedsted, and Bedding, 1 Chair and Old Close Stool

In the first Chamber

1 Bed Bedsted and Bedding 3 small Chairs 1 Arm D^{o}. – a Chest of Drawers & a Joint Stool

In ye Second Chamber

3 small Chairs & a long stool

In ye Shop

an Old Cubboard a large Old Table, Working Tools and an Old Tub.

RELIEF: William Buck was in receipt of a pension of 3s. per week when this inventory was taken. He had received this for a number of years prior to his goods being appraised by the parish. It is unknown if he received additional support from parochial authorities, since overseers' accounts only note the distribution of pensions to claimants (NRO PD 122/38).

FURTHER INFORMATION: William Buck is also referred to as Robert Buck in poor law records. He was probably living on his own in Winfarthing, Norfolk, when his goods were appraised by the parish officers but had settlement in Stratton St. Mary. There is a note in the accounts recalculating the outgoings of the parish due to William Buck 'being departed this Life' dated 7 November 1774 (NRO PD 122/38).

216. James Gill, 4 March 1793

NRO PD 122/38 Stratton St. Mary Vestry Minutes, 1783–1812.

4th March 1793.

A true & perfect Inventory / taken then / of the Househould furniture &c. of James Gill, – by us, whose Hands are hereunder written. Viz –

In the Bed room

Bed and Bedstead, Blankets and Sheets, Leather Trunk & small square Table

In the Pantry

~~Three~~ Four Killers, Washing Stool and Meal Hutch

In the Chamber

Bed ~~and~~ Bedstead, & Coverlid – 2 small Beer Vessels – Lye leach – Riving Beetle & Wedges –

In the Kitchen

Two old square Tables, – a Chest of Drawers – 4 Chairs – 2 Pottage Pots.

Thos Stannard James Aldis
John Fryer

RELIEF: James Gill had been in receipt of poor relief for several years before this inventory was made. It is, however, difficult to determine the precise nature of this as poor relief papers for Stratton St. Mary only list the total amounts of money expended per pauper during the 1790s. Nevertheless, records from the 1780s show that James Gill received money and goods from the parish, and was paid 1s. to 2s. 6d. per week to look after 'Meadows's Bastard' children (NRO PD 122/38–39; NRO PD 122/54).

FURTHER INFORMATION: James Gill was born around 1736 and was approximately 57 years old when this inventory was taken. He was buried on Christmas day 1795 at the age of 59 years old. It is unknown who Thomas Stannard, John Fryer, and James Aldis were (NRO PD 122/3; NRO PD 122/38–39; NRO PD 122/54).

217. William Martin, 21 June 1816

NRO PD 122/39 Stratton St. Mary Vestry Minutes, 1814–1832.

June, 21, 1816. An Inventory of the Goods an<d> Chattles of W^{m}. Martin of Pulham Husbandman taken by M^{r}. Stanley, Overseer of Stratton St Mary

Six Elm small Chairs, & one great Chair 2 Tables, Meal hutch, and two Keelers A pail, Lyeletch, Boiler, Frying pan, & Linin hor<se> Bed and Bedstead, blankets, sheets, & Coverlid Little bedstead, Chest, three Chamber chairs.

RELIEF: William Martin had been in receipt of poor relief for several years before this inventory was made. It is, however, difficult to determine the precise nature of this as records for Stratton St. Mary only list the total amounts of money expended per pauper during the 1810s. Nevertheless, records indicate that William Martin was given either regular or casual relief in the form of money during this decade (NRO PD 122/38–39; NRO PD 122/54).

FURTHER INFORMATION: William Martin was a husbandman and was living in Pulham, Norfolk, but had settlement in Stratton St. Mary (NRO PD 122/38–39; NRO PD 122/54).

DAMAGE: Ink spill on several parts of the page. Page torn on lines 1 and 5, cutting off the words 'an<d>' and hor<se>'.

218. Ben Kent, 10 April 1822

NRO PD 122/39 Stratton St. Mary Vestry Minutes, 1814–1832.

April 10th. 1822. An Inventory of the Effects of Ben. Kent of Starstan taken by the Oversee<r> of Stratton St. Mary,

Stump bedstead, with flight bed pair of blankets sheet & coverlid Stump bedstead with feather bed pair of sheets & coverlid, deal box, wash keeler stool & shelf, copper boiler, iron D°, – water pa<il> oak meal hutch, 2 leaf tables, square table, tea table, six elm chairs, coal grate fire pan <Pr> tongs & pot iron, bellows, tea kettle iron rake three tin'd fork & shovel.

RELIEF: Ben Kent had been in receipt of poor relief for several years before this inventory was made. It is, however, difficult to determine the precise nature of this as parish sources for Stratton St. Mary lack detail during the 1810s. Nonetheless, they reveal that Ben Kent was given 2s. per week in April 1823. He may have been receiving this when this inventory was taken. He and his wife and children were also provided with clothing, linen, and shoes from the parish on occasion (NRO PD 122/39).

FURTHER INFORMATION: Ben Kent was married and his wife may have been called Phoebe. The couple had children according to the vestry minutes, but it is unknown how many they had. The inventory and vestry minutes demonstrate that Ben Kent and his family lived in Starston, Norfolk, but had settlement in Stratton St. Mary. The names of the overseer(s) who made this inventory are unknown (NRO PD 122/39).

DAMAGE: Left-hand side of the page is ripped, cutting off the letters of the words 'Oversee<r>' (line 2) and 'pa<il>' (line 5). '<Pr>' on line 6 is illegible as the writing has faded.

Surlingham pauper inventories

Three pauper inventories have been located for Surlingham in a set of overseers' accounts which cover the years 1739 to 1764. The inventories were written by the incumbent overseers and are scattered throughout the volume. Also included in the accounts are two inventories which could not be categorised and one goods-taken inventory (NRO PD 611/38).

219. John Durrant, 30 October 1747

NRO PD 611/38 Surlingham Overseers' Accounts, 1739–1764.

1747: October ye 30 An Account of John Durrants Goods in the Town of Surlingham as followeth

first a Beed as it Stand: 2 Chists 1 Jointed Stool & Slip 2 Chairs 2 hakes 1 pair of Tongs 1 fire-pan 1 Cittle 1 poriage pot 1 pall 1 Gridgiron 1 Pair of Bellows 1 frieng-pan 2 Beer vesels 1 Killer 1 Brewing Tubb 1 peuter Dish 3 Stone Bottles 1 Sive 1 Speet 1 Dragning Crome 2 Hatchets 1 Hook 1 matthook 1 fur Jobb 1 over whart-Saw 1 Garden Rake 1 Shod Scuppet 1 Spade 1 Looking Glase 1 Smothing Iron and heats 1 Lead Ston wait 1 Lade half Ston wait ~~1 Pair of Draws 1 Ovle Table 6 Chairs~~ 1 Sythe 1 Turnip how 3 Iron weeges

RELIEF: John Durrant was in receipt of casual relief when this inventory was made. For example, between Easter 1747 and Easter 1748, he was given casual relief 'several times' totalling £1 8s. 6d. (NRO PD 611/38).
DUBIOUS TERMS: Line 7: 'fur Jobb' – unknown term. Line 8: 'Shod Scuppet' – unknown term; possibly a coal scuppet.

220. John Balls, 21 January 1762

NRO PD 611/38 Surlingham Overseers' Accounts, 1739–1764.

Jan = 21th. 1762 An Account then Taken of Jo<hn> Ballses houseld Goods made by us Robt Franks Church warden and Robt aldys Overseer of the parish of Surlingham as Followeth

one Bedstead with a Feather Bed & Curtins
one Coverley with two Blankets
one Bolster with one piller

one Chest of Dwerers with one Chist
one Trunk with one Great Chier

RELIEF: John Balls started to receive 2s. per week when this inventory was taken. He also received money from the parish when 'at need' (NRO PD 611/38).

DAMAGE: Line 1: Ink spill on 'Jo<hn>'.

221. Mary/Widow Clarke, 22 April 1762

NRO PD 611/38 Surlingham Overseers' Accounts, 1739–1764.

An Account Taken And made of the wd^{o} Clarkes Househod Goods by me Robt Aldys Overseer this 22th Day of April 1762 as Followeth
One bed & bedstead with Curttins & Vallants
2 Porrage potts A Peel & forke
one fryin pan one Roastron & pottiron
five Chairs A Twellting frame 2 tables 3 Stools
A pair of Bellows A pair of Toangs 3 Candlesticks
A Cobbard A Dresser A Lyeleech A hamer
2 Cillers one tubb one Large Chist A Lanton
A Sive A Linnen Basket A table Cloath
one Covlay 2 blankets 2 pair of Sheets
A bolster A piller A Tunel 2 hanks
a Large mate pott A Small Earthen pott
And 3 Secks

RELIEF: Widow Clarke's husband, Edward, died around April 1762 and the parish subsequently started to give Widow Clarke 4s. per week. In addition, the parish paid for Edward Clarke's funeral and rent (£1 6s. 6d.), gave Widow Clarke money when she was 'in need', and provided the Clarke children with clothing (NRO PD 611/38).

FURTHER INFORMATION: Widow Clarke's forename was Mary and she had at least one son and one daughter when the inventory was taken. Overseers' accounts indicate that Widow Clarke had been removed from an unknown parish to her home parish of Surlingham with her children in early 1762 (NRO PD 611/38).

DUBIOUS TERMS: Line 13: 'mate' – probably metal or meat.

Tharston pauper inventory

Only one pauper inventory has been located for Tharston from a set of overseers' accounts dated 1777–1793. It is located at the back of the volume and is in the handwriting of George Coleman, who was an overseer for the parish at various points over the 1780s and 1790s. Also included in the volume is a goods-taken inventory of Widow Ropes' goods which were taken by the parish, c.1780–1793 (NRO PD 708/84).

222. John Riches, no date (probably c.1780–1793)

NRO PD 708/84 Tharston Draft Overseers' Accounts, 1777–1793.

An Invetory of ye Goods of John Riches

A Peel fork 4 pair of Nippers 46 Lasts Iron Kettel a pair of Drawers Boot Jack four Tubs Iron Pott Quarter of Peck frying pan Bowl Skillet two Tables ~~five~~ 7 Chairs A Corner Cubbord Looking Glass pail 4 Swill Tubs Spit fire pan tongs Hake Bullow's purr Dust pan pair of Dog Irons Wheel Barrow Lanthorn Warming Pan Lye Leach two Candle Sticks two Boxes Coffer Cheast Bed as it Stand with Curtains and all furniture a Short Ladder Beetle Spade Mattock two Hoes Iron Rake four Vessels two Ale Stools a Large Bottle Chaff Sive Skep and Hog Stool Syder Press and throw

RELIEF: John Riches was continually noted as a pauper between the 1780s and 1790s, however because the inventory could not be precisely dated it is not possible to establish what the exact nature of relief was when the inventory was taken. Nonetheless, John Riches received relief on a frequent basis from the parish. During the early 1790s, for example, he received a pension of 2s. 6d. per week from parochial authorities. He was also given money from the parish when he was 'at Need' and sick, and provided with clothing and fuel (NRO PD 708/84; NRO PD 708/88; NRO PD 708/90).

FURTHER INFORMATION: The inventory was probably made between 1780 and 1793, based on the patterns of relief given to John Riches and the distinctive handwriting of the overseer (George Coleman) who wrote the inventory. John Riches was married and his wife's name was possibly Mary. A Robert Riches is mentioned in overseers' accounts for the parish, but it is unknown whether he was any relation of John Riches (NRO PD 708/84; NRO PD 708/88; NRO PD 708/90).

DUBIOUS TERMS: Line 5: 'Bullow's purr' – pair of bellows. Line 9: 'Chaff Sive' – an item for sieving chaff but also possibly a chaffer/chaffing dish and sieve.

Trowse pauper inventories

The three pauper inventories from Trowse were written on loose sheets of paper, found among a range of other inventories which were made for reasons such as arrears of rent (NRO PD 216/90).

223. Widow Dictarson, 7 December 1694

NRO PD 216/90 Trowse Inventories, 1694–1786.

An Inventory of the goods of the widdow dictarson in the towne howse in trowse newton and an Agree ment made betwen the town above Said and har sun and dauter to take theare mother to keepe at on Shilling six pence per weeke in the towne of porland and when thay find themselves Greved to returne har and the Goods agayne to the inhabitants in the afore said parrish or the mony thay are allowed at december y[e] 7: 94

		li s d
Impris	One bed and bed Steade and Curtons and vallonds as it Stand	1 – 15 – 0
	2 tabels and 2 Joynt Stooles and 2 playne Stooles and 2 Chayers	0 – 8 – 0
	One Iron pott and one ould bras-Cittell and one Keepe	0 – 10 – 0
	one deske and 1 bocks and wooll Reele ...	0 – 4 – 0
	One hake and roasttorn and one par of tongs and one friing pan	0 – 2 – 6
	Two new petty Coates and one Gowne and one neck Skarfe and one Long Skarfe ...	0 – 15 – 4
	The totall is –	3 – 14 – 10

Besn Ceverall Small things that ar not foriseid and wee agree to this account witness ~~my~~ our hands the day and yeare above written –

his marke
John X King
Mary X King
her marke

RELIEF: Trowse poor relief sources are inconsistent and lack detail. Extant records and the inventory, however, show that Widow Dictarson was a pauper and was provided with housing from the parish. Her children were also given 1s. 6d. per week towards her care (NRO PD 216/90; NRO PD 216/92).

FURTHER INFORMATION: Widow Dictarson was living in Trowse townhouse (parish-provided housing) when this inventory was made. Widow Dictarson moved out of the townhouse soon after the inventory was made to live with her son and daughter (John King and Mary King) in Poringland, Norfolk, around four miles to the south of Trowse (NRO PD 216/90).

DUBIOUS TERMS: Line 20: 'Besn' – unknown term, possibly besides.

224. Elizabeth King, 12 April 1749

NRO PD 216/90 Trowse Inventories, 1694–1786.

An Inventory of the Goods of Elizabeth King late Fuller

In the Ketchen

One Bed as it stands – a Chest of Draws – Six Chairs A Fire range Firepan & Tongues & Bellows –

Upon the Chamber

One Bed as it stands – In the Closett Ditto – one Iron pot one Kittle

Then agreed with the Churchwardens & Overseers of Trowse newton for Eighteen pence a Week for Twelve Months for which I am to keep Alice & Elizabeth the two Childris of my wives and from that time I am to keep them for a Shilling P Week so long as there is reason for them the said Officers of Trowse to allow it, but for the said Officers to allow no more than a shilling P week, if they should I acknowledge they have & shall have a right to take the above Goods of theers above mentiond as witness my hand this Twelwth Day of Aprill 1749

Witniss the Mark

Thom[s]. Linsey John X King

of

RELIEF: Poor relief sources are inconsistent for Trowse. Extant records and the inventory, however, show that Elizabeth King was a pauper and that her husband was given 1s. 6d. per week to look after her children (NRO PD 216/90; NRO PD 216/92).

FURTHER INFORMATION: Elizabeth King was married to John King. She may have been previously married to somebody with the surname Fuller and had two children from this: Alice and Elizabeth. These children, however, could have instead potentially been John King's children. The inventory was made to allow John King relief to help raise his wife's children, but to also ensure that he did not ask for too much from the parish. It is unknown who Thomas Linsey was or whether he was a churchwarden or overseer of the poor for Trowse (NRO PD 216/1; NRO PD 216/90; NRO PD 216/92).

225. Widow Cullender, 10 June 1750

NRO PD 216/90 Trowse Inventories, 1694–1786.

An account of the household goods of the widow Cullender

A Blue Bed and Curtins and other nesscecarys ther to belong
A Napkin press
half a Dozen Chairs
a dale Box
a pair Bellows
a pail and Ciller and tin Boiler
a brown Table

Taken by John Robkins June 18: 1750

RELIEF: Widow Cullender is noted as a pauper in various poor relief records, but no information could be found as to when relief started or what the exact nature of it was (NRO PD 216/90; NRO PD 216/92).

FURTHER INFORMATION: It is unknown who John Robkins was or whether he was a parish officer, such as a churchwarden or overseer of the poor (NRO PD 216/90; NRO PD 216/92).

Wighton pauper inventory

Only one pauper inventory has been located for Wighton, written in an unknown hand on a loose sheet of paper (NRO PD 553/79)

226. Mary Shearling, 18 February 1819

NRO PD 553/79 Wighton Inventory, 1819.

Inventory of the Houshold Furniture of Mary Shearling
A Clock
A 4 Post Bedstead & Beding
7 Chairs 2 of them Arm'd
2 Beds upstairs with Beding
1 Chest of Drawers
2 Round Tables
1 Bedstead
1 Glass & 1 swing d^{o}

Wainscot Table
9 Chairs 4 of y^{m} mahogany
3 Tubs
1 Corner Cupboard
1 Hanging d^{o}
1 Deal Table
2 Brass Candlesticks
1 Table with 4 Drawers
1 mahogony Tea Tray
1 Toasting Fork
1 Poker 2 p^{r} Tongs 1 Firepan
2 Boilers & 3 Saucepan's
Wighton Feby 18th 1819

RELIEF: Mary Shearling was in receipt of 7s. per week when this inventory was taken. Overseers' papers indicate that she was also sometimes given additional money, rent payments, and clothing from the parish (NRO PD 553/56).

FURTHER INFORMATION: Mary Shearling was widowed and had at least two children (a girl and a boy) living with her when this inventory was made (NRO PD 553/56).

DUBIOUS TERMS: Line 9: 'Glass' – looking glass.

Winfarthing pauper inventory

The inventory from Winfarthing is written on a loose sheet of paper in the hand of one of the incumbent overseers (Robert Woods or Phillip Browne) (NRO PD 78/66).

227. John Crowe and Martha Smith, 29 January 1816

NRO PD 78/66 Winfarthing Inventories, 1816.

Crowes Goods
Taken – Jan 29th 1816

Kitchen
Small Table.
Meal Hatch
Chest of Drawers
Desk
7 Chairs
Bowl
Pail
2 Stools
Round Table
30 H. Clock
Small Looking Glass
Hanging Shelf
Shelf
2 Keeler's
Ley Letch
Coal Hod
Frying Pan

Spice Drawers
Spinning Wheel Reel
Box Iron Heater & Rest
Small Shelf
Hair Broom

Chamber
Stool & Childs Chair
mattock & 2 Helves
Spinning Wheel Iron Rake
Small Table Reel Coal Gate
2 Cobb Irons Fender
Vessel 2 Chairs 2 Slates
2 Drawers 2 Spits
Bedstead & Bed as it Stands

Martha Smith's Goods
Bedstead Shelf
Chest of Drawers
Keeler
Table
Leaf Table
1 Chair
~~Ley~~ Pail

RELIEF: John Crowe and his wife were in receipt of casual relief when this inventory was made. For example, between January and February 1816 the couple were given 8s. in total when 'at need'. Martha Smith appears to have been living with John Crowe. She was also a pauper and received money from the parish when she was sick and 'at need'. In April 1816, she is noted as receiving 1s. per week (NRO PD 78/59).

FURTHER INFORMATION: John Crowe was married and was born around 1746, meaning that he was approximately 70 years old when this inventory was taken. He was buried on 15 February 1824 in Winfarthing at the age of 78. His place of residence was noted as the parish poorhouse in 1824. There are a William, George, and Noah Smith noted in overseers' accounts for the parish during the mid–1810s, but it is unknown whether they were any relation of Martha Smith (NRO PD 78/59). There is also a second inventory of Martha Smith's goods at John Crowe's house. It is undated but it is written on the back of a scrap piece of paper which has the date 1816 on it. Each of the items is ticked off in pencil, except the spinning wheel which has been crossed out in a different hand to the original. This suggests that the items were taken by the parish when she died and then checked off. The inventory is as follows (NRO PD 78/8; NRO PD 78/66):

The Goods of the late Martha Smith at John Crowe's

Chest of Drawers
2 Tables
2 Reels
2 Spinning Wheels
Washing Keeler
Earthen Pot
2 Dishes
Porridge Pot
Bason & Two Spoons
Huckaback Towel
A Piece of Patch Work
An Old Blanket
Bedstead Cord and Mat
a Pail
A large Damask Table Cloth
An Iron Sauce Pan

Yelverton with Alpington pauper inventories

Three pauper inventories survive in a set of overseers' accounts for the parish dated 1720–1748. They are found next to the disbursements and expenses of the overseers in 1738, 1739, and 1742. A list of goods given to the pauper Mary Copping in 1740 is also included in the volume (NRO PD 316/46).

228. Lucy Wigg, 13 July 1738

NRO PD 316/46 Yelverton with Alpington Overseers' Accounts, 1720–1748.

July: y^{e}: 13: <u>1738</u> An Enventerry of the goods & Chattells of Lucy Wigg Singell woman Collectioner of ye Town of yellver toun taken by Henry Leverrett overseere of ye pore of ye Said parish ye day & yeare a foresad – –

one tronke one Small Coberd one Samall box one freying pan a wollrelle one Skillett one porridge pott a pwooendish fire pane two gall pott two goshes & a Small drinking pott two bottells a Lanthon one paile one Long Earthing pott one boule one Stule one Candell Stick one Leylen: one bedd as itt Stands four bottels one flour pott three Cillers a byle of a paill one Chare one baskett one Sive one Chisst one Chamber pott one pair of bollers one Jent stule .... The day & year a bove Said this Inventrey was takeing by me in ye presentes of

of
ye mark X John Goderd:
Richard: Tilney:
Churchwarden

of
ye Mark H Henry Leverret
overseere

RELIEF: Lucy Wigg was in receipt of 9d. per week when this inventory was made and in the following weeks her pension rose to 1s. 6d. per week. She gave birth to a son around mid–1738 and the parish paid the costs of delivering the baby and for clothing and blankets (NRO PD 316/46). The inventory also states that she was a 'Collectioner'.

FURTHER INFORMATION: Lucy Wigg was a single woman and had at least one son out of wedlock, who was baptised John on 6 August 1738. Overseers' accounts note 'Children' on one occasion, suggesting that Lucy Wigg may have had more than one child. John Goderd does not appear to have held a position in the parish and it is unknown whether this was the same John Goderd whose goods were appraised on 30 July 1739 **(229)** (NRO PD 316/2; NRO PD 316/46).

DUBIOUS TERMS: Line 5: 'pwooendish' – possibly wooden dish or proving dish. Line 7: 'Leylen' – possibly lye letch. Line 8: 'byle' – bail.

229. John Goderd, 30 July 1739

NRO PD 316/46 Yelverton with Alpington Overseers' Accounts, 1720–1748.

July: y^e: 30: <u>1739</u>
An account of ye goods & Chattels of John Goderd Colecttinor of ye parrish of yellvertoun taken by John Briggs & Richard Tilney as followeth –

one bedd pillou & bouster & bedd Stad & all other things thare to be Langing one worming pan & one fryin pan one Iern pott 2 Jented Stules one Chare one Larg Stone bottell one paile 2 Littell Cillers one boule one Copp 2 trukes one pair boullows one Rosstonn one Laspen a pair toungs one Coufer a Large hammer a Cobert one Candelstik 2 Muggs ....

RELIEF: John Goderd appears to have been in receipt of around 1s. per week when this inventory was made. He had received this since around Michaelmas 1738 and was also given cash on occasion. The parish may have also paid his rent between Michaelmas 1739 and Easter 1740 (costing 15s.) (NRO PD 316/46). The inventory also states that he was a 'Colecttinor'.

FURTHER INFORMATION: John Goderd is also referred to as John Goodwell in overseers' accounts for the settlement. Goody Goderd/Godwell is mentioned in poor relief records, but it is unknown whether she was any relation of John Goderd. John Briggs was overseer of the poor in July 1739. Richard Tilney was a churchwarden for the parish (NRO PD 316/46)

DUBIOUS TERMS: Line 7: 'Laspen' – possibly latch pan.

230. John Levek, 5 May 1742

NRO PD 316/46 Yelverton with Alpington Overseers' Accounts, 1720–1748.

May: y^e: 5: 1742
An Account of ye Gudes of John Levek Colectshinor of ye toun of yelverton taken by^e George Kemp Gen^tt Oversere & Henry Leveritt Church Warden –

One bedd & beddstad: 2: blankets one bouster 2: Seeths one Ruog Korttings & Rads – –
4: Cherss one table one Spining wele one boox one Iron pott one friing pan one tronk fier pan tongs & hake ....

of ye Mark X Sarah wittnes: Charmberlin	of ye Mark: H : Henry Leveret Richard Tilne

RELIEF: Poor law records were poorly kept during the 1740s and so it is not possible to fully reconstitute the relief that John Levek and his family received. Nevertheless, overseers' accounts indicate that John Levek was given money from the parish on occasion and that his wife received 9d. per week. It is also possible that the parish paid 10s. towards their rent and that they had been removed from another, unknown, parish when this inventory was made (NRO PD 316/46). The inventory also states that John Levek was a 'Colectshinor'.

FURTHER INFORMATION: John Levek was married. It is unknown who Sarah Chamberlin was. Henry Leveret was a churchwarden or overseer and Richard Tilney was a churchwarden (NRO PD 316/46).

Appendices

Appendix 1: List of pauper inventories by settlement

No.	Reference number (NRO)	Date	Name
Ashwellthorpe			
1	PC 88/1	16 Jul 1695	Ann Turner
2	PC 88/1	26 Jan 1710/11	Widow Hill
3	PC 88/1	2 Nov 1720	Mary Hill
4	PC 88/2	1 Oct 1754	Edward Rushbrook
5	PC 88/2	1 Oct 1754	Constance Huggin
6	PC 88/2	1 Oct 1754	Widow Cooper
Besthorpe			
7	PD 309/52	10 Oct 1776	Widow Stephenson
8	PD 309/53	10 Jul 1803	John Dunnett
Bressingham			
9	PD 111/170	27 Dec 1693	Widow Tiller
10	PD 111/170	17 Feb 1717/18	Henry Wells
11	PD 111/114	25 May 1719	Ann Route
12	PD 111/170	16 Sep 1719	Thomas Surgon
13	PD 111/114	22 Oct 1724	Ann Hart
14	PD 111/170	14 Dec 1727	William Car
15	PD 111/114	7 Feb 1759	Widow Brister
16	PD 111/114	7 Feb 1759	Ann Burrows
17	PD 111/170	11 Mar 1773	William Adkins
18	PD 111/170	16 Oct 1773	Henry Fisher/Harrison
19	PD 111/170	5 Nov 1773	Mary Bravenett
20	PD 111/114	8 Oct 1814	William Arnold
21	PD 111/114	n.d.	— Hernwell
Brockdish			
22	PD 477/43	13 Mar 1804	John Minter
Bunwell			
23	PD 712/49	15 Apr 1771	Mary Coleman
Carbrooke			
24	MC 29412, 1025X2	4 Sep 1787	John Daniels
Cawston			
25	PD 193/93	14 Dec 1699	Widow Penell
26	PD 193/93	14 Dec 1699	Widow Garby
27	PD 193/93	14 Dec 1699	Widow Paten / Ann Clayton
28	PD 193/93	14 Dec 1699	Widow Woods

No.	Reference number (NRO)	Date	Name
29	PD 193/93	14 Dec 1699	Widow Reed
30	PD 193/93	14 Dec 1699	Richard Ladrken
31	PD 193/93	14 Dec 1699	Robert Land
32	PD 193/93	14 Dec 1699	Widow Bloume
33	PD 193/93	14 Dec 1699	Dorothy Ridge
34	PD 193/93	14 Dec 1699	Matthew Matthews
35	PD 193/93	14 Dec 1699	Richard Barker/Barber
36	PD 193/93	14 Dec 1699	Widow Greenwood
37	PD 193/93	14 Dec 1699	John Kenen
38	PD 193/93	14 Dec 1699	Henry Blackburn
39	PD 193/93	14 Dec 1699	Thomas Barker/Barber
40	PD 193/93	14 Dec 1699	Edward Martin
41	PD 193/93	14 Dec 1699	William Bridge
42	PD 193/93	14 Dec 1699	Andrew Allen
43	PD 193/93	14 Dec 1699	Widow Wilson
Forncett St. Peter			
44	PD 421/133	12 Jan 1784	Thomas Cullams
45	PD 421/133	c.1784	Martha Smith
Gissing			
46	PD 50/71	c.1720-1750s	Widow Watling
47	PD 50/44	c.1720-1740s	Widow Tutell
48	PD 50/45	4 Nov 1756	John Smith
Hapton			
49	PD 236/51	15 Apr 1796	William Read (junior)
50	PD 236/51	No date	Mary Huson
East Harling			
51	PD 219/114	9 Apr 1821	Rhoda Wretham
52	PD 219/114	9 Apr 1821	Widow Whitehead
53	PD 219/114	12 Oct 1821	George Orsborne
54	PD 219/114	16 Nov 1825	— Parker
West Harling			
55	PD 219/114	23 Jan 1779	Widow Doe
56	PD 219/114	4 Jul 1803	Esther Turner
Hilgay			
57	PD 382/45	27 Mar 1805	William Johnson
Hingham			
58	PD 575/128	26 Sep 1710	Robert Coper
59	PD 575/128	c.1723-1727	Widow Osburn
60	PD 575/128	8 Jun 1724	Widow Little
61	PD 575/128	23 Mar 1724/25	Widow Man

No.	Reference number (NRO)	Date	Name
62	PD 575/128	16 Nov 1725	Widow Flowars
63	PD 575/128	c.1726-1728	William Burgany
64	PD 575/128	c.1727-1732	Widow Dawson
65	PD 575/128	c.29 Mar 1728	John Larthman (junior)
66	PD 575/128	30 Aug 1731	Widow Norton
Holme-next-the-Sea			
67	PD 629/50	7 Jun 1752	Susan Greves
68	PD 629/50	29 Nov 1766	Thomas Trips
69	PD 629/50	7 May 1770	Widow Holybrad
Hopton			
70	PD 563/49	1 May 1731	Robert Pycrass
Horningtoft			
71	PD 642/35	2 Dec 1771	Widow Pratt
72	PD 642/35	9 Dec 1772	Martha Ralph
73	PD 642/35	24 May 1773	Frances Smith
Ingworth			
74	PD 521/26	25 Dec 1769	Dan Heagon
75	PD 521/26	14 Nov 1774	Tom Storey
Letton			
76	MC 76/50, 534X10	20 Sep 1759	Widow Wix [Wise]
77	MC 76/50, 534X10	1762	Widow Bannett
78	MC 76/50, 534X10	14 Apr 1769	Widow Elvey
Loddon			
79	PD 595/22	26 Nov 1751	Alexander Wade
Martham			
80	PD 710/68	14 Oct 1758	Elizabeth Bland (younger)
81	PD 710/68	14 Oct 1758	Mary Crosshold
82	PD 710/68	14 Oct 1758	Mary Wright
83	PD 710/68	14 Oct 1758	Widow Conyard
84	PD 710/68	14 Oct 1758	Elizabeth Bland (elder)
85	PD 710/68	18 Dec 1764	Widow/Priscilla Myhill
86	PD 710/68	18 Dec 1764	John Brunson
87	PD 710/68	18 Dec 1764	Widow/Mary Piercon
88	PD 710/68	18 Dec 1764	Robert Howell (elder)
89	PD 710/68	16 Mar 1768	Edward Knights
90	PD 710/68	16 Dec 1771	Widow Elizabeth Smith
91	PD 710/68	14 Feb 1772	Roger Riches

No.	Reference number (NRO)	Date	Name
Great Moulton with Little Moulton			
92	PD 489/29	3 Jul 1693	Sara Hubert
93	PD 489/29	3 Jul 1693	Margaret Smith
94	PD 489/29	24 Jul 1699	Widow Tackling
95	PD 489/29	7 Jan 1701/2	Henry and Susan Barret
96	PD 489/29	18 Oct 1710	Josh Miller
97	PD 489/29	6 Aug 1722	John Church
98	PD 489/29	15 Sep 1735	Widow Blake
99	PD 489/29	29 Aug 1737	Widow Townsend
100	PD 489/29	11 Jul 1738	Widow Cock
101	PD 489/29	11 Jul 1738	James Hilling
102	PD 489/30	28 Sep 1748	Robert Websdale
103	PD 489/30	c.1740-1754	Richard Pottel
104	PD 489/30	14 Oct 1754	Widow Moor
105	PD 489/30	14 Oct 1754	Widow Parish
106	PD 489/30	14 Oct 1754	Widow Pyman
107	PD 489/30	14 Oct 1754	Widow Porter
108	PD 489/30	14 Oct 1754	Amy Hammond
109	PD 489/30	14 Oct 1754	Widow Hilling
110	PD 489/30	14 Oct 1754	Edmund Trixon
111	PD 489/30	14 Oct 1754	Widow Pottle
112	PD 489/30	14 Oct 1754	Sarah Harvey
113	PD 489/30	1756	Robert Roberts
114	PD 489/31	19 Apr 1762	Widow Moor
115	PD 489/31	19 Apr 1762	Widow Parish
116	PD 489/31	19 Apr 1762	Chris Collers
117	PD 489/31	7 May 1764	John Blake
118	PD 489/51	21 Oct 1767	Susan Buck
119	PD 489/31	c.1760s	Jemimah Parish
120	PD 489/31	c.1760s	John Nudds
121	PD 489/31	c.1760s	John Church
Norwich, St. Mary in the Marsh			
122	PD 499/79	14 May 1734	Lady/Jemima Pleasant
123	PD 499/79	26 Jun 1772	Samuel Hunt
Redenhall with Harleston and Wortwell			
124	PD 295/102	8 May 1708	Susan Aldred
125	PD 295/102	1710	Robert Burton
126	PD 295/93	23 Mar 1713/14	Widow Bottwright
127	PD 295/102	20 Jun 1731	Widow Reed
128	PD 295/102	26 Jun 1731	Thomas Self
129	PD 295/102	26 Jun 1731	Flegg Pettow
130	PD 295/102	26 Jun 1731	Jane Branch
131	PD 295/102	26 Jun 1731	Ann Green
132	PD 295/102	26 Jun 1731	William Afsey (senior)
133	PD 295/102	26 Jun 1731	Ann Burton

No.	Reference number (NRO)	Date	Name
134	PD 295/102	26 Jun 1731	Elizabeth Trew
135	PD 295/102	26 Jun 1731	Widow Todd
136	PD 295/102	26 Jun 1731	Elizabeth/Widow Goldspink
137	PD 295/102	26 Jun 1731	Lettice/Widow Flattman / Henry Branch
138	PD 295/102	10 Nov 1731	Lionel Lawson
139	PD 295/102	8 Dec 1731	John Andrews
140	PD 295/102	29 Dec 1733	Widow Chamberlaine
141	PD 295/102	15 Jun 1734	Samuel Harman
142	PD 295/102	21 Nov 1737	Lettice Flattman
143	PD 295/102	29 Sep 1738	Nicholas Burley (junior)
144	PD 295/102	29 Sep 1738	Widow Todd
145	PD 295/102	27 Nov 1738	Godfrey Goodrum
146	PD 295/102	15 Jan 1738/39	Susan Burrows
147	PD 295/102	2 Feb 1738/39	James Keely
148	PD 295/102	2 Jun 1739	Widow Searls
149	PD 295/102	6 May 1740	Ann/Widow Alexander
150	PD 295/102	10 May 1740	Mary Gower
151	PD 295/102	4 Jul 1740	Widow Catchpool
152	PD 295/102	4 Jul 1740	Robert Garrard
153	PD 295/102	4 Jul 1740	Widow Salter
154	PD 295/102	11 Jul 1740	John Cupper
155	PD 295/102	6 Jan 1740/41	Francis Semmons
156	PD 295/102	11 Dec 1742	Isaac Day
157	PD 295/102	11 Dec 1742	Frances Metchels
158	PD 295/102	17 Jun 1743	Elizabeth Twist
159	PD 295/117	24 Jun 1744	Ann Capon
160	PD 295/102	15 Apr 1745	Elizabeth Trew
161	PD 295/117	29 Nov 1745	Amey Gardner
162	PD 295/102	3 Jan 1745/46	Widow Catchpool
163	PD 295/117	8 Apr 1746	Alexander Bazer
164	PD 295/117	6 Oct 1746	John Brown
165	PD 295/117	18 Feb 1752	Widow Meek
166	PD 295/117	3 Mar 1762	Phillip Knight
167	PD 295/106	24 Dec 1828	Michael Aggus
Shelton			
168	PD 358/41	28 Oct 1692	Anne Roberts
169	PD 358/41	9 Feb 1693/94	John Hatton (junior)
170	PD 358/41	22 May 1696	Widow Hatton
171	PD 358/41	21 May 1700	Francis Karrington
172	PD 358/41	31 Jul 1700	Barbara Jermyn
173	PD 358/41	15 Nov 1709	Jeremy Nudds
174	PD 358/41	16 Apr 1712	William Jermyn
175	PD 358/41	6 Aug 1713	Goodman Dunnen
176	PD 358/41	3 Feb 1718/19	Joseph Bateman
177	PD 358/41	12 Oct 1719	Francis Baker

No.	Reference number (NRO)	Date	Name
178	PD 358/41	3 Feb 1722/23	Katherine Jex
179	PD 358/41	2 Mar 1723/24	Mary/Widow Frances
180	PD 358/41	5 Mar 1728/29	Christiana/Widow Bateman
181	PD 358/42	26 Oct 1741	Ann Milles
182	PD 358/42	28 Sep 1742	Widow Thrower
183	PD 358/42	28 Sep 1743	John Francis (junior)
184	PD 358/42	30 Jul 1746	Widow Fulcher
185	PD 358/42	18 Jan 1747/48	John Frances (senior)
186	PD 358/42	12 Jul 1748	Henry Brown
187	PD 358/42	23/30 Apr 1751	Thomas Taylor (junior)
188	PD 358/42	29 Sep 1753	William Brett
189	PD 358/42	8 Feb 1762	Mary Taylor
Shimpling			
190	PD 102/32	9 Jun 1785	Widow Long
Shipdham			
191	PD 337/158	24 May 1720	John Dorman
192	PD 337/158	24 May 1720	Ealles Platfoot
193	PD 337/158	24 May 1720	John Doughty
194	PD 337/158	24 May 1720	Widow Allcock
195	PD 337/158	24 May 1720	Widow Reeves
196	PD 337/158	24 May 1720	Widow Adkens
197	PD 337/158	24 May 1720	Widow Ouldham
198	PD 337/158	24 May 1720	Sarah Tillets
199	PD 337/158	24 May 1720	Widow Simonds
200	PD 337/158	24 May 1720	Widow Mallett
201	PD 337/158	24 May 1720	Widow Fuller
202	PD 337/158	24 May 1720	— Rice
203	PD 337/158	24 May 1720	William Bright
204	PD 337/158	24 May 1720	Widow Fish
205	PD 337/158	24 May 1720	Widow Ranson
206	PD 337/158	24 May 1720	Widow Bright
207	PD 337/158	24 May 1720	Widow Stagg
208	PD 337/158	24 May 1720	Margaret Bowl
209	PD 337/158	24 May 1720	Widow Head
210	PD 337/158	24 May 1720	Ann Wright
211	PD 337/158	24 May 1720	Elizabeth Brett
212	PD 337/158	24 May 1720	Widow Gilldens
213	PD 337/158	24 May 1720	Widow Stimpson
Stratton St. Mary			
214	PD 122/54	27 Jan 1774	Widow Booty
215	PD 122/54	30 Jul 1774	William Buck
216	PD 122/38	4 Mar 1793	James Gill
217	PD 122/39	21 Jun 1816	William Martin
218	PD 122/39	10 Apr 1822	Ben Kent

No.	Reference number (NRO)	Date	Name
Surlingham			
219	PD 611/38	30 Oct 1747	John Durrant
220	PD 611/38	21 Jan 1762	John Balls
221	PD 611/38	22 Apr 1762	Mary/Widow Clarke
Tharston			
222	PD 708/84	c.1780-1793	John Riches
Trowse			
223	PD 216/90	7 Dec 1694	Widow Dictarson
224	PD 216/90	12 Apr 1749	Elizabeth King
225	PD 216/90	10 Jun 1750	Widow Cullender
Wighton			
226	PD 553/79	18 Feb 1819	Mary Shearling
Winfarthing			
227	PD 78/66	29 Jan 1816	John Crowe / Martha Smith
Yelverton with Alpington			
228	PD 316/46	13 Jul 1738	Lucy Wigg
229	PD 316/46	30 Jul 1739	John Goderd
230	PD 316/46	5 May 1742	John Levek

Appendix 2: List of pauper inventories by surname

No.	Reference number (NRO)	Name	Date	Parish of settlement
196	PD 337/158	Widow Adkens	24 May 1720	Shipdham
17	PD 111/170	William Adkins	11 Mar 1773	Bressingham
132	PD 295/102	William Afsey (senior)	26 Jun 1731	Redenhall with Harleston and Wortwell
167	PD 295/106	Michael Aggus	24 Dec 1828	Redenhall with Harleston and Wortwell
124	PD 295/102	Susan Aldred	8 May 1708	Redenhall with Harleston and Wortwell
149	PD 295/102	Ann/Widow Alexander	6 May 1740	Redenhall with Harleston and Wortwell
194	PD 337/158	Widow Allcock	24 May 1720	Shipdham
42	PD 193/93	Andrew Allen	14 Dec 1699	Cawston
139	PD 295/102	John Andrews	8 Dec 1731	Redenhall with Harleston and Wortwell
20	PD 111/114	William Arnold	8 Oct 1814	Bressingham
177	PD 358/41	Francis Baker	12 Oct 1719	Shelton
220	PD 611/38	John Balls	21 Jan 1762	Surlingham
77	MC 76/50, 534X10	Widow Bannett	1762	Letton
35	PD 193/93	Richard Barker/ Barber	14 Dec 1699	Cawston
39	PD 193/93	Thomas Barker/ Barber	14 Dec 1699	Cawston
95	PD 489/29	Henry and Susan Barret	7 Jan 1701/2	Great Moulton with Little Moulton
180	PD 358/41	Christiana/ Widow Bateman	5 Mar 1728/29	Shelton
176	PD 358/41	Joseph Bateman	3 Feb 1718/19	Shelton
163	PD 295/117	Alexander Bazer	8 Apr 1746	Redenhall with Harleston and Wortwell
38	PD 193/93	Henry Blackburn	14 Dec 1699	Cawston
117	PD 489/31	John Blake	7 May 1764	Great Moulton with Little Moulton
98	PD 489/29	Widow Blake	15 Sep 1735	Great Moulton with Little Moulton

No.	Reference number (NRO)	Name	Date	Parish of settlement
84	PD 710/68	Elizabeth Bland (elder)	14 Oct 1758	Martham
80	PD 710/68	Elizabeth Bland (younger)	14 Oct 1758	Martham
32	PD 193/93	Widow Bloume	14 Dec 1699	Cawston
214	PD 122/54	Widow Booty	27 Jan 1774	Stratton St. Mary
126	PD 295/93	Widow Bottwright	23 Mar 1713/14	Redenhall with Harleston and Wortwell
208	PD 337/158	Margaret Bowl	24 May 1720	Shipdham
137	PD 295/102	Henry Branch / Lettice/Widow Flattman	26 Jun 1731	Redenhall with Harleston and Wortwell
130	PD 295/102	Jane Branch	26 Jun 1731	Redenhall with Harleston and Wortwell
19	PD 111/170	Mary Bravenett	5 Nov 1773	Bressingham
211	PD 337/158	Elizabeth Brett	24 May 1720	Shipdham
188	PD 358/42	William Brett	29 Sep 1753	Shelton
41	PD 193/93	William Bridge	14 Dec 1699	Cawston
206	PD 337/158	Widow Bright	24 May 1720	Shipdham
203	PD 337/158	William Bright	24 May 1720	Shipdham
15	PD 111/114	Widow Brister	7 Feb 1759	Bressingham
186	PD 358/42	Henry Brown	12 Jul 1748	Shelton
164	PD 295/117	John Brown	6 Oct 1746	Redenhall with Harleston and Wortwell
86	PD 710/68	John Brunson	18 Dec 1764	Martham
118	PD 489/51	Susan Buck	21 Oct 1767	Great Moulton with Little Moulton
215	PD 122/54	William Buck	30 Jul 1774	Stratton St. Mary
63	PD 575/128	William Burgany	c.1726-1728	Hingham
143	PD 295/102	Nicholas Burley (junior)	29 Sep 1738	Redenhall with Harleston and Wortwell
16	PD 111/114	Ann Burrows	7 Feb 1759	Bressingham
146	PD 295/102	Susan Burrows	15 Jan 1738/39	Redenhall with Harleston and Wortwell
133	PD 295/102	Ann Burton	26 Jun 1731	Redenhall with Harleston and Wortwell
125	PD 295/102	Robert Burton	1710	Redenhall with Harleston and Wortwell

No.	Reference number (NRO)	Name	Date	Parish of settlement
159	PD 295/117	Ann Capon	24 Jun 1744	Redenhall with Harleston and Wortwell
14	PD 111/170	William Car	14 Dec 1727	Bressingham
151	PD 295/102	Widow Catchpool	4 Jul 1740	Redenhall with Harleston and Wortwell
162	PD 295/102	Widow Catchpool	3 Jan 1745/46	Redenhall with Harleston and Wortwell
140	PD 295/102	Widow Chamberlaine	29 Dec 1733	Redenhall with Harleston and Wortwell
97	PD 489/29	John Church	6 Aug 1722	Great Moulton with Little Moulton
121	PD 489/31	John Church	c.1760s	Great Moulton with Little Moulton
221	PD 611/38	Mary/Widow Clarke	22 Apr 1762	Surlingham
27	PD 193/93	Ann Clayton / Widow Paten	14 Dec 1699	Cawston
100	PD 489/29	Widow Cock	11 Jul 1738	Great Moulton with Little Moulton
23	PD 712/49	Mary Coleman	15 Apr 1771	Bunwell
116	PD 489/31	Chris Collers	19 Apr 1762	Great Moulton with Little Moulton
83	PD 710/68	Widow Conyard	14 Oct 1758	Martham
6	PC 88/2	Widow Cooper	1 Oct 1754	Ashwellthorpe
58	PD 575/128	Robert Coper	26 Sep 1710	Hingham
81	PD 710/68	Mary Crosshold	14 Oct 1758	Martham
227	PD 78/66	John Crowe / Martha Smith	29 Jan 1816	Winfarthing
44	PD 421/133	Thomas Cullam	12 Jan 1784	Forncett St. Peter
225	PD 216/90	Widow Cullender	10 Jun 1750	Trowse
154	PD 295/102	John Cupper	11 Jul 1740	Redenhall with Harleston and Wortwell
24	MC 29412, 1025X2	John Daniels	4 Sep 1787	Carbrooke
64	PD 575/128	Widow Dawson	c.1727-1732	Hingham
156	PD 295/102	Isaac Day	11 Dec 1742	Redenhall with Harleston and Wortwell

No.	Reference number (NRO)	Name	Date	Parish of settlement
223	PD 216/90	Widow Dictarson	7 Dec 1694	Trowse
55	PD 219/114	Widow Doe	23 Jan 1779	West Harling
191	PD 337/158	John Dorman	24 May 1720	Shipdham
193	PD 337/158	John Doughty	24 May 1720	Shipdham
175	PD 358/41	Goodman Dunnen	6 Aug 1713	Shelton
8	PD 309/53	John Dunnett	10 Jul 1803	Besthorpe
219	PD 611/38	John Durrant	30 Oct 1747	Surlingham
78	MC 76/50, 534X10	Widow Elvey	14 Apr 1769	Letton
204	PD 337/158	Widow Fish	24 May 1720	Shipdham
18	PD 111/170	Henry Fisher/Harrison	16 Oct 1773	Bressingham
137	PD 295/102	Lettice/Widow Flattman / Henry Branch	26 Jun 1731	Redenhall with Harleston and Wortwell
142	PD 295/102	Lettice Flattman	21 Nov 1737	Redenhall with Harleston and Wortwell
62	PD 575/128	Widow Flowars	16 Nov 1725	Hingham
185	PD 358/42	John Frances (senior)	18 Jan 1747/48	Shelton
183	PD 358/42	John Francis (junior)	28 Sep 1743	Shelton
179	PD 358/41	Mary/Widow Frances	2 Mar 1723/24	Shelton
184	PD 358/42	Widow Fulcher	30 Jul 1746	Shelton
201	PD 337/158	Widow Fuller	24 May 1720	Shipdham
26	PD 193/93	Widow Garby	14 Dec 1699	Cawston
161	PD 295/117	Amey Gardner	29 Nov 1745	Redenhall with Harleston and Wortwell
152	PD 295/102	Robert Garrard	4 Jul 1740	Redenhall with Harleston and Wortwell
216	PD 122/38	James Gill	4 Mar 1793	Stratton St. Mary
212	PD 337/158	Widow Gilldens	24 May 1720	Shipdham
229	PD 316/46	John Goderd	30 Jul 1739	Yelverton with Alpington
136	PD 295/102	Elizabeth/ Widow Goldspink	26 Jun 1731	Redenhall with Harleston and Wortwell
145	PD 295/102	Godfrey Goodrum	27 Nov 1738	Redenhall with Harleston and Wortwell

No.	Reference number (NRO)	Name	Date	Parish of settlement
150	PD 295/102	Mary Gower	10 May 1740	Redenhall with Harleston and Wortwell
131	PD 295/102	Ann Green	26 Jun 1731	Redenhall with Harleston and Wortwell
36	PD 193/93	Widow Greenwood	14 Dec 1699	Cawston
67	PD 629/50	Susan Greves	7 Jun 1752	Holme-next-the-Sea
108	PD 489/30	Amy Hammond	14 Oct 1754	Great Moulton with Little Moulton
141	PD 295/102	Samuel Harman	15 Jun 1734	Redenhall with Harleston and Wortwell
13	PD 111/114	Ann Hart	22 Oct 1724	Bressingham
112	PD 489/30	Sarah Harvey	14 Oct 1754	Great Moulton with Little Moulton
170	PD 358/41	Widow Hatton	22 May 1696	Shelton
169	PD 358/41	John Hatton (junior)	9 Feb 1693/94	Shelton
209	PD 337/158	Widow Head	24 May 1720	Shipdham
74	PD 521/26	Dan Heagon	25 Dec 1769	Ingworth
21	PD 111/114	— Hernwell	n.d.	Bressingham
3	PC 88/1	Mary Hill	2 Nov 1720	Ashwellthorpe
2	PC 88/1	Widow Hill	26 Jan 1710/11	Ashwellthorpe
101	PD 489/29	James Hilling	11 Jul 1738	Great Moulton with Little Moulton
109	PD 489/30	Widow Hilling	14 Oct 1754	Great Moulton with Little Moulton
69	PD 629/50	Widow Holybrad	7 May 1770	Holme-next-the-Sea
88	PD 710/68	Robert Howell (elder)	18 Dec 1764	Martham
92	PD 489/29	Sara Hubert	3 Jul 1693	Great Moulton with Little Moulton
5	PC 88/2	Constance Huggin	1 Oct 1754	Ashwellthorpe
123	PD 499/79	Samuel Hunt	26 Jun 1772	Norwich, St. Mary in the Marsh
50	PD 236/51	Mary Huson	No date	Hapton
172	PD 358/41	Barbara Jermyn	31 Jul 1700	Shelton
174	PD 358/41	William Jermyn	16 Apr 1712	Shelton
178	PD 358/41	Katherine Jex	3 Feb 1722/23	Shelton
57	PD 382/45	William Johnson	27 Mar 1805	Hilgay

No.	Reference number (NRO)	Name	Date	Parish of settlement
171	PD 358/41	Francis Karrington	21 May 1700	Shelton
147	PD 295/102	James Keely	2 Feb 1738/39	Redenhall with Harleston and Wortwell
37	PD 193/93	John Kenen	14 Dec 1699	Cawston
218	PD 122/39	Ben Kent	10 Apr 1822	Stratton St. Mary
224	PD 216/90	Elizabeth King	12 Apr 1749	Trowse
89	PD 710/68	Edward Knights	16 Mar 1768	Martham
166	PD 295/117	Phillip Knight	3 Mar 1762	Redenhall with Harleston and Wortwell
30	PD 193/93	Richard Ladrken	14 Dec 1699	Cawston
31	PD 193/93	Robert Land	14 Dec 1699	Cawston
65	PD 575/128	John Larthman (junior)	c.29 Mar 1728	Hingham
138	PD 295/102	Lionel Lawson	10 Nov 1731	Redenhall with Harleston and Wortwell
230	PD 316/46	John Levek	5 May 1742	Yelverton with Alpington
60	PD 575/128	Widow Little	8 Jun 1724	Hingham
190	PD 102/32	Widow Long	9 Jun 1785	Shimpling
200	PD 337/158	Widow Mallett	24 May 1720	Shipdham
61	PD 575/128	Widow Man	23 Mar 1724/25	Hingham
40	PD 193/93	Edward Martin	14 Dec 1699	Cawston
217	PD 122/39	William Martin	21 Jun 1816	Stratton St. Mary
34	PD 193/93	Matthew Matthews	14 Dec 1699	Cawston
165	PD 295/117	Widow Meek	18 Feb 1752	Redenhall with Harleston and Wortwell
157	PD 295/102	Frances Metchels	11 Dec 1742	Redenhall with Harleston and Wortwell
96	PD 489/29	Josh Miller	18 Oct 1710	Great Moulton with Little Moulton
181	PD 358/42	Ann Milles	26 Oct 1741	Shelton
22	PD 477/43	John Minter	13 Mar 1804	Brockdish
104	PD 489/30	Widow Moor	14 Oct 1754	Great Moulton with Little Moulton
114	PD 489/31	Widow Moor	19 Apr 1762	Great Moulton with Little Moulton
85	PD 710/68	Priscilla/Widow Myhill	18 Dec 1764	Martham
66	PD 575/128	Widow Norton	30 Aug 1731	Hingham

No.	Reference number (NRO)	Name	Date	Parish of settlement
173	PD 358/41	Jeremy Nudds	15 Nov 1709	Shelton
120	PD 489/31	John Nudds	c.1760s	Great Moulton with Little Moulton
53	PD 219/114	George Orsborne	12 Oct 1821	East Harling
59	PD 575/128	Widow Osburn	c.1723-1727	Hingham
197	PD 337/158	Widow Ouldham	24 May 1720	Shipdham
119	PD 489/31	Jemimah Parish	c.1760s	Great Moulton with Little Moulton
105	PD 489/30	Widow Parish	14 Oct 1754	Great Moulton with Little Moulton
115	PD 489/31	Widow Parish	19 Apr 1762	Great Moulton with Little Moulton
54	PD 219/114	— Parker	16 Nov 1825	East Harling
27	PD 193/93	Widow Paten / Ann Clayton	14 Dec 1699	Cawston
25	PD 193/93	Widow Penell	14 Dec 1699	Cawston
129	PD 295/102	Flegg Pettow	26 Jun 1731	Redenhall with Harleston and Wortwell
87	PD 710/68	Mary/Widow Piercon	18 Dec 1764	Martham
192	PD 337/158	Ealles Platfoot	24 May 1720	Shipdham
122	PD 499/79	Lady/Jemima Pleasant	14 May 1734	Norwich, St. Mary in the Marsh
107	PD 489/30	Widow Porter	14 Oct 1754	Great Moulton with Little Moulton
103	PD 489/30	Richard Pottel	c.1740-1754	Great Moulton with Little Moulton
111	PD 489/30	Widow Pottle	14 Oct 1754	Great Moulton with Little Moulton
71	PD 642/35	Widow Pratt	2 Dec 1771	Horningtoft
70	PD 563/49	Robert Pycrass	1 May 1731	Hopton
106	PD 489/30	Widow Pyman	14 Oct 1754	Great Moulton with Little Moulton
72	PD 642/35	Martha Ralph	9 Dec 1772	Horningtoft
205	PD 337/158	Widow Ranson	24 May 1720	Shipdham
49	PD 236/51	William Read (junior)	15 Apr 1796	Hapton
29	PD 193/93	Widow Reed	14 Dec 1699	Cawston
127	PD 295/102	Widow Reed	20 Jun 1731	Redenhall with Harleston and Wortwell

No.	Reference number (NRO)	Name	Date	Parish of settlement
195	PD 337/158	Widow Reeves	24 May 1720	Shipdham
202	PD 337/158	— Rice	24 May 1720	Shipdham
222	PD 708/84	John Riches	c.1780-1793	Tharston
91	PD 710/68	Roger Riches	14 Feb 1772	Martham
33	PD 193/93	Dorothy Ridge	14 Dec 1699	Cawston
168	PD 358/41	Anne Roberts	28 Oct 1692	Shelton
113	PD 489/30	Robert Roberts	1756	Great Moulton with Little Moulton
11	PD 111/114	Ann Route	25 May 1719	Bressingham
4	PC 88/2	Edward Rushbrook	1 Oct 1754	Ashwellthorpe
153	PD 295/102	Widow Salter	4 Jul 1740	Redenhall with Harleston and Wortwell
148	PD 295/102	Widow Searls	2 Jun 1739	Redenhall with Harleston and Wortwell
128	PD 295/102	Thomas Self	26 Jun 1731	Redenhall with Harleston and Wortwell
155	PD 295/102	Francis Semmons	6 Jan 1740/41	Redenhall with Harleston and Wortwell
226	PD 553/79	Mary Shearling	18 Feb 1819	Wighton
199	PD 337/158	Widow Simonds	24 May 1720	Shipdham
90	PD 710/68	Widow Elizabeth Smith	16 Dec 1771	Martham
73	PD 642/35	Frances Smith	24 May 1773	Horningtoft
48	PD 50/45	John Smith	4 Nov 1756	Gissing
93	PD 489/29	Margaret Smith	3 Jul 1693	Great Moulton with Little Moulton
45	PD 421/133	Martha Smith	c.1784	Forncett St. Peter
227	PD 78/66	Martha Smith / John Crowe	29 Jan 1816	Winfarthing
207	PD 337/158	Widow Stagg	24 May 1720	Shipdham
7	PD 309/52	Widow Stephenson	10 Oct 1776	Besthorpe
213	PD 337/158	Widow Stimpson	24 May 1720	Shipdham
75	PD 521/26	Tom Storey	14 Nov 1774	Ingworth
12	PD 111/170	Thomas Surgon	16 Sep 1719	Bressingham
94	PD 489/29	Widow Tackling	24 Jul 1699	Great Moulton with Little Moulton
189	PD 358/42	Mary Taylor	8 Feb 1762	Shelton
187	PD 358/42	Thomas Taylor (junior)	23/30 Apr 1751	Shelton
182	PD 358/42	Widow Thrower	28 Sep 1742	Shelton
9	PD 111/170	Widow Tiller	27 Dec 1693	Bressingham

No.	Reference number (NRO)	Name	Date	Parish of settlement
198	PD 337/158	Sarah Tillets	24 May 1720	Shipdham
135	PD 295/102	Widow Todd	26 Jun 1731	Redenhall with Harleston and Wortwell
144	PD 295/102	Widow Todd	29 Sep 1738	Redenhall with Harleston and Wortwell
99	PD 489/29	Widow Townsend	29 Aug 1737	Great Moulton with Little Moulton
134	PD 295/102	Elizabeth Trew	26 Jun 1731	Redenhall with Harleston and Wortwell
160	PD 295/102	Elizabeth Trew	15 Apr 1745	Redenhall with Harleston and Wortwell
68	PD 629/50	Thomas Trips	29 Nov 1766	Holme-next-the-Sea
110	PD 489/30	Edmund Trixon	14 Oct 1754	Great Moulton with Little Moulton
1	PC 88/1	Ann Turner	16 Jul 1695	Ashwellthorpe
56	PD 219/114	Esther Turner	4 Jul 1803	West Harling
47	PD 50/44	Widow Tutell	c.1720-1740s	Gissing
158	PD 295/102	Elizabeth Twist	17 Jun 1743	Redenhall with Harleston and Wortwell
79	PD 595/22	Alexander Wade	26 Nov 1751	Loddon
46	PD 50/71	Widow Watling	c.1720-1750s	Gissing
102	PD 489/30	Robert Websdale	28 Sep 1748	Great Moulton with Little Moulton
10	PD 111/170	Henry Wells	17 Feb 1717/18	Bressingham
52	PD 219/114	Widow Whitehead	9 Apr 1821	East Harling
228	PD 316/46	Lucy Wigg	13 Jul 1738	Yelverton with Alpington
43	PD 193/93	Widow Wilson	14 Dec 1699	Cawston
76	MC 76/50, 534X10	Widow Wix [Wise]	20 Sep 1759	Letton
28	PD 193/93	Widow Woods	14 Dec 1699	Cawston
51	PD 219/114	Rhoda Wretham	9 Apr 1821	East Harling
210	PD 337/158	Ann Wright	24 May 1720	Shipdham
82	PD 710/68	Mary Wright	14 Oct 1758	Martham

Appendix 3: List of pauper inventories by date

No.	Reference number (NRO)	Name	Date	Parish of settlement
168	PD 358/41	28 Oct 1692	Anne Roberts	Shelton
92	PD 489/29	3 Jul 1693	Sara Hubert	Great Moulton with Little Moulton
93	PD 489/29	3 Jul 1693	Margaret Smith	Great Moulton with Little Moulton
9	PD 111/170	27 Dec 1693	Widow Tiller	Bressingham
169	PD 358/41	9 Feb 1693/94	John Hatton (junior)	Shelton
223	PD 216/90	7 Dec 1694	Widow Dictarson	Trowse
1	PC 88/1	16 Jul 1695	Ann Turner	Ashwellthorpe
170	PD 358/41	22 May 1696	Widow Hatton	Shelton
94	PD 489/29	24 Jul 1699	Widow Tackling	Great Moulton with Little Moulton
42	PD 193/93	14 Dec 1699	Andrew Allen	Cawston
35	PD 193/93	14 Dec 1699	Richard Barker/Barber	Cawston
39	PD 193/93	14 Dec 1699	Thomas Barker/Barber	Cawston
38	PD 193/93	14 Dec 1699	Henry Blackburn	Cawston
32	PD 193/93	14 Dec 1699	Widow Bloume	Cawston
41	PD 193/93	14 Dec 1699	William Bridge	Cawston
27	PD 193/93	14 Dec 1699	Ann Clayton / Widow Paten	Cawston
26	PD 193/93	14 Dec 1699	Widow Garby	Cawston
36	PD 193/93	14 Dec 1699	Widow Greenwood	Cawston
37	PD 193/93	14 Dec 1699	John Kenen	Cawston
30	PD 193/93	14 Dec 1699	Richard Ladrken	Cawston
31	PD 193/93	14 Dec 1699	Robert Land	Cawston
40	PD 193/93	14 Dec 1699	Edward Martin	Cawston
34	PD 193/93	14 Dec 1699	Matthew Matthews	Cawston
25	PD 193/93	14 Dec 1699	Widow Penell	Cawston
29	PD 193/93	14 Dec 1699	Widow Reed	Cawston
33	PD 193/93	14 Dec 1699	Dorothy Ridge	Cawston
43	PD 193/93	14 Dec 1699	Widow Wilson	Cawston
28	PD 193/93	14 Dec 1699	Widow Woods	Cawston
171	PD 358/41	21 May 1700	Francis Karrington	Shelton
172	PD 358/41	31 Jul 1700	Barbara Jermyn	Shelton
95	PD 489/29	7 Jan 1701/2	Henry and Susan Barret	Great Moulton with Little Moulton
124	PD 295/102	8 May 1708	Susan Aldred	Redenhall with Harleston and Wortwell
173	PD 358/41	15 Nov 1709	Jeremy Nudds	Shelton

No.	Reference number (NRO)	Name	Date	Parish of settlement
58	PD 575/128	26 Sep 1710	Robert Coper	Hingham
96	PD 489/29	18 Oct 1710	Josh Miller	Great Moulton with Little Moulton
125	PD 295/102	1710	Robert Burton	Redenhall with Harleston and Wortwell
2	PC 88/1	26 Jan 1710/11	Widow Hill	Ashwellthorpe
174	PD 358/41	16 Apr 1712	William Jermyn	Shelton
175	PD 358/41	6 Aug 1713	Goodman Dunnen	Shelton
126	PD 295/93	23 Mar 1713/14	Widow Bottwright	Redenhall with Harleston and Wortwell
10	PD 111/170	17 Feb 1717/18	Henry Wells	Bressingham
176	PD 358/41	3 Feb 1718/19	Joseph Bateman	Shelton
11	PD 111/114	25 May 1719	Ann Route	Bressingham
12	PD 111/170	16 Sep 1719	Thomas Surgon	Bressingham
177	PD 358/41	12 Oct 1719	Francis Baker	Shelton
47	PD 50/44	c.1720-1740s	Widow Tutell	Gissing
46	PD 50/71	c.1720-1750s	Widow Watling	Gissing
196	PD 337/158	24 May 1720	Widow Adkens	Shipdham
194	PD 337/158	24 May 1720	Widow Allcock	Shipdham
208	PD 337/158	24 May 1720	Margaret Bowl	Shipdham
211	PD 337/158	24 May 1720	Elizabeth Brett	Shipdham
206	PD 337/158	24 May 1720	Widow Bright	Shipdham
203	PD 337/158	24 May 1720	William Bright	Shipdham
191	PD 337/158	24 May 1720	John Dorman	Shipdham
193	PD 337/158	24 May 1720	John Doughty	Shipdham
204	PD 337/158	24 May 1720	Widow Fish	Shipdham
201	PD 337/158	24 May 1720	Widow Fuller	Shipdham
212	PD 337/158	24 May 1720	Widow Gilldens	Shipdham
209	PD 337/158	24 May 1720	Widow Head	Shipdham
200	PD 337/158	24 May 1720	Widow Mallett	Shipdham
197	PD 337/158	24 May 1720	Widow Ouldham	Shipdham
192	PD 337/158	24 May 1720	Ealles Platfoot	Shipdham
205	PD 337/158	24 May 1720	Widow Ranson	Shipdham
195	PD 337/158	24 May 1720	Widow Reeves	Shipdham
202	PD 337/158	24 May 1720	— Rice	Shipdham
199	PD 337/158	24 May 1720	Widow Simonds	Shipdham
207	PD 337/158	24 May 1720	Widow Stagg	Shipdham
213	PD 337/158	24 May 1720	Widow Stimpson	Shipdham
198	PD 337/158	24 May 1720	Sarah Tillets	Shipdham
210	PD 337/158	24 May 1720	Ann Wright	Shipdham
3	PC 88/1	2 Nov 1720	Mary Hill	Ashwellthorpe
97	PD 489/29	6 Aug 1722	John Church	Great Moulton with Little Moulton

No.	Reference number (NRO)	Name	Date	Parish of settlement
178	PD 358/41	3 Feb 1722/23	Katherine Jex	Shelton
59	PD 575/128	c.1723-1727	Widow Osburn	Hingham
179	PD 358/41	2 Mar 1723/24	Mary/Widow Frances	Shelton
60	PD 575/128	8 Jun 1724	Widow Little	Hingham
13	PD 111/114	22 Oct 1724	Ann Hart	Bressingham
61	PD 575/128	23 Mar 1724/25	Widow Man	Hingham
62	PD 575/128	16 Nov 1725	Widow Flowars	Hingham
63	PD 575/128	c.1726-1728	William Burgany	Hingham
64	PD 575/128	c.1727-1732	Widow Dawson	Hingham
14	PD 111/170	14 Dec 1727	William Car	Bressingham
65	PD 575/128	c.29 Mar 1728	John Larthman (junior)	Hingham
180	PD 358/41	5 Mar 1728/29	Christiana/ Widow Bateman	Shelton
70	PD 563/49	1 May 1731	Robert Pycrass	Hopton
127	PD 295/102	20 Jun 1731	Widow Reed	Redenhall with Harleston and Wortwell
132	PD 295/102	26 Jun 1731	William Afsey (senior)	Redenhall with Harleston and Wortwell
137	PD 295/102	26 Jun 1731	Henry Branch / Lettice/ Widow Flattman	Redenhall with Harleston and Wortwell
130	PD 295/102	26 Jun 1731	Jane Branch	Redenhall with Harleston and Wortwell
133	PD 295/102	26 Jun 1731	Ann Burton	Redenhall with Harleston and Wortwell
136	PD 295/102	26 Jun 1731	Elizabeth/ Widow Goldspink	Redenhall with Harleston and Wortwell
131	PD 295/102	26 Jun 1731	Ann Green	Redenhall with Harleston and Wortwell
129	PD 295/102	26 Jun 1731	Flegg Pettow	Redenhall with Harleston and Wortwell
128	PD 295/102	26 Jun 1731	Thomas Self	Redenhall with Harleston and Wortwell
135	PD 295/102	26 Jun 1731	Widow Todd	Redenhall with Harleston and Wortwell
134	PD 295/102	26 Jun 1731	Elizabeth Trew	Redenhall with Harleston and Wortwell

No.	Reference number (NRO)	Name	Date	Parish of settlement
66	PD 575/128	30 Aug 1731	Widow Norton	Hingham
138	PD 295/102	10 Nov 1731	Lionel Lawson	Redenhall with Harleston and Wortwell
139	PD 295/102	8 Dec 1731	John Andrews	Redenhall with Harleston and Wortwell
140	PD 295/102	29 Dec 1733	Widow Chamberlaine	Redenhall with Harleston and Wortwell
122	PD 499/79	14 May 1734	Lady/Jemima Pleasant	Norwich, St. Mary in the Marsh
141	PD 295/102	15 Jun 1734	Samuel Harman	Redenhall with Harleston and Wortwell
98	PD 489/29	15 Sep 1735	Widow Blake	Great Moulton with Little Moulton
99	PD 489/29	29 Aug 1737	Widow Townsend	Great Moulton with Little Moulton
142	PD 295/102	21 Nov 1737	Lettice Flattman	Redenhall with Harleston and Wortwell
100	PD 489/29	11 Jul 1738	Widow Cock	Great Moulton with Little Moulton
101	PD 489/29	11 Jul 1738	James Hilling	Great Moulton with Little Moulton
228	PD 316/46	13 Jul 1738	Lucy Wigg	Yelverton with Alpington
143	PD 295/102	29 Sep 1738	Nicholas Burley (junior)	Redenhall with Harleston and Wortwell
144	PD 295/102	29 Sep 1738	Widow Todd	Redenhall with Harleston and Wortwell
145	PD 295/102	27 Nov 1738	Godfrey Goodrum	Redenhall with Harleston and Wortwell
146	PD 295/102	15 Jan 1738/39	Susan Burrows	Redenhall with Harleston and Wortwell
147	PD 295/102	2 Feb 1738/39	James Keely	Redenhall with Harleston and Wortwell

No.	Reference number (NRO)	Name	Date	Parish of settlement
148	PD 295/102	2 Jun 1739	Widow Searls	Redenhall with Harleston and Wortwell
229	PD 316/46	30 Jul 1739	John Goderd	Yelverton with Alpington
103	PD 489/30	c.1740-1754	Richard Pottel	Great Moulton with Little Moulton
149	PD 295/102	6 May 1740	Ann/Widow Alexander	Redenhall with Harleston and Wortwell
150	PD 295/102	10 May 1740	Mary Gower	Redenhall with Harleston and Wortwell
151	PD 295/102	4 Jul 1740	Widow Catchpool	Redenhall with Harleston and Wortwell
152	PD 295/102	4 Jul 1740	Robert Garrard	Redenhall with Harleston and Wortwell
153	PD 295/102	4 Jul 1740	Widow Salter	Redenhall with Harleston and Wortwell
154	PD 295/102	11 Jul 1740	John Cupper	Redenhall with Harleston and Wortwell
155	PD 295/102	6 Jan 1740/41	Francis Semmons	Redenhall with Harleston and Wortwell
181	PD 358/42	26 Oct 1741	Ann Milles	Shelton
230	PD 316/46	5 May 1742	John Levek	Yelverton with Alpington
182	PD 358/42	28 Sep 1742	Widow Thrower	Shelton
156	PD 295/102	11 Dec 1742	Isaac Day	Redenhall with Harleston and Wortwell
157	PD 295/102	11 Dec 1742	Frances Metchels	Redenhall with Harleston and Wortwell
158	PD 295/102	17 Jun 1743	Elizabeth Twist	Redenhall with Harleston and Wortwell
183	PD 358/42	28 Sep 1743	John Francis (junior)	Shelton
159	PD 295/117	24 Jun 1744	Ann Capon	Redenhall with Harleston and Wortwell

No.	Reference number (NRO)	Name	Date	Parish of settlement
160	PD 295/102	15 Apr 1745	Elizabeth Trew	Redenhall with Harleston and Wortwell
161	PD 295/117	29 Nov 1745	Amey Gardner	Redenhall with Harleston and Wortwell
162	PD 295/102	3 Jan 1745/46	Widow Catchpool	Redenhall with Harleston and Wortwell
163	PD 295/117	8 Apr 1746	Alexander Bazer	Redenhall with Harleston and Wortwell
184	PD 358/42	30 Jul 1746	Widow Fulcher	Shelton
164	PD 295/117	6 Oct 1746	John Brown	Redenhall with Harleston and Wortwell
219	PD 611/38	30 Oct 1747	John Durrant	Surlingham
185	PD 358/42	18 Jan 1747/48	John Frances (senior)	Shelton
186	PD 358/42	12 Jul 1748	Henry Brown	Shelton
102	PD 489/30	28 Sep 1748	Robert Websdale	Great Moulton with Little Moulton
224	PD 216/90	12 Apr 1749	Elizabeth King	Trowse
225	PD 216/90	10 Jun 1750	Widow Cullender	Trowse
187	PD 358/42	23/30 Apr 1751	Thomas Taylor (junior)	Shelton
79	PD 595/22	26 Nov 1751	Alexander Wade	Loddon
165	PD 295/117	18 Feb 1752	Widow Meek	Redenhall with Harleston and Wortwell
67	PD 629/50	7 Jun 1752	Susan Greves	Holme-next-the-Sea
188	PD 358/42	29 Sep 1753	William Brett	Shelton
6	PC 88/2	1 Oct 1754	Widow Cooper	Ashwellthorpe
5	PC 88/2	1 Oct 1754	Constance Huggin	Ashwellthorpe
4	PC 88/2	1 Oct 1754	Edward Rushbrook	Ashwellthorpe
108	PD 489/30	14 Oct 1754	Amy Hammond	Great Moulton with Little Moulton
112	PD 489/30	14 Oct 1754	Sarah Harvey	Great Moulton with Little Moulton
109	PD 489/30	14 Oct 1754	Widow Hilling	Great Moulton with Little Moulton
104	PD 489/30	14 Oct 1754	Widow Moor	Great Moulton with Little Moulton

No.	Reference number (NRO)	Name	Date	Parish of settlement
105	PD 489/30	14 Oct 1754	Widow Parish	Great Moulton with Little Moulton
107	PD 489/30	14 Oct 1754	Widow Porter	Great Moulton with Little Moulton
111	PD 489/30	14 Oct 1754	Widow Pottle	Great Moulton with Little Moulton
106	PD 489/30	14 Oct 1754	Widow Pyman	Great Moulton with Little Moulton
110	PD 489/30	14 Oct 1754	Edmund Trixon	Great Moulton with Little Moulton
48	PD 50/45	4 Nov 1756	John Smith	Gissing
113	PD 489/30	1756	Robert Roberts	Great Moulton with Little Moulton
84	PD 710/68	14 Oct 1758	Elizabeth Bland (elder)	Martham
80	PD 710/68	14 Oct 1758	Elizabeth Bland (younger)	Martham
83	PD 710/68	14 Oct 1758	Widow Conyard	Martham
81	PD 710/68	14 Oct 1758	Mary Crosshold	Martham
82	PD 710/68	14 Oct 1758	Mary Wright	Martham
15	PD 111/114	7 Feb 1759	Widow Brister	Bressingham
16	PD 111/114	7 Feb 1759	Ann Burrows	Bressingham
76	MC 76/50, 534X10	20 Sep 1759	Widow Wix [Wise]	Letton
121	PD 489/31	c.1760s	John Church	Great Moulton with Little Moulton
120	PD 489/31	c.1760s	John Nudds	Great Moulton with Little Moulton
119	PD 489/31	c.1760s	Jemimah Parish	Great Moulton with Little Moulton
220	PD 611/38	21 Jan 1762	John Balls	Surlingham
189	PD 358/42	8 Feb 1762	Mary Taylor	Shelton
166	PD 295/117	3 Mar 1762	Phillip Knight	Redenhall with Harleston and Wortwell
116	PD 489/31	19 Apr 1762	Chris Collers	Great Moulton with Little Moulton

No.	Reference number (NRO)	Name	Date	Parish of settlement
114	PD 489/31	19 Apr 1762	Widow Moor	Great Moulton with Little Moulton
115	PD 489/31	19 Apr 1762	Widow Parish	Great Moulton with Little Moulton
221	PD 611/38	22 Apr 1762	Mary/Widow Clarke	Surlingham
77	MC 76/50, 534X10	1762	Widow Bannett	Letton
117	PD 489/31	7 May 1764	John Blake	Great Moulton with Little Moulton
86	PD 710/68	18 Dec 1764	John Brunson	Martham
88	PD 710/68	18 Dec 1764	Robert Howell (elder)	Martham
85	PD 710/68	18 Dec 1764	Priscilla/Widow Myhill	Martham
87	PD 710/68	18 Dec 1764	Mary/Widow Piercon	Martham
68	PD 629/50	29 Nov 1766	Thomas Trips	Holme-next-the-Sea
118	PD 489/51	21 Oct 1767	Susan Buck	Great Moulton with Little Moulton
89	PD 710/68	16 Mar 1768	Edward Knights	Martham
78	MC 76/50, 534X10	14 Apr 1769	Widow Elvey	Letton
74	PD 521/26	25 Dec 1769	Dan Heagon	Ingworth
69	PD 629/50	7 May 1770	Widow Holybrad	Holme-next-the-Sea
23	PD 712/49	15 Apr 1771	Mary Coleman	Bunwell
71	PD 642/35	2 Dec 1771	Widow Pratt	Horningtoft
90	PD 710/68	16 Dec 1771	Widow Elizabeth Smith	Martham
91	PD 710/68	14 Feb 1772	Roger Riches	Martham
123	PD 499/79	26 Jun 1772	Samuel Hunt	Norwich, St. Mary in the Marsh
72	PD 642/35	9 Dec 1772	Martha Ralph	Horningtoft
17	PD 111/170	11 Mar 1773	William Adkins	Bressingham
73	PD 642/35	24 May 1773	Frances Smith	Horningtoft
18	PD 111/170	16 Oct 1773	Henry Fisher/Harrison	Bressingham
19	PD 111/170	5 Nov 1773	Mary Bravenett	Bressingham
214	PD 122/54	27 Jan 1774	Widow Booty	Stratton St. Mary
215	PD 122/54	30 Jul 1774	William Buck	Stratton St. Mary
75	PD 521/26	14 Nov 1774	Tom Storey	Ingworth
7	PD 309/52	10 Oct 1776	Widow Stephenson	Besthorpe
55	PD 219/114	23 Jan 1779	Widow Doe	West Harling
222	PD 708/84	c.1780-1793	John Riches	Tharston

No.	Reference number (NRO)	Name	Date	Parish of settlement
44	PD 421/133	12 Jan 1784	Thomas Cullam	Forncett St. Peter
45	PD 421/133	c.1784	Martha Smith	Forncett St. Peter
190	PD 102/32	9 Jun 1785	Widow Long	Shimpling
24	MC 29412, 1025X2	4 Sep 1787	John Daniels	Carbrooke
216	PD 122/38	4 Mar 1793	James Gill	Stratton St. Mary
49	PD 236/51	15 Apr 1796	William Read (junior)	Hapton
56	PD 219/114	4 Jul 1803	Esther Turner	West Harling
8	PD 358/42	10 Jul 1803	John Dunnett	Besthorpe
22	PD 477/43	13 Mar 1804	John Minter	Brockdish
57	PD 382/45	27 Mar 1805	William Johnson	Hilgay
20	PD 111/114	8 Oct 1814	William Arnold	Bressingham
227	PD 78/66	29 Jan 1816	John Crowe / Martha Smith	Winfarthing
217	PD 122/39	21 Jun 1816	William Martin	Stratton St. Mary
226	PD 553/79	18 Feb 1819	Mary Shearling	Wighton
52	PD 219/114	9 Apr 1821	Widow Whitehead	East Harling
51	PD 219/114	9 Apr 1821	Rhoda Wretham	East Harling
53	PD 219/114	12 Oct 1821	George Orsborne	East Harling
218	PD 122/39	10 Apr 1822	Ben Kent	Stratton St. Mary
54	PD 219/114	16 Nov 1825	— Parker	East Harling
167	PD 295/106	24 Dec 1828	Michael Aggus	Redenhall with Harleston and Wortwell
21	PD 111/114	No date	— Hernwell	Bressingham
50	PD 236/51	No date	Mary Huson	Hapton

Glossary of inventory terms

This glossary is not comprehensive and some terms are open to further interpretation. It is recommended that readers use a range of glossaries to aid their understanding of the inventories. Some of the most useful include:

Bristow, Joy, *The Local Historian's Glossary of Words and Terms*, 3rd edn. (Newbury, 2001).

Milward, Rosemary, *A Glossary of Household and Farming Terms from Sixteenth-century Probate Inventories*, 3rd edn. (Chesterfield, 1986).

Moore, John S., *The Goods and Chattels of our Forefathers: Frampton Cotterell and district probate inventories, 1539-1804* (London, 1976), pp. 290-340.

Oxford English Dictionary (http://www.oed.com/).

Terms

Adze	Similar to an axe but with the blade at a right angle to the handle. Used for cutting or slicing wood
Ale stool	Stool used for placing casks of beer on
Andirons	Metal supports, typically in pairs, used for holding burning wood in a fireplace
Anker	Cask or keg that holds beer, wine, or spirits, typically 10 gallons (45.46 litres)
Anvil	Block used for hammering and shaping metal
Ark	Type of storage unit similar to a box or chest
Ash tub	Tub for ashes and household rubbish. Also possibly a Mash/mashing tub
Ass	Donkey
Auger	Carpenter's tool for making holes in wood
Awl	Tool used for making holes in materials (often leather or cloth). Also known as a piercer, pricker, or bodkin
Back iron	Probably a fireback or thick iron plate placed at the back of a hearth (also known as an iron back)
Bail	The hooped sides or handles of a pail, kettle, or similar item
Bear	Case or covering for a pillow or bolster. Also sometimes a spelling mistake for 'beer'
Bed stould	Bedstead
Beetle	Thick-headed hammer usually made out of wood. Similar to a mallet
Bell metal	An alloy of copper and tin

Bill	Agricultural implement with a wooden handle and iron blade used for pruning, cutting wood, and trimming hedges
Board	Table top without the legs/supports
Bocks	Box
Boiler/boyler	Cooking vessel for boiling food. Possibly synonymous with Kettle
Boll	Bowl
Bolster	Long pillow
Bolting hutch	Hutch used for storing or sifting meal, bran, or other cereals
Boot jack	Item used for taking shoes and boots off
Bott/butt	Large cask used for storing food and drink
Box iron	Clothes iron heated by an iron wedge (heater) being placed into its cavity
Buffet stool	Footstool
Cettell	Kettle or Settle
Chaff	Collective term for husks of separated corn or other grain; but also possibly refuse
Chaffer	Dish used to hold burning fuel to heat food. Often used alongside a chaffing dish
Chaffing dish	Dish used to hold food over a chaffer
Cheeks	Sides of a fire grate
Cheese press	Appliance used for pressing curd and removing moisture in cheese making
Cheyney	Type of worsted or wool
Chive/chiver	A knife
Close stool	A chair or stool with lid over a hole for relieving oneself. A chamber pot is often concealed underneath the hole. Also known as a necessary stool and a night stool/convenience
Coal hod	Coal bucket used for holding, carrying, and pouring coal. Also known as a coal scuttle
Cob irons	Pair of iron supports used for holding spits or another term for Andirons
Collectioner	Somebody who is in receipt of poor relief
Coule/cowle	Possibly a vat/trough used in domestic production such as brewing or washing
Counterpane	Bedding/cover for a bed
Coverlet/coverlid/covrin	Bedding/cover for a bed
Crab harrow	See Harrow
Cream pot	Vessel used for holding milk while cream is forming, or a vessel used for storing cream
Crome	A claw/hook used on the land for removing the boughs of trees and weeds
Crow	A trivet that rotates, or an agricultural tool of some sort
Dale	Deal wood
Desk	In early modern times desks were portable boxes which were used for writing or reading on. Sometimes they had sloping lids and locks. Legs were later added to them
Dough trough	Vessel in which bread is mixed, kneaded, and left to rise

Drage/draget	Mixed cereals
Draging crome	Crome used for cereal production
Dredging box	Box with holes in used for sprinkling flour
Dripping pan	Pan placed under roasting meat to catch fat drippings
Faggots	Bundle of sticks (firewood)
Fender	Metal frame placed around a fireplace to stop burning fuel from rolling out into the room
Fire irons	Umbrella term used to describe implements for attending the hearth, such as a poker, tongs, and fire shovel
Fire pan	Metal pan used for holding burning fuel in place
Fire shovel	Shovel used for placing fuel on the fire or for removing ashes from the hearth
Firkin	Small cask used to hold a variety of foodstuffs, such as beer, ale, fish, or butter
Flag spade	Spade used for digging flags (peat)
Flags	Peat
Flat iron	Clothes iron heated by being placed next to a fire
Flesh fork	Fork used for moving meat out of a pot
Flock	Wool, cotton, and other textile refuse used for stuffing mattresses, pillows, bolsters, and cushions etc
Flyer	Part of the spinning wheel that twists the thread
Form	Bench
Furze	Ulex (also known as gorse or whin), often used as fuel for heating bread ovens
Gallipot	Small glazed earthenware pot, often used for making ointments and medicines
Goch/gotch	Big-bellied earthenware pot or jug
Grate	Frame of metal bars used to hold fuel in place. Principally used with coal
Gridiron/grill iron	Cooking implement formed of parallel bars of metal (generally iron) on short legs placed on or near the fire to grill or toast food
Hack	Tool used for breaking/chopping, an agricultural implement for breaking up earth or pulling up root vegetables, or a pick used for breaking stone
Hake	Hook used for hanging pots
Handiron	See Andirons
Hank	Rope used for fastening items together
Harrow	A heavy frame of timber or iron with iron teeth for breaking up ploughed land
Hatch	See Hutch
Hatchet	One-handed axe with a short handle
Heater	Piece of iron which is heated and placed into the cavity of a box iron or similar clothes iron
Heckle/hickle	Implement for splitting, straightening, and combing flax or hemp fibres for spinning
Helve	Handle of a tool/implement such as a broom, chisel, or hammer etc
Hods	Buckets/tubs of some sort

Hoe	Long-handled agricultural tool with a thin blade at the end
Hog stool	Probably a meat stool
Horse	Frame or stand for placing items onto, such as clothing, linen, or barrels
Hough	See Hoe
Hutch	Wooden box with a lid for storage
Imprimis	Latin to denote the first item on an inventory
Iron/ironing box	See Box iron
Jack	Mechanical device for turning a spit for roasting meat, or a bottle used for holding liquid (for example, a leather jack)
Keeler/killer	Shallow tub/vessel used for household purposes/cooling liquids
Keep	Type of cupboard, sometimes used for storing food
Kettle	Cooking vessel with handle(s) used for boiling food. Not to be confused with modern-day kettles used for boiling water or tea kettles. Possibly synonymous with Boiler
Kid	Small wooden tub used for domestic purposes
Kive	Tub or vat used for brewing
Last	Wooden mould of a foot which shoemakers use to shape or repair boots and shoes
Latch pan	See Dripping pan
Latten	Metal alloy resembling brass
Leaf table	Table with a hinged or removable leaf
Letch	Vessel used to hold lye
Livery cupboard	Freestanding cupboard with doors used for storing food and drink
Long stool	Bench/form
Low stool	Footstool
Lye/lie	Alkaline solution primarily made out of vegetable ashes, used for washing clothes and linen
Lye/lie letch	Vessel used for making lye or washing clothing and linen with lie
Maid	Clothes horse
Mash/mashing tub	Vessel used to mix malt and hot water to form wort in the brewing process
Mattock	Agricultural tool similar to a pick, with a right-angled blade at the end of the handle
Meal chest/hutch	Chest used to store meal
Meat stool	Stand used for cutting meat or killing livestock
Mess/mesh(ing) tub	Mash/mashing tub
Milk sieve	Sieve used to filter out the impurities in milk
Minging hutch/trough	Mixing tub, particularly used in bread making
Mole spade	Spade used for digging out and killing moles
Napkin press	Device used to press and store napkins
Nest of drawers	Small set of chest of drawers, often placed on a table
Nest of spice drawers	Small set of drawers used for holding spices
Nippers	Pincers used for grasping objects, often used by shoemakers

Pattens	Thick-soled overshoes, generally made out of wood or metal and held on to one's feet by iron, cloth, or leather bands. They were used to raise the wearer above the dirty ground
Peck	Large container (generally 2 gallons; c.9.1 litres) used to hold dry goods
Peel	Long-handled pole with a flat disc at the end used to move loaves in and out of an oven
Pipkin	Small earthenware pot or pan. Also a drinking vessel or bottle
Poke	Bag, sack, or pouch
Porridge pot	Pot used for cooking porridge
Porringer	Small bowl, typically with a handle, used to hold porridge, soup, or stew etc
Portmanteau	Case, trunk, or bag for carrying clothing
Posnet	Tripod metal cooking pot with a long handle. Possibly synonymous with Skillet
Pot iron	Iron frame for placing pots on
Pottage pot	Pot used for cooking pottage, soups, and stews etc
Powdering tub	Tub used for salting or pickling food such as meat and fish
Press cupboard	Cupboard, typically large with shelves and doors, used to hold clothing and linen
Quant	A pole for propelling a barge or punt
Quart	Measurement equalling two pints (2.27 litres)
Rack	Rack typically used for holding plates
Reel	Spinning-related item. Either the spool of a spinning wheel, or a frame used to hold bobbins, but also sometimes the spinning wheel itself
Roast/roasting iron	See Gridiron
Rug	Bed covering/linen
Rutter	Spade or other implement for cutting turf (peat)
Safe	Ventilated cupboard used for storing meat
Salt box	Box for holding salt for domestic use
Scuppet	Spade used to make trenches and ditches
Seg/segging chair	Chair partially or wholly made from basketwork, such as wood splints, rush (sedge), runners, and cane
Settle	Long wooden bench with arms and a high back
Shiften/shiftening	Change of linen
Sifter	Sieve or fire shovel
Sile dish	Sieve/strainer used for milk
Sithe	Scythe
Skep/skeep	Basket/hamper; a specific quantity of grain, malt, or charcoal etc.; or a bee-hive
Skillet	Metal cooking pot with three or four legs and a long handle. Possibly synonymous with Posnet
Skimmer	Utensil with a long handle and a spoon-like end used for removing fat or scum from a cooking pot, milk, or ashes from the hearth
Slice	Fire shovel
Slip	Covering and/or padding of a stool, chair, or similar item
Smoothing iron	See Box iron

Snuffer	Tool used for snuffing out candles, rushlights, or similar items
Spice drawers	See Nest of spice drawers
Stave	Barrel or parts that make up the sides of the barrel
Strike	A dry measure of a bushel or half bushel (36.37 or 18.18 litres), depending upon the locality, or a wooden measuring vessel, often cylindrical
Stump bedstead	Bedstead without posts
Swift	See Reel
Swill tub	Vessel for holding pig feed
Swing glass	Looking glass suspended on hinges
Tartin/tarting	Tartan or tarlatan (muslin)
Tea caddy	Small container for storing tea
Tent bed	Bed with hangings and covered sides
Tester	Canopy or wood used as a covering over a bed
Thane chair	Thrown (turned) chair
Tick	Fabric casing into which chaff, flock, feathers etc.were placed to make a mattress, bolster, or pillow etc
Till	Probably a small box
Tow wheel	Spinning wheel for making coarse tow yarn
Trencher	Wooden plate
Trestles	Supports for a table top or board
Trickle bed	See Truckle/trundle bed
Trippet	See Trivet
Trivet	Tripod stand used for placing pots, kettles, or other vessels close to or on the fire
Trow	Trough
Truckle/trundle bed	Low-lying bed, often on wheels, generally stored underneath a standing bedstead when not in use
Tunel/tunnel	Either a funnel, barrel, or an alternative name for a dough trough
Turf	Peat
Turn	Spinning wheel
Twilting frame	Quilting frame used for stretching out the material while making a quilt
Valance	Material border that hangs around the bed
Wainscot	Oak boards/boarding
Wheel	Spinning wheel
Wort sieve	Sieve for removing the impurities from wort during the brewing process
Yoke	A bar or pole placed across a person's shoulders for carrying pairs of baskets or pails

Primary sources

This section lists all the reference numbers for the pauper inventories that are transcribed in this volume (highlighted in bold). In most cases, the pauper inventories were found on loose pieces of paper or at the fronts and backs of overseers' accounts, vestry minutes, and other miscellaneous parish records. The list also includes the resources that were consulted to verify that each source was a pauper inventory and that the person in the inventory was a pauper.

Canterbury Cathedral Archives and Library, Canterbury

Wingham

U3/269/16/1 — Case for opinion, 1766.

Dorset History Centre, Dorchester

Lydlinch

PE-LYD/OV/1/1 — Overseers' accounts, 1734–1781.

Swanage

PE-SW/OV/1/5 — Overseers' accounts, 1752–1780.

Essex Record Office, Chelmsford

Ardleigh

D/P 263/12/8 — Overseers' accounts, 1821–1824.

Colchester

D/P 245/18/11 — Order to seize estate of Elizabeth Hart to defray her lunacy maintenance, 1770.

Fyfield

D/P 144/8/1 — Parish book, 1648–1732.

Stock

D/P 54/18/1 — Bond to maintain a pauper for three years in consideration of receiving his goods, 1629.

Kent History Library Centre, Maidstone

Brabourne

P41/5/1 — Churchwardens' assessments and disbursements, 1693–1735.

Deal

De/JQs1 — Quarter sessions book, 1719–1778.

Ightham

P202/8/1 — Vestry church volume, 1782–1813.

Lenham

P224/12/2	Overseers' assessments and disbursements, 1748–1760.

Otford

P279/8/2	Public vestry book, 1820–1838.

Smarden

P339/11/3	Poor rate book, 1675–1690.

Lancashire Record Office, Preston

Cowpe Lenches, New Hall Hey, and Hall Carr

MBRA/acc9017/11	Overseers' accounts, 1806–1850.

Norfolk Record Office, Norwich

Ashill

PD 548/71	Inventories, 1780–1786.

Ashwellthorpe

PC 88/1	Town book, 1693–1798.
PC 88/2	Overseers' accounts, 1741–1775.

Besthorpe

PD 309/12	Overseers' accounts, 1730–1813.
PD 309/52	Inventory of Widow Stephenson's goods, 1776.
PD 309/53	Inventory of John Dunnett's goods, 1803.

Bressingham

PD 111/1	Parish registers (baptisms, marriages, and burials), 1559–1742.
PD 111/89	Overseers' accounts, 1688–1729.
PD 111/170	Inventories, 1693–1773.
PD 111/114	Inventories, 1719–1815.
PD 111/111	Applications for relief, 1737–1834.
PD 111/93	Overseers' vouchers, 1737–1838.
PD 111/117	Miscellaneous overseers' papers, 1759–1827.
PD 111/90	Overseers' accounts, 1809–1821.

Brockdish

PD 477/43	Overseers' accounts, 1772–1811.

Bunwell

PD 712/49	Overseers' accounts, 1756–1776.

Carbrooke

MC 2941/2, 1025X2	Overseers' accounts, 1776–1803.

Cawston

PD 193/93	Inventories, 1699, 1826.

Forncett St. Peter

PD 421/133	Overseers' accounts, 1778–1791.

Gissing

PD 50/44	Town book, 1688–1741.
PD 50/71	Inventories, 1726–1742.
PD 50/45	Overseers' accounts, 1741–1759.

Hapton	
PD 236/51	Inventories, 1796–1831.
Harling, East	
PD 219/94	Overseers' accounts, 1809–1828.
PD 219/9	Parish register (marriages), 1813–1837.
PD 219/14	Parish register (burials), 1813–1854.
PD 219/114	Inventories, 1821–1825.
Harling, West	
PD 27/21	Overseers' accounts, 1771–1828.
Hilgay	
PD 382/41	Overseers' accounts, 1800–1810.
PD 382/45	Overseers' vouchers, 1804–1805.
Hingham	
PD 575/2	Parish register (baptisms, marriages, and burials), 1683–1753.
PD 575/124	Lists of poor people in receipt of weekly collection, 1700–1746.
PD 575/128	Inventories, 1706–1731.
PD 575/126	Overseers' bills, 1710–1746.
Holme-next-the-Sea	
PD 629/50	Overseers' accounts, 1704–1783.
PD 629	Parish register (baptisms, marriages, and burials), 1704–1868.
Hopton	
PD 563/49	Overseers' accounts, 1718–1842.
Horningtoft	
PD 642/35	Overseers' accounts, 1689–1775.
PD 642/2	Parish register (baptisms, marriages, and burials), 1698–1812.
Ingworth	
PD 521/26	Town book, 1768–1798.
Letton	
PD 359/3	Parish registers (baptisms, marriage and burials), 1716–1786.
MC 76/50, 534X10	Overseers' accounts, 1744–1791.
Loddon	
PD 595/22	Overseers' accounts, 1720–1752.
Marlingford	
PD 404/54	Town book, 1776–1829.
Martham	
PD 710/68	Overseers' accounts, 1744–1785.
Great Moulton with Little Moulton	
PD 489/29	Overseers' accounts, 1695–1738.
PD 489/38	Overseers' bills and receipts, 1722–1836.
PD 489/30	Overseers' accounts, 1747–1757.
PD 489/31	Overseers' accounts, 1757–1764.
PD 489/51	Inventories, 1767–1770.

Norwich	
PD 499/45	Overseers' accounts, 1722–1759.
PD 499/79	Inventories, 1734–1772.
PD 499/46	Overseers' accounts, 1759–1788.
Redenhall with Harleston and Wortwell	
PD 295/93	Overseers' accounts, 1692–1721.
PD 295/95	Overseers' accounts, 1698–1766.
PD 295/3	Parish register (baptisms, marriages, and burials), 1707–1831.
PD 295/102	Overseers' order book, 1708–1743.
PD 295/94	Overseers' accounts, 1721–1751.
PD 295/113	Miscellaneous overseers' papers, 1732–1743.
PD 295/103	Overseers' order book, 1743–1772.
PD 295/117	Inventories, 1744–1762.
PD 295/98	Overseers' accounts, 1798–1808.
PD 295/101	Overseers' accounts, 1827–1832.
PD 295/106	Overseers' order book, 1828–1831.
Shelton	
PD 358/1	Parish register (baptisms, marriages, and burials), 1557–1744.
PD 358/41	Overseers' accounts, 1670–1734.
PD 358/61	Various papers, 1704–1769.
PD 358/42	Various accounts and papers, 1735–1779.
PD 358/2	Parish register (baptisms, marriages, and burials), 1744–1796.
Shimpling	
PD 102/32	Churchwardens' accounts, 1761–1810.
PD 102/36	Town book, 1769–1799.
Shipdham	
PD 337/158	Inventories, 1720.
Stratton St. Mary	
PD 122/2	Parish registers (baptisms, marriages, and burials), 1749–1783.
PD 122/54	Accounts of weekly collections of the poor, 1770–1813.
PD 122/3	Parish registers (baptisms and burials), 1783–1812.
PD 122/38	Vestry minutes, 1783–1812.
PD 122/39	Vestry minutes, 1814–1832.
Surlingham	
PD 611/38	Overseers' accounts, 1739–1764.
Tharston	
PD 708/88	Overseers' accounts, 1768–1797.
PD 708/84	Draft overseers' accounts, 1777–1793.
PD 708/90	Overseers' accounts, 1797–1813.
Trowse	
PD 216/90	Inventories, 1694–1786.
PD 216/1	Parish registers (baptisms, marriages, and burials), 1695–1778.
PD 216/92	Overseers' vouchers, 1720–1856.
Walsingham, Little	
PD 582/108	Order for distress against William Groom, 1820.

Wighton

PD 553/79	Inventory, 1819.

Winfarthing

PD 78/59	Overseers' accounts, 1811–1828.
PD 78/8	Parish registers (burials), 1813–1877.
PD 78/66	Inventories, 1816.

Yelverton with Alpington

PD 316/2	Parish registers (baptisms, marriages, and burials), 1715–1800.
PD 316/46	Overseers' accounts, 1720–1748.

Record Office for Leicestershire, Leicester and Rutland, Wigston

Ullesthorpe

DE 400/64	Order to distrain, 1830.

Wigan Archives Service, Leigh

Abram

TR/Ab/5–7	Particulars of disbursements of the overseers, constables, and supervisors, c.1691–1800.

Bibliography

Printed primary sources

Cirket, Alan F., ed., *Samuel Whitbread's Notebooks 1810–11, 1813–14* (Bedford, 1971).

Clare, John, *The Parish: A satire*, ed., Eric Robinson (London, 1985).

Copy of the Poll for the Knights of the Shire for the County of Norfolk (Norwich, 1734).

King, Steven, Thomas Nutt, and Alannah Tomkins, eds., *Narratives of the Poor in Eighteenth-century Britain*, vol. 1, *Voices of the poor: poor law depositions and letters* (London, 2006).

Kussmaul, Ann, ed., *The Autobiography of Joseph Mayett of Quainton (1783–1839)* (Chesham, 1986).

Melling, Elizabeth, ed., *Kentish Sources*, vol. 4, *The poor* (Maidstone, 1964).

Morgan, Gwenda, and Peter Rushton, eds., *The Justicing Notebook (1750–64) of Edmund Tew, Rector of Boldon* (Woodbridge, 2000).

Paley, Ruth, ed., *Justice in Eighteenth-century Hackney: The justicing notebook of Henry Norris and the Hackney petty sessions book* (London, 1991).

Robinson, Eric, ed., *John Clare's Autobiographical Writings* (Oxford, 1983).

Sokoll, Thomas, ed., *Essex Pauper Letters, 1731–1837* (Oxford, 2001).

White, Anne, and Mary Clapinson, eds., *The Compton Census of 1676: A critical edition* (Oxford, 1986).

Published contemporary sources

Burn, Richard, *The History of the Poor Laws* (London, 1764).

Burn, Richard, *The Justice of the Peace and Parish Officer*, 4 vols., 12th edn. (London, 1772).

Cobbett, William, *Two-penny Trash: Politics for the poor* (London, 1831).

Davies, David, *The Case of Labourers in Husbandry* (London, 1795).

Dickinson, William, *A Practical Exposition of the Law relative to the Office and Duties of a Justice of the Peace*, 2 vols. (London, 1813).

Eden, Frederic Morton, *The State of the Poor*, 3 vols. (London, 1797).

Gardiner, Robert, *Compleat Constable*, 3rd edn. (London, 1708).

Jacob, Giles, *The Compleat Parish-officer*, 10th edn. (London, 1744).

Kent, Nathaniel, *Hints to Gentlemen of Landed Property* (London, 1775).

Nevill, Samuel, *The Acts of the General Assembly of the Province of New-Jersey, from the year 1753*, 2 vols. (Woodbridge, NJ, 1761).

Nolan, Michael, *A Treatise of the Laws for the Relief and Settlement of the Poor*, 3 vols., 4th edn. (London, 1825).

Pigot and Co.'s National Commercial Directory (London, 1830).

Scott, John, *Observations on the Present State of the Parochial and Vagrant Poor* (London, 1773).

Williams, Thomas Walter, *The Whole Law relative to the Duty and Office of a Justice of the Peace*, 4 vols., 3rd edn. (London, 1812).

Wooler, Thomas Jonathan, *Every Man his own Attorney* (London, 1830).

Newspapers

Chester Courant and Anglo Welsh Gazette.
Evening Mail.
Newcastle Courant.
Royal Cornwall Gazette, Falmouth Packet, and Plymouth Journal.
The Bury and Norwich Post, or Suffolk, Essex, Cambridge, Ely, and Norfolk Telegraph.
The Hull Packet Humber Mercury or Yorkshire and Lincolnshire Advertiser.
The Ipswich Journal; and Suffolk, Norfolk, Essex, and Cambridgeshire Advertiser.
The Manchester Courier and Manchester General Advertiser.
The Northampton Mercury.
The Public Ledger and Daily Advertiser.

Official publications

British Parliamentary Papers, 1803–4, XIII, *Abstract of Answers and Returns... relative to the Expenses and Maintenance of the Poor in England.*

British Parliamentary Papers, 1834, XXIX.1, *Report from his Majesty's Commissioners for Inquiring into the Administration and Practical Operation of the Poor Laws. Appendix A: Reports of assistant commissioners, part II.*

British Parliamentary Papers, 1834, XXXIX.1, *Report from his Majesty's Commissioners for Inquiring into the Administration and Practical Operation of the Poor Laws. Appendix F: Foreign Communications.*

National Census, 1801–1831.

Published secondary works

Agnew, Jean-Christophe, 'Coming up for Air: Consumer culture in historical perspective', in Brewer and Porter, *World of Goods*, pp. 19–39.

Arkell, Tom, Nesta Evans, and Nigel Goose, eds., *When Death do us Part: Understanding and interpreting the probate records of early modern England* (Oxford, 2000).

Banks, J. A., 'The Social Structure of Nineteenth century England as seen through the Census', in Lawton, *Census and Social Structure*, pp. 179–223.

Batchelor, Jennie, and Cora Kaplan, eds., *Women and Material Culture, 1660–1830* (Basingstoke, 2007).

Baugh, Daniel A., 'The costs of Poor Relief in South-east England, 1790–1834', *Economic History Review*, 28 (1975), pp. 50–68.

Beaudry, Mary C., 'Words for Things: Linguistic analysis of probate inventories', in Beaudry, *Documentary Archaeology*, pp. 43–50.

Beaudry, Mary C., ed., *Documentary Archaeology in the New World* (Cambridge, 1988).

Beaudry, Mary C., *Findings: The material culture of needlework and sewing* (New Haven, 2006).

Beckett, John, and Catherine Smith, 'Urban Renaissance and Consumer Revolution', *Urban History*, 27 (2000), pp. 31–50.

Bedell, John, 'Archaeology and Probate Inventories in the Study of Eighteenth-century Life', *Journal of Interdisciplinary History*, 31 (2000), pp. 223–245.

Blaug, Mark, 'The Myth of the Old Poor Law and the making of the New', *Journal of Economic History*, 23 (1963), pp. 151–184.

Blaug, Mark, 'The Poor Law Report reexamined', *Journal of Economic History*, 24 (1964), pp. 229–245.

Borsay, Peter, *The English Urban Renaissance: Culture and society in the provincial town 1660–1770* (Oxford, 1989).
Botelho, L. A., *Old Age and the English Poor Law, 1500–1700* (Woodbridge, 2004).
Boulton, Jeremy, 'Going on the Parish: The parish pension and its meaning in the London suburbs, 1640–1724', in Hitchcock, King, and Sharpe, *Chronicling Poverty*, pp. 19–46.
Boyer, George R., *An Economic History of the English Poor Law 1750–1850* (Cambridge, 1990).
Brewer, John, and Roy Porter, eds., *Consumption and the World of Goods* (London, 1993).
Brewer, John, and John Styles, eds., *An Ungovernable People: The English and their law in the seventeenth and eighteenth centuries* (London, 1980).
Briggs, Chris, P. M. Kitson, and S. J. Thompson, eds., *Population, Welfare and Economic Change in Britain 1290–1834* (Woodbridge, 2014).
Bristow, Joy, *The Local Historian's Glossary of Words and Terms*, 3rd edn. (Newbury, 2001).
Broad, John, 'Parish Economies of Welfare', *Historical Journal*, 42 (1999), pp. 985–1006.
Broad, John, 'Housing the Rural Poor in Southern England, 1650–1850', *Agricultural History Review*, 48 (2000), pp. 151–170.
Brundage, Anthony, *The English Poor Laws, 1700–1930* (London, 2002).
Burman, Barbara, and Jonathan White, 'Fanny's Pockets: Cotton, consumption and domestic economy, 1780–1850', in Batchelor and Kaplan, *Women and Material Culture*, pp. 31–51.
Buxton, Anthony, *Domestic Culture in Early Modern England* (Woodbridge, 2015).
Cherry, Steven, *Mental Health Care in Modern England: The Norfolk Lunatic Asylum/St. Andrew's Hospital, 1810–1998* (Woodbridge, 2003).
Clark, Peter, ed., *The Cambridge Urban History of Britain*, vol. 2, *1540–1840* (Cambridge, 2000).
Clark, Peter, and Paul Slack, *English Towns in Transition 1500–1700* (Oxford, 1976).
Corfield, Penelope J., *The Impact of English Towns 1700–1800* (Oxford, 1982).
Corfield, Penelope J., 'East Anglia', in Clark, *Cambridge Urban History*, pp. 31–48.
Cornford, Barbara, 'Inventories of the Poor', *Norfolk Archaeology*, 35 (1970–1973), pp. 118–125.
Coward, Barry, *The Stuart Age: England, 1603–1714*, 3rd edn. (Harlow, 2003).
Daunton, M. J., *Progress and Poverty: An economic and social history of Britain 1700–1850* (Oxford, 1995).
de Vries, Jan, *European Urbanization 1500–1800* (London, 1984).
de Vries, Jan, 'The Industrial Revolution and the Industrious Revolution', *Journal of Economic History*, 54 (1994), pp. 249–270.
de Vries, Jan, *The Industrious Revolution: Consumer behaviour and the household economy 1650 to present* (Cambridge, 2008).
Digby, Anne, *Pauper Palaces* (London, 1978).
Douglas, Mary, and Baron C. Isherwood, *The World of Goods: Towards an anthropology of consumption* (London, 1979).
Dunkley, Peter, 'Paternalism, the Magistracy and Poor Relief in England, 1795–1834', *International Review of Social History*, 24 (1979), pp. 371–397.
Dunkley, Peter, *The Crisis of the Old Poor Law in England 1795–1834: An interpretive essay* (London, 1982).

Dyer, Alan, 'Small Market Towns 1540–1700', in Clark, *Cambridge Urban History*, pp. 425–450.

Dyson, Richard, 'Welfare Provision in Oxford during the latter stages of the Old Poor Law', *Historical Journal*, 52 (2009), pp. 943–962.

Dyson, Richard, The Extent and Nature of Pauperism in five Oxfordshire Parishes, 1786–1832', *Continuity and Change*, 28 (2013), pp. 421–449.

Ellis, Joyce, 'Regional and County Centres', in Clark, *Cambridge Urban History*, pp. 673–704.

Ellis, Joyce, *The Georgian Town 1680–1840* (Basingstoke, 2001).

Emmison, F. G., *The Relief of the Poor at Eaton Socon, 1706–1834* (Aspley Guise, 1933).

Englander, David, *Landlord and Tenant in Urban Britain 1838–1918* (Oxford, 1983).

Estabrook, Carl B., *Urbane and Rustic England: Cultural ties and social spheres in the provinces 1660–1780* (Manchester, 1998).

Evans, Adrian B., 'Enlivening the Archive: Glimpsing embodied consumption practices in probate inventories of household possessions', *Historical Geography*, 36 (2008), pp. 40–72.

Fideler, Paul A., *Social Welfare in Pre-industrial England* (London, 2006).

Findlen, Paula, ed., *Early Modern Things: Objects and their histories, 1500–1800* (London, 2013).

Fine, Ben, *The World of Consumption: The material and cultural revisited*, 2nd edn. (London, 2002).

Fine, Ben, and Ellen Leopold, *The World of Consumption* (London, 1993).

Floud, Roderick, Jane Humphries, and Paul Johnson, eds., *The Cambridge Economic History of Modern Britain*, vol. 1, *1700–1870*, 2nd edn. (Cambridge, 2014).

Floud, Roderick, Jane Humphries, and Paul Johnson, eds., *The Cambridge Economic History of Modern Britain*, vol. 2, *1870 to the present*, 2nd edn. (Cambridge, 2014).

Fraser, Derek, *The Evolution of the British Welfare State*, 4th edn. (London, 2009).

Freeman, Michael, 'Transport', in Langton and Morris, *Atlas of Industrializing Britain*, pp. 80–93.

French, Henry, *The Middle Sort of People in Provincial England 1600–1750* (Oxford, 2007).

French, Henry, 'An Irrevocable Shift: Detailing the dynamics of rural poverty in southern England, 1762–1834', *Economic History Review*, 68 (2015), pp. 769–805.

French, Henry, 'How Dependent were the "Dependent Poor"? Poor relief and the life-course in Terling, Essex, 1752–1834', *Continuity and Change*, 30 (2015), pp. 193–222.

Goggin, Maureen Daly, and Beth Fowkes Tobin, eds., *Women and the Material Culture of Needlework and Textiles, 1750–1950* (Farnham, 2009).

Green, Adrian, 'Heartless and Unhomely? Dwellings of the poor in East Anglia and north-east England', in McEwan and Sharpe, *Accommodating Poverty*, pp. 69–101.

Hamling, Tara, and Catherine Richardson, eds., *Everyday Objects: Medieval and early modern material culture and its meaning* (Farnham, 2010).

Hammond, J. L., and Barbara Hammond, *The Village Labourer, 1760–1832: A study in the government of England before the reformation bill*, 2nd edn. (London, 1920).

Hampson, E. M., *The Treatment of Poverty in Cambridgeshire 1597–1834* (Cambridge, 1934).

Harley, Joseph, 'Material Lives of the Poor and their Strategic use of the Workhouse during the final decades of the English Old Poor Law', *Continuity and Change*, 30 (2015), pp. 71–103.

Harley, Joseph, 'Consumption and Poverty in the Homes of the English Poor, c. 1670–1834', *Social History*, 43 (2018), pp. 81–104.

Harley, Joseph, 'Pauper Inventories, Social Relations and the Nature of Poor Relief under the Old Poor Law, England c. 1601–1834', *Historical Journal*, 62 (2019), pp. 375–398.

Harris, Bernard, *The Origins of the British Welfare State: Social welfare in England and Wales, 1800–1945* (London, 2004).

Hatcher, John, *The History of the British Coal Industry*, vol. 1, *Before 1700: towards the age of coal* (Oxford, 1993).

Head-König, Anne-Lise, ed., *Inheritance Practices, Marriage Strategies and Household Formation in European Rural Societies* (Turnhout, 2012).

Healey, Jonathan, *The First Century of Welfare: Poverty and poor relief in Lancashire 1620–1730* (Woodbridge, 2014).

Hindle, Steve, 'Power, Poor Relief, and Social Relations in Holland Fen, c. 1600–1800', *Historical Journal*, 41 (1998), pp. 67–96.

Hindle, Steve, *On the Parish? The micro-politics of poor relief in rural England c. 1550–1750* (Oxford, 2004).

Hindle, Steve, 'Dependency, Shame and Belonging: Badging the deserving poor, c. 1550–1750', *Cultural and Social History*, 1 (2004), pp. 6–35.

Hindle, Steve, 'Technologies of Identification under the Old Poor Law', *The Local Historian*, 36 (2006), pp. 220–236.

Hitchcock, Tim, Peter King, and Pamela Sharpe, 'Introduction: Chronicling poverty – the voices and strategies of the English poor, 1640–1840', in Hitchcock, King, and Sharpe, *Chronicling Poverty*, pp. 1–18.

Hitchcock, Tim, Peter King, and Pamela Sharpe, ed., *Chronicling Poverty: The voices and strategies of the English poor, 1640–1840* (Basingstoke, 1997).

Hitchcock, Tim, and Robert Shoemaker, *London Lives: Poverty, crime and the making of a modern city, 1690–1800* (Cambridge, 2015).

Holmes, Vicky, *In Bed with the Victorians: The life-cycle of working-class marriage* (Cham, 2017).

Horrell, Sara, 'Consumption, 1700–1870', in Floud, Humphries, and Johnson, *Cambridge Economic History of Modern Britain*, vol. 1, pp. 237–263.

Hoskins, Lesley, 'Social, Economic and Geographical Differences in mid-Nineteenth-century Homes: The evidence from inventories', *Regional Furniture*, XXVIII (2013), pp. 93–119.

Hoskins, W. G. 'The Leicestershire Farmer in the Seventeenth century', *Agricultural History*, 25 (1951), pp. 9–20.

Hurl-Eamon, Jennine, 'Love Tokens: Objects as memory for plebeian women in early modern England', *Early Modern Women: An Interdisciplinary Journal*, 6 (2011), pp. 181–186.

Hussey, David, and Margaret Ponsonby, *The Single Homemaker and Material Culture in the long Eighteenth century* (Farnham, 2012).

Innes, Joanna, 'The King's Bench Prison in the later Eighteenth Century: Law, authority and order in a London debtors' prison', in Brewer and Styles, *An Ungovernable People*, pp. 250–298.

Innes, Joanna, *Inferior Politics: Social problems and social policies in eighteenth-century Britain* (Oxford, 2009).
Jones, Peter, and Steven King, eds., *Obligation, Entitlement and Dispute under the English Poor Laws, 1600–1900* (Cambridge, 2015).
Kain, Roger J. P., John Chapman, and Richard R. Oliver, *The Enclosure Maps of England and Wales 1595–1918* (Cambridge, 2004).
Kent, Joan, 'The Rural "middling sort" in Early Modern England, circa 1640–1740: Some economic, political and socio-cultural characteristics', *Rural History*, 10 (1999), pp. 19–54.
Kent, Joan, and Steven King, 'Changing Patterns of Poor Relief in some English Rural Parishes circa 1650–1750', *Rural History*, 14 (2003), pp. 119–156.
King, Peter, 'Pauper Inventories and the Material Lives of the Poor in the Eighteenth and early Nineteenth Centuries', in Hitchcock, King, and Sharpe, *Chronicling Poverty*, pp. 155–191.
King, Peter, *Crime, Justice and Discretion in England 1740–1820* (Oxford, 2000).
King, Peter, 'The Summary Courts and Social Relations in Eighteenth-century England', *Past and Present*, 183 (2004), pp. 125–172.
King, Peter, *Crime and Law in England, 1750–1840: Remaking justice from the margins* (Cambridge, 2006).
King, Peter, 'The Rights of the Poor and the Role of the Law: The impact of pauper appeals to the summary courts, 1750–1834', in Jones and King, *Obligation, Entitlement and Dispute*, pp. 235–262.
King, Steven, 'Chance Encounters? Paths to household formation in early modern England', *International Review of Social History*, 44 (1999), pp. 23–46.
King, Steven, *Poverty and Welfare in England 1700–1850: A regional perspective* (Manchester, 2000).
King, Steven, 'Negotiating the Law of Poor Relief in England, 1800–1840', *History*, 96 (2011), pp. 410–435.
King, Steven, 'Too Poor to Marry? "Inheritance", the poor and marriage/household formation in rural England 1800–1840s', in Head-König, *Inheritance Practices*, pp. 127–152.
King, Steven, *Writing the Lives of the English Poor, 1750s–1830s* (London, 2019).
King, Steven, and Geoffrey Timmins, *Making Sense of the Industrial Revolution* (Manchester, 2001).
King, Steven, and Alannah Tomkins, eds., *The Poor in England 1700–1850: An economy of makeshifts* (Manchester, 2003).
Langton, John, and R. J. Morris, eds., *Atlas of Industrializing Britain, 1780–1914* (London, 1986).
Law, C. M., 'Some notes on the Urban Population of England and Wales in the Eighteenth century', *The Local Historian*, 10 (1972), pp. 13–26.
Lawton, Richard, ed., *The Census and Social Structure: An interpretation guide to nineteenth century censuses for England and Wales* (London, 1978).
Lees, Lynn Hollen, *The Solidarities of Strangers: The English poor laws and the people, 1700–1948* (Cambridge, 1998).
Lemire, Beverly, *The Business of Everyday Life: Gender, practice and social politics in England, c. 1600–1900* (Manchester, 2005).
Maegraith, Janine, and Craig Muldrew, 'Consumption and Material Life', in Scott, *Oxford Handbook of Early Modern European History*, pp. 369–397.
Malcolmson, Robert W., *Life and Labour in England 1700–1780* (London, 1981).

Marshall, John D., *The Old Poor Law 1795–1834* (London, 1968).
Martin, E. W., ed., *Comparative Development in Social Welfare* (London, 1972).
Martins, Susanna Wade, *A History of Norfolk* (Chichester, 1984).
Martins, Susanna Wade, *Norfolk: A changing countryside* (Chichester, 1988).
McEwan, Joanne, and Pamela Sharpe, ed., *Accommodating Poverty: The housing and living arrangements of the English poor, c. 1600–1850* (Basingstoke, 2011).
McInnes, Angus, *The English Town, 1660–1760* (London, 1980).
McKendrick, Neil, 'Introduction', in McKendrick, Brewer, and Plumb, *Consumer Society*, pp. 1–6.
McKendrick, Neil, 'The Consumer Revolution of Eighteenth-century England', in McKendrick, Brewer, and Plumb, *Consumer Society*, pp. 9–33.
McKendrick, Neil, John Brewer, and J. H. Plumb, *The Birth of a Consumer Society: The commercialisation of eighteenth-century England* (London, 1982).
McKenney, Jenny, 'The "Bossy Shield": Money, sex, sentiment, and the thimble', *Lumen*, 34 (2015), pp. 1–23.
Milward, Rosemary, *A Glossary of Household and Farming Terms from Sixteenth-century Probate Inventories*, 3rd edn. (Chesterfield, 1986).
Mintz, Sidney W., *Sweetness and Power: The place of sugar in modern history* (New York, 1985).
Moore, John S., *The Goods and Chattels of our Forefathers: Frampton Cotterell and district probate inventories, 1539–1804* (London, 1976).
Morrison, Kathryn, *The Workhouse: A study of poor-law buildings in England* (Swindon, 1999).
Muldrew, Craig, *Food, Energy and the Creation of Industriousness: Work and material culture in agrarian England, 1550–1780* (Cambridge, 2011).
Neeson, J. M., *Commoners: Common right, enclosure and social change in England, 1700–1820* (Cambridge, 1993).
Neuman, Mark, *The Speenhamland County: Poverty and the poor laws in Berkshire 1782–1834* (London, 1982).
Nicholls, George, *A History of the English Poor Law*, vol. 2 (London, 1854).
Offer, Avner, 'Consumption and Affluence, c. 1870–2010', in Floud, Humphries, and Johnson, *Cambridge Economic History of Modern Britain*, vol. 2, pp. 205–228.
Orlin, Lena Cowen, 'Fictions of the Early Modern English Probate Inventory', in Turner, *Culture of Capital*, pp. 51–83.
Ottaway, Susannah R., *The Decline of Life: Old age in eighteenth-century England* (Cambridge, 2004).
Overton, Mark, *Agricultural Revolution in England: The transformation of the agrarian economy, 1500–1850* (Cambridge, 1996).
Overton, Mark, 'Prices from Probate Inventories', in Arkell, Evans, and Goose, *When Death do us Part*, pp. 120–141.
Overton, Mark, Jane Whittle, Darron Dean, and Andrew Hann, *Production and Consumption in English Households, 1600–1750* (London, 2004).
Oxley, Geoffrey W., *Poor Relief in England and Wales 1601–1834* (London, 1974).
Patten, John, *English Towns 1500–1700* (Folkestone, 1978).
Pennell, Sara, '"For a crack or flaw despis'd": Thinking about ceramic durability and the "everyday" in late seventeenth- and early eighteenth-century England', in Hamling and Richardson, *Everyday Objects*, pp. 27–40.
Pennell, Sara, *The Birth of the English Kitchen, 1600–1850* (London, 2017).

Pounds, Norman J. G., *Hearth & Home: A history of material culture* (Bloomington, 1989).
Poynter, J. R., *Society and Pauperism: English ideas on poor relief, 1795–1834* (London, 1969).
Priestly, Ursula, and Penelope J. Corfield, 'Rooms and Room use in Norwich Housing, 1580–1730', *Post-Medieval Archaeology*, 16 (1982), pp. 93–123.
Rawcliffe, Carole, and Richard Wilson, eds., *Norwich since 1550* (London, 2004).
Reay, Barry, *Rural Englands: Labouring lives in the nineteenth century* (Basingstoke, 2004).
Riello, Giorgio, '"Things Seen and Unseen": The material culture of early modern inventories and their representation of domestic interiors', in Findlen, *Early Modern Things*, pp. 125–150.
Rowntree, B. Seebohm, *Poverty: A study of town life*, 3rd. ed. (London, 1902).
Rubin, G. R., and David Sugarman, eds., *Law, Economy and Society, 1750–1914: Essays in the history of English law* (Abingdon, 1984).
Scott, Hamish, ed., *The Oxford Handbook of Early Modern European History, 1350–1750*, vol. 1, *Peoples and place* (Oxford, 2015).
Shammas, Carole, *The Pre-industrial Consumer in England and America* (Oxford, 1990).
Sharpe, Pamela, '"The bowels of compation": A labouring family and the law, c. 1790–1834', in Hitchcock, King, and Sharpe, *Chronicling Poverty*, pp. 87–108.
Shave, Samantha A., 'The Dependent Poor? (Re)constructing the lives of individuals "on the parish" in rural Dorset, 1800–1832', *Rural History*, 20 (2009), pp. 67–97.
Shave, Samantha A., 'The Impact of Sturges Bourne's Poor Law reforms in Rural England', *Historical Journal*, 56 (2013), pp. 399–429.
Shave, Samantha A., *Pauper Policies: Poor law practice in England, 1780–1850* (Manchester, 2017).
Shaw-Taylor, Leigh, 'Labourers, Cows, Common rights and Parliamentary Enclosure: The evidence of contemporary comment c. 1760–1810', *Past and Present*, 171 (2001), pp. 95–126.
Shepard, Alexandra, *Accounting for Oneself: Worth, status, and the social order* (Oxford, 2015).
Slack, Paul, *Poverty and Policy in Tudor and Stuart England* (London, 1988).
Smith, Richard M., ed., *Land, Kinship and Life-cycle* (Cambridge, 1984).
Smith, Woodruff D., *Consumption and the Making of Respectability, 1600–1800* (London, 2002).
Sneath, Ken, 'A Consumer Revolution in Huntingdonshire?', *The Local Historian*, 41 (2011), pp. 229–238.
Snell, K. D. M., *Annals of the Labouring Poor: Social change and agrarian England, 1660–1900* (Cambridge, 1985).
Snell, K. D. M., *Parish and Belonging: Community, identity and welfare in England and Wales* (Cambridge, 2006).
Sokoll, Thomas, *Household and Family among the Poor: The case of two Essex communities in the late eighteenth and early nineteenth centuries* (Bochum, 1993).
Stapleton, Barry, 'Inherited Poverty and Life-cycle Poverty: Odiham, Hampshire, 1650–1850', *Social History*, 18 (1993), pp. 339–355.
Stearns, Peter N., *Debating the Industrial Revolution* (London, 2015).
Stobart, Jon, 'A History of Shopping: The missing link between retail and consumer revolutions', *Journal of Historical Research in Marketing*, 2 (2010), pp. 342–349.

Stobart, Jon, *Sugar and Spice: Grocers in provincial England 1650–1830* (Oxford, 2013).
Stobart, Jon, and Mark Rothery, 'Fashion, Inheritance and Family', *Cultural and Social History*, 11 (2014), pp. 385–406.
Styles, John, 'Manufacturing, Consumption and Design in Eighteenth-century England', in Brewer and Porter, *World of Goods*, pp. 527–554.
Styles, John, 'Fashion, Textiles and the Origins of Industrial Revolution', *East Asian Journal of British History*, 5 (2016), pp. 161–189.
Sugarman, David, and G. R. Rubin, 'Towards a New History of the Law and Material Society in England 1750–1914', in Rubin and Sugarman, *Law, Economy and Society*, pp. 1–123 and i-lxviii.
Sweet, Rosemary, *The English Town: Government, society and culture* (Harlow, 1999).
Tate, W. E., *The Parish Chest: A study of the records of parochial administration in England*, 3rd edn. (Cambridge, 1969).
Taylor, James S., 'The Unreformed Workhouse, 1776–1834', in Martin, *Comparative Development*, pp. 57–84.
Taylor, James S., 'The Impact of Pauper Settlement 1691–1834', *Past and Present*, 73 (1976), pp. 42–74.
Taylor, James S., *Poverty, Migration, and Settlement in the Industrial Revolution: Sojourners' narratives* (Palo Alto, 1989).
Tebbutt, Melanie, *Making Ends Meet: Pawnbroking and working-class credit* (Leicester, 1983).
Thirsk, Joan, *The Agrarian History of England and Wales*, vol. 5, *1640–1750*: Parts 1–2 (Cambridge, 1984–1985).
Thompson, E. P., *The Making of the English Working Class* (London, 1991, reprint of 1963 ed.).
Thompson, S. J., 'Population Growth and Corporations of the Poor, 1660–1841', in Briggs, Kitson, and Thompson, *Population, Welfare and Economic Change*, pp. 189–225.
Tomkins, Alannah, *The Experience of Urban Poverty, 1732–82: Parish, charity and credit* (Manchester, 2006).
Trentmann, Frank, ed., *The Oxford Handbook of the History of Consumption* (Oxford, 2012).
Turner, Henry S., ed., *The Culture of Capital* (London, 2002).
Turner, Michael, *English Parliamentary Enclosure: Its historical geography and economic history* (Folkestone, 1980).
Vickery, Amanda, *Behind Closed Doors: At home in Georgian England* (New Haven, 2009).
Voth, Hans-Joachim, *Time and Work in England 1750–1830* (Oxford, 2000).
Wales, Tim, 'Poverty, Poor Relief and Life-cycle: Some evidence from seventeenth century Norfolk' in Smith, *Land, Kinship and Life-cycle*, pp. 351–404.
Weatherill, Lorna, *Consumer Behaviour and Material Culture in Britain 1660–1760*, 2nd edn. (London, 1996).
Webb, Sidney, and Beatrice Webb, *English Local Government: English poor law history*, part 1, *The old poor law* (London, 1927).
Wild, John, *Tetney, Lincolnshire: A history* (Grimsby, 1901).
Williams, Karel, *From Pauperism to Poverty* (London, 1981).
Williams, Samantha, *Poverty, Gender and Life-cycle under the English Poor Law 1760–1834* (Woodbridge, 2011).

Wilson, Richard, 'The Textile Industry', in Rawcliffe and Wilson, *Norwich*, pp. 219–241.

Wrigley, E. A., 'Urban Growth and Agricultural Change: England and the continent in the early modern period', *Journal of Interdisciplinary History*, 15 (1985), pp. 683–728.

Wrigley, E. A., 'Rickman Revisited: The population growth rates of English counties in the early modern period', *Economic History Review*, 62 (2009), pp. 711–735.

Wrigley, E. A., *The Path to Sustained Growth: England's transition from an organic economy to an industrial revolution* (Cambridge, 2016).

Wrigley, E. A., and R. S. Schofield, *The Population History of England 1541–1871* (London, 1981).

Unpublished secondary works

Brewer, John, 'The Error of our Ways', Lecture to the Cultures of Consumption programme, The Royal Society, 2003, Working paper no. 12 [From: www.consume.bbk.ac.uk/ publications.html. Accessed 26/11/2010].

Harley, Joseph, 'Consumption and the Life-cycle of English Paupers: The perspective from Essex, 1750–1834', (M.A. thesis, University of Warwick, 2011).

Harley, Joseph, 'Material Lives of the English Poor: A regional perspective, c. 1670–1834' (Ph.D. thesis, University of Leicester, 2016).

Harrison, C. J., ed., 'Glossary of Wills and Inventories from three Tudor/Jacobean Towns' (unpublished paper, University of Keele, 2001).

Hitchcock, Tim, 'The English Workhouse: A study of institutional poor relief in selected counties, 1696–1750' (D.Phil. thesis, University of Oxford, 1985).

Mather, Ruth, 'The Home-Making of the English Working Class: Radical politics and domestic life in late-Georgian England, c. 1790–1820' (Ph.D. thesis, Queen Mary, University of London, 2016).

Newman, A. E., 'The Old Poor Law in east Kent, 1606–1834: A social and demographic analysis', (Ph.D. thesis, University of Kent, 1979).

Sneath, Ken, 'Consumption, Wealth, Indebtedness and Social Structure in Early Modern England' (Ph.D. thesis, University of Cambridge, 2008).

Online sources

Oxford English Dictionary (http://www.oed.com/).

Index of persons

Index of subjects